D0849744

OLIVER TWIST

THE GARLAND DICKENS BIBLIOGRAPHIES
(General Editor: Duane DeVries)
Vol. 2

GARLAND REFERENCE LIBRARY
OF THE HUMANITIES
Vol. 385

The Garland
Dickens Bibliographies

Duane DeVries
General Editor

Our Mutual Friend
compiled by Joel J. Brattin
and Bert G. Hornback

David Copperfield
compiled by Richard J. Dunn

Hard Times
compiled by Sylvia Manning

Dickens's Christmas Books,
Christmas Stories, and Other
Short Fiction
compiled by Ruth F. Glancy

Oliver Twist
compiled by David Paroissien

OLIVER TWIST
An Annotated Bibliography

David Paroissien

GARLAND PUBLISHING, INC. • NEW YORK & LONDON
1986

Library of Congress Cataloging-in-Publication Data

Paroissien, David.
   Oliver Twist : an annotated bibliography.

   (The Garland Dickens bibliographies ; vol. 2) (The
Garland reference library of the humanities ; vol. 385)
   Includes index.
   1. Dickens, Charles, 1812–1870. Oliver Twist—
Bibliography.   I. Title.   II. Series: Garland Dickens
bibliographies ; v. 2.   III. Series: Garland reference
library of the humanities ; v. 385.
Z8230.P37   1986   [PR4567]   016.823'8   82-49136
ISBN 0-8240-9198-1 (alk. paper)

Printed on acid-free, 250-year-life paper
Manufactured in the United States of America

CONTENTS

PART 2. STUDIES

PART 3. BACKGROUND AND
RELATED STUDIES

PREFACE

Oliver Twist: An Annotated Bibliography, like its companions in The Garland Dickens Bibliographies, shares the same practical objectives. Each editor sets out to annotate a reasonably complete listing of notes, articles, books, and other publications specific to his focus. By providing readers with a full description of the various editions of the novel in question and an account of Dickens's involvement with the work during the period of its composition, each editor also hopes to enhance the bibliography's usefulness and compile a volume that serves both the student and the serious scholar. Ideally, each editor attempts to furnish a reference tool that covers a spectrum of interests appropriate to his or her particular focus.

I have found *Oliver Twist* a challenging assignment, a novel at once broadly appealing and also capable of attracting readers with quite specific interests. An examination of the Table of Contents provides support for this point. *Oliver Twist* elicited considerable comment among Victorian reviewers, many of whom praised the work for its realism, its humor, and its compassion. Others, locating the novel in the literary context of Newgate or crime fiction of the nineteenth century, saw more ominous implications in its success and warned readers against the novel's putative ability to demoralize or corrupt. Because *Oliver Twist* also proved successful, first on the stage and later as a source for film versions, the novel has occasioned extensive commentary among those interested in both media. As a novel with a powerful Semitic figure—at once appealing and repulsive—*Oliver Twist* has attracted many Jewish writers and scholars; and because George Cruikshank illustrated the novel, critics concerned with the reputation of one of Victorian England's greatest artists have written about his controversial contribution to the novel in some detail. Moreover, as a novel intimately connected with the Poor

Law Amendment Act of 1834—a piece of social legislation no less important in its appropriate sphere than the Reform Bill of 1832 and the Abolition of Slavery in the British Empire in 1833 in theirs—we see yet another instance of how *Oliver Twist* provides the opportunity for extensive discourse of a special focus. Finally, and most pervasively, as an enduringly and perennially popular novel, *Oliver Twist* has generated a substantial body of critical studies, whose ebb and flow I comment on in the Introduction. In Part 2 of this study, I have attempted to impose some order on this broad domain by employing various chronological and thematic categories to which readers can go for sought information.

With respect to the overall arrangement, I have divided *Oliver Twist: An Annotated Bibliography* into three parts—Text, Studies, and Background and Related Studies—and then subdivided them into the following sixteen sections: (I) *Oliver Twist* in Progress, Dickens's Letters Concerning the Novel, the Manuscript, and His Agreements with Publishers; (II) Major Editions; (III) Commentary on the Text; (IV) Bibliographical Studies; (V) Dickens's Reading Adaptations; (VI) Stage Adaptations; (VII) Film, Musical, Radio, and Television Adaptations; (VIII) Prose Adaptations; (IX) Contemporary Reviews; (X) *Oliver Twist* and the Newgate Novel; (XI) Reception by Dickens's Contemporaries; (XII) Criticism; (XIII) Special Studies; (XIV) Related Writings of Dickens; (XV) the Poor Laws; and (XVI) Historical Background. Sections III, IV, V, VII, XI, XII, XIII, XV, and XVI are arranged alphabetically, by author. Sections II, IX, and X are arranged chronologically. Sections I and VI are divided into a chronological arrangement of works followed by an alphabetical arrangement of commentary. Section VIII employs both a chronological and alphabetical means of arrangement, while section XIV is thematic, listing first *Sketches by Boz* and then subsequent works of Dickens bearing on *Oliver Twist* and Dickens's continuing interest in children and the Poor Laws, prostitution, capital punishment, and Jews. Within each of the sixteen major divisions, the items are numbered consecutively. As a result, all cross references include both a Roman numeral and an Arabic number.

Anonymous reviews of *Oliver Twist* annotated in sections IX and X are listed by title unless I have been able to include names previously supplied by other scholars. All reviews ascribed to John Forster are drawn from the identifications made by Kathleen Tillotson in her Appendix F (IX. 40) of the Clarendon edition of *Oliver Twist*; those names I have taken from Philip Collins's anthology of reviews (IX. 39) are acknowledged in the bibliographical citation. The identifications in IX. 34 and IX. 35 are mine. All authors listed in the *Household Words* entry (XIV. 3) are taken from Anne Lohrli's study of the *Household Words* Office Book (1973).

Occasional entries among the chronological listing of editions of 1867–1983 rely on information taken from John B. Podeschi's *Dickens: The Gimbel Collection* (IV. 19), as do several entries in Section VII, where I cover unauthorized prose versions of *Oliver Twist*. One entry I placed tentatively but received confirmation too late to list the entry correctly: II. 34 should carry the date [1970] and not appear, as it does, between II. 33 and II. 35. The absence of full bibliographical information relating to some of the editions in this section originates in a difficulty scholars sometimes encounter. On several occasions I received photographic copy of relevant editorial matter but no word about the total pagination or volume number, if the book appeared as part of a series. For these omissions I apologize.

Other limitations are deliberate. I chose not to include citations to reviews of the books I annotated unless the reviews were so important as to deserve their own entry. This bibliography also ignores all works published in foreign languages; similarly, it excludes all dissertations, except in three notable cases. I examined Richard P. Fulkerson's (V. 47) and Walter Lazenby's (V. 51) because so little reliable information about the adaptations of Dickens's novels for the theatre is available. I read Richard A. Vogler's study of Cruikshank because I became compulsive about the question of the illustrator's controversial role in *Oliver*

Twist and did my best to annotate documents about his claims as widely as I could.

To authors whose names lack appropriate foreign accents I apologize; the print wheel I selected did not provide them. For the same reason I wrote "pounds" (sterling) throughout.

D.P.   17 July 1985

ABBREVIATIONS

AL	*American Literature*
AYR	*All the Year Round*
Berg Collection	Henry W. and Albert A. Berg Collection, New York Public Library
BNYPL	*Bulletin of the New York Public Library*
CE	*College English*
Cent R	*Centennial Review*
CLAJ	*College Language Association Journal*
CLS Bulletin	*Charles Lamb Society Bulletin*
DiS	*Dickens Studies*
DSA	*Dickens Studies Annual*
DSN	*Dickens Studies Newsletter*
ELH	*English Literary History*
ES	*English Studies*
F	John Forster, *The Life of Charles Dickens*
HLB	*Harvard Library Bulletin*
HSL	*Hartford Studies in Literature*
HW	*Household Words*
JETT	*Journal of English Teaching Techniques*
JFI	*Journal of the Folklore Institute*
KN	*Kwartalnik neofilologiczny (Warsaw)*
L&P	*Literature and Psychology*
MLN	*Modern Language Notes*
MP	*Miscellaneous Pieces*
N	*Nonesuch Letters*, edited by Walter Dexter
N&Q	*Notes and Queries*
NCF	*Nineteenth-Century Fiction*
NYPL	New York Public Library
P	*Pilgrim Letters*
PBSA	*Papers of the Bibliographical Society of America*
PMLA	*Publication of the Modern Language Association of America*

PULC	*Princeton University Library Chronicle*
QQ	*Queen's Quarterly*
RES	*Review of English Studies*
SoR	*Southern Review (Adelaide)*
SNNTS	*Studies in the Novel*
SRAZ	*Studia romanica et anglica zagrabiensia*
TLS	[London] *Times Literary Supplement*
UT	*Uncommercial Traveller*
UTQ	*University of Texas Quarterly*
VPN	*Victorian Periodicals Newsletter*
VS	*Victorian Studies*
YES	*Yearbook of English Studies*
YR	*Yale Review*
YULG	*Yale University Library Gazette*

INTRODUCTION

I

"I have thrown my whole heart and soul into *Oliver Twist*," Dickens informed Richard Bentley, his publisher, on 27 January 1837, "and most confidently believe he will make a feature in the work, and be very popular."[1] That was a bold forecast one week before the serial's debut in *Bentley's Miscellany*, especially from a young author yet to complete his first novel, *The Pickwick Papers*. But Dickens spoke with assurance because he had an excellent subject and because he sensed the story's appeal. He knew that the opening chapters attacked the government's attempts in the 1830's to reform the laws regulating Britain's poor. He could also gauge from his own literary experience the appeal of tested formulas involving narratives of crimes and their punishments. And perhaps at some intuitive level he sensed his power to produce what Graham Greene calls Dickens's "secret prose," words capable of plumbing the domain of romance, fairy tale, and myth.

Oliver Twist's reception and the novel's continued popularity into the twentieth century amply justify Dickens's confident declaration to Richard Bentley in January 1837. From Queen Victoria to her humblest literate subjects, enthusiasm for the story swept British society, especially after Dickens's publisher brought out a completed version of the novel in November 1838, four months before the final serial number. Within less than a year, multiple versions of *Oliver Twist* made their way into readers' hands. Some editions of the text came in three expensive volumes; other publishers pirated the novel and reprinted it in cramped double columns, selling the whole narrative for only a penny. Even less commonly known to present-day readers are the clumsily arranged extracts focussing on a single character and simplistic plot summaries popular for much of the century. Such versions of *Oliver Twist* were made available by unscrupulous publishers, who cut up the novel with impunity and furnished cheap reading material for self-taught readers of the lower classes.

The numerous theatrical adaptations of *Oliver Twist* which flourished at the same time represent another aspect of the book's widespread success. Before Dickens published the complete text of the novel in November 1838, theatrical entrepreneurs in London produced four adaptations of *Oliver Twist*, a distinction rare even among Dickens's other works, which were also widely and unlawfully adapted for the stage. Concern about the harmful consequences of depicting on stage thieves and murderers led to a ban on theatrical versions of *Oliver Twist* by the Lord Chamberlain and checked their proliferation between about 1841 and 1860. After this interval, the novel resumed its vogue among adapters and prospered in theatres throughout Britain until the beginning of World War One.

In the United States no comparable national censor stepped in to interdict what many Victorians considered a seditious play. Consequently adaptations from London, hybrid versions of the same, and genuine American stage versions of *Oliver Twist* became staples in cities all over the United States, continuing throughout the nineteenth century. Later, movie versions of the novel eclipsed those of the stage, although *Oliver Twist* must surely occupy a unique place among Dickens's works for being put to such ingenious use as teaching American immigrants English by employing marionettes in dramatized version of the novel to reinforce familiar words and a basic vocabulary. This scheme was undertaken in the Bronx in 1937 under the auspices of the WPA Federal Theater Project with financial support from New York City and the U.S. Government.[2]

What accounts for the novel's initial success? The intense topicality of the early chapters of *Oliver Twist* provides one reason for the book's popularity and the favorable reception of the first issues of *Bentley's Miscellany*. Dickens's contemporaries, for example, recognized in his "glance at the new Poor Law Bill," as he described his work to a friend, a biting attack on the Poor Law Amendment Act of 1834. Dickens's objections to the Act, like those of many of his readers, focussed on specific provisions of the new government legislation—dietary regulations for the inhabitants of workhouses, the separation of married paupers by sex, the abolition of "outdoor relief," and so on—issues widely debated in the press and Parliament following the publication in 1834 of the Report prepared by members of the Royal Commission on the Poor Laws. In this respect, the novel's opening represents the extension of a contentious national debate along predictable and firmly established lines. Dickens's comments in the novel do little to illuminate the conceptual changes implicit in the Act of 1834. Rather, their value for readers in 1837 appears to lie in the intensity with which Dickens opposed the Malthusian and Benthamite principles guiding a new pattern of public administration, one which replaced the old notion of Christian charity with a new secular and social ideal of philanthropy.

Victorian readers also responded to the novel's fictional qualities. *Oliver Twist* offered terror and excitement and not simply instruction and polemics. The threats to which Dickens subjects his helpless orphan protagonist and the dark, ominous city Oliver encounters serve to draw readers into the narrative and absorb their attention. Equally compelling in this respect are the novel's notable characters, the pompous beadle, the brutal housebreaker, his penitent mistress and the devilish receiver of stolen property. Each transcends the social and historical context Dickens drew upon when he created them and retains a freshness and power capable of affecting modern readers as well. Such is the nature of a classic, a work that surpasses its cultural context and knows few boundaries.

By shifting our perspective, we can see another dimension of *Oliver Twist*'s appeal. Family misfortunes deprived Dickens of the security one usually associates with a middle-class upbringing, substituting for a conventional, uninterrupted education a period of intense misery during which Dickens worked for his living in humiliating conditions. As a hungry twelve-year-old, he acquired sufficient self-discipline to divide his small wage into seven daily allotments and master impulse buying when he passed shops stuffed with food. He also gained a knowledge of London's dark alleys and filthy courts almost unparalleled among his literary and artistic contemporaries. Frowzy dens and "the great black world of Crime and Shame,"[3] readers soon recognize, constitute the London that Dickens explores in *Oliver Twist*.

The terror and bewilderment Oliver experiences upon his arrival in the metropolis reflect powerful lessons Dickens conveyed to contemporary readers. Glancing at the demographic shifts that characterize Britain's industrial development in the early nineteenth century, one sees two major trends. For the fortunate, arriving in London conferred social mobility upon those who could use the city's anonymity to escape class boundaries and exploit through hard work the many opportunities for success London offered. For the unfortunate, like many characters in the novel, London resembled a vast sink of privation. Abandoned children and destitute adults turned to thievery and other crimes, while girls and young women fell into "the weed-choked well" inhabited by the Nancys of real life.

Still, the reception of *Oliver Twist* in 1837 was not completely favorable. A strident minority of Victorian reviewers of *Oliver Twist* claimed that the novel corrupted its readers. By depicting too freely the "melancholy shades of life," they argued, Dickens ran counter to his professed sympathy for the poor, whose interest in crime he abetted rather than checked by investing his villains with false glamour.

Other opponents of *Oliver Twist* linked the novel with the productions of the "School of Criminal Romance," an invidious comparison which implicitly accused Dickens of capitalizing on the sensational works of William Harrison Ainsworth and Bulwer Lytton. The critics of Newgate ficton also charged that the popular crime novels distorted the real nature of thieves, murderers, and prostitutes by presenting them as good people wronged by an unsympathetic society.

Thackeray, the most intelligent and articulate of these critics, added other objections. He maintained that no writer sensitive to his public could tell the whole truth about such evil characters without violating accepted codes of literary propriety. He also shared the view that the rash of stage versions of *Oliver Twist* and *Jack Sheppard* following their appearance in *Bentley's Miscellany* in 1837 and 1839 encouraged practicing and potential criminals, an opinion put so forcefully by others that, as mentioned earlier, the Lord Chamberlain's office interdicted dramatizations of these crime stories for nearly twenty years. Controvery continued to haunt performances of *Oliver Twist* in the 1860's, when the graphic violence of Nancy's murder on stage materialized as another issue, a concern which reappeared over one hundred years later. In 1962, MP's in the House of Commons raised questions about a BBC television version of the novel shown to British audiences at a time generally reserved for family viewing.

Dickens did not really find an opportunity to reply to his critics until 1841; the reason for this delay is tied to the publishing history of *Oliver Twist*.

In a way, chance openings with different publishers led to the writing of *Oliver Twist*. Through a common friend, Dickens met John Macrone, his first publisher. Macrone's confidence in the marketability of the sketches of London life Dickens had written for various journals and newspapers led to the republication of these essays in collected form as *Sketches by Boz* (First Series, February 1836), a work which, in turn, brought further contracts. A second publishing firm, Chapman and Hall, approached Dickens with a proposal that led to the commencement of *The Pickwick Papers* as a serial in March 1836, while Macrone, encouraged by the public's response to "Boz," signed a second contract with Dickens for "Gabriel Vardon," as Dickens originally referred to *Barnaby Rudge*. Later that summer, a third publisher, Richard Bentley, lured Dickens from Macrone by offering him more money for not one but two novels. Dickens's involvement with Bentley subsequently increased when the latter asked him to edit a new monthly periodical, a collection of humorous articles "from the pens of eminent writers," and contribute something of his own to each issue as well.

The language of the agreement Dickens signed on 4 November 1836 specified the amount but not the nature of the matter Dickens contracted to supply every month. This vagueness hinders critics from determining exactly when Dickens first thought of *Oliver Twist*, but the unspecific phrase, "original article of his own writing," must have been an advantage in not pinning Dickens down to a particular subject with *Pickwick* incomplete and two other novels promised to Bentley. The contract also contained other attractive features. Serving as editor insured Dickens a predictable income in addition to the money he earned as an author. And, by a separate arrangement between the publisher and the artist, Bentley put George Cruikshank, Britain's foremost graphic artist, at Dickens's disposal as the journal's illustrator.

An editor's monthly salary and the added security of Cruikshank's reputation constituted tangible benefits, although they did not bring lasting satisfaction to the author, who quickly understood that his own commercial value far exceeded the terms of the 1836 contract. This awareness led to considerable tension between Bentley and Dickens, to which the publisher responded by attempting to hold Dickens to the provisions of the original agreement and the author by insisting on better payment and threatening to withhold *Oliver Twist*. On two occasions, Dickens acted on his word. In October 1837, he substituted a second Mudfog Paper for the serial installment and the following September he held back *Oliver Twist*'s eighteenth number. Dickens excused himself by saying that the rush to finish the manuscript in time for its publication as a novel in November 1838 made impossible the preparation of the monthly installment. A more likely interpretation of his action suggests that he did not want to undermine the success of the novel in book form by revealing too early its exciting climax.

By such tactics Dickens demonstrated that he held the whip hand, despite his legal subservience to Bentley implicit in the various contracts he signed with the publisher. A similar conflict of wills characterizes Dickens's relationship with Cruikshank, although the gestures prove less overt and must be read more carefully. The interpretation accepted by literary critics generally stresses Dickens's ascendancy over the illustrator, the faithful executor in a visual medium of the author's literary commands. Significant work by John Harvey and Richard A. Vogler forces a radical revision of this view and requires one to evaluate with precision both the relationship between Dickens and Cruikshank and their respective roles in *Oliver Twist*. But the arguments of Harvey and Vogler do not alter the consensus that once the Inimitable had defined himself he knew that he could stand without any assistance from the Illustrious. Some sense of their rivalry may be inferred from Dickens's silence about Cruikshank's help when he published *Oliver Twist* as a book in November 1838. In this edition and in later ones Dickens made no reference to Cruikshank's role, a courtesy all the more conspicuously absent when we recall the gracious tribute he paid the illustrator in the 1836 Preface to *Sketches by Boz*, where Dickens readily acknowledged Cruikshank's help.

After the publication of *Oliver Twist* in three volumes in 1838 Dickens temporarily detached himself from the novel. Under the terms of the original contract, Bentley paid Dickens a lump sum for the book's copyright and reserved for himself the profit from all future sales. Such an arrangement represented standard practice at the time, although to an author like Dickens with a rising reputation the agreement proved less satisfying because it denied him a share in his own increasing market value. The successive editions of *Oliver Twist* that Bentley published between 1838 and 1840, therefore, elicited little attention from their author, and no opportunity to answer—with a Preface—his critics until Chapman and Hall, who had remained Dickens's principal publishers since *The Pickwick Papers*, bought Bentley's interest in the novel and drew up an entirely new contract. By paying Dickens royalties from all future sales and naming him the book's sole proprietor, Chapman and Hall revived his interest in the work. Dickens proposed a new edition of *Oliver Twist* and wrote what he termed "an interesting preface" in March 1841 to stimulate public enthusiasm for the novel, secure in the knowledge that his rekindled commitment could in no way benefit Bentley.

The 1841 Preface was Dickens's opportunity to reply to his critics—those "jolter-headed enemies" of the novel, whom he deeply resented—and, coincidentally, of course, to arouse renewed interest in *Oliver Twist* and its social concerns. A mixture of reason and indignation characterizes this document, a critical manifesto comparable in tone and intensity to Émile Zola's reply to his detractors in 1880, whom he confronted in his volume of essays entitled *Le Roman expérimental*.

In part, Dickens based his response on an analysis of the eighteenth-century literary tradition to which *Oliver Twist* belonged. Henry Fielding and others, he pointed out, used Newgate as a mirror held up to nature to reveal social truths, in this case the affinity between the upper and lower classes. In both groups, the same corrupt morality could be observed, except that wealth and titles protected the great and saved them from the gallows, where those without privilege and rank often ended their lives. At the same time, Dickens clearly lost patience with reviewers when they railed at him for presenting life as it really is. It is useless to discuss whether Nancy's devotion to the brutal Sikes is "natural or unnatural, probable or improbable, right or wrong," he countered, adding emphatically, "IT IS TRUE." By this he meant true to two realities: the social and the divine. Nancy's behavior, he explained, was something he had tracked "through many profligate and noisome ways" some years before he dealt with it in fiction. "It is [also] emphatically God's truth," he noted, that a genuine religious impulse could survive even among London's most "depraved and miserable breasts."

Later developments in Dickens's career suggest that the arguments he expressed in the 1841 Preface originated from conviction rather than from an expedient position adopted simply to silence his opponents. Several of the themes he explored in *Oliver Twist*, for example, reappeared in subsequent novels, whose focus on neglected children, crime, and poverty indicates the extent of his interest in subjects indiscriminately labelled sensational or exploitive by hostile reviewers. Furthermore, his philanthropic work and the issues he championed as a journalist and public speaker provide additional proof of his sincerity.

Dickens's efforts on behalf of Ragged Schools and prostitutes, for example, two focal points of his charitable pursuits with Angela Burdett Coutts, have an obvious affinity with the social themes of the novel. These endeavors also show a personal willingness to work practically for the principles of support and help the novel advocates.

A similar case for continuity can be made for the essays Dickens published in the *Examiner* attacking the system of baby "farming" he satirized in Chapter Two of *Oliver Twist*, the opposition he expressed to public executions in the *Daily News* and the *Times*, and his contributions to *Household Words* and *All the Year Round* from 1850 onwards. Many of his magazine articles returned to the issues he examined in the novel, touching on the importance of schools for children, a concern for public health, and the ever-present need to improve England's Poor Laws, a subject to which he reverted in his last complete novel, *Our Mutual Friend* (1864–65).

Interest in a very different aspect of *Oliver Twist*, however, characterizes Dickens's involvement with the novel towards the end of his life when he resolved in 1868 to adapt the last part of the narrative for performance during his Farewell Series of public readings. Comments by Dickens in his letters reveal how seriously he prepared, first testing the reading before an invited audience and then modifying the text so as to include Sikes's death in the three chapters he carefully adapted from the final scenes of *Oliver Twist*. At the same time, Dickens's correspondence is less explicit about why he wanted to add "the Oliver Twist murder," as he referred to it, although we can infer from the letters his realization that Nancy's murder offered spectacular histrionic possibilities. Performing the scene also gave Dickens the chance to prove his indisputable mastery of a form of public entertainment he had done much to establish when he began reading professionally in 1858. By all accounts, he succeeded, earning almost unanimous and unqualified praise from his contemporaries for the brilliance of the *Sikes and Nancy* reading.

Some modern critics, by contrast, tend to view Dickens's success more ambiguously, seeing in the exhaustive demands the scene required an unconscious but powerful impulse to shorten his life. Edgar Johnson, for example, goes as far as to argue that in adding the strenuous *Sikes and Nancy* episode to his repertoire of readings Dickens was "sentencing himself to death." He took this course, Johnson contends, because by this late stage of his life Dickens had "ceased to care what happened," arguing that a combination of domestic and personal disappointments rendered Dickens careless of his health and alienated from middle-class society.[4] Viewing the *Sikes and Nancy* episode in these terms unquestionably affords a different perspective. Whether one accepts or rejects Johnson's interpretation depends on one's willingness to remove *Oliver Twist* from the Victorian context we have just examined.

II

Oliver Twist has continued to remain one of Dickens's most popular novels, generating in the years following its publication a sustained critical discourse, whose central issues frequently engage both early and modern critics.

Several of Dickens's reviewers, for example, spoke approvingly of his verisimilitude, finding a fidelity of observation in *Oliver Twist* comparable to that of the camera obscura. Comparisons with realistic painters were also common, so that the early notices often referred to figures like Ostade, Teniers, Wilkie, Hogarth, and Cruikshank. Another reviewer compared Oliver to "a sort of London Ulysses" who encounters not mythic beasts and enchanting maidens but genuine criminals, the offspring of a real urban hell where people rather than shades suffer in genuine misery. Less fancifully, John Forster summed up much of the laudatory early criticism of the novel with his simple assertion that in Dickens's writings "we find reality."

Many modern critics agree, especially those who emphasize the book's topicality and the importance of the workhouse chapters. In them and in the closing account of Fagin in the condemned cell several locate the novel's greatest power and praise

Dickens for his ability to make palpable the workhouse, the parish, and the prison. By showing his contemporaries the folly of their punitive response to poverty, these critics argue, Dickens isolated an important social truth: the flaw in the policies of the reformers, men whose well meaning but rigid efforts to improve society tended to go astray. The parish workhouse under the efficient but heartless regimen of applied Benthamism more likely induced criminal behavior among able-bodied paupers than provided an incentive to work, as the reformers intended. Dickens conveys his sense of their failure in the novel's original subtitle, "The Parish Boy's Progress." Oliver's essential goodness, of course, saves him from the criminal life a parish boy might have lived, a twist to the plot sterner champions of realism ignore.

For those who lament the protagonist's transformation into a middle-class hero who is finally established in domestic ease, *Oliver Twist* still offers some consolation. Its treatment of adult criminals like Sikes and Fagin reveals a masterly hand, one which is realistic at several levels. Near unanimity exists that the presentation of Sikes after he murders Nancy and the depiction of Fagin after his arrest contain not only some of the best narrative prose and psychological realism in the novel but some of the best examples of each in the world's literature.

The intensity of Dickens's involvement with Fagin merits a word of caution, especially to those who argue that Dickens is so completely caught up with his outlaws that the kinship he expresses towards the fence and his gang is greater than his disgust. Approaching the novel from this perspective leads some critics to overstate the novel's subversive elements by locating Dickens's "greatest moments" exclusively in the scenes of death and violence. In a similar vein, others insist that an anarchic intelligence pervades the novel, delighting in the amorality of London's underworld and sympathizing with its inhabitants. Compared with the bland good people the criminals certainly appear to advantage and fire Dickens's imagination in ways that Mr. Brownlow and Mrs. Maylie fail to. This fact did not escape Victorian readers. But modern critics go too far when they deny

Dickens's intention to castigate thieves and murderers and read biographical implications into his ability to explore the criminal mind. As Philip Collins suggests, one can admit the complexity of Dickens's outlook and his ability to write convincingly about criminals without granting that he was an outcast himself.

Twentieth-century critics occupy firmer ground when they express reservations about the formulaic attitudes toward Jews which Dickens embraced in his portrait of Fagin. Commentators have pointed out that Dickens does little to individualize his fence, relying only on a few conventional touches to establish his Jewishness—his occupation, avarice, and the hooked nose of Cruikshank's illustrations. That is exactly the point: in a culture that has denigrated Jews for several hundred years a writer can easily tap centuries of accumulated hatred merely by repeating the epithet, "The Jew."

A chorus of protests rebukes Dickens for the "vile prejudice" he encouraged towards Jews and occasions modern commentators to ask what one can "do" about Fagin. Apart from confronting him forthrightly, a response not always evident among critics, few possibilities exist. Some writers futilely debate the extent to which Dickens did or did not share the stereotypical attitudes he depicts. Some argue against the undesirability of democratic societies attempting to censor works with anti-Semitic elements. Others explain Fagin historically, the defense Dickens himself chose when Eliza Davis, a contemporary Jewish woman, protested that his portrait of the fence admitted only a negative interpretation. Nevertheless, granting Fagin's historical verisimilitude does not explain how Dickens dredged out of the collective folklore of Western culture an image of the Jew before which Gentiles should bow their heads.

My own view is that Dickens embraced conventionally offensive attitudes to Jews in apparent innocence and did not pause to question them until Mrs. Davis admonished him in 1862. However unsatisfactory Riah might appear to modern eyes, Dickens's good Jew in *Our Mutual Friend* deserves consideration as an act of atonement, a genuine effort by the creator of Fagin to upstage the Western tradition of the odious Jew with a revised figure. As

a wise, compassionate man, an individual at one with Jenny
Wren and Lizzie Hexam in their imaginative Golden Bower far
above the gritty reality of smoky London, Riah stands out as a
newly-minted persona, representing Dickens's attempt to reverse
the fraternity of Jewish villains so prominent in Western culture.
The textual revisions to the 1867 edition of *Oliver Twist* offer
further evidence of a reappraisal. And although Dickens began
to substitute "Fagin" or a personal pronoun for the repetitive
epithet only at Chapter 34, such revisions suggest that Dickens
took Mrs. Davis's reproof to heart. Reading the revised text, we
see that Fagin stands alone as an individual and not simply as
"the Jew," as he does in the earlier editions of the novel.
"Nothing extenuate,/Nor set down aught in malice," Mrs. Davis
urged Dickens, quoting *Othello* to evident effect, if we assume
that a new sensitivity towards Jews prompted the textual
changes.

Assessing the novel's artistry has been a major concern of
twentieth-century critics and presents fewer problems. The language of *Oliver Twist* reveals many of the accomplishments that
characterize Dickens's greatest novels, sharing some of the
richness in the varieties of prose rhythm, dialogue, and linguistic
textures we commonly associate with them. In the early chapters, Dickens's anger at those who cloak their political intentions
in abstract terminology and jargon suggests a vigilance to linguistic abuse comparable to that of George Orwell and Arthur
Koestler, two writers equally sensitive to the ways enemies of
humanity obscure their designs by mouthing slogans and reducing people to mathematical equations. Later, when the action
develops, narrative and description predominate, as Dickens
seizes the opportunity to explore the growing complexity of city
life and probe its "secret spots." The phrase belongs to Osbert
Sitwell, who cites *Oliver Twist* as the forerunner of the modern
thriller in which the narrator, like the detective, unravels a tale of
crime and uses coincidence as a device to connect the seemingly
distinct parts of urban life. Sitwell also praises Dickens for his
ability to accomplish one of fiction's greatest challenges: the
transformation of a comic character into one capable of great

heroism. In the scene in which Charley Bates throws himself on Nancy's murderer, Sitwell argues, Dickens "rises on the wings of his genius," as he brings about the metamorphosis of Bates without a break in the character's continuity.

Other critics, by contrast, show less interest in the various aspects of the novel's realism and explore how *Oliver Twist* operates on other levels as well. Its world, as J. Hillis Miller contends, has much in common with dream and poetic symbolism, so that the claustrophobia of Fagin's den comes from the references to the labyrinth and the devil of myth rather than from the topographical exactness with which Dickens describes Field Lane in Holborn. Several other writers, some independently and some following Miller, pursue similar arguments, so we now commonly speak of the mythic, folkloric, and fairy tale elements of *Oliver Twist*, recognizing in the waif's struggle against evil a battle with several dimensions.

Taken as a whole, however, the novel's artistic reputation varies. Modern critics generally agree that *Oliver Twist* lacks the compositional richness of the major novels, even though, in embryonic form, it reveals some affinity with them. Different centers of interest exist, separate groups of characters are drawn together, foreshadowing and symbolism heighten the narrative. But *Oliver Twist* remains flawed in a fundamental way: plot and theme fail to coincide. Not all writers employ the same critical terminology, but among those who point to this weakness a consensus exists that the novel explores two contradictory truths. One half of *Oliver Twist* examines the symbolic role of Providence, a divine power that protects the child-hero and delivers him to his bourne. The other focuses on the consequences of social injustice and suggests how the victims of an oppressive state are pushed relentlessly towards crime.

Dickens's failure to unite these two disparate threads prompts a good deal of misunderstanding, particularly among those who find the second a more worthy concern and attack the protagonist for his lack of realism. Had Oliver come down to posterity as a feral child of the slums, these critics would have been delighted. Instead, Dickens chose to present him as the embodiment of indelible goodness, one whose innate gentility, courteous manners, and standard English signify the imprint not of the workhouse but heaven. Annoyed critics sometimes respond by insulting Oliver with various tags, most frequently those of a political cast. But the fact remains that Dickens valued middle-class attributes and saw no incongruity in rewarding his spiritual hero with the material benefits of comfort, education, and domesticity.

Modern readers nevertheless are likely to question Dickens's lack of realism and complain that Oliver strains their credulity. Later in his career, Dickens created portraits of goodness that present fewer problems, protagonists like Esther Summerson and Amy Dorrit who are convincing because they are equipped with an inner life. Oliver lacks a psychological dimension and works primarily as an allegorical figure embodying the writer's view that the blessed triumph: "I wished to show, in little Oliver, the principle of Good surviving through every adverse circumstance, and triumphing at last," Dickens explains in the Preface to the 1841 edition. This statement suggests the futility of expecting Oliver to act as an individual responsible for his own destiny, no matter how hard the modern sensibility finds Dickens's view to accept. For taking goodness seriously and making it palpable constitute two of his most enduring concerns. Readers, he believed, should be encouraged, a professional conviction he championed throughout his career.

Dickens's later novels offer a bleak view of Victorian society, where life's "sombre colours" emanate from its institutions and the social order rather than from "the jaundiced eyes and hearts" of individuals, as specified by the narrator of *Oliver Twist*. Yet by insisting that not all is "dark and gloomy," the narrator affirms "the real hues," whose delicate vision Dickens never forsook, even in his most pessimistic works. To the novelist, the emissaries of light remained no less powerful than those of darkness, a truth he always tried to convey to his readers. *Oliver Twist*, like all Dickens's fiction, combines a "sharp anatomization of humbug" with cheerful views[5] and urges readers to live life "along the moral plane." Like Orwell, who coins the phrase in his essay on the novelist, Dickens rejoiced in life's ineffable worth and exuded a common sense feeling that people are capable of becoming a little more humane and a little more civilized. After nearly a century and a half of critical commentary on *Oliver Twist,* that much is clear.

NOTES

1. *The Letters of Charles Dickens, Volume One: 1820–1839*, The Pilgrim Edition, ed. Madeline House and Graham Story (Oxford: Clarendon Press, 1965), p. 227.

2. "Marionettes to Teach Foreign-Born English," *New York Herald Tribune*, 20 April 1937, p. 19.

3. Dickens to Angela Burdett Coutts, 4 January 1854, in *The Heart of Charles Dickens*, ed. Edgar Johnson (New York: Duell, Sloan and Pearce, 1952), p. 252.

4. Edgar Johnson, *Charles Dickens: His Tragedy and Triumph*, 2 vols. (New York: Simon and Schuster, 1952), II, 1104.

5. *The Letters of Charles Dickens, Volume Four: 1844–1846*, The Pilgrim Edition, ed. Kathleen Tillotson (Oxford: Clarendon Press, 1977), p. 328.

ACKNOWLEDGMENTS

A study of this kind inevitably accumulates many debts. Of the institutions and individuals who have provided support of various kinds, I am most anxious to record my gratitude to the following: John D. Kendall, Librarian of the University of Massachusetts, Amherst, and the staff of the Interlibrary Loan Office, particularly Edla Holm, for her constant assistance in locating books and periodicals; Professor Vincent J. DiMarco, Chairman, Department of English, University of Massachusetts, Amherst, for his enthusiastic and extremely effective support for the project throughout its multiple stages; to Professor Murray M. Schwartz, Dean of the Faculty of Humanities and Fine Arts, for support to cover some of the costs of the preparation of the manuscript; and the University of Massachusetts, for providing funds for travel to the Dickens House, London. At the Dickens House, David Parker, the Curator, introduced me to the collection, while Kevin Harris proved a most friendly and helpful assistant, whose work on my behalf enabled me to make full use of the time I had available. Elsewhere, several librarians answered questions and provided me with copies of materials I sought. I would like to acknowledge the help I received from Lisa Backman, N. F. Nash, and Catherine Stover. I also owe particular thanks to Alan M. Cohn, Joseph Donohue, Louis James, Alec Lucas, Meredith Raymond, Harry Stone, and J. P. Wearing, all of whom answered questions and helped in various ways. Richard Fulkerson most kindly sent me a copy of the relevant chapters from his dissertation. I wish to thank Mary Coty for her fast and expert typing. Most especially, I want to take this opportunity to thank Duane DeVries, general editor of the series, for his advice, support, and help: throughout, he has proved a superb editor.

PART I
TEXT

I. OLIVER TWIST IN PROGRESS: DICKENS'S LETTERS CONCERNING THE NOVEL, THE MANUSCRIPT, AND HIS AGREEMENTS WITH PUBLISHERS

1. Dickens, Charles. **The Letters of Charles Dickens.** Volume One 1820-1839. The Pilgrim Edition. Ed. Madeline House and Graham Storey. Oxford: Clarendon Press, 1965, passim.

The letters assembled by the editors of Volume One provide a detailed account of how Dickens made his debut as the editor of **Bentley's Miscellany** in January 1837, began **Oliver Twist** as a serial the next month, and also continued to write and publish **The Pickwick Papers** in monthly parts. From February 1837 to April 1839, **Oliver Twist** appeared in the **Miscellany** as the magazine's new attraction, running continuously except for three breaks. See II. 1. This second novel soon swept its readers along and quickly affected Dickens too, giving him energy to sustain two serial works simultaneously between February and October 1837, when **The Pickwick Papers** and **Oliver Twist** overlapped.

From the first, Dickens exuded optimism about **Oliver Twist**, taking "a great fancy" to his protagonist (p. 225) and warming up even more when he thought about the "great things" he hoped to do with Nancy (p. 328). In order to resist the temptation of working too hard, he told John Forster in November 1837, he had to apply himself "to the labour of being idle" in order to keep his hands off "Fagin and the rest of them in the evenings" (p. 328). On another day, Dickens confidently introduced himself to a respected reporter from whom he wanted help arranging a visit to Hatton Garden court so that he could watch Mr. Laing at work and use his observation of this notoriously severe police magistrate as the basis for Chapter 12 in the novel when Oliver appears before Mr. Fang (p. 267). Later that year, he thanked the owner of **The Statistical Journal** for sending him on request a copy of his magazine (pp. 315-16n.). The tables about juvenile delinquency, Dickens explained, proved most useful, evidently helping his understanding of the problem and thus contributing to the novel. From the opening chapters onwards, the various threads of **Oliver Twist** appear, then, to have fallen readily into place. By 20 October 1838, he had completed the manuscript of the novel, applying himself to its close with "hearty energy" as he sent Sikes to the Devil and "disposed" of Fagin.

The extant letters referring to the early history of **Oliver Twist** provide less definitive information about the novel's genesis, a subject of dispute among scholars. According to Kathleen Tillotson (XII. 201), a comment Dickens made to H.W. Kolle in December 1833 suggests that he had in mind a general notion of a work based on London life at this early date. Shortly after the **Monthly Magazine** published Dickens's first story, "A Dinner at Poplar Walk," in December 1833, he informed Kolle that "The Monthly people" had requested more pieces. If we close our treaty, Dickens wrote, he intended to "commence a series of papers ... called **The Parish,**" for which he had been noting down materials "for some time past." If these succeeded, he added, he would cut his "proposed Novel up into little Magazine Sketches" and try to publish them in **The Metropolitan.** Some of this material found its way into

3

Sketches by Boz, 1836 (XIV. 1), but this reference and certain others, argues Tillotson, "indicate a long incubation for the novel" (II. 48). Burton M. Wheeler, by contrast, notes that the assumption that Dickens referred to Oliver Twist in the letter to Kolle lacks support and suggests instead that he spoke of Sketches by Boz, which he was writing at the time (XII. 210). On this, and other grounds, Wheeler, therefore, cautions readers about Tillotson's "long incubation" theory.

Specific references to Oliver Twist, in fact, do not appear in Dickens's correspondence until after he agreed to edit Bentley's journal and had written his first paper for the Miscellany, the "Public Life of Mr. Tulrumble." This humorous sketch fulfilled the terms he had agreed upon with Bentley in November 1836 to supply monthly "an original article of his own writing" in addition to his editorial duties. But some time between its completion on 5 December 1836 and the end of the year, Dickens changed his mind, deciding instead to write a continuous piece of prose fiction for serial distribution rather than the unconnected articles the contract permitted. Extant evidence provides no further clues about the precise date of the novel's genesis, although we can infer that work on Oliver Twist began around this time from the letter Dickens sent George Cruikshank, the novel's illustrator. On 9 January 1837 Dickens expressed his willingness to the artist to "settle our illustration" for the first serial number of Oliver Twist and apologized for the delay, promising "to behave better next time" and deliver the manuscript earlier (p. 221). Thus during the Christmas period of 1836, Dickens assumed the triple labor of writing Oliver Twist and The Pickwick Papers and serving also as the editor of a monthly journal.

Personal details in the letters convey some sense of the strain these tasks imposed. The "vagaries" of his first "son and heir," he writes, rob him of a night's sleep and leave him in a "woeful plight" (p. 355), while an unexpected visitor stops in and forces Dickens to stop too, just as he was "in the humour for writing" (p. 346). On other occasions he grumbles about having to sit with his wife, just as he had fallen on Oliver "tooth and nail," or complains that his work gets in "the most foggy perspective" he ever saw it in after an attack of illness (pp. 387 and 419). Nothing, however, shook and unnerved Dickens so greatly as the sudden death of Mary Hogarth, his young sister-in-law, on 7 May 1837. This loss left him prostrate with grief and unable to write the serial installments of Oliver Twist and The Pickwick Papers for a month.

For the writer who works at home amidst a growing family, domestic interruptions become part of his lot, a situation Dickens apparently accepted even if his letters during this period suggest a testy attitude that contrasts sharply with H. Burnett's account of him working happily in company (I. 3). One source of annoyance during the composition of Oliver Twist, however, grew beyond proportions Dickens could control, as comments in his letters about Richard Bentley indicate.

The Pilgrim editors call Bentley "one of the most prominent of Victorian publishers" (p. 164n.). He was also a shrewd business man, as his initial dealings with Dickens suggest. John Macrone, of course, deserves recognition among Dickens's publishers for his willingness to bring out his first book, Sketches by Boz. Bentley, however, played a greater role in Dickens's early career as an author, first by luring him from Macrone in August 1836 with a higher offer for the projected novel ("Gabriel Vardon") Dickens had promised Macrone in May 1836 (I. 6), and second, by engaging Dickens in the November of the same year to edit a monthly journal. Under the terms of the November contract, Bentley agreed to pay Dickens twenty pounds a month for his services as editor and a further twenty-one pounds as a contributor to the publication in return for sixteen pages of original writing each month.

To a young and inexperienced author, the prospect of an annual salary close to five hundred pounds must have been a "cool" one, as Joe Gargery might say.

When Dickens defaulted on his obligation to Macrone by cancelling the agreement for "Gabriel Vardon," he acted in his own interest, as he saw it. Bentley, however, demonstrated a similar ruthlessness, despite the generous contracts he negotiated in 1836 with Dickens, in whom he saw a promising and remunerative author. As Dickens's letters to Bentley show, relations between the two soon deteriorated, with Bentley revealing a determination to make the best of his partnership with Dickens matched only by the author's will to best his publishers.

Signs of tension appeared as early as July 1837, when Dickens, having considered "the subject very carefully" offered his "fixed conclusion" about his current agreement with Bentley (p. 284). Inflexible language like that from Dickens meant trouble. Understand, he warned Bentley, you either agree to the alterations I propose (increasing the copyright price of Oliver Twist and also raising the sum for Barnaby Rudge), or "I shall abide by the strict letter of my agreement respecting the Miscellany" (p. 284). This statement, perhaps a covert threat to discontinue Oliver Twist but still contribute sixteen pages of unconnected articles each month, Bentley chose to ignore temporarily. As Dickens's impatience grew when he received no response, he referred to Bentley in the unflattering terms Sikes used for Fagin. "No news, as yet," Dickens reported to Forster some weeks later, "from the 'infernal, rich, plundering, thundering old Jew'" (p. 292).

To show that he meant business when Bentley remained silent, Dickens suspended the October installment of Oliver Twist, attaching to the wrapper of the Miscellany the public explanation that "The great length of the proceedings of the Mudfog Association prevents the insertion of the usual continuation this month" (p. 301n.). A compromise followed which allowed the serial to stay on course, but Bentley unwisely played Scrooge next year by deducting money from Dickens when his monthly contributions totalled less than sixteen pages. Looking over the journal's sales, Dickens discovered in May 1838 how "some thirty or forty pounds" had been taken from him. Evidently the strong resentment with which Dickens expressed himself had some effect on Bentley because no further references to the accounts occur again. "Presumably Bentley made some conciliatory move," the Pilgrim editors conclude (pp. 401-02 and n.).

No gesture from Bentley would fully satisfy Dickens, unless the publisher released him from his original agreement to write Barnaby Rudge--(see I. 5)--and renegotiated the copyright terms for Oliver Twist. That novel, as the Miscellany's sales demonstrated each month, was capable of generating "immense profits" for his antagonist and a "paltry, wretched, miserable sum" for himself, Dickens complained to Forster on 21 January 1839. Why, he continued, should he struggle "in old toils" and waste energy filling the pockets of others, "while for those who are nearest and dearest to me I can realise little more than a genteel subsistence"? (pp. 493-94). The language of this letter, written after Bentley had published Oliver Twist in three volumes in November 1838 but before the serial version had finished in the Miscellany, conveys the extent to which Dickens's struggle with Bentley had become an obsession. Resigning therefore as editor on 31 January 1839 proved a necessary first step for Dickens to rid himself of a connection that had grown hateful to him. But peace of mind eluded him until he "burst the Bentleyean bonds" altogether by buying his way out of the contract to write Barnaby Rudge and purchasing the copyright of Oliver Twist in 1840. See I. 6.

In comparison with this protracted struggle, the other irritants that accompanied Dickens's success with Oliver Twist assume minor importance.

Within a year of the serial's commencement, stage versions of the novel began to appear as unscrupulous hacks capitalized on the story's popularity and presumed to finish the novel before Dickens had completed it. See VI. 1-3. Another worry, particularly in the later stages of the book, developed when Cruikshank failed to heed the text carefully and produced illustrations Dickens thought little of. See Dickens XIII. 14.

Scattered references to **Oliver Twist** also appear in Dickens's later correspondence and are conveniently indexed in volumes II-V of the Pilgrim Letters. Because the Pilgrim volumes do not presently go beyond 1849, readers interested in Dickens's comments about the reading version of **Oliver Twist** he prepared in 1869 and his occasional later references to **Oliver Twist** and its various editions must consult volume III of the Nonesuch Letters. For the **Sikes and Nancy** reading, see V. 4-7.

2. ———. **Oliver Twist; or, The Parish Boy's Progress.** By Boz. Illustrated by George Cruikshank. Bound manuscript. 2 vols. In the Forster Collection at the Library of the Victoria and Albert Museum, London.

The incomplete autograph manuscript consists of 474 folios (9.2 in. x 7.6 in.) containing twenty-two chapters of the novel (twenty-three chapters, chs. 12-13 and chs. 23-43 according to the final form of the chapter division). F.G. Kitton (IV. 16) notes that these chapters were found at Richard Bentley's office and purchased by Forster at Sotheby's for fifty pounds on 23 July 1870. The missing fragments, Kitton adds, were lost or destroyed during the clearing out of the publisher's warehouse in the absence of his son, George Bentley. Also missing are the concluding ten chapters of **Oliver Twist** (chs. 44-53), which Richard Bentley sold on 31 October 1838 to the Philadelphia publishers, Carey, Lea and Blanchard, who used them instead of early proofs for the preparation of their three volume edition of the novel published in 1839 (III. 18).

Some scraps of the manuscript, however, survive elsewhere. The Berg Collection possesses three leaves from Chapter 10 and two leaves from Chapter 15; one half leaf from Chapter 10 is in Dickens House; and the Gimbel Collection at Yale University has 1 1/3 leaves of Chapter 15. In the first passage, Barney waits on Fagin and Sikes at the Cripples; in the second, Oliver loses his way in Clerkenwell.

Unlike the middle and later novels, **Oliver Twist** was apparently composed without reference to any working notes or memoranda, although in a letter to Georgina Hogarth on 29 July 1857, Dickens refers to a "Newgate collection" he kept in his study of old cuttings, pamphlets, and pictures about the prison (N, II, 864-65), some of which he possibly drew upon when he wrote the novel. These papers seem to have disappeared, as have the proofs of **Oliver Twist,** of which there is no record of their existence.

Although only about two-fifths of the manuscript survive, the 474 folios hold considerable interest for scholars wishing to study Dickens at work during the first draft of the novel. The relative absence of the heavy deletions and interlinings that characterize his later manuscripts suggests a fluency, ease, and certainty of purpose, whose onward movement the legible and bold hand seems to confirm. Elaborating on this point in her introduction to the Clarendon edition of **Oliver Twist** (II. 48), Tillotson notes that Dickens appears to hesitate only when introducing a new scene or character or when writing a speech of particular importance to the plot.

The critical apparatus of the Clarendon edition allows the interested reader to make his own study of the many changes Dickens introduced at the earliest stage of the novel's composition. At the same time, one needs to note that Tillotson's decision to include "only the more important" of the manuscript deletions severely restricts a systematic scrutiny of the extant manuscript pages. Tillotson states that she provides only those deletions which indicate "a substantial change of intention, or illuminate the process of finding the aptest expression." These sensible limitations serve her editorial purpose as she conceives it but her policy frustrates the almost unique opportunity this manuscript provides, because of its legibility, to study the many fascinating examples of how Dickens altered his manuscript either as he wrote or at some unspecified time prior to sending it to the printers. Cf. Tanselle (III. 16). Among the many easily legible cancellations not recorded in the Clarendon apparatus are numerous instances of Dickens's condensing expressions and eliminating descriptive phrases, often after a line of dialogue, and removing repetitious words. Other examples show him adopting concrete expressions by altering a general "said" to a more specific "croaked," or by expanding short phrases and adding additional words. Sometimes these are for comic effect, such as the "fat old woman" who sits up with Oliver at night when he recuperates at Mr. Brownlow's and falls into "a series of short naps" during which she tumbles forward, moans, and chokes, instead of going to sleep for short intervals. On another occasion, Dickens remembers a minor but significant detail associated with one of his characters. When introducing the apothecary's apprentice sent by the parish to attend old Sally before she dies (ch. 24), Dickens refers to the youth's preoccupation with making a toothpick out of a quill. In the ensuing exchange between the apprentice and Mrs. Corney, Dickens initially forgets the young man's interest in his teeth, but later inserts a phrase about the toothpick with a caret, a necessary connecting reference in view of the final description of the apprentice planting himself before the fire and making good use of his instrument before leaving the scene. The manuscript is available on microfilm as "Manuscripts of Charles Dickens from the Forster Collection in the Victoria and Albert Museum, London," Film No. 96738 (Micro Methods Ltd. East Ardsley, Wakefield, Yorkshire), reel I.

3.   Burnett, Henry. "Words of Remembrance." In Frederic G. Kitton. A Supplement to Charles Dickens By Pen and Pencil, Including Anecdotes and Reminiscences Collected from his Friends and Contemporaries. London: Frank T. Sabin, 1890, pp. 7-8.

Notes how in Dickens's early days his untiring energy caused friends to worry that he was overworking while editing the **Miscellany** and writing both **The Pickwick Papers** and Oliver Twist. "His habit, for a limited time," writes Burnett, "was to retire to his study after supper about ten o'clock--and write till one, as a rule; but now and then the rule would be forgotten through the interest taken by him in his work, when the study-door would remain locked on the wrong side of his bed until two, and sometimes three o'clock in the morning, he feeling that the action of his mind--or the essence of it--was impeded in the daytime, that it could be brought with greater ease under control when silence reigned within and without, and there was freedom from noise, light, heat, distraction by a multitude of callers, and other hindrances." To this Kitton adds in a footnote Georgina Hogarth's comment that Dickens only worked thus in the **very, very,** early days." Within her knowledge, which dates only from 1843, she says of his working habits that "he rarely wrote in the night." For most of Dickens's career, the mornings were his normal time for writing.

4. Kitton, Frederic G. "Oliver Twist." In his **The Novels of Charles
    Dickens: A Bibliography and Sketch.** London, 1897; rpt. New York:
    AMS Press, 1975, pp. 29-30.

Quotes Henry Burnett's description of Dickens at work on a monthly
portion of **Oliver Twist** as Burnett (Dickens's brother-in-law), his wife, Fanny
Dickens, and Catherine Dickens sat cosily by the fire one evening enjoying a
chat at 48 Doughty Street, London. When Dickens found that he and
Catherine had visitors, he returned to his study, where he had been writing,
brought down the manuscript of **Oliver Twist,** seated himself at a little round
table in the corner of the room, and recommenced working. As the feather of
Dickens's pen moved rapidly from one side of the paper to the other, his
visitors, at his bidding, talked on, with Dickens putting in an occasional word.
"It was interesting to watch, upon the sly," writes Burnett, "the mind and the
muscles working (or, if you please, **playing**) in company, as new thoughts were
being dropped upon the paper. And to note the working brow, the set of the
mouth, with the tongue tightly pressed against the closed lips, as was his
habit."

5. Morgan, E.S. Untitled Manuscript. Collection of the Papers of Richard
    Bentley. University of Illinois. 23 pp.

In July 1837, E.S. Morgan, Bentley's chief accountant and aide, prepared
a "brief retrospect" of his associations with Bentley and Henry Colburn which
contributes to but does not settle the debate about when Dickens began
composing **Oliver Twist.** Wheeler (XII. 210) cites Morgan to support his
contention that Dickens did not start writing the novel "earlier ... than 1837,"
referring to Morgan's note that Dickens originally intended to commence
Oliver Twist in the first number of the **Miscellany** in January 1837. This
intention, Morgan writes, was frustrated by an attack of influenza. "I
remember calling upon him [Dickens] at his lodgings at Furnivals Inn for
Copy," Morgan recalls, "when he explained to me the cause of the delay,
promising that the opening chapter should be delivered in time for the 2nd
Number, to appear on the 1st of February, 1837."
Two points about this statement are worth noting. First, it tells nothing
about either the scope or proposed length of the story Dickens contemplated.
Second, it may contain errors of fact or interpretation, for which Morgan
himself makes tentative provision, apologizing for his "enfeebled powers of
brain" and "this imperfect sketch" of his professional life.

6. Dickens, Charles. "Agreements with Publishers." Appendix C. In
    Pilgrim Letters, Vol. I (I. 1), 647-80.

Between 22 August 1836 and 2 July 1840 Dickens and Richard Bentley
signed nine formal agreements, three of which are of special importance to
Oliver Twist and the vexed question of the novel's exact genesis. Dickens's
relationship with Bentley began in 1836 when he signed an agreement on 22
August to deliver two three-volume novels, selling the copyright of each to
the publisher for five hundred pounds a novel. The first, untitled but actually
planned as "Gabriel Vardon," as Dickens initially thought of **Barnaby Rudge,**
was the novel he had originally promised to John Macrone, whom he left when
Bentley doubled the copyright payment. The second represented something
far less specific, appearing in the contract simply as Dickens's "next novel" of
three volumes.
Three months later, Dickens drew closer to Bentley when he agreed on 4

November 1836 to edit a new monthly publication consisting of "articles of a humorous nature from the pens of eminent writers" and to supply each month "an original article [my emphasis] of his own writing ... of about a sheet of 16 pages." This contract, readers should note, made no further reference to the nature of the article, leaving the matter entirely within Dickens's hands. Such an arrangement undoubtedly suited him, but in the absence of any record of his intentions makes impossible the precise dating of the inception of Oliver Twist. Existing records, in fact, suggest that if Dickens had any definite plans for his monthly contribution at the time he may well have contemplated a series of loosely connected papers, something closer to Sketches by Boz than to The Pickwick Papers, the novel he already had in progress. In a draft of a Prospectus for the Miscellany, Dickens wrote that his objective as editor was to place before the public "a feast of the richest comic humour." He also affirmed his intention to avoid publishing extracts from books and to concentrate on "original articles," which, as the exclusive copyright of the publisher, will be found "nowhere else, and will never be collected in any other form." The Prospectus proves nothing about the evolution of Oliver Twist, although its language and last stipulation suggest that if Dickens contemplated an extended piece of fiction--in effect, a third novel--he kept his own counsel. As we know from existing letters, he said nothing to Bentley until early 1837, by which time he had committed himself to his "glance at the new poor Law Bill," as he described the opening chapters of Oliver Twist to a friend on 28 January 1837.

Within the next eight months, however, the contractual status of the novel changed radically when Dickens and Bentley signed another agreement on 28 September 1837. This document represents Bentley's de facto acceptance of Oliver Twist as one of the two novels Dickens had promised to deliver in 1836, a concession he won only after a bitter and protracted fight since Bentley understandably saw Dickens's proposal to make Oliver Twist serve a double purpose as a violation of the letter and spirit of the August and November agreements. But because Bentley wished to retain Dickens as his author and because he had no answer to his threat to discontinue Oliver Twist and resign from the Miscellany Bentley was forced to concede. Thus in a single move, Dickens reduced his debt to Bentley from two novels to one and altered the status of Oliver Twist, defining it as a three volume novel he had never originally planned. Under the terms of the September agreement, Oliver Twist would continue as a serial, after which Dickens would deliver the remainder of the manuscript in return for five hundred pounds. In view of these developments, scholars interested in the gestation of Oliver Twist can only lament the absence of relevant facts and note that Dickens began work on it in fulfillment of an agreement to write a series of articles but at some point early in 1837 altered his mind and thought of it as a full-length novel, whose copyright he later sold to Bentley while also receiving a monthly salary for the same individual installments.

The remaining agreements trace an increasingly tense relationship between two strong-willed men, whose inflexibility and hostility to each other eventually drove them apart. First, Dickens resigned as the editor of the Miscellany on 31 January 1839 but agreed to deliver Barnaby Rudge at a later date for two thousand pounds, a potential fourfold increase of the original sum. But in spite of this contract, signed by both parties on 27 February 1839, Dickens remained antagonistic and did not rest until he escaped Bentley's net altogether, which he did with the help of Chapman and Hall in the final agreement of 2 July 1840. In return for release from the agreement to write Barnaby Rudge, Dickens paid 2,250 pounds (advanced by his new publishers) for the rights, stock, and plates of Oliver Twist. For the text of this contract, see P, II, 471-75.

7. Fitzgerald, Percy. "Boz and his Publishers II: Richard Bentley and his Miscellany." Part One. The Dickensian, 3 (February 1907), 33-37; Part Two (March 1907), 70-73; Part Three (April 1907), 93-96.

Combines Fitzgerald's personal recollections of Bentley with an outline of Dickens's relationship with the publisher from the time he began editing the Miscellany to their eventual separation in 1840. Fitzgerald downplays the intensity of the quarrel and tries to provide a balanced account of Bentley, who, he thinks, behaved with "great moderation."

8. Gettmann, Royal A. "Agreements." In his A Victorian Publisher: A Study of the Bentley Papers. Cambridge: Cambridge Univ. Press, 1960, pp. 76-118.

An even-handed account of the almost epic quarrel between Dickens and Bentley, whose origin Gettmann traces to the standard nineteenth-century practice of arranging for future, unpublished manuscripts by selling their copyright to a publisher for a fixed sum. A far better procedure, he concludes, would have been for Dickens to have sold one book at a time, after the manuscript was ready for the press. In that way, Dickens's market value could have increased without the constraints imposed by negotiating a price for Barnaby Rudge and the other unnamed novel far in advance of their composition. See Dickens (I. 6). Gettmann censures Bentley for the niggardly manner in which he deducted small sums from Dickens when his contributions to the Miscellany failed to amount to sixteen pages. He also notes how Forster, Johnson, and other biographers have uncritically sided with Dickens, whose poor conduct Gettmann notes. Excessive pride and Dickens's easy recourse to righteous indignation, "that cheapest of virtues," writes Gettmann, as a way of solving a crisis prompted not only over-blown but "even sanctimonious" behavior from the novelist.

9. Johnson, Edgar. "The Break with Bentley." In his Charles Dickens: His Tragedy and Triumph. 2 Vols. New York: Simon and Schuster, 1952, I, 234-52. Also published as "Dickens Clashes with his Publishers." The Dickensian, 46 (Winter 1949-1950), 10-17, and 46 (Spring 1950), 76-83.

Narrates dramatically and succinctly the highlights of Dickens's protracted duel with Bentley. Johnson writes with unrestrained admiration for the will and tenacity Dickens showed, although he recognizes that Bentley deserves some sympathy. At every stage in their struggle, he notes, Bentley "had the law on his side." At the same time, the publisher "bristled with difficult traits," clashing inevitably with Dickens when he turned authoritarian and demanded his rights. Johnson also recognizes that much of the trouble between the two originated in the practice common at the time of publishers paying a lump sum for the absolute purchase of a copyright. This procedure worked when an author's reputation remained stable, but it was naturally unsatisfactory to Dickens, "whose popularity constantly outstripped every attempted readjustment." The revisions Dickens demanded, he concludes, represented "a common-sense view of fairness even if they were not embodied in contractual law."

10. Patten, Robert L. "Dickens and the Burlington Street Brigand." In his Charles Dickens and His Publishers. Oxford: Clarendon Press, 1978, pp. 75-87.

Distinguishes two major areas of friction between Dickens and Bentley: Dickens's annoyance with Bentley's interference with the editorial policies of the **Miscellany** and money. Patten sees Dickens as clearly the victor, wringing concession after concession from a tough opponent who had the law on his side but used his advantage clumsily. Patten comments that at times Dickens behaved "outrageously"; he also thinks that Dickens exaggerated the smallness of his payment for **Oliver Twist.** Instead of the wretchedly small sums Dickens complained of, he received almost eight hundred pounds. This amount, writes Patten, nearly equals "that Bentley had given Maria Edgeworth in 1834 for an edition of 3,000 copies of **Helen**" and one "considerably above Bentley's average offer" of slightly more than 250 pounds for an edition of 1,000. But if Dickens used deplorable methods, Patten concludes, his grievances were real.

II. EDITIONS

EDITIONS OF OLIVER TWIST 1837-1867 (chronological listing)

1. **Oliver Twist; or, The Parish Boy's Progress.** By Boz. Illustrated by George Cruikshank. Bentley's Miscellany, 1 (February 1837) to 5 (April 1839).

First published in the Miscellany in twenty-four monthly parts and contributed in fulfillment of Dickens's agreement in November 1836 to supply Bentley with sixteen pages of writing a month. A serialized novel, readers should note, was not part of Dickens's original plan, although once the idea of Oliver Twist developed after he had written his first Mudfog contribution to the Miscellany (I. 1), Dickens quickly threw his "whole heart and soul" into the novel's production. "[I] most confidently believe," he wrote to Bentley on 24 January 1837, that Oliver "will make a feature in the work, and be very popular" (P, I, 227).

Initially, Dickens had trouble supplying his serial quota for each month, producing only 10 1/2 pages for February and 12 or 12 1/2 for the next three numbers. To supplement these contributions, Dickens also wrote "The Pantomime Life" and "Some Particulars Concerning a Lion," submitted to the Miscellany as part of another feature, "Stray chapters by Boz," for the April and May issues respectively. Later that year, Dickens's installments settled down to an average of about fifteen pages, increasing only to a full sixteen in July 1838 after he discovered Bentley's pettiness in docking his payments when the monthly contributions fell short (I. 1). Irregularities in the serial's length do not occur again until the final numbers in 1839. In January, Dickens resigned as editor and allowed the remaining chapters of Oliver Twist to be squeezed in and made to fit around its new serial successor, Jack Sheppard.

After beginning Oliver Twist in February 1837, Dickens failed to contribute his serial installments on three occasions. Mary Hogarth's death on 7 May 1837 so upset him that he issued no monthly number of either Oliver Twist or The Pickwick Papers, placing in the June issue of the Miscellany an announcement to the effect that he had been compelled "to seek a short interval of rest and quiet." (For the text of this announcement, see P, I, 266-67n.) Later, disputes with Bentley in the summer of 1837 led Dickens to suspend his October contribution, putting in its stead the second of his Mudfog papers, the "Full Report of the First Meeting of The Mudfog Association for the Advancement of Everything." Finally, in the summer of 1838, Dickens held back his September contribution, ostensibly because he was busy finishing the manuscript, but in fact as a means of ensuring that the serial did not end before Bentley published the novel in book form. In place of the serial, Dickens included his third Mudfog paper, the "Full Report of the Second Mudfog Association for the Advancement of Everything." In February 1839 Dickens also published a farewell to his readers, "Familiar Epistle from a Parent to a Child, Aged Two Years and Two Months," which offset the 7 1/2 pages of Oliver Twist appearing the next month.

In Chapter 1 of the serial, Dickens described Oliver's birthplace as "the town of Mudfog," a fictitious name for Chatham originally coined for his opening contribution to the periodical, the "Public Life of Mr. Tulrumble,

Once Mayor of Mudfog." By using the name again, Dickens connected **Oliver Twist** with the Mudfog papers, presumably as a transition designed to link the novel with his first essay in January 1837. In subsequent revisions to the novel, Dickens eliminated the "Mudfog" reference and substituted "in a certain town" for Oliver's birthplace.

Cruikshank's twenty-four illustrations appeared one per issue for each of the monthly installments of **Oliver Twist**, with the exception of the eighteenth number (October 1838), which lacked its appropriate illustration, "The evidence destroyed." Subsequently this one was added to number twenty (December 1838), making two illustrations in this particular installment. Cruikshank's "Church" plate was used as the final illustration for **Oliver Twist** in the **Miscellany**.

2.   **Oliver Twist; or, The Parish Boy's Progress.** By "Boz." In 3 volumes.
     London: Richard Bentley, 1838.

As Tillotson points out (III. 17), Dickens never originally thought of **Oliver Twist** as a three-volume novel and did not propose its publication in this form until July 1837 (P, I, 284). He did this, she argues, as "a sop to Bentley," to whom Dickens had previously promised **Barnaby Rudge** in a prior agreement. With two serials on hand (**Oliver Twist** and **The Pickwick Papers**), Dickens had no time to work on **Barnaby Rudge** and he hoped that by substituting **Oliver Twist** as a three-volume publication for the former he could gain time to fulfill his original contract. In September 1837 Bentley agreed to bring out **Oliver Twist** in book form as well as a serial, naming midsummer 1838 as the publication date for the book. Dickens failed to make this deadline but managed to deliver the manuscript on 20 October 1838, five days ahead of the new due date. Twelve days later, Bentley advertised **Oliver Twist** for publication on 7 November; the book appeared two days later and sold for twenty-five shillings.

The rapid production necessitated by this schedule led to several printing errors, all of which complicate the textual and bibliographical history of **Oliver Twist** and account for the confusing designations collectors have used to distinguish one "edition" from the next. Because Dickens was away on a brief holiday in Wales during the printing of the final volume, he never saw the plates Cruikshank designed for volume three (XIII. 14). In his absence he also missed the opportunity to oversee the title-page and the final pages of the text. However, in a compromise between author and publisher, Dickens reduced from five to one the number of plates he wanted Cruikshank to redesign, while Bentley accepted a new title-page. This revision substituted "Charles Dickens" for "Boz" and also made reference on the title-page to Dickens as "Author of **The Pickwick Papers.**" Trade orders of the first impression (528 had been accepted and put aside) nevertheless went out, a necessity to which Forster and Dickens agreed. The copies all bore the inscription "By Boz" on the title-page and included the "Fireside" plate (XIII. 14) as the final illustration to volume three. "It is not clear," notes Tillotson (III. 17), "whether the new title or the new plate was ready first," for several variants exist. Some copies combine the "Boz" title with the redesigned "Church" plate (XIII. 14), while at least one is known in which the "Charles Dickens" title appears with the "Fireside" plate. Further variants occur with the list of Cruikshank's illustrations (added upon Dickens's request), which appears with both the "Boz" and "Charles Dickens" title-pages. Cruikshank contributed twenty-four plates, nine of which were in volume one, seven in two, and eight in three. Readers interested in the collation and the printing history of the volumes of the various "editions" should consult Tillotson's

"Descriptive List of Editions" in the Clarendon **Oliver Twist** and her article on this edition (XII. 17).

A comparison of the manuscript, the text in **Bentley's Miscellany**, and that of the 1838 edition shows that Dickens revised **Oliver Twist** in serial form at the proof stage. He also revised volumes one and two a little further but more or less ignored volume three. Copy for volumes one and two was taken from printed magazine installments, while volume three was set from the manuscript. Tillotson (III. 17) states that Dickens showed little interest in the final serial chapters, whose copy came from volume three of the novel, allowing them to be awkwardly cut in order to fit in with Ainsworth's new work in the **Miscellany, Jack Shepherd**. She does note, however, the chapters for the December number, in which Dickens removed the word "pilaster" from the description of Noah's hiding place on London Bridge and substituted "pier or pedestal" in one place and "pier" in another **(Oliver Twist**, ch. 46). These revisions appear in a single copy of the "Charles Dickens" issue seen by Tillotson, thus giving rise to the distinction between the "pilaster" and "pier" copies of the second issue.

3.   **Oliver Twist.** By Charles Dickens. Author of "The Pickwick Papers." In 3 volumes. London: Richard Bentley, 1838.

Published within a few days of the "Boz" issue with the new title page and Cruikshank's revised "Church" plate in volume three.

4.   **Oliver Twist.** By Charles Dickens. Author of "The Pickwick Papers." In 3 volumes. "Second" edition. London: Richard Bentley, 1838.

A "fictitious" second edition published on 17 December 1838. Tillotson states that "there is no reason to suppose that Dickens had anything whatever" to do with this edition (III. 17).

5.   **Oliver Twist.** By Charles Dickens. Author of "The Pickwick Papers" and "Nicholas Nickleby." A New edition. In 3 volumes. London: Richard Bentley, 1839.

A so-called "New edition" published late in October 1839 which Bentley brought out to capitalize on Dickens's success with **Nicholas Nickleby.** Tillotson writes that she has seen only one copy with the title-page matching Bentley's advertisements for this edition as he described it on 21 and 28 October 1839 (III. 17).

6.   **Oliver Twist.** By Charles Dickens, (Boz!) Author of "Pickwick Papers," "Nicholas Nickleby [Nickleby Vol. II]," "Sketches of Every day life," etc. In 2 volumes. Philadelphia: Lea and Blanchard, 1839.

The first American edition of **Oliver Twist** published on 18 or 19 December 1838, probably at fifty cents. This edition appeared without illustrations. For the book's textual history and that of its immediate successor (II. 7), see Tillotson's Appendix A (III. 18) in her edition of the Clarendon **Oliver Twist.**

7.   **Oliver Twist.** By Charles Dickens, (Boz,) Author of "Pickwick Papers," "Nicholas Nickleby," "Sketches of Every day Life," etc. Philadelphia: Lea and Blanchard, 1839.

Published on 2 February 1839, probably at $1.00 or $1.25. This edition included twenty-four illustrations by J. Yeager, who redrew Cruikshank's plates, using the "Fireside" plate for the final illustration, not Cruikshank's revised plate.

8.   Dickens, Charles. **Oliver Twist; or, The Parish Boy's Progress.** Paris: Baudry's European library, 1839. 367 pp.

The earliest Continental reprint of **Oliver Twist,** evidently from one of the three-volume editions in 1838 or 1839, in Baudry's Collection of Ancient and Modern British Authors, volume 229.

9.   **Oliver Twist; or, The Parish Boy's Progress.** By "Boz." In 3 volumes. London: Richard Bentley, 1840.

Bentley's last edition of **Oliver Twist,** for which he used the title-page Dickens disliked and a completely reset third volume. Tillotson (III. 17) suggests that Bentley designed this edition to cash in on the imminent appearance of **Master Humphrey's Clock,** Dickens's new weekly periodical for Chapman and Hall, which began in March 1840. When Dickens and Bentley signed their final agreement (July 1840), Dickens repurchased the unsold stock of this edition and used it as the basis for the so-called "Third edition" of 1841. See II. 10.

10. Dickens, Charles. **Oliver Twist; or, The Parish Boy's Progress.** In 3 volumes. Third edition. With an Introduction by the author. London: Chapman and Hall, 1841.

Reissues the sheets Bentley prepared for his edition of 1840 (III. 9) under the name of Dickens's new publishers, Chapman and Hall. In July 1840, the latter purchased all Bentley's remaining stock of **Oliver Twist**--"1002 copies ... in quires (not bound) fit for sale"--together with the copyright and plates by Cruikshank for 2,250 pounds. Some weeks before the principals signed the agreement, Dickens suggested to Forster that with a new title-page and "an interesting Preface," Chapman and Hall could bring out **Oliver Twist** "as a new edition." This proposal did not mature, however, until 15 May 1841, by which time Dickens had finished **The Old Curiosity Shop** and begun the long-awaited **Barnaby Rudge.**

The Preface Dickens wrote in April 1841 constitutes an aggressive defense of the book's moral purpose and an attempt by the author to disassociate himself from writers who sympathized with thieves as seductive and amiable fellows (P, II, 20-24). Readers would find no falsely glamorized accounts of highwaymen and criminals in his pages, he warned, because he had allied himself with the work of Hogarth, where "miserable reality" prevails. Dickens did this, he explains, to serve society by showing thieves "as they really are," with "the great, black, ghastly gallows" hurrying near at their backs. He admits that delicate readers might question such an aim but avows that he did not willingly "offend the ear," taking encouragement from the maxim laid down by "the greatest men in the world" that "a lesson of the purest good may ... be drawn from the vilest evil." Dickens refers to Nancy as a prostitute and defends her devotion to Sikes as not only natural but "TRUE." Her affection and "redeeming traits," he continues, are "emphatically God's truth," which He leaves "in such depraved and miserable breasts" as hers, "the last fair drop of water at the bottom of the dried-up weed-choked well."

11. ____. **Oliver Twist; or, The Parish Boy's Progress.** Vol. 36 of
Tauchnitz's Collection of British Authors. Leipzig: Bernhard
Tauchnitz, 1843. 438 pp.

Includes Dickens's 1841 Preface and the text without illustrations.
Tauchnitz also reprinted the Charles Dickens Edition Preface and text after
1867, with a reset 1843 title-page, notes Tillotson (II. 48).

12. ____. **The Adventures of Oliver Twist; or, The Parish Boy's Progress.**
Illustrated by George Cruikshank. A new edition, revised &
corrected. To be completed in ten numbers. London: Bradbury and
Evans, [1846].

Two factors, Tillotson comments, brought about this important edition in
parts. First, for all the excellence of Dickens's 1841 Preface, his introduction
had not worked as a selling device, leaving by May 1844 over 600 of the 1,002
copies delivered by Bentley to Chapman and Hall unsold. Second, because
Dickens was best known by this time as the author of five novels published in
parts, bringing **Oliver Twist** into line as a publication in parts represented an
"obvious final step." See Tillotson (II. 48). On 1 January 1846, Bradbury and
Evans began issuing the novel in ten monthly installments at one shilling each;
they also issued a one-volume edition of the parts on 26 September 1846 at
eleven shillings. In this form, the title-page bore the subtitle, **The Adventures
of Oliver Twist; or The Parish Boy's Progress,** after which came Dickens's
name as author, and then this inscription: "With twenty-four illustrations on
steel, By George Cruikshank. A new edition, revised and corrected. London:
Bradbury and Evans, 1846."
Describing the text as "A new edition, revised and corrected," was, for
once, "strictly true," writes Tillotson. This edition, she adds, was more
thoroughly revised "than any other in the whole history of Dickens's work" (II.
48), a judgment which accounts for her controversial decision to use the 1846
edition as her copy-text for the Clarendon **Oliver Twist.** See various entries
(III. 1, 2, 7, and 16) for comments about her choice of copy-text. Dickens
reprinted his 1841 Preface, together with Cruikshank's twenty-four plates,
retouched, re-bitten, and added to by J. Findlay (Tillotson, Appendix E, XIII.
57). Cruikshank also contributed to this edition a specially designed wrapper,
incorporating eleven scenes from the novel. Tillotson reproduces the wrapper
as the frontispiece to her edition. This new edition in 1846 marks Dickens's
first use of **The Adventures of Oliver Twist** as the novel's title.

13. ____. **The Adventures of Oliver Twist.** With a frontispiece by
George Cruikshank. London: Chapman and Hall, 1850.

The Cheap edition, based on a corrected copy of the 1846 text and issued
by Chapman and Hall in weekly and monthly parts, at 1 1/2d. and 7d., between
1 December 1849 and 1 April 1850. Chapman and Hall also published this
edition in a single volume at 3s. 6d. on 20 April 1850. Cruikshank designed a
special woodcut frontispiece showing Oliver standing before Mr. Bumble and
Mrs. Mann.
In a new, topical Preface written specially for this edition in March 1850,
Dickens directed his remarks exclusively to the problem of sanitary reform,
an issue he had recently addressed at the first meeting of the Metropolitan
Sanitary Association. See also Dickens (XVI. 7). Seconding several
resolutions proposed and passed on 6 February 1850, Dickens also endorsed
some remarks made by Dr. Charles Blomfield, Bishop of London. In

his speech, Blomfield noted the relative cheapness of basic sanitary measures and reflected upon the urgent need for action in areas like Jacob's Island, the slum Dickens describes in Chapter 50 of **Oliver Twist.** Soon after accounts of the meeting appeared in the press, Sir Peter Laurie, a magistrate and former Lord Mayor of London, poked fun at Blomfield and Dickens as misguided and misinformed reformers, claiming that Jacob's Island never had existed, except in Dickens's fiction. In retaliation, Dickens used the occasion of this Preface to comment on Laurie's ignorant remarks and ridicule his opponent. Turning Laurie's poor logic on the man himself, Dickens sarcastically noted how Newgate prison ceased to exist when Fielding wrote about it, Bath when Smollett sent Roderick Random there and, evidently, Jacob's Island when Dickens referred to it in **Oliver Twist.** Now, continued Dickens, the same reasoning must apply to Sir Peter Laurie himself, whom he described earlier in **The Chimes** as the foolish Alderman Cute, who wants to "Put down" everything. "For SIR PETER LAURIE having been himself described in a book," Dickens concluded, "it is but too clear that there CAN be no such man!"

14. ____. The Adventures of Oliver Twist. London: Chapman and Hall; and Bradbury and Evans, 1858.

Part of a collected library edition, first proposed by Bradbury and Evans in September 1857 and published on 4 December 1858 at six shillings a volume. In the prospectus issued in October 1857, each text was described as "carefully revised by the author," a claim not consistent with this edition of **Oliver Twist,** which Dickens's publishers based on the 1850 text. Dickens, however, did make minor substantive changes to the 1846 Preface, which he included in this edition. **Oliver Twist** and its companions in this series had no illustrations except for a vignette title-page by H.K. Browne showing Bumble and Oliver outside Mrs. Mann's cottage. When this edition was reissued in 1861-62, the publishers included the illustrations, adding Cruikshank's original plates to **Oliver Twist** and raising the price to 7s. 6d.

15. ____. The Adventures of Oliver Twist. With eight illustrations. London: Chapman and Hall, 1867.

The third volume in the Charles Dickens Edition, of which Chapman and Hall printed 25,000 copies for distribution at three shillings a copy. This edition of **Oliver Twist,** published on 1 August, became the standard text and is the one probably most familiar to present-day readers of Dickens. To it Dickens added a descriptive headline "attached to every right-hand page," as a new feature (see Appendix C of the Clarendon **Oliver Twist** II. 48); each volume in the series also carried on every cover a facsimile of the author's signature to indicate "his present watchfulness over his own Edition." Most notable of the changes Dickens made in 1867 is his alteration of "the Jew" to either "Fagin" or "He," beginning with Chapter 32 and continuing throughout the text, except for Chapters 34 and 35. See also Dickens (XIII. 78) and various entries under Fagin and anti-Semitism. In a prospectus published in the **Athenaeum** on 4 May 1867, Dickens's publishers promised a legible and cheap volume, with "a flowing open page," free from double columns, and eight of the original illustrations "selected as the best." Tillotson provides a list of these in her Appendix E (XIII. 57) and notes that perhaps Dickens himself made the choice. Dickens included the 1841 Preface but reduced its length by almost half.

16. ____. Adventures of Oliver Twist. With **Pictures from Italy** and **Ameri-can Notes.** Diamond Edition. Boston: Ticknor and Fields, 1867. 237 pp.

This edition bears a printed note, dated 2 April 1867, by Dickens, stating that Ticknor and Fields have become by a special arrangement between the novelist and his English publishers "the only authorized representatives in America of the whole series" of his books. This edition has a Preface and text (both undated) and ten illustrations by Sol Eytinge, Jr.

EDITIONS OF OLIVER TWIST 1867-1983 (chronological listing)

17. Dickens, Charles. The Adventures of Oliver Twist. New Illustrated Library Edition. New York: Hurd and Houghton, 1876. xxix + 438 pp.

Introduction by Edwin P. Whipple (XII. 17), Cruikshank's illustrations, and the 1867 Preface (undated) with an unspecified text.

18. ___. The Adventures of Oliver Twist. London: Macmillan, 1892. xxxii + 394 pp.

Introduced by Charles Dickens, Jr. (XII. 6), who states that he has reprinted the 1838 three-volume edition of the novel. The complete texts of Dickens's Prefaces of 1841 and 1850 appear in the Introduction.

19. ___. The Adventures of Oliver Twist. Vol. 3 of the Gadshill Edition. London: Chapman and Hall, 1897. x + 509 pp.

Specifies the use of the 1867 text, includes the original illustrations, and provides (undated) Dickens's 1867 Preface. Introduction and notes by Andrew Lang (XII. 12).

20. ___. Oliver Twist; or, The Parish Boy's Progress. 2 vols. The Temple Edition. London: J.M. Dent, 1899. 566 pp.

Walter Jerrold contributes a brief "Bibliographical Note" in which he makes several factual errors about the novel's origin, its interruptions in the Miscellany, and the date of its first publication in three volumes. Jerrold also discusses Dickens's trouble with adapters and refers to the objections some readers had to Fagin. Jerrold specifies that this edition is based on the 1846 text. He quotes from the 1841 Preface but does not provide Dickens's Introduction in full.

21. ___. Oliver Twist. Vol. 4 of the Autograph Edition. London: Chapman and Hall, 1900.

Introduction by Richard Garnett (XII. 9).

22. ___. Oliver Twist. Rochester Edition. London: Methuen, 1900. xxi + 501 pp.

Introduction by George Gissing (XII. 10) and "Notes Chiefly Topographical" by F.G. Kitton (XIII. 154).

23. ___. Oliver Twist. Vols. 9-10 of the National Edition. London: Chapman and Hall, 1906. 532 pp.

A handsome edition, which specifies the 1867 text, provides all three of Dickens's Prefaces, Cruikshank's original illustrations, including the "Fireside" plate and a facsimile of the cover of the 1846 edition of **Oliver Twist** in ten parts. This edition also reproduces H.K. Browne's cover design for the People's Edition in 1850 and the vignette title-page he drew for the Library Edition of 1858.

24. ___. **The Adventures of Oliver Twist.** Vol. 3 of Biographical Edition. London: Chapman and Hall, 1906. xv + 330 pp.

Includes Cruikshank's illustrations, the 1867 Preface (undated), and the running headlines Dickens added to the Charles Dickens Edition. The copy-text of this edition is unspecified; A[rthur] W[augh] provides a Biographical Introduction (XII. 207).

25. ___. **Oliver Twist.** Everyman's Library. London, 1907; rpt. London: Dent, 1975. xiii + 423 pp.

A paperback edition without illustrations and lacking a note about the text and the Preface, both of which appear to be based on the 1867 Charles Dickens Edition. Introduction by G.K. Chesterton (XII. 54).

26. ___ **The Adventures of Oliver Twist or The Parish Boy's Progress.** Vol. 27 of Centenary Edition. London: Chapman and Hall, 1910. xviii + 509 pp.

Reprints Dickens's Prefaces to the Third Edition (1841), the first Cheap Edition (1850), and the Charles Dickens Edition (1867). A brief bibliographical note explains that this edition is based on Dickens's emended text of 1867. Cruikshank's original illustrations accompany the text.

27. ___. **Oliver Twist.** Vol. 15 of the London Edition. London: Caxton, n.d. [circa 1910?] 316 pp.

Gives no reference to the text or to the Preface used but provides "Editorial Notes" (pp. ix-xvi), which gloss the place names and some of the buildings mentioned in the novel.

28. ___. **The Adventures of Oliver Twist.** Vol. 18 of The Waverley Dickens. London: The Waverley Book Company, n.d. [1912] xiv + 312 pp.

Provides the 1867 Preface and text without specifying the publisher's choice of copy-text. Charles Pears contributes four illustrations; Fred Barnard's drawing of Sikes is also reproduced, in color. The small type-face makes this an unattractive edition, which A.C. Benson introduces (XII. 28).

29. ___. **The Adventures of Oliver Twist.** New York: Macmillan, 1918. xxvii + 472 pp.

Introduction by Frank W. Pine (XII. 167).

30. ___. **Oliver Twist.** Vol. 3 of National Library Edition. Boston: Charles E. Lauriat, 1923. xxv + 541 pp.

Provides Dickens's Prefaces of 1841, 1850, and 1867 and specifies that this edition is based on the revised text of the 1867 Charles Dickens Edition. Twelve illustrations by Cruikshank accompany the novel.

31. ____. **Oliver Twist.** The Nonesuch Dickens. London: The
     Nonesuch Press, 1937. 418 pp.

A sumptuous edition designed by Francis Meynell to "end all editions of
Dickens" by bringing together the complete corpus of his writings in a
collective enterprise hitherto without parallel in cost and scope. Limited to
subscribers only, 877 sets were prepared, each with one of the original plates
assigned to it for distribution as an inducement to wealthy collectors. Arthur
Waugh oversaw the editorial committee, on which he served together with
Walter Dexter, Thomas Hatton, and Hugh Walpole. The textual editors chose
the 1867 version of **Oliver Twist** because the text "was carefully prepared and
proof-read by Dickens himself" for the Charles Dickens Edition of 1867 (II.
15). They also provided all three of Dickens's Prefaces, with dates, all
Cruikshank's illustrations for the novel, including a facsimile of the 1846
cover, and H.K. Browne's engraved title-page for the 1858 Library Edition.
The page-headlines Dickens added in 1867 appear in the margins against the
relevant passages.

32. ____. **Oliver Twist.** Great Illustrated Classics. New York: Dodd,
     Mead, 1941. vii + 541 pp.

Includes a brief, inconsequential introduction by May Lamberton Becker
based on her remarks about the autobiographical nature of the novel in her
biography, **Introducing Charles Dickens** (New York: Dodd, Mead, 1940). This
edition makes no reference to its copy-text, provides the 1867 Preface
(undated), and reproduces fifteen of Cruikshank's twenty-four illustrations.

33. ____. **Oliver Twist.** In CEBCO Classics for Enjoyment Series. New
     York: College Entrance Book Co., 1947. 335 pp.

Adapted for prospective college students by Mabel Dodge Holmes, who
provides an abridged and radically altered text which retains Dickens's
dialogue but little else as he originally wrote it. The text is lightly annotated;
facts about Dickens's life and discussion questions relating to the novel
appear at the end of this edition. The degree to which Holmes has rewritten
the novel leads one to conjecture that this edition could hinder rather than
help college-bound students.

34. ____. **Oliver Twist.** Amsco Literature Series. New York: Amsco
     School Publications, n. d. 412 pp.

A short note states that the text has been prepared "with careful
attention to a faithful presentation of the author's work and to literary
scholarship," of which this paperback edition presents little evidence. The
publishers make no reference to the copy-text, omit all Dickens's Prefaces,
and provide no introductory information for their readers, presumably high
school and college students.

35. ____. **The Adventures of Oliver Twist or The Parish Boy's
     Progress.** London: Todd Publishing Group, 1948. 160 pp.

A note explains that this arranged and abridged text has been prepared
for those who lack the time to read long novels. The Modern Reading Library,
the writer continues, has reduced but not re-written the original, cutting the
text to 50,000 words by deleting long digressions, subplots and minor

characters, and "the less essential paragraphs of description, which are not often acceptable to the busy reader of today." The editors ignore Dickens's Prefaces and provide no information about the text, although they do admit to bringing up to date the punctuation and spelling "in some cases."

36. ____. The Adventures of Oliver Twist. London: Paul Elek and World Film Publications, 1948. 324 pp.

An unabridged, cheap edition of the novel illustrated with scenes from Cineguild's 1947 film version of the novel (VII. 18).

37. ____. Oliver Twist. New York: Washington Square Press, 1948.

Cited by Patten in his review of paperback editions of Oliver Twist (III. 13) but unavailable for annotation. Patten notes that in 1957 Edgar Johnson contributed an introduction based mainly on his comments on the novel in his biography (XII. 121).

38. ____. The Adventures of Oliver Twist. The Oxford Illustrated Dickens. London: Oxford Univ. Press, 1949. xxvi + 415 pp.

Includes Cruikshank's twenty-four illustrations and an Introduction by Humphry House (XII. 111). Long regarded by critics as a standard hard-cover text, this edition provides no information about its copy-text, reprints the 1867 Preface without identifying it, and treats casually the text's accidental and substantive changes.

39. ____. Oliver Twist. The Novel Library. London: Hamish Hamilton, 1950. xx + 511 pp.

Includes the 1867 Preface and reprints, unacknowledged, the text of the Charles Dickens Edition. The small but readable pages and lack of illustrations suggest an inexpensive edition. Graham Greene provides a short but excellent introduction best known to readers in its reprinted form, "The Young Dickens," in his The Lost Childhood and Other Essays (XII. 97).

40. ____. Oliver Twist. London: Collins, 1954.

Introduction by Kenneth Hayens (XII. 102).

41. ____. Oliver Twist. Signet Classic. New York: New American Library, 1961. xxii + 496 pp.

A paperback edition which provides the text of Dickens's Prefaces of 1841, 1850, and 1867 and an Afterword by Edward LeComte (XII. 136). A note on the text specifies that this edition is based on the Charles Dickens Edition of 1867, whose spelling and punctuation "have been brought into conformity with modern British usage."

42. ____. The Adventures of Oliver Twist. The Heritage of Literature Series. London: Longman, 1961. lii + 523 pp.

A paperback edition which includes the 1867 Preface but does not specify the choice of copy-text. S.H. Burton (XII. 43) provides an Introduction and notes.

43. ____. **The Adventures of Oliver Twist.** New York: Holt, Rinehart and Winston, 1962. xxxiii + 411 pp.

Introduction by J. Hillis Miller (XII. 151). This paperback includes a chronological outline of Dickens's life, a list of suggested readings, and the 1867 Preface, but omits textual notes, annotations, and Cruikshank's illustrations. Miller follows the 1867 text but does not give the descriptive headlines Dickens added in 1867.

44. ____. **Oliver Twist.** Ed. Doris Dickens. London: Michael Joseph, 1962. 354 pp.

A note on the jacket explains that Doris Dickens has edited her great-grandfather's novel "with loving care" to ensure "a smooth flow in the narrative without in anyway detracting from the original." As a result of these silent changes, three chapters are dropped. Ronald Searle, a well-known British caricaturist and cartoonist, illustrates the text.

45. ____. **Oliver Twist.** New York: Airmont Books, 1962.

Cited by Patten in his review of paperback editions of **Oliver Twist** (III. 13) but unavailable for annotation. The biographical introduction, Patten notes, contains numerous factual errors.

46. ____. **Oliver Twist.** London: Blackie, 1963.

Introduction by A.R. Tomkins (XII. 202).

47. ____. **Oliver Twist.** Ed. Peter Fairclough. Penguin English Library Edition. Harmondsworth: Penguin, 1966. 490 pp.

Fairclough's textual policy represents an abrogation of editorial integrity infrequently encountered in editions which offer "reliable texts" and promise something sufficiently authoritative for classroom use. In his "Note on the Text" (pp. 28-29), he states that he has retained Dickens's "later version" of his treatment of the Maylies and Mr. Brownlow not because he has chosen a later (unspecified) copy-text, but because he approves of the elimination of the "crude and clumsy early writing" Dickens made in his subsequent revisions to these figures. Reversing himself on another comparable issue, Fairclough ignores "almost all" of the instances where Dickens later dropped the oaths uttered by the criminals and by Dr. Losberne because he prefers the earlier, oath-sprinkled text, which, he thinks, lends versimilitude to the thieves and makes Losberne "more engaging." As for the changes Dickens added in 1867 relating to Fagin, "on the whole," he keeps the emended reading of "Fagin" for the phrase "the Jew." In Chapters 35 to 39, where Dickens dropped material from the manuscript version of **Oliver Twist** to accommodate the restrictions of space imposed by the monthly numbers of **Bentley's Miscellany,** Fairclough restores some of the dropped passages. These appear in the text without indication, following the policy of silent changes to which Fairclough adheres throughout. Dickens's "eccentric punctuation" is similarly emended and refurnished according to what Fairclough judges "the correct punctuation."

This paperback edition reprints the 1858 Preface (i.e., Dickens's Introduction of 1841), provides a brief Appendix on the Poor Law, a partial gloss of thieves' slang, and Cruikshank's twenty-four illustrations. The editor indicates the novel's original serial divisions; Angus Wilson contributes an introduction (XII. 214).

48. ____. **Oliver Twist**. Ed. Kathleen Tillotson. The Clarendon Dickens.
     Oxford: Clarendon Press, 1966. lxv + 403 pp.

The inaugural volume of the Clarendon Dickens, whose origin lies in
various essays by John Butt and Kathleen Tillotson which present their
investigations into Dickens's working habits as an author and discuss the
issues that arise when editing his works (III. 4-6; 17). This edition of **Oliver
Twist**, they state in their General Preface, establishes "a critical text" free
from the corruptions reprints typically accumulate; the editors also provide
an apparatus of variants designed to show "Dickens's progressive revisions."
After defining briefly an editor's responsibility to include also a history of the
novel's composition and publication, Butt and Tillotson turn to an issue crucial
to any editor of a Dickens novel: what constitutes a valid text when an author
at proof stage frequently adjusted his manuscript to the fixed size of his
monthly or weekly installment?

As general editors, Butt and Tillotson do not use their joint Preface to
discuss the theoretical principles American textual scholars typically apply to
the issue of textual authority but offer instead views based on their extensive
experience with Dickens as he prepared his works for publication. When his
galley-proofs revealed "over-matter," they explain, Dickens customarily
"retrench[ed]" by deleting passages; if he were short, he added a paragraph or
two to give his readers full measure. Thus Dickens apparently ignored his
manuscript when reading proof, they argue, and saw his "principal task" as
that of adjusting the amount he had written to the number of pages available,
leading Butt and Tillotson to state their policy for dealing with this situation
as follows: "All deletions required for adjusting the size of an instalment are
printed in the textual apparatus, while all additions made for the same
purpose are left in the text and recorded in the apparatus."

The application of this procedure proves useful to Tillotson and allows
her in the case of **Oliver Twist** to simplify a textual situation more than
ordinarily complicated by the existence of seven substantive texts: (1) the
incomplete manuscript of Chapters 12 and 13 and 23 through 43; (2) the
Miscellany monthly parts set mainly from the manuscript and revised in proof;
(3) Bentley's three-volume edition of 1838, whose first two volumes were set
from the **Miscellany** text, revised by Dickens, and the last one from the
manuscript; (4) the 1846 edition, thoroughly revised by Dickens and printed
from an annotated 1841 text; (5) the Cheap edition of 1850; (6) the Charles
Dickens Edition of 1867; and (7) Chapters 44 through 51 of the 1838
Philadelphia edition, which were set from the portion of the manuscript
Dickens sent to America after Bentley had finished with it.

Two principal factors account for Tillotson's decision to select the 1846
edition as her copy-text. First, because she sticks firmly to the position she
and Butt announced for treating manuscript matter Dickens excised or added
in proof so as to fit the sixteen pages allotted to him in the **Miscellany**,
Tillotson can ignore the manuscript as one possible authority for emending her
text. "It might be supposed," she argues, "that an author writing
simultaneously for a magazine and for volume publication would later replace
passages excised for no other reason than length; there would have been
ample room, for his three volumes contain a less than average amount of
text. But no instance of such restoration is found in any novel of Dickens's,
whether because the process would be complicated under pressure of time, or
in order to keep faith with the serial-publishers, or, most likely, because once
a decision was taken he did not look back." Second, she argues forcefully that
the 1846 text was the only one Dickens revised thoroughly and corrected
"throughout its length." As proof, she cites the attention Dickens gave to both

the book's structure and text. Beside redividing four chapters and adding the transitions these changes necessitated, Dickens reworked extensively the book's punctuation according to the new, rhetorical system he developed after experimenting with the oral delivery of his books to a group of friends. So thorough are these changes, Tillotson concludes, that the text cannot be said to have achieved stability until 1846. Until then, she comments, "Dickens was still writing his novel." Thereafter, the text steadily deteriorated. Subsequent revisions prove "cursory," she argues, and were made by Dickens "for non-literary reasons" and as condescensions "to certain changes of taste." Tillotson presents in her Introduction a detailed analysis of the kinds of revisions Dickens made both to the manuscript and to the various texts he published. In addition to her table of editorial emendations to her copy-text, Tillotson also provides a useful Descriptive List of Editions, the text, with variants, of the Prefaces Dickens later wrote, and a list of the Descriptive Headlines he added in 1867. A table comparing the installments in the **Miscellany** and the chapter divisions in the book editions appears at the back, as do the following: an appendix about the Philadelphia editions of 1839–39 (III. 18), one on Cruikshank's illustrations (XIII. 57), a brief account of the 'Sikes and Nancy' reading version of the novel (V. 23), the most comprehensive list of contemporary responses to **Oliver Twist** in print (IX. 40), a glossary of thieves' slang and cant, and an 1837 map of London. For further discussion of the general editors' textual policy, see articles by John Butt (III. 3–6). For a vigorous dissent from her choice of copy-text, see especially Bowers (III. 2), and Altick (III. 1), Cribb (III. 7) and Tanselle (III. 8).

49. _____. Oliver Twist. New York: Lancer Books, 1968.

Cited by Patten in his review of paperback editions of **Oliver Twist** (III. 13) but unavailable for annotation.

50. _____. **Oliver Twist**. In Heron Books Series, **Books That Have Changed Man's Thinking**. Geneva: Heron Books, 1970. xvi + 509 pp.

Courtlandt Canby, the editor of the Series, writes in a Foreword that Dickens changed man's thinking by introducing middle-class readers to the criminal underworld and by exposing them to all classes of society and the harsh facts of social injustice in early Victorian England. Arthur Calder-Marshall contributes a short biographical Introduction and a longer Appreciation (XII. 45).

51. _____. **Oliver Twist**. Enriched Classics Series. New York: Washington Square Press, 1975. 457 pp.

An inexpensive paperback edition which includes a Reader's Supplement as a center inset. The supplement, prepared under the supervision of an editorial committee directed by Harry Shefter, provides perfunctory comments about the novel's autobiographical elements, its social and historical context, and a number of stills from David Lean's film version of the novel. Reproductions of nineteenth-century drawings and photographs are included as well, some of which are inadequately identified or confusingly labelled. Seventeen short extracts constitute the remainder of the supplement, providing a variety of responses to the novel taken from both contemporary reviewers and recent critics. The text lacks an Introduction, Prefaces, and a note about its provenance.

52. ____. **Oliver Twist.** London: Pan Books, 1980. 461 pp.

A serviceable paperback edition based specifically on the text of 1867.
In a textual note, Ian Ousby mentions that he has corrected obvious misprints,
indicated the novel's monthly installments with asterisks, and included the
1841 Preface. Ousby also provides a glossary of slang, light annotations to
the text, and a useful introduction (XII. 159).

53. ____. **Oliver Twist.** Bantam Classic Series. Toronto: Bantam
Books, 1981. 419 pp.

A paperback edition of the novel specifically based on the Charles
Dickens Edition of 1867. Apart from the 1867 Preface, the text stands alone,
without notes or an Introduction.

54. ____. **Oliver Twist.** Bantam Classic Series. Toronto: Bantam
Books, 1982. xix + 424 pp.

The second printing of the earlier Bantam paperback edition (II. 53) with
the addition of Irving Howe's Introduction (XII. 112) and a brief bibliography
of recent biographical and critical books on Dickens.

55. ____. **Oliver Twist.** The World's Classics. Oxford: Oxford Univ.
Press, 1982. xxviii + 363 pp.

A paperback edition which reproduces the text of the Clarendon **Oliver
Twist** (II. 48) without the variant readings and the textual apparatus.
Kathleen Tillotson contributes a new Introduction (XII. 199), explanatory
notes, and her glossary of thieves' cant and slang from the Clarendon edition.
The Prefaces of 1841 and 1850 are also included, as are eight of Cruikshank's
illustrations. This edition represents an important contribution to the
paperback market, making available for the first time a scholarly text at a
cheap price. Unfortunately, the small typeface and poor quality of the paper
give the book little visual appeal.

56. ____. **Oliver Twist.** London: Macmillan Education, 1983. xxiv +
413 pp.

A paperback edition of the novel in the Macmillan Students' Novels series
designed specifically for British students taking "Ordinary" level
examinations. Guy Williams (XII. 212) provides some introductory comments
and light annotations to the text, but makes no reference to his copy-text.
He also includes the 1867 Preface without specifying its date.

III. COMMENTARY ON THE TEXT: SCHOLARSHIP CONCERNING THE
PUBLICATION AND TEXTUAL MATTERS

Introductory Note:

Several entries in the following section assume some acquaintance with developments in editorial theory since 1950 when W.W. Greg challenged the past practice of determining an authoritative text and incorporating into it all substantive and accidental alterations. In basic form, Greg proposed that an editor differentiate between the **substantives,** or actual wording of a text, and the **accidentals,** or the spelling, punctuation, and capitalization, and recognize for each a different authority. Greg also suggested that the editor base his text on an author's manuscript and insert into that all substantive or other alterations from later editions which his editorial judgment passes as authoritative. Greg specified a manuscript or the earliest edition set from it as being most likely to reflect the author's treatment of the accidentals. See "The Rationale of Copy-Text," **Studies in Bibliography,** 3 (1950), 19-36. Greg's theories form the basis of Fredson Bowers's textual work and that of the Center for Edition of American Authors. See Fredson Bowers, "Textual Criticism," **The Aims and Methods of Scholarship in Modern Languages and Literatures,** ed. James Thorpe (New York: MLA, 1963), pp. 23-42, and **Statement of Editorial Principles and Procedures: A Working Manual for Editing Nineteenth-Century American Texts** (New York: MLA, 1972).

1.   Altick, Richard D. Untitled review of the Clarendon **Oliver Twist.** VS, 11 (March 1968), 415-16.

Agrees with Tillotson's choice of copy-text (II. 48) but argues that this "perennially vexatious question" admits more than one solution. An equally sound case, Altick thinks, can be made for an earlier text, one that "faithfully represents the book in its pristine form." Such an edition, Altick contends, would have as much value as one reflecting an author's second thoughts because by reading **Oliver Twist** in its serial form or in the 1838 version we see the novel "at the most critical moment of its life."

2.   Bowers, Fredson. "Kathleen Tillotson, ed., Charles Dickens: **Oliver Twist.**" A Review. NCF, 23 (September 1968), 226-39.

An important review of the Clarendon **Oliver Twist** challenging Tillotson's editorial methods and her choice of copy-text. Bowers recognizes that the 1846 edition (II. 12) conveys Dickens's intentions at that time but he disputes its ultimate superiority over the surviving chapters of the manuscript and other authoritative sources. That part of **Bentley's Miscellany** set from the manuscript, the latter chapters of the 1838 Philadelphia edition (III. 18), and the revised texts of 1850 (II. 13) and 1867 (II. 15), he comments, all deserve some consideration. Modern textual theory, Bowers argues, acknowledges the validity of different sources and seeks to establish an eclectic text, one which combines those readings closest to the author's intentions as they are apparent in all forms of the text. Tillotson, by contrast, proves too timorous an editor by relying upon a single source--the

1846 edition--and by rejecting authoritative readings from both earlier and later documents. Instead of producing a definitive and critical text, Bowers states, Tillotson provides "a critical reprint," a hybrid achievement which essentially relies on a single authority and relegates to the textual apparatus all other variant readings.

Substantial and perhaps irreconcilable assumptions underlie the differences between Bowers and Tillotson on these crucial issues of textual policy. For example, Bowers finds Tillotson's treatment of matter present in the manuscript that Dickens cut out or added at proof stage debatable. One might as well reverse her procedure, he continues, by arguing that an editor concerned with the prime evidence of the manuscript could construct a critical text more faithful to Dickens's original literary intentions by restoring to it those passages Dickens excised solely upon consideration of their length. Similarly, an editor working with this intention would relegate to the textual apparatus the material Dickens added when he found it necessary to expand into the space allotted to him by the serial installment. Under these conditions of "addition and subtraction for part publication," Bowers writes, "it would appear to be a lack of boldness in the editorial decision to print as an integral part of a critical text those extra passages added only for length but to acquiesce in the removal of the excised material and to reprint it only in the apparatus."

Bowers also questions the importance Tillotson attaches to the revised punctuation system Dickens introduced in 1846, a factor which proved decisive in her view for making that form of the novel her copy-text. Bowers agrees that the eccentric punctuation with its pauses for the voice rather than conventional syntactical relationship incontrovertibly reflects Dickens's intentions between 1844-45, but he points out that Tillotson makes no strong case for Dickens's continued adherence to that system. Since Dickens's punctuation seems to have reverted "pretty largely to normal" after 1846, Bowers argues, "a serious doubt obtains whether a passing enthusiasm, no matter how authoritative, should be retained when it is present in what is, after all, a revised edition [the 1846 text] and thus departs from the original concept of the accidentals."

Further evidence of Tillotson's "arbitrary editorial procedure" appears in her apparent refusal to take seriously the revisions Dickens made after 1846. Occasionally, she will admit, for example, a dialect form from 1850 or 1867, but generally she takes the view that in 1846 Dickens established the text "once and for all." In one instance, however, Bowers approves, agreeing with Tillotson's decision not to incorporate one series of changes Dickens made in 1867, whereby he substituted Fagin's name or a pronoun for the epithet "the Jew." "Most modern editors would agree that such post-facto toning down of possibly offensive readings divorced from literary considerations should be rejected," writes Bowers. In this case, Bowers and Tillotson both deny Dickens the right to change his mind, seeming to imply that his response to Mrs. Davis's reproof (XIII. 78) was irrelevant because it was made on non-literary grounds. How this change can be said to represent something other than the author's final literary intentions Bowers does not explain.

Readers should note that Bower's dissent remains principled throughout and reflects a genuinely different approach to the problems editorial work poses. Essentially, Tillotson's procedures imply a position of editorial humility, whereby the scholar defends a choice of text as the one most nearly representative of the author's final intention. Because Dickens took such trouble revising and correcting **Oliver Twist** in 1844-45, Tillotson reasons--with some plausibility--that this text best represents Dickens's view of how **Oliver Twist** should appear. Bowers, by contrast, assigns to the editor a greater challenge--and perhaps a more presumptuous one of divining the author's final intentions by synthesizing more than one source. This procedure, Bowers insists, must be consistent with a sound theoretical position capable of constructing how errors occurred and how changes in the text were transmitted from one version to the next. Most useful in his view, and an opinion also shared by the Center for Editions of American authors, are the "revolutionary textual theories" of Walter Greg, whose ideas Tillotson ignores, preferring instead her own ability, seasoned by long familiarity with Dickens's working habits, to judge the moment when Dickens put his novel aside, content not to look back.

3.   Butt, John. **"David Copperfield:** From Manuscript to Print." RES, NS 1 (1950), 247-51.

Describes how the problem of "over-matter" arose in Dickens's manuscripts when corrections and interlineations made it difficult for him to estimate his serial contribution, whose exact length he never knew until he received the proofs. The additions or deletions Dickens made at this stage pose a problem, Butts argues, because the editor of a definitive text must weigh the importance of corrections made solely to fulfill the serial quota. Giving an example from **David Copperfield,** Butt comments that an editor would have "an arguable case if he [decided] that many of [Dickens's] deletions in proof must be added to the standard text and many of the additions relegated to the apparatus."

4.   ____. "Dickens's Manuscripts." YULG, 36 (April 1962), 149-61.

Recounts how the grandson of Richard Bentley, Dickens's publisher, discovered the surviving two-thirds of the **Oliver Twist** manuscript at the end of the century. Butt also comments briefly on how Dickens usually corrected proof. It was not his "invariable practice," Butt writes, to consult his manuscript, which often remained at the printer's. Consequently Dickens allowed plausible errors to pass and also invented new readings on occasions to correct errors made by the type-setter.

5.   ____. "Editing a Nineteenth-Century Novelist (Proposals for an Edition of Dickens)." In **English Studies Today.** Ed. G.A. Bonnard. Berne: Francke Verlag. 2nd ser. (1961), pp. 187-95.

Comments on the "peculiar value" of Dickens's proofs for revealing the paragraphs Dickens added or cut out when he failed to calculate exactly his serial quota. Of the troublesome issue of the "over-matter," Butt states that Dickens removed passages simply because there was no room for them, and not because he disliked them. He concludes, therefore, that a case surely exists for restoring them, even though Dickens ignored them in subsequent editions. "It would be inadvisable to replace them in the text," he continues, "but they might occupy a prominent position at the foot of the page, in type larger than that to be used for recording variants." This opinion, a modification of Butt's above (III. 3) and the one he held jointly with Tillotson (II. 48), moves closer to the answer the two propose in their General Preface to the Clarendon **Oliver Twist** in 1965 (II. 48).

6.   ____, and Kathleen Tillotson. "Dickens as a Serial Novelist." In their **Dickens at Work.** 1957; rpt. London: Methuen, 1968, pp. 13-34.

Comments generally on how, "When forced to lop and crop," Dickens frequently cut at the expense of comedy as he prepared his proofs for serial publication. Butt and Tillotson furnish examples from **Dombey and Son, David Copperfield, Bleak House,** and **The Mystery of Edwin Drood,** to which they add this reflection: "The future editor of Dickens will have to consider restoring these passages to the text, since they were removed only because of the fortuitous demands of serial publication." Cf. Butt (III. 5).

7.   Cribb, Timothy. Untitled review of the Clarendon **Oliver Twist.** RES, NS 19 (February 1968), 87-91.

Discusses intelligently the problem of "over-matter" Dickens deleted in proof and examines the issues involved in deciding upon its status. Cribb contributes a common-sense view that Dickens implicitly accepted the conditions and consequences of committing his works to serial form and points out that he went in "with his eyes open." Why, therefore, should deletions in proof assume greater value than those made in manuscript? Cribb also notes that throughout the various collected and revised editions of his works Dickens oversaw, he never bothered to restore the excised over-matter. What he put in print and left in print, Cribb concludes, "represents his authorial and conclusive act of choice."

To these points Cribb adds a rejoinder from the other side. Proof deletions "made solely for arbitrary quantitative requirements," he suggests, are clearly different from manuscript revisions. Moreover, it is precisely "the exigencies and contingent corruptions of local circumstance from which an editor seeks to purify his text," he responds. Cribb also notes how Butt and Tillotson have at different times proposed different answers to this editorial problem. See III. 3, III. 5, III. 6, and II. 48.

8.   Dexter, Walter. **"Bentley's Miscellany."** The Dickensian, 33 (Autumn 1937), 232-38.

A useful compilation of Dickens's incidental contributions to the **Miscellany.** Dexter provides the texts of Dickens's various addresses to his readers, his announcements suspending the monthly numbers for June and October 1837, a list of Dickens's initial contributors, and a reproduction of the journal's monthly wrapper designed by Cruikshank.

9.   Grubb, Gerald Giles. "On the Serial Publication of **"Oliver Twist."** MLN, 56 (April 1941), 290-94.

Corrects factual errors made by Charles Dickens, Jr., in his Introduction to **Oliver Twist** (XII. 6), Eckel (IV. 10), and Hatton and Cleaver (IV. 14). All three, Grubb notes, failed to record that the serial publication of **Oliver Twist** in the **Miscellany** had two other interruptions in addition to the one in June 1837, which arose when Dickens suspended the number because of the death of Mary Hogarth (I. 1). For details about **Oliver Twist's** serialization in the **Miscellany,** see II. 1. Grubb notes that Dickens's anxiety about finishing **The Pickwick Papers** and the strain of editing the journal put him behind in October 1837. He remains at a loss, however, to explain why no serial installment of **Oliver Twist** appeared in September 1838, unaware that Dickens's determination to complete the final chapters of the manuscript before 25 October so absorbed him that he delayed the September number by a month. For further comments on Dickens's motive for the delay, see II. 1.

10. Lauterbach, Charles E., and Edward S. Lauterbach. "The Nineteenth
     Century Three-Volume Novel." PBSA, 51 (1957), 263-302.

A useful examination of the mechanical and bibliographical aspects of
the Victorian "three-decker," complete with tables and comparative data
about word count and length. The Lauterbachs' conclusion that **Oliver Twist**
fell short of comparable three-volume works remains valid as a general
observation, although the facts they assemble about its word count, blank
pages, and generous typography need qualification. While **Oliver Twist** lacked
the appropriate bulk of the typical three-decker, Dickens, in fact, gained no
advantage, as they argue, by producing fewer words than his contract
originally called for because the agreement they use as their basis for
judgment applies to **Barnaby Rudge** and not **Oliver Twist**. When Dickens
signed on with Bentley on 22 August 1836 to write a three-volume novel of
960 pages and with twenty-five lines to a page, the book he had in mind was
Barnaby Rudge. By presenting **Oliver Twist** as the outcome of this contract,
the Lauterbachs draw an erroneous conclusion: Dickens may have got the
better of Bentley in conflicts with his publisher but not because he produced
16,920 words fewer than he had at first agreed to.

11. Muir, Kenneth. Untitled review of the Clarendon **Oliver Twist**.
     MLR, 63 (July 1968), 687-88.

Muir approves of Tillotson's choice of copy-text (II. 48), but he thinks
some of the passages Dickens discarded are worth reinstating in the reading
text. Muir cites as one example Sikes's argumentative response to Fagin in
Chapter 39, which Dickens cut solely as an expedient and for no literary
purpose. See Clarendon **Oliver Twist** (II. 48), pp. 260-61n.

12. Nowell-Smith, Simon. "The 'Cheap Edition' of Dickens's Works. [First
     Series] 1847-1852." **The Library**, 5th ser., 2 (September 1967), 245-51.

Describes in some detail the form and appearance of the Cheap Edition
of Dickens's early works, a series which began on 27 March 1847 with the
issue of **The Pickwick Papers** in weekly numbers, in parts (four numbers
combined), and in a single volume. Nowell-Smith also provides the full text of
the Prospectus Dickens wrote, first published in Part Seven of **Dombey and
Son** (April 1847), announcing this edition of his early works. His purpose,
wrote Dickens, was to reproduce his recent books "in a shape which shall
render them easily accessible as a possession by all classes of society."
Dickens also expresses his hope to become, "in his new guise, a permanent
inmate of many English homes."

13. Patten, Robert L. "Reviews--Paperback Editions: **Oliver Twist**."
     DSN, 3 (September 1972), 84-92.

A judicious essay reviewing eight paperback versions of **Oliver Twist**
available at the time. Patten finds little praise for the textual policies of the
various editions, where casual practice, the omission of information, and
carelessness seem to prevail. The Rinehart text, on balance, he thinks, proves
the "least objectionable." Helpful introductions by J. Hillis Miller (XII. 151)
and Angus Wilson (XII. 214), he notes, provide some substance, but not one
edition under review approaches the standards set by Norton for their critical
editions.

14. _____. "'So Much Paints about One Chalk-faced Kid': The Clarendon
       Oliver Twist." DiS, 3 (October 1967), 160-68.

Notes that Tillotson's decision to select the 1846 edition as her copy-text
will not please those readers who want restored to the definitive text the
manuscript passages Dickens cut out in proof for reasons of space (II. 48).
Similarly, her failure to register Dickens's final modifications will upset
others. But the 1846 text, with significant manuscript readings and
substantive later revisions recorded in the apparatus, Patten concludes, "is
probably the best compromise text we can establish."

15. Schweitzer, Joan. "The Chapter Numbering in *Oliver Twist*." PBSA,
       60 (1966), 337-48.

Describes the variant chapter divisions evident in the different textual
versions of *Oliver Twist*. When Dickens published the novel as a monthly
serial in *Bentley's Miscellany* between February 1837 and April 1839, he
divided the text into three Books, each with twenty-two, fourteen, and fifteen
chapters respectively. Twice in the serial version he divided chapters (49 and
51) in two to fit the serial scheme, not because the chapter endings occurred
naturally (see *Miscellany*, Book III, chs. 11 and 13). When Dickens revised the
text of *Oliver Twist* in 1846 and 1867-68, he removed these divisions but
divided Chapter 44 into two parts (i.e., *Miscellany*, III, 7). Further changes of
this kind made in 1846 and in later editions include Chapter 29 (*Miscellany*, II,
7) and Chapter 37 (*Miscellany*, III, 1), thus bringing the total number of
chapters to fifty-three in the later editions as opposed to the original
fifty-one. Schweitzer also notes how Dickens added a transition to Chapter
12 in 1846, so that instead of ending with Oliver's fainting away when Mr.
Brownlow remarks on the portrait above his head, as the text did in the
Miscellany, the added sentence takes the reader back to "the two young
pupils" before the chapter ends with the youths returning to Fagin's den.
    Tillotson (III. 17) points out that the awkward cuts in the final chapters
occurred because Dickens stopped reading serial proofs of *Oliver Twist* after
the novel's publication in three volumes in December 1838. (From November
on, copy for the serial came from the printed sheets of volume III.) The last
serial chapters of *Oliver Twist*, Tillotson also notes, had to fit in with the
unwieldy installments of *Jack Sheppard*, the journal's new attraction and
successor to Dickens's novel.

16. Tanselle, G. Thomas. "Problems and Accomplishments in the Editing of
       the Novel." SNNTS, 7 (Fall 1975), 344-50.

A wide ranging and important survey of recent British and American
editing with detailed comments on the Clarendon texts of Dickens, including
Oliver Twist. Tanselle acknowledges the impressiveness of Tillotson's
achievement, but he judges that her edition falls short in two respects. The
first of these is her selection of the 1846 edition (II. 12) as her copy-text and
her incorporation of Dickens's idiosyncratic punctuation, whose status he
thinks she fails to make clear. Cf. Bowers (III. 2). Since Tillotson suggests in
her Introduction that Dickens returned to more conventional practice after
1846, Tanselle wonders if the 1846 punctuation is appropriate for a text
designed to reflect Dickens's ultimate wishes. It is possible, he argues, that
the accidentals of an earlier edition "might be a better representation of
Dickens's final wishes" than the system he introduced in 1846. Using the
surviving portion of the manuscript, the *Miscellany* text set from the

manuscript up to October 1838, and the remaining chapters of the 1838 Philadelphia edition (III. 18) also set from the manuscript (I. 2), one could create an eclectic copytext and then emend that, Tanselle suggests, with later authorial variants, both substantive and accidental. Instead, Tillotson gives the benefit of the doubt to the 1846 text and more or less ignores the earlier materials.

The other area in which Tanselle finds the Clarendon Oliver Twist inadequate is in the editor's handling of the textual apparatus. By not providing all the factual information about all the variants in the manuscript, her own emendations, and other changes in form, Tillotson leaves too much to her individual judgment. "A critical text naturally depends upon critical judgment," Tanselle notes, "but the purpose of an apparatus is to document that judgment with factual information."

17. Tillotson, Kathleen. "Oliver Twist in Three Volumes." The Library, 5th Ser., 18 (June 1963), 113-32.

A densely packed and informative reconstruction of the printing history and bibliographical features of the various three-volume imprints of Oliver Twist published between 1838 and 1841. Tillotson begins with Dickens's advice to Richard Bentley on 3 October 1838 to get the printing of the first three volume edition "in hand." Thereafter she follows Dickens's dealings with Bentley until July 1840, when, according to the terms of the last agreement between them, the publisher returned the copyright of the novel to Dickens. See I. 6. Between those two dates, Bentley published five issues or editions of Oliver Twist in three volumes, whose complicated textual history Tillotson felt driven to explore when she set out to discover how so many doubtful readings in the 1846 text (II. 12) originated from the earlier issues. The errors stemmed, Tillotson shows, from two principal causes: (1) in December 1838, when Dickens parted with the copyright after the publication of the first three-volume edition, he lost all financial interest in the book's sale. As a result, Tillotson thinks, Dickens did not touch the text of Oliver Twist for seven years, until he made his "most thorough revision of all" in 1846; (2) the increasing friction between Bentley and Dickens led the publisher to advertise and market as many "editions" of Oliver Twist as he could. As Tillotson demonstrates, Bentley used the term "edition" lightly, even fictitiously, one consequence of which is the difficulty bibliographers have had distinguishing one imprint from the next. "It seems a long time since I believed in all innocence" in the chief distinctions, writes Tillotson, after discovering that "the actual words inside the covers presented a more complicated picture" than the cherished 'Boz' title-page, 'Charles Dickens' title-page, Fireside and Church plate, 'London Bentley' on spine, "Sadleir A' and 'Sadleir B' labels, with which collectors hitherto designated "editions" of the novel.

The bibliographical details that characterize Bentley's five issues of Oliver Twist in three volumes defy brief condensation; the interested reader will find Tillotson's "Descriptive List of Editions 1838-1867" in her Introduction to the Clarendon edition (II. 48) a succinct summary of the complications she unravelled. To the prose narrative she provides in this account, Tillotson also adds a useful chronicle of the novel's origin, not as a three-volume novel (cf. III. 10), but as the outgrowth of Dickens's November 1836 agreement with Bentley to supply "an original article of his own writing" of "about one sheet" each month. Wanting a sop for Bentley, to whom he had promised another three volume novel (Barnaby Rudge) in an earlier contract, Dickens first offered Oliver Twist as a three-volume novel as well as a serial in July 1837. In the following September, Bentley named Midsummer 1838 as the publishing date for **Oliver Twist** as a book and Dickens agreed to provide the remainder of the copy--i.e., that part of the novel not yet serialized in the **Miscellany**--by 1 May. This, comments Tillotson, was "a crazy piece of optimism" on Dickens's part which he soon revised. Two more deadlines followed, first some time in September and then 25 October, which Dickens beat by five days. Twelve days after he received the completed manuscript, Bentley advertised **Oliver Twist** for publication on 7 November 1838, thereby initiating the tangled printing history Tillotson investigates.

18.   ____. "The Philadelphia Editions of 1838-39." Appendix A. In the Clarendon edition of **Oliver Twist** (II. 48), pp. 372-81.

Reconstructs the textual history of Lea and Blanchard's one-volume and two-volume editions of **Oliver Twist** (II. 7 and 6), both of which were printed early in December 1838 but were delayed in their publication pending the arrival of Cruikshank's illustrations. The two-volume edition appeared on 19 December 1838 without illustrations; the one-volume edition was published on 2 February 1839 with a full complement of illustrations, each redrawn by J. Yeager.

After collating each text with her copy-text, Tillotson confirms the validity of the Philadelphia firm's published claim--taken by Wilkins (IV. 24) as a mendacious piece of advertising--that a large portion of the last part of the novel was set from the manuscript, which Dickens sent to Lea and Blanchard in accordance with the terms they negotiated with him and Bentley. Her collation of Chapters 43 to 53--that part of the Philadelphia edition set from the manuscript--also allows Tillotson to establish superior readings which take precedence over subsequent English editions, where textual errors occurred and went undetected by either Dickens or Forster. The Appendix provides a full list of the substantive variants.

IV. BIBLIOGRAPHICAL STUDIES

1. Carr, Sister Mary Callista, comp. **Catalogue of the Dickens Collection at the University of Texas.** Austin: Univ. of Texas Press, 1961, pp. 55-60.

Lists various American and British editions of the novel in the Humanities Research Center at the University of Texas, Austin. The collection also includes a limited number of plagiarisms, parodies, dramatizations, and translations of **Oliver Twist**.

2. _____. **A Catalogue of the VanderPoel Dickens Collection at the University of Texas.** Austin: Univ. of Texas Press, 1968, pp. 60-66.

A reissue of IV. 1 augmented by additional items from Halstead VanderPoel's collection of Dickensiana.

3. Churchill, R.C. **A Bibliography of Dickensian Criticism 1836-1975.** New York: Garland, 1975. 314 pp.

Attempts to "do justice to all periods of criticism" by assembling chronologically arranged entries divided into multiple topics. Overlapping categories and imprecision in the bibliographical citations sometimes undermine this aim, making the work frustrating for the specialist and of doubtful value to the novice. Churchill provides thirty-three entries for **Oliver Twist** in the section on entries for individual works, but the reader who checks other sections will find useful references to the novel elsewhere. Citations often include references to reviews and quotations from the pieces annotated. When these are full, as they are in the section "Radical and Reformer," the extracts prove helpful. Churchill's apparent fondness for his own writings on Dickens and generous cross-referencing of his opinions with those of other writers tend to exaggerate his importance as a Dickens critic, so much so that references to Churchill in the Index outnumber Forster (by ten) and run ahead of such notables as House, Orwell, and several others.

4. Cohn, Alan. M., and K.K. Collins. **The Cumulated Dickens Checklist 1970-1979.** Troy, N.Y.: Whitson Publishing Company, 1982. 391 pp.

Extends the cut-off date of Gold's compilation (IV. 13), which ends with items published up to 1968, and includes materials from 1980, despite the dates of coverage specified by the title. Cohn and Collins arrange their bibliography, which is based on their quarterly Checklist published in DSN (IV. 5), in the following five sections: Dickens's works; critical, scholarly, and biographical publications about him; reprints; doctoral dissertations; and a selection of miscellanea. Within each division, entries are listed alphabetically by the author's name, consecutively numbered, and lightly annotated. The authors have also added a most useful Subject Index for each of Dickens's works. Under **Oliver Twist**, for example, they list fifty-four separate headings, many of which are further divided into subheadings. The volume is fully cross-referenced and the entries on books list reviews.

36   Text

5. _____. "The Dickens Checklist." DSN, 1 (September 1970), to date.

An invaluable and exhaustive quarterly compilation of editions, secondary sources, dissertations, reviews, adaptations, and miscellaneous Dickens items. Includes nothing published prior to 1970 except those books on Dickens which were reviewed in 1970. Incorporated in IV. 4.

6.   Coleman, Edward D. "The Jew in English Drama: An Annotated Bibliography." BNYPL, 42 (1938), 827-50 and 919-32; 43 (1939), 42-52, 374-78, and 443-58; and 44 (1940), 361-72, 429-44, 495-504, 543-68, 620-34, 675-98, 777-88, and 843-66. Also published as The Jew in English Drama: An Annotated Bibliography, 1943; rpt. New York: NYPL and KTAV Publishing House, Inc., 1970, pp. 68-70.

This bibliography presents a complete and annotated list of printed plays of Jewish interest based on materials in the NYPL, the Library of Congress, Harvard College Library, and Coleman's own collection. Coleman defines "of Jewish interest" to mean whenever one or more characters in a play is designated in the dramatis personae as a Jew, whenever the text clearly indicates that a character is to be taken as such, or when the author gives his character an unmistakably Jewish name.

For more specific information about the dramatic versions of Oliver Twist that Coleman records, see entry VI. 42 in the section Stage Adaptations: Commentary.

7.   Collins, Philip. "Charles Dickens." In The New Cambridge Bibliography of English Literature. Ed. George Watson. Cambridge: Cambridge Univ. Press, 1969, III, 779-850. Also available in offprint form from Dickens House, London.

Includes a brief section on Oliver Twist, providing some titles of early editions, a partial list of reviews, and a selective survey of criticism of the novel. Collins's general sections on Critical Studies and Shorter Studies include books and articles treating Oliver Twist, but the reader cannot distinguish them from the other entries because the format excludes any systematic annotation.

8.   _____. "Charles Dickens." In Victorian Fiction: A Second Guide to Research. Ed. George H. Ford. New York: MLA, 1978, pp. 34-113.

Updates and supplements Nisbet (IV. 18) by adding further subdivisions--characterization, plot and narration, style and language, illustrations, Dickens and society, London, industrialism, women--and studies of individual novels. Entries on Oliver Twist (pp. 88-89) comment very briefly on general essays on the novel and such aspects of its background as orphan literature, the workhouse, and crime.

9.   Dunn, Frank T., comp. A Cumulative Analytical Index to The Dickensian 1905-1974. Hassocks: The Harvester Press, 1976, pp. 130-31 and passim.

An author-subject guide to articles on Oliver Twist appearing in The Dickensian. When using this volume, readers should check entries under characters, locales, and topics because the main entries under individual works do not aim at completeness or provide reliable cross-referencing.

Dickens's alleged anti-Semitism appears, for example, under Dickens III, Personal, while references to A.S. Laing, the alleged original of Mr. Fang, follow alphabetical entries under Laing and do not appear in the section on Oliver Twist.

10. Eckel, John C. **The First Editions of the Writings of Charles Dickens: Their Points and Values.** 1913; rev. and enlarged, New York: Maurice Inman, 1932, pp. 59-63.

Nisbet (IV. 18) calls Eckel Dickens's standard bibliographer but notes (pp. 48-50) several other authorities who demonstrate his shortcomings. The value of this volume with respect to **Oliver Twist** lies principally in Eckel's description of the various issues of the first book edition of the novel, a point of concern to bibliographers and collectors but often one of less interest to scholars and critics. The first three-volume edition of the novel published by Richard Bentley in 1838, notes Eckel, appeared as **Oliver Twist: or, The Parish Boy's Progress** by "Boz" and comprises the following issues: (1) the first issue with Cruikshank's "Fireside" plate in volume three (II. 2), many copies of which Bentley distributed before stopping their circulation at Dickens's request; (2) the second issue with the substituted plate, "Rose Maylie and Oliver"; (3) the third, which shortened the full title to **Oliver Twist** and replaced "By Boz" with "By Charles Dickens, Author of The Pickwick Papers."

Eckel also provides information about two other lesser variants in the first issue: (1) some copies omitted the London,/Bentley imprint at the base of the spine, making these, Eckel thinks, "the very earliest form of the binding"; (2) some include "a List of Illustrations" added when someone noticed that Cruikshank's name had been entirely omitted in the book. "This list," reasons Eckel, "was in the nature of an interpolation" and represents a later printing. "The paper does not correspond with the texture of that in the book; it was whiter and it was cut shorter. With or without the list there is no marring of a first edition--it resolves itself into the question of priority of issue."

Tillotson's descriptive list of editions in the Clarendon **Oliver Twist** (II. 48) and her longer prose summary of the bibliographical features of the early editions in III. 17 surpass Eckel, although she presents confusingly the information about copies of **Oliver Twist** published with the "Fireside" plate in the Clarendon Appendix on the illustrations (pp. 393 and 396).

11. Edgar, Herman Le Roy, and R.W.G. Vail. "Early American Editions of the Works of Charles Dickens." BNYPL, 33 (May 1929), 302-19.

Provides a checklist of titles owned by the NYPL but makes no claim to a definitive study of the history and publication of Dickens's works in America since they began to appear from 1834 onwards. The opening chapter of **Oliver Twist** was first published in New York in 1837, together with the "Public Life of Mr. Tulrumble"; Carey, Lea and Blanchard published the first two chapters of the novel in Philadelphia the same year, including with them sketches and tales from the **Miscellany** and the Library of Fiction by other authors. Thereafter, four American editions of **Oliver Twist** appeared between 1838 and 1839: two in New York and two in Philadelphia, only one of which has any textual significance (see III. 18). Three other editions of **Oliver Twist** appeared in 1842.

12. Fenstermaker, John J. **Charles Dickens, 1940-1975: An Analytical Subject Index to the Periodical Criticism of the Novels and Christmas Books.** Boston: G.K. Hall, 1979, pp. 51-60.

Fenstermaker defines as his objective the attempt to make readily accessible a major portion of the scholarly activity Dickens's works have supported since 1940. Towards this end, he provides a valuable topical key to the journal articles appearing in English during the major reassessment of Dickens's reputation since Wright (XII. 219), Edmund Wilson (V. 24), House (XII. 111) and others. The section on **Oliver Twist** includes 64 entries whose usefulness to the reader becomes apparent when one examines the subject index preceding the bibliographical citations. Each of the seventeen categories (standard for each of the individual novels) is, in turn, variously broken down into topics of increasing specificity. Thus one can learn at a glance under **Oliver Twist** which characters have drawn the most comment (Fagin), what literary influences and parallels commentators have detected, and how critics have variously defined the novel's themes. Fenstermaker's thoroughness constitutes an additional strength since he frequently identifies, through his seventeen subject categories, articles on an aspect of an individual novel that the title conceals, as is the case with Sucksmith's essay, "The Secret of Immediacy" (XIII. 146), or Steig's on Inspector Bucket (XIII. 145).

13.   Gold, Joseph, comp. "**Oliver Twist.**" In his **The Stature of Dickens: A Centenary Bibliography.** Toronto: Univ. of Toronto Press, 1971, pp. 122-27.

A selective but useful general bibliography emphasizing critical and biographical writing since 1870. The section on **Oliver Twist** includes little on Dickens's relationship with Cruikshank, the Sikes and Nancy reading, and dramatic adaptations of the novel. Instead Gold lists Introductions to the text and provides a survey of writings covering social and artistic issues. Entries appear in their order of publication, not alphabetically.

14.   Hatton, Thomas, and Arthur H. Cleaver. **A Bibliography of the Periodical Works of Charles Dickens: Bibliographical, Analytical, and Statistical.** London: Chapman and Hall, 1933, pp. 213-24.

Provides an authoritative and full bibliographical description of the 1846 parts issue of **Oliver Twist**, published in ten monthly numbers between January and October (II. 12). Complete sets of the parts, notes Cleaver, are "the utmost rarity" irrespective of their condition. This edition included Cruikshank's twenty-four plates, together with a front wrapper drawing depicting eleven scenes and incidents from the novel specially designed and etched by Cruikshank for the occasion.

15.   Kitton, Frederic G. **Dickensiana: A Bibliography of the Literature Relating to Charles Dickens and His Writings.** London, 1886, rpt. New York: Haskell House, 1971. 510 pp.

Entries grouped under ten headings. Kitton's volume still proves useful because he includes generous verbatim extracts from the works he cites, numbers each entry, and cross-references thoroughly. Miller (IV. 17) follows a similar format and updates Kitton's work. The volume lacks an index.

16.   _____. "**Oliver Twist.**" In his **The Novels of Charles Dickens: A Bibliography and Sketch** (I. 4), pp. 27-42.

Provides a useful introduction to non-textual matters relating to the novel. Kitton presents briefly some of the details of Dickens's financial arrangements with Richard Bentley about Oliver Twist, indicates how some of Dickens's contemporaries responded to the novel, discusses Cruikshank's claim to have inspired various characters--see XIII. 10-11--and lists the different editions of the novel published up to 1850. Kitton notes correctly that the first number of Oliver Twist did not appear in the Miscellany until February 1837, and he refers to the story's interruption in June, when Dickens was prostrated with grief over the death of his sister-in-law. But Kitton fails to note that installments of Oliver Twist also failed to appear in October 1837 and September 1838. See I. 1 and II. 1.

17.   Miller, William. The Dickens Student and Collector: A List of Writings Relating to Charles Dickens and his Works, 1836-1945. Cambridge, Mass.: Harvard Univ. Press, 1946. 351 pp.

Focuses primarily on biographical materials and collects relatively ignored items such as reviews of Forster's Life, tributes to Dickens in verse, topographical writings, and parodies and plagiarisms of his works. Miller's bibliography holds little interest for the modern scholar because recent, specialized bibliographies provide a more extensive guide to critical writing and reviews of the novels. Miller bases his subject arrangement on Kitton's 1886 bibliography (IV. 16), enters authors chronologically, and annotates briefly and occasionally. For a detailed assessment of the strengths and inadequacies of Miller's bibliography, see Philo Calhoun and Howell J. Heaney in their "Dickensiana in the Rough," PBSA, 41 (1947), 293-320.

18.   Nisbet, Ada. "Charles Dickens." In Victorian Fiction: A Guide to Research. Ed. Lionel Stevenson. Cambridge: Harvard Univ. Press, 1966, pp. 44-153.

Subdivides Dickens criticism into social realism, imagination and symbolism, self-revelation, craftsmanship, lure of the theatre, precursors and imitators, foreign influence, and humor. This essay provides an indispensable starting point for any serious Dickens student, but its broad topics create obstacles for the reader interested only in the criticism of a single work.

19.   Podeschi, John B. Dickens and Dickensiana: A Catalogue of The Richard Gimbel Collection in the Yale University Library. New Haven: Yale Univ. Press, 1980, passim.

An important catalogue of a rich and diversified collection of first editions, translations, adaptations, plagiarisms, simplified popular versions of Dickens's novels, collected editions, and manuscripts of Dickens's work now housed at the Beinecke Library, Yale. Podeschi arranges his catalogue according to a clearly organized plan and provides full and accurate information for each entry.

20.   Rosenbach, A.S.W. A Catalogue of The Writings of Charles Dickens in the Library of Harry Elkins Widener. Philadelphia: privately printed, 1918, pp. 31-37.

An important collection of first editions now housed in the Widener Memorial Room and available for use in the Houghton reading room, Harvard University. Among them are a copy of the first issue of the first edition of Oliver Twist in three volumes (II. 2), with its suppressed plate, "Fireside

Scene," in volume three, and two copies of the second issue of the first edition with the substituted plate, "Rose Maylie and Oliver" in the church (II. 3). Inserted in one of these copies are Cruikshank's original drawings of (1) Oliver escaping being bound apprentice to the sweep; (2) Monks and Fagin looking in on Oliver asleep at his desk, with a sketch of Nancy in the upper corner; (3) a page of studies with a note in Cruikshank's writing: "Sketches for 'Oliver Twist.' Suggestions to Mr. C. Dickens The **Writer**." This was the drawing upon which Cruikshank based his later claim to joint authorship of the novel (XIII. 10-11). The collection also includes nine other drawings on thin paper, the original tracings Cruikshank used for the first edition of the novel.

21.   Sadleir, Michael. "Charles Dickens." In his **XIX Century Fiction: A Bibliographical Record Based on His Own Collection.** 2 vols. London: Constable, 1951, I, 104-07.

    Describes Sadleir's remarkable collection of Dickens's work in octavo first editions in cloth, including the first three volume "Boz" issue of **Oliver Twist** in 1838 with the "Fireside" plate and a copy Sadleir calls "partially second issue." This edition has "Boz" on all the spines but "By Charles Dickens" on the title-page of volume one.

22.   Smith, Walter E. **Charles Dickens in the Original Cloth: A Bibliographical Catalogue of the First Appearance of His Writings in Book Form in England with Facsimiles of the Bindings and Titlepages.** Part One. Los Angeles: The Heritage Bookshop, 1982, pp. 30-37.

    A bibliographical catalogue providing book collectors, dealers, and librarians with descriptions of Dickens's novels as they appeared in the original cloth bindings of their first editions in book form. Sixteen entries for **Oliver Twist** follow in chronological order, each with a photograph of the title-page and binding, as well as information about the collation, contents, internal flaws, and illustrations. Smith's notes on **Oliver Twist** succinctly and accurately summarize the main features distinguishing (and complicating) the novel's early publishing history.

23.   Wilkins, William Glyde. **First and Early American Editions of the Works of Charles Dickens.** Cedar Rapids, 1910; rpt. New York: Burt Franklin, 1968, pp. 13-16.

    Provides some help but not the definitive guide through the tangled history of early American publications of Dickens's works. Wilkins thinks that the first part of **Oliver Twist** to see publication in America was the first two chapters of the novel. These were published in 1837 by Carey, Lea, and Blanchard of Philadelphia in volume two of their **Tales and Sketches**, a compilation of articles from Richard Bentley's **Miscellany**, together with Dickens's Mudfog papers in volume one and the two opening chapters of **Oliver Twist** in volume two. Wilkins describes an American reprint of the **Miscellany** by the New York firm of William and Jemima Welker as "the first American edition of the entire work." This version included Cruikshank's plates redrawn by an American artist. Wilkins also notes that Carey, Lea, and Blanchard began an edition of **Oliver Twist** in parts in 1838 and completed it early in 1839, shortly before they issued the complete work in two volumes. For the textual and publishing history of this important edition, see III. 18.

24.   "The Year's Work in Dickens Studies." **The Dickensian,** 64 (September 1968) to date.

A selective though useful annual survey of essays and notes on Dickens published mainly in American and British journals. Michael Slater began the series, handing it to Malcolm Andrews (1970-77), who afterwards relinquished it to Jean Elliott, the present author. The survey appears as a continuous narrative, although the topics under which entries are presented vary from issue to issue as the author devises different categories to describe the contributions of a given year.

V. DICKENS'S READING ADAPTATIONS: SIKES AND NANCY

1. Bowen, W.H. "The Medical History of Charles Dickens." In his **Charles Dickens and His Family: A Sympathetic Study.** Cambridge: W. Heffer & Sons, 1956, pp. 134-59.

Bowen's careful examination of Dickens's medical history and his cautious inferences about the reasons for Dickens's premature death at fifty-eight usefully counter those who argue that the paid Readings caused the novelist's death. This chapter also leads one to question Edgar Johnson's assertion (V. 18) that in deciding to add "the murder of Nancy to his repertory, he was sentencing himself to death."

Bowen concedes that evidence exists to support the contention that the Readings hastened Dickens's end. The writer's nervousness about railway travel after he escaped without serious physical harm from the Staplehurst accident in June 1865, the fact that the reading tours required extensive travel, and the resulting anxiety, together with the exhaustion and sleeplessness after the evening performances, all added extra strain to the work Dickens undertook in the years his health severely declined. At the same time, Bowen suggests that Dickens's recuperative powers eased some of the burden; he also argues that Dickens's efficient staff and his inflexible resolution to live quietly while travelling moderated the toll. Bowen's most persuasive argument, however, rests on his analysis of Dickens's health in the late sixties.

As a life-long victim of renal colic--a degenerative disease which manifests itself through arteriosclerosis--Dickens exhibited two classic symptoms of that affliction. As the walls of his body's smaller arteries (arterioles) weakened, collapsed, and eventually destroyed brain tissue, Dickens suffered from incipient paralysis from 1865 onwards in his left side and particularly in his left foot. Similarly, as the channels of his blood vessels narrowed, the intensified resistance put his heart muscle under greater strain and led to an altered pulse rate and signs diagnosed by his doctors as "heart irritability." To these conditions was added gout, a disease which increases the tendency towards degenerative changes in the kidney because there is in gout "some factor present antagonistic to renal efficiency."

Dickens sought help from the most eminent physicians of his day, including Sir Thomas Watson, who gave permission, with reservations, for the Readings to be resumed after Dickens broke down at Preston in April 1869. Bowen also points out that Dickens's regimen of exercise and his ability to recover his health after a short rest served to promote a sense of well being rather than hasten his "chronic persistent disease," whose progressive deterioration continued "whatever his mental and physical activities might be." Bowen passes quickly over the details of Dickens's final stroke, but adds that his falling unconscious after returning to his desk, much against his usual custom, was consistent with Dickens's "whole medical history." Dickens fell to the floor shortly after a period of "sustained creative effort," when the blood flow to his brain would be at its maximum. "This should be remembered when it is stated that his Readings, which, broadly speaking, involved physical and emotional rather than mental strain, were the cause of his premature death."

2.   Collins, Philip, ed. "Sikes and Nancy." In his **Charles Dickens: The**
      Public Readings. Oxford: Clarendon Press, 1975, pp. 465-86.

Collins's headnote provides a brief account of Dickens's growth of
interest in the reading, his preparation of the text, first reading with a
private audience, and his adoption of the episode for public performances.
Referring to the texts of the reading, Collins describes the first one Dickens
had privately printed in or about September 1868. In this Dickens divides the
narrative into three parts, concluding the reading with the killing of Nancy.
To it he later added three manuscript pages, "a brilliantly condensed version
of parts of chs. 48 and 50, concluding with the death of Sikes and his dog."
Dickens devised this extra narrative on the suggestion of Charles Kent and
Wilkie Collins. See V. 5 and V. 20. This prompt-copy, now in the Berg
Collection, provides interesting evidence of Dickens's rewriting of the last
hours of Sikes. "Events," Collins points out, "are seen through Sikes's eyes
which had not been presented that way in the novel."
      Dickens performed the revised text in public and had a new edition of it
privately printed, incorporating the extension into the narrative. No copy of
this edition with stage directions in Dickens's hand appears to have survived.
Fortunately, a copy formerly owned by Adeline Billington, an actress Dickens
admired, does. In it she transcribed from Dickens's personal prompt-copy,
lent to her for the purpose, all his elaborate underlinings and stage
directions. Billington's copy is now in the Suzannet Collection at Dickens
House. Because it represents the latest stage of Dickens's text, Collins uses
it as the copy-text for his present edition, to which he adds a footnote record
of some variants in the Berg copy.

3.   ———. "'Sikes and Nancy': Dickens's Last Reading." TLS, 11 June
      1971, pp. 681-82.

Describes in detail the "Billington" copy of the **Sikes and Nancy**
reading--see also Collins (V. 2)--and comments on the exaggerated stories
surrounding Dickens's performances of the murder. Dickens gave the reading
four times a week, not ten (a figure based, Collins thinks, on a misreading of
"fourth" in Dickens's letter to Alexander Russel in N, III, 708); ladies fainted
at a reading of "David Copperfield" and "The Trial from Pickwick" on 25
January 1869, not at Clifton on the twentieth, whence Dickens wrote
Georgina Hogarth that he had given "by far the best Murder yet done." Past
critics, writes Collins, erred by "mentally conflating" extracts from two
different letters cited by Forster in his chapter on the "Last Readings" (Life,
XI, i), inferring incorrectly as Collins himself does in his **Dickens and Crime**
(XII. 60), that Dickens's phrase the "contagion of fainting" described the
effect of the reading from **Oliver Twist** not **David Copperfield.** Cf. also P, I,
439n.
      Speculation about Dickens's reasons for preparing the murder for public
performances concludes Collins's note. Unlike those who see Dickens
projecting into the scene his own lawless feelings, deep antagonism to
Victorian society, and suicidal impulses, Collins suggests that two practical
factors may have affected his decision to offer the reading. First, Dickens's
Farewell Series faced increasing competition from other recitalists; second,
Thomas Hood's poem about a murderer, "The Dream of Eugene Aram,"
enjoyed great popularity. Both considerations, Collins thinks, may have
influenced Dickens's intention to devise something equally sensational from
the end of **Oliver Twist,** which offered "very similar histrionic possibilities."

4.   ———. "The Text of Dickens' Readings." BNYPL, 74 (June 1970),
      360-80.

Gives the particulars of the Berg's twenty-one reading texts or "prompt-copies" of the volumes Dickens used in his career as a public reader between 1858 and 1870. Among these octavo size personal copies, each approximately 8 1/2 by 5 1/2 inches, the Berg has the original prompt-book of **Sikes and Nancy** printed by William Clowes in 1868 (V. 6) and the later prompt-copy, privately printed by C. Whiting (V. 7). This one, bound in paper wrappers, included the expanded ending in which Sikes and his dog die. Collins also described two "trade" editions of the public readings: Bradbury and Evans's special "Reading Editions" of those pieces Dickens had in his repertoire by June 1858 and the nine readings, issued both in pairs and then in a collected edition, published by Ticknor and Fields in Boston between 1868-69. **Sikes and Nancy** appears in none of these.

5.   Dickens, Charles. **The Letters of Charles Dickens.** Volume III 1858-
       1870. The Nonesuch Dickens. Ed. Walter Dexter. Bloomsbury: The
       Nonesuch Press, 1938, passim.

Later in Dickens's career his interest in **Oliver Twist** returned when he set to work preparing an addition to his repertoire of paid readings for his Farewell Season of 1868-69. Five years before Dickens first performed "the Oliver Twist murder," he wrote to W.H. Brookfield that he had been experimenting with it by himself "but have got something so horrible out of it that I am afraid to try it in public" (N, III, 353). No further reference to the murder appears in the Nonesuch Letters until October 1868. Early that autumn Dickens put together "a short reading" which he thought would provide a new attraction to the last tour and satisfy his own ambitions. "I wanted to leave behind me the recollection of something very passionate and dramatic," he wrote to Forster in November, "done with simple means, if the art would justify the theme" (N, III, 679).

Two practical concerns occupied Dickens soon after he turned his attention to the novel. Although he never doubted his ability to "perfectly petrify" an audience with the murder, he hesitated about the advisability of performing something so "very powerful." He also developed second thoughts about where to end the reading. Initially, he planned to finish after Nancy's murder, but questions from Wilkie Collins and Charles Kent led him to reconsider. After a trial reading, both urged Dickens to culminate the reading with Sikes's death.

In order to test the reading's effect on an audience, Dickens assembled about one hundred guests on 14 November 1868 in St. James's Hall, London, where, his figure "completely isolated" by the use of a back screen, two "wings" at the sides and curtains all round, Dickens held everyone spell-bound in an astonishing display of histrionic skill. "[T]he public have been looking out for a sensation these last fifty years or so," Dickens reported Mrs. Mary Ann Keely, the actress, as saying, "and by Heaven they have got it!" (N, III, 687). Cf. also Edmund Yates (V. 25). Forster responded less enthusiastically, voicing doubts on aesthetic grounds and objecting that regular performances would exhaust Dickens, in which opinion Charley, the novelist's eldest son, concurred. See V. 12.

Dickens's mind, however, was set. Perform he would, although at first he demurred about the advisability of getting in Sikes's fall. "[B]elieve me," he wrote to Kent, "no audience on earth could be held for ten minutes after the girl's death" (N, III, 678). Later he told Collins that he had put together "in a very short space" the conclusion his two friends had suggested (N, III, 681). Dickens describes how he "cut about the [novel's] text with great care" in a letter to Forster (III, 674). See also Philip Collins (V. 2) for the changes Dickens made when he adapted the conclusion of **Oliver Twist** to the reading version.

Dickens gave his first public performance of the murder on 5 January 1869; thereafter he read the episode regularly until his health gave way in April 1869, at which time his doctor ordered him to stop the tour. Dickens complied, bitterly disappointed that he should have to abandon the remaining readings. He did, however, obtain his physician's consent to give a short London Farewell Series of twelve readings before retiring completely on 15 March 1870.

Critics united in an almost unanimous chorus of superlatives to describe the **Sikes and Nancy** reading, into which Dickens threw every theatrical resource at his command. "TWO MACBETHS!" exclaimed an aging Macready (N, III, 704), whose praise may be taken to mean that Macready thought Dickens revealed a power comparable to his own performances of Macbeth when the famous actor was in his prime. Alternatively, as Philip Collins suggests on the basis of his own experience reading **Sikes and Nancy**, the performance is "'two Macbeths' in terms of the physical and emotional strain on the performer" (XII. 60).

6.   ____. **Sikes and Nancy: A Reading** from Oliver Twist. [London]: William Clowes, n.d., pp. 79-112.

The original text of the reading privately printed around September 1868 and bound with Dickens's reading version of **The Chimes.** Collins notes (V. 2 and V. 4) that this prompt-copy now belongs to the Berg Collection of the New York Public Library. Dickens divided the narrative into three chapters, basing sections I and II on **Oliver Twist** Chapters 45 and 46 and section III mainly on Chapter 47. This version, the first Dickens put together, ends with dawn breaking as Sikes leaves the house after murdering Nancy. Many stage-directions in Dickens's hand appear in the margins. Among the revisions noted by Collins in his article describing the Berg's collection of reading texts (V. 4) are those Dickens made to Sikes's oaths, typically deleting "Damme's" and "Hell's Fire!" or changing an oath to "Hello!" To this Berg copy are appended three manuscript pages, Dickens's condensed version of Chapters 48 and 50, of **Oliver Twist**, in which Sikes and his dog fall to their deaths. These three pages represent roughly three-and-a-half printed pages; overall, the reading equals only one third of the length of the corresponding chapters in the novel.

7.   ____. **Sikes and Nancy: A Reading.** [London]: C. Whiting, n.d., pp. 3-47.

A privately printed version of the revised text, incorporating the new ending Dickens added upon the advice of his friends (V. 5 and V. 20). Dickens used this new printed edition as his prompt-copy but no record of the existence of the actual copy he used survives. A copy of his stage-directions exists, however, in a printed copy of the Whiting text Dickens gave Adeline Billington, who transcribed from his reading copy, lent to her for the purpose, all Dickens's markings into her personal copy. This item is now in the Suzannet Collection at Dickens House and represents the latest stage of Dickens's text.

8.   ____. **Sikes and Nancy: A Reading** by Charles Dickens. Ed. J. Harrison Stonehouse. London: Henry Sotheran, 1921. xii + 58 pp.

Reprints the text of the reading copy formerly owned by Mrs. Billington but without her annotations (V. 2), together with a concise account of Dickens's preparations of the text and the changes he made after the experimental reading on 14 November 1868. Stonehouse also quotes from several contemporaries of Dickens who wrote about the performances and discusses briefly Dickens's failing health during his farewell series of readings. Stonehouse incorrectly attributes the 1869 essay in **Tinsleys' Magazine** (V. 25) to James Payn.

9. ____. **Sikes and Nancy.** Ed. Philip Collins. In his **Charles Dickens The Public Readings** (V. 2), pp. 472-86.

Reprints the "Billington" prompt-copy together with footnotes recording some variants in the Berg text (V. 6). Throughout, Dickens refers to Fagin as Fagin and only once calls him "the Jew."

10. ____. **Sikes and Nancy.** Ed. Philip Collins. London: The Dickens House, 1982. vii + 47 pp.

A facsimile of the privately-printed second version of the murder of Nancy that Dickens gave to Adeline Billington, in which she transcribed his inked-in underlinings and additions after borrowing Dickens's own desk-copy. Collins provides a brief introduction covering some of the material he discusses in the Headnote to the **Sikes and Nancy** text in his **Charles Dickens: The Public Readings** (V. 2). Copies of this Facsimile Reading Copy may be bought at the Dickens House.

11. ____. **Sikes and Nancy and Other Public Readings.** Ed. Philip Collins. Oxford: Oxford Univ. Press, 1983, pp. 229-46.

An abbreviated paperback version of Collins's edition of **The Public Readings** (V. 2) with a new, shorter Introduction. Collins provides the same text of **Sikes and Nancy** as he did in 1975 with its footnotes recording variants in the Berg text but condenses his headnote commenting on how Dickens adapted and prepared the reading for performance.

12. Dickens, Charles, Jr. "Glimpses of Charles Dickens." Part II. **The North American Review,** 160 (June 1895), 677-84.

Recalls one of Charley's first work experiences as his father's private secretary and sub-editor of **All the Year Round** in the autumn of 1868. Alone in the library at Gadshill, Charley heard what appeared to be "a tremendous row going ... on outside." Initially, he attributed the disturbance to a quarrel between local tramps, but when the sounds of a violent altercation continued, he stepped into the garden to investigate. At the other end of the meadow he found his father "striding up and down, gesticulating wildly, and, in the character of **Mr. Sikes,** murdering **Nancy,** with every circumstance of the most aggravated brutality." The dramatic performance impressed Charley greatly, but he resolutely stuck to his admonition. "The finest thing I have ever heard," he responded after his father acted the episode for him again that evening, "but don't do it."

13. Dolby, George. "The 'Final Farewell' Tour in the United Kingdom." In his **Charles Dickens as I Knew Him: The Story of the Reading Tours**

in Great Britain and America (1866-1870). London, 1885; rpt. New
York: Haskell House, 1970, passim.

Records the unsuccessful struggle of Dickens's reading manager to
persuade his "Chief" not to perform the murder, whose impact on Dickens's
health Dolby regarded as "one of the greatest dangers we had to contend
against." He adds: "The terrible force with which the actual perpetration of
this most foul murder was described was of such a kind as to render Mr.
Dickens utterly prostrate after its delivery." The other readings, too, drove
up Dickens's pulse to high levels, but Dolby gives his opinion that their after
effects were not so serious as when Dickens left the stage exhausted after
performing the murder.

14. Fitzgerald, Percy. "The Reading Tours." In his Memoirs of Charles
     Dickens. Bristol and London, 1913; rpt. New York: Benjamin Blom,
     1971, pp. 56-62.

Useful for Fitzgerald's briefly expressed dissenting view about the
powerful effects of the murder. "It was a gruesome thing enough, but
somewhat overstrained and melodramatic."

15. Fitzsimons, Raymund. "Murderous Instincts." In his The Charles
     Dickens Show: An Account of his Public Readings 1858-1870. London:
     Geoffrey Bles, 1970, pp. 142-69.

Recounts Dickens's preparation, practice, and delight in performing
successfully the Sikes and Nancy reading, together with the reactions of
various friends about Dickens's declining health during the Farewell Tour of
1868-70.

16. Hollingshead, John. "Dickens." In his According to My Lights.
     London: Chatto & Windus, 1900, pp. 11-19.

Hollingshead notes in this essay that he was told "on good authority" that
a day or two before Dickens died "he was found in the grounds of Gadshill,
acting the murder scene between Sikes and Nancy."

17. Hollingsworth, Keith. The Newgate Novel 1830-1847: Bulwer,
     Ainsworth, Dickens, & Thackeray. Detroit: Wayne State Univ. Press,
     1963, pp. 123-25.

Finds Nancy's murder full of "stagey pathos," a "forced" episode "by no
means a necessity of the plot." Dickens wrote it, Hollingsworth argues, to
capitalize on Newgate sensationalism and to express his own "obsession with
murderers." Hollingsworth endorses Edmund Wilson's hypothesis that
Dickens's identification with murderers originated in the psychic trauma of
his childhood despair (V. 24) and agrees with Edgar Johnson that Dickens's
insistence upon performing the murder later in life led to his premature death
(V. 18).

18. Johnson, Edgar. "Last Rally." In his Charles Dickens: His Tragedy and
     Triumph (I, 9), II, 1095-1114.

Speculates that by adding the Sikes and Nancy reading to his repertoire against the advice of his doctors and his friends Dickens "sentence[d]

himself to death." He recklessly expended his "waning energies," Johnson thinks, because by this late stage of his life Dickens "had ceased to care what happened." His marriage had proved unsuccessful, Ellen Ternan, in some way, "failed his need," his children worried and disappointed him, and his earlier "gleaming hopes" for a better world had given way to deep pessimism about England's apparent decline and loss of moral initiative and direction. Little therefore remained in Dickens's life, argues Johnson, other than the destructive excitement of the readings, to which the novelist returned with the same compulsiveness with which John Jasper in **The Mystery of Edwin Drood** sought relief from the world in his murderous opium fantasies.

19.   Kennethe, L.A. [Pseud. Walter Dexter]. "The Unique Reading Books."
      The Dickensian, 39 (Spring 1943), 75-78.

Notes the sale of Dickens's reading version of **Sikes and Nancy** in New York in 1938 for $7,500. The text, specially printed by William Clowes (see V. 6), was bound with the reading version of **The Chimes**, and had appended three pages of manuscript in Dickens's hand in which he added his condensed description of Sikes's flight and fall from the roof. This former prompt-copy, now in the Berg Collection, is described fully by Collins (V. 4).

20.   Kent, Charles. "Sikes and Nancy." In his **Charles Dickens as a Reader**.
      London: Chapman and Hall, 1872, pp. 253-62.

Describes Dickens's experimental rehearsal of the reading on 14 November 1868, which Dickens announced as a "Private Trial of the Murder in Oliver Twist." Although Kent felt skeptical about the undertaking, the performance quickly dissipated his doubts. The murder scene, he adds, "immeasurably surpassed anything" Dickens had ever achieved before and proved a "splendid ... piece of tragic acting." Kent comments on the brilliance with which Dickens stepped instantaneously in and out of the principal roles, moving from Fagin, "high shouldered" with bird-like claws, to a long-limbed, chuckle-headed Bolter, and thence to "the burly ruffian" Sikes, and finally to Nancy. In her suppressed emotion, foreboding of horror, and last "gasping, shrieking apostrophes," Kent thought, Dickens's genius revealed itself most persuasively.
Kent also speaks of his reservations about the original ending, which, in his judgment, finished too abruptly with the murder. By adding a condensed version of Sikes's flight and eventual death, Dickens achieved an even more stunning effect, as he conveyed the emotions Sikes experiences. In the murderer's horror, Kent saw an avenging voice not only against Sikes but "all who ever outraged ... the sanctity of human life." Above all, Kent believed that this last scene sublimated an incident "of the ghastliest terror into a homily of burning eloquence."

21.   **Mr. Charles Dickens's Farewell Readings.** London: J. Mallett, n.d., 4 pp.

A rare pamphlet which collects a number of contemporary rave reviews of the **Sikes and Nancy** reading. Dickens House owns a copy.

22.   Robinson, Kenneth. **Wilkie Collins: A Biography.** London: Bodley Head,
      1951, p. 243.

Quotes Collins's opinion that the **Sikes and Nancy** reading "did more to kill Dickens than all his works put together."

23.   Tillotson, Kathleen. "'Sikes and Nancy': The Reading Version." Appendix D. In the Clarendon edition of **Oliver Twist** (II. 48), pp. 389-91.

Recounts briefly Dickens's growth of interest in the reading, his first draft, the private performance, and his subsequent lengthening of the reading to include Sikes's flight and death.

24.   Wilson, Edmund. "Dickens: The Two Scrooges." In his **Wound and the Bow: Seven Studies in Literature.** Boston, 1941; rpt. London: Methuen, 1961, passim.

Wilson remarks briefly on Dickens's motives for beginning the public readings and comments on the murder of Nancy by Sikes, from which Dickens "obviously derived" satisfaction by horrifying people. Wilson speculates that perhaps the scene represented symbolically "his behaviour in banishing his wife." Into it Dickens threw himself with "hysterical" passion, "as if reading it had become at this point in his life a real means of self-expression." In Wilson's words, the murder took on "something of the nature of an obsessive hallucination," in whose threads Wilson sees Dickens's self-destructiveness and evidence of his profound alienation from society.
This interpretation of the murder accords with Wilson's general thesis that the destruction of Dickens's childhood at the blacking factory and his father's imprisonment destined him to respond to the cruelty of organized society in one of two roles: "that of the criminal or that of the rebel." Wilson sees Dickens as playing both, especially the criminal in his later career, as his psychological insight into the mind of the murderer increases with the author's own sense of isolation and outlawry. **The Mystery of Edwin Drood,** argues Wilson, carries "the theme of the criminal ... to its logical development in his fiction" and presents John Jasper as "an insoluble moral problem which is identified with his own."

25.   Yates, Edmund. "Mr. Charles Dickens's New Reading." **Tinsleys' Magazine,** 4 (February 1869), 60-64.

Documents Yates's view that the **Sikes and Nancy** reading finally allowed Dickens to give "his dramatic genius full vent." As one who attended the private reading on 14 November 1868, Yates saw Dickens warm with excitement and "fl[i]ng aside his book" as he "acted the scene of the murder." Dickens's Fagin appeared, his back bent but without shrugged shoulders, husky voiced and speaking with a slight lisp "but no nasal intonation." "[T]he conventional attributes are omitted, the conventional words are never spoken; and the Jew fence, crafty and cunning even in his bitter vengeance, is there before us, to the life," Yates states. Unlike Kent (V. 20), Yates argues that "Artistically speaking, the story of Sikes and Nancy ends" when she is murdered. The audience's wild excitement, he thought, died when she died, "and the rest was somewhat of an anti-climax."

VI. STAGE ADAPTATIONS OF OLIVER TWIST

PRODUCTIONS (CHRONOLOGICAL LISTING)

1. a Beckett, Gilbert A. **Oliver Twist.** St. James's Theatre, London. 27
    March 1838.

The first recorded adaptation of **Oliver Twist,** which was produced and
staged before Dickens wrote the thrilling incidents connected with the
conclusion of the Sikes-Nancy story. Working with the incomplete novel, a
Beckett, argues Fawcett (VI. 45), accented the humor in the thieves' kitchen,
at the undertaker's, and among the ludicrous parish officials. Fulkerson (VI.
48), who has read the manuscript, notes that a Beckett followed the novel in
outline "(without [my emphasis] the workhouse and Sowerberry scenes)" until
the attempted robbery, when his own invention had to take over. In this
version, the thieves break into Mr. Brownlow's and not Mrs. Maylie's house,
where they are suddenly ambushed by the police. In the resulting confusion,
Sikes accidentally shoots Fagin dead before the police arrest him. This
production, note the Pilgrim editors, was "Pulverized by the critics" and taken
off at once (P, I, 388n). For further comments about a Beckett's adaptation,
see Fulkerson (VI. 48). No published version of a Beckett's play exists, but the
manuscript he submitted for licensing survives in the collection of plays in the
British Museum from the Lord Chamberlain's office (B.M. Add. 42945, ff.
683-70).

2. Barnett, Charles Zachary. **Oliver Twist, or, The Parish Boy's Progress.**
    A Drama in Three Acts. Pavilion Theatre, London. 21 May 1838.

Another short-lived adaptation put on at a large East-end theatre
specializing in "Melodrama of a rough type, farce, pantomime, etc.,"
according to Charles Dickens, Jr., writing in his **Dickens's Dictionary of
London** in 1879. Fulkerson (VI. 48) calls this play an improvement over a
Beckett's (VI. 1) because Barnett used Nancy more effectively and gave the
plot against Oliver greater coherency. But the adaptation also suffers from
many defects, amongst which the invented ending stands out. During the
attempted robbery at Mr. Brownlow's, a wounded Oliver shoots Monks just as
Bumble enters with the police to arrest Fagin and Sikes. Oliver is then
revealed as Mr. Brownlow's grandson and Monks as the old man's nephew, who
had turned Mr. Brownlow against his daughter, Oliver's mother, after she had
spurned him and run away to marry a soldier. In addition, Barnett names
Monks as Nancy's seducer.
Two printed versions of Barnett's adaptation exist. One appears in
Duncombe's British Theatre (volume 29) and gives the text of the Pavilion
production in May 1838; the second, written apparently after Dickens
completed **Oliver Twist,** substitutes an ending closer to that of the novel.
Published versions of this revised text are available in Lacy's Acting Edition
(volume 33) and in French's Acting Edition (no. 494). Fulkerson notes that the
Lacy's version is usually attributed to Thomas Hailes Lacy (VI. 7), whose text
he describes as "a scissors-and-paste plagiarism using scenes from Barnett's
play for Act I and the first half of Act II, and then using slightly abbreviated

scenes from Almar's play [VI. 3] for the end of Act II and all of Act III."
Fulkerson adds that he has found no evidence that "this compilation" was ever
performed. But cf. Pierce (VI. 57), who lists an Adelphi version of **Oliver
Twist**, produced by Frederick Yates and adapted by T.H. Lacy on 25 February
1839, and Charles Dickens, Jr., who also refers to this production in his
Introduction to **Oliver Twist** in 1892 (II. 18).

3.   Almar, George. **Oliver Twist**. A Serio-Comic Burletta, in Three Acts.
       Royal Surrey Theatre, London. 19 November 1838.

This version opens with Bumble courting Mrs. Corney and also shows
Oliver working for Mr. Sowerberry as his apprentice. The drama includes
scenes at Fagin's, Oliver's trial, rescue, and recapture, and follows the main
outline of Dickens's narrative until the ending, making this in the words of
Morley (VI. 55) "a stage transcript" of the novel. Nevertheless, Almar's
adaptation ends hastily, omitting Fagin's trial and execution.

The Pilgrim editors note that this was the most successful of the
contemporary adaptations of **Oliver Twist** and that it ran for eighty nights,
ending in February 1839 (P, I, 388n). Forster (XII. 7) records that when
Dickens visited the Surrey Theatre in the middle of the first scene "he laid
himself down upon the floor in a corner of the box and never rose from it until
the drop scene fell." Contemporary reviewers seemed to share Dickens's
reaction. The music and drama critic in **The Athenaeum** on 24 November
1838 (p. 844) briefly dismissed the production as the penalty Dickens paid for
his popularity, while the reviewer in **The Examiner** gave it a very poor notice
on 25 November 1838, praising only the striking scenic effects, the boy-actor
who played Oliver, and the youth who played Noah Claypole (p. 742).

Almar's text exists in the following acting editions: Webster's Acting
National Drama (no. 64); Dicks' Standard Plays (no. 293); and French's
Standard Drama (no. 228). Coleman (VI. 42) notes that a prompter's copy is in
the NYPL. Morley (VI. 55) comments that Almar's version subsequently ran in
New York; Lazenby (VI. 51) notes that later American versions of **Oliver
Twist** grew out of Almar's play, in a slightly shorter four-act form, rather
than from the novel directly.

4.   Greenwood, Thomas. **Boz's Oliver Twist; or, the Parish Boy's Progress**.
       Sadler's Wells Theatre, London. 3 December 1838.

This version starred Mrs. Honner as Oliver and her husband, Robert, the
joint manager of Sadler's Wells with Greenwood, as Fagin. In a letter to
Frederick Yates, Dickens commented that he had never seen Mrs. Honner act,
adding that "from the mere circumstance of her being a Mrs, I should say at
once that she was 'a many sizes too large' for Oliver Twist." Casting "a very
sharp girl of thirteen or fourteen" as Oliver might work, Dickens continued,
but otherwise "the character would be an absurdity" (P, I, 388), a warning
many producers appeared to overlook. As Morley observes (VI. 55), actresses
frequently took Oliver's part, a fact also true in America, where stage
handbills of adaptations in the Gimbel Collection--see Podeschi (VI.
58)--frequently name women in this role. The reviewer for **The Town**,
December 1838, wrote favorably of this version, praising Robert Honner's
Fagin and his overall production of the play. See clipping in the Harvard
Theatre Collection (VI. 49).

5.   Stirling, Edward. **Oliver Twist, a New Version**. City of London
       Theatre, London. 3 December 1838.

The fifth of the early versions of **Oliver Twist** performed before Coyne's adaptation at the Adelphi (VI. 6). Fulkerson (VI. 48) doubts the existence of a script of this play, but Podeschi (IV. 19) records a copy of a number two in a weekly series, the "Penny Pictorial Play," whose title reads as follows: **Oliver Twist; or, The Parish Boy's Progress. A Domestic Drama, in Three Acts. Dramatised from 'Boz's' Celebrated Work of that Name, and as Performed at the City of London Theatre** (London: H. Beale, n.d. 8 pp.). This adaptation crudely reduces Dickens's plot. Act one opens with Oliver arriving in London and beginning work almost immediately as a thief, until Mr. Brownlow enters, rescues Oliver, and takes him in. In the second act, Sikes and Nancy drag Oliver off from Brownlow's. A small role is allotted to Bumble; and the rest of the action develops around the attempted robbery at Chertsey. In the compressed final act, Oliver is rescued, Sikes wounded, and then attended by Nancy, whom he murders off stage. Pierce (VI. 57) lists the City of London production in December 1838 as anonymous but ascribes a second version performed there in the following March to Stirling. Cf. Nicoll (VI. 56), who does not record this production and who credits Stirling with the Adelphi performance in March 1839 (VI. 6). For details of the cast performing at the City of London Theatre in December 1838, see an advertisement in **The Town** (Harvard Theatre Collection).

6.   Coyne, Joseph Stirling. **Oliver Twist; based on Charles Dickens's Novel.** Adelphi Theatre, London. 25 February 1839.

Confusion about the authorship of this stage version exists. Nicoll (VI. 56), citing the **Catalogue of Additions to the Manuscripts in the British Museum: Plays Submitted to the Lord Chamberlain 1825-1851**, gives Edward Stirling as the author (BM Add. 42950); the **Times** reviewer (26 February 1839, p. 5), Coleman (VI. 42), and others cite Coyne. Pierce, on the other hand, names T.H. Lacy: see comments in VI. 57 and VI. 7. Referring to the two acts of the play which survive in the Lord Chamberlain's collection, Fulkerson (VI. 48) writes that the adapter made economical cuts by dropping the workhouse scenes. He preserved some of the comedy of Bumble and Mrs. Corney, adds Fulkerson, but placed more emphasis on the thieves and made Nancy the leading character. Act Two featured the attempted robbery and showed Nancy struggling to help Oliver, ending with her meeting with Rose.

Before this version was produced at the Adelphi on 25 February 1839, Dickens had written in March 1838 to Frederick Yates, actor-manager of the theatre, proposing to dramatize **Oliver Twist** for the beginning of the September season, several months before he had finished the novel. Nothing came of this proposal or of a later attempt to interest W.C. Macready (XI. 16) in a stage version of **Oliver Twist.** Yates, however, did produce Coyne's adaptation and take the role of Fagin. With "your name as the Jew," wrote Dickens in March 1838, "and mine as the author [we] would knock any other attempts quite out of the field. I do not however see the least possibility of any other Theatre being able to steal a march upon you" (P, I, 388-89).

The fact that this production ran for only fourteen nights (P, I, 388n) appears to undercut this prediction. The music and drama critic of **The Athenaeum** found the cast powerful. The writer praised Mrs. Yates as Nancy and Mrs. Keeley as Oliver; "every inch" of O. Smith looked the burglar, he added, commending the actor for raising "the brutality of the character almost to the sublime of low tragedy." But the play's weakness, he concluded, lay in its very poor dramatic version of the story (p. 174).

7.   Lacy, Thomas Hailes. **Oliver Twist.** Adelphi Theatre, London. 25 February 1839.

Noted only by Pierce (VI. 57) and Charles Dickens, Jr., who, commenting on early adaptations of **Oliver Twist**, tentatively gives Lacy as the author of a version of the story "successfully produced at the Adelphi with Yates as Fagin, Mrs. Yates as Nancy, and 0. Smith as Sikes" (II. 18). For comments about the published version of the text and its ascription to Lacy, see entry VI. 57.

8.   Murray, William Henry Wood. **Oliver Twist**. Theatre Royal, Edinburgh. 23 March 1840.

No text of Murray's adaptation appears to have survived, but all major sources agree about the date of this production. The playbill in the Gimbel Collection--see Podeschi (VI. 58)--announcing **Oliver Twist** on 8 November 1849 at the same theatre may also be another production by Murray, the actor-manager of the Adelphi, Edinburgh, and the Theatre Royal from 1830 to 1848.

9.   Mordaunt, John. **Oliver Twist**. Marylebone Theatre, London. 9 June 1856.

Coleman (VI. 42) and Nicoll (VI. 56) both list a revival of this new dramatic version of the novel at the Alexander Theatre, Camden Town, London, on 10 April 1869. Fulkerson (VI. 48) notes that the 1856 adaptation appeared during the one year that William Bodham Donne, Deputy Examiner and later Examiner of Plays, was not in charge of licensing between 1849 and 1874. Donne--see Stottlar (VI. 61)--appears to have continued the policy of denying London theatres permission to perform **Oliver Twist** during a twenty-year period, despite the fact that the Lord Chamberlain had licensed early dramatic versions of the novel. A likely time for the implementation of this ban is some date shortly after Parliament passed the Theatres' Regulation Act on 14 August 1843 (**Hansard's Parliamentary Debates**, vol. 71, p. 690). The intention of this legislation was to enlarge the power of the Lord Chamberlain to censor plays, hitherto confined only to London's patent theatres, and to make him responsible, not local city and borough magistrates, for granting licenses to perform plays of any kind throughout the metropolitan area of London. By doing so, proponents of the Bill argued, one responsible person could work to improve dramatic art and forbid the performance of any drama likely to threaten "the promotion of good manners and decorum, or ... the public peace" (**Hansard**, vol. 70, p. 1350; vol. 71, p. 690).

More than twenty years later, dissatisfaction with the 1843 Theatres' Regulation Act prompted the formation of a Parliamentary Select Committee, appointed in March 1866, to inquire into the operation of licensing regulations and practice in the Metropolis (**Hansard**, vol. 181, pp. 344-45 and p. 1695). Testifying before this Committee on 20 and 23 April 1866, W.B. Donne used **Oliver Twist** and **Jack Sheppard** as examples of plays that had been stopped by Lord De la Warr (Lord Chamberlain, 1841-46) as a result of "representations from the different [London] parishes" in which they were performed. Dramas founded on burglaries and robberies, Donne later explained, "had a bad influence" and his office refused to license them, especially after dramatic versions of **Oliver Twist** provoked "a great many letters from parents and masters requesting that such pieces should not be exhibited, because they had an ill effect on their sons and apprentices." New plays turning on such plots, Donne added, "are not now recommended for license." See **British Parliamentary Papers: Stage and Theatre**, vol. 2 (Shannon: Irish Univ. Press), 107; 112-13.

Information about titles of plays refused a license among the papers Donne supplied to the Select Committee reveals that between 1852 and 1865 the Lord Chamberlain's office approved 2,797 plays and denied licenses to nineteen, of which Jack Sheppard was one. The fact that Oliver Twist does not appear on this list corroborates testimony to the Committee from Spencer Ponsonby, the Comptroller in the Lord Chamberlain's office, that the theatre managers quickly came to learn what was allowable and did not waste money submitting scripts for approval, with a reading fee, when they knew the likely negative response. This practice, which resulted in the de facto censorship of Oliver Twist, presumably accounts to some extent for its absence from the stage in London from about 1841 onwards, until a later generation of adapters challenged the Lord Chamberlain's prevailing interpretation of presumed threats to public peace and decorum. See the following entries. No text of Mordaunt's adaptation appears to have survived.

10. Jefferson, Joseph. **Oliver Twist**. Winter Garden Theatre, New York. 2 February 1860.

See Lazenby (VI. 51) for a detailed summary and analysis of Jefferson's refurbished version of Almar's (VI. 3) adaptation. The changes, Lazenby notes, were so extensive as to make Jefferson's "a new play," although in the text published by Samuel French (New York, 1861), he receives no credit. Jefferson, too, makes no reference to his adaptation in his **Autobiography** (New York, 1897), but, adds Lazenby, T. Allston Brown, Joseph N. Ireland, and George C.D. Odell, all authorities on the history of the American stage, testify to his having done it.

11. Oxenford, John. **Oliver Twist**. New Queen's Theatre, London. 11 April 1868.

Oxenford's new version of the novel appears to have become a focal point for those who sought to challenge the Lord Chamberlain's opposition to dramatic performances of **Oliver Twist**. In an extract from the **Leeds Intelligencer** of March 1868, one of the paper's writers commented on a report from the **Pall Mall Gazette** that the Lord Chamberlain had interdicted the performance of **Oliver Twist** at the New Queen's Theatre. "How public morality can be affected by the production of ... [this] work of unquestionable morality, we cannot conceive." The writer surmised that the "preposterous" veto was based on the fact that thieves and pickpockets were among the characters and noted that this version of the novel had played in Leeds and elsewhere with immense success. (Quoted in **The Dickensian**, 23 [1927], 160.)

Several other newspapers added to the protest, alleging that the Lord Chamberlain had refused to license Oxenford's adaptation and that all plays based on Dickens's celebrated novel "were interdicted in London as being offensive to parish beadles." On 3 April 1868, J. Brady, an Irish M.P., questioned Gathorne Hardy, Secretary of State for the Home Department, about this policy, asking Hardy if he approved of the Lord Chamberlain's "consideration for the feelings of the parish authorities." Hardy replied that "many years ago" Oliver Twist and Jack Sheppard had been prohibited because they were considered capable of doing "a great deal of harm." The Secretary assured Brady that Oxenford's adaptation had been licensed and added that the Lord Chamberlain "had not been petitioned by the parish beadles." Thus the question, he concluded, "was altogether founded in a mistake." (See **Hansard's Parliamentary Debates**, vol. 191, pp. 834-35.)

No text of Oxenford's adaptation appears to exist, but Fulkerson (VI. 48), working from a lengthy review in the **Examiner** (18 April 1868, p. 249), sketches its main outlines. He notes that Oxenford simplified the plot and introduced the improbable denouement of Monks exposing Fagin to the police and compromising his dispute with Oliver in return for an annuity, if he left England. Inevitably the criminals played a major role, but in an apparent attempt to secure Donne's approval, Oxenford gave less emphasis to Nancy's bloody death--she swoons after Sikes shoots her--and avoided showing precisely how her murderer met his end. Writing in **The Athenaeum** for 18 April 1868 (p. 567), the music and drama critic praised the acting of the leading characters and noted that this costly production with abundant accessories played to a full house.

12.   Johnstone, John Beer. **Oliver Twist.** Surrey Theatre, London. 18 May 1868.

Noted by Coleman (VI. 42). An unidentified review on 23 May 1868 in the Harvard Theatre Collection (VI. 49) provides details about the cast and comments favorably on this production as a successful, well-staged adaptation. A second newspaper notice (5 August 1905) refers to a revival of Johnstone's version (also at the Surrey), calling his and Oxenford's adaptation (VI. 11) "the last two important **Oliver Twist** plays" till Oswald Brand's (VI. 17).

13.   Toole, J.L. **The Artful Dodger.** Lyceum Theatre, New York. 15 February 1875.

A successful sketch by a British actor, whom Pierce (VI. 57) lists as first starring in this piece in 1868, presumably in London, although she gives no further details. Lazenby (VI. 51) refers to the Lyceum playbill of the date above, which notes that Toole had played the Dodger 3,000 times. The sketch included Fagin, Fang, Monks, Mr. Brownlow, Oliver, a police officer, and a bookseller. It began with Oliver meeting the Dodger on the road to London and ended in the magistrate's court.

Some confusion, Lazenby points out, exists about an earlier play by the same title, which ran in New York from 1843-48. This, he writes, was "the composition of Ben DeBar, ... and was not at all Dickensian in its dramatis personae." Such adaptations based on a single story line, Lazenby later adds, were quite common, as plays with titles such as **Micawber, Jingle, Dolly Varden, Gabriel Grub,** and **Jo** attest.

14.   Searle, Cyril [Joseph Seale]. **Nancy Sikes.** Olympic Theatre, London. 9 July 1878.

Harrison Grey Fiske in **The New York Mirror Annual** (1888), p. 124, lists Searle as an Englishman who came to New York in 1869 and who married Rose Eytinge in 1881. Lazenby (VI. 51) comments that Searle's new version of **Oliver Twist** was "essentially [Joseph] Jefferson's play [VI. 10] starring Nancy." Playing Sikes, Searle evidently introduced a good deal of bloodshed and horror, the effect of which, according to the reviewer in **The Athenaeum** on 13 July 1878, was to make this version "a brutal and degrading melo-drama." If ever the interference of authority "to prevent the employment of the stage as a means of national debasement could be justified," he continued, "it would be justified with regard to such a work." **Nancy Sikes** closed with graphic details of the murder of Nancy, played by Rose Eytinge, making the finale, **The Athenaeum** critic thought, about as healthy an entertainment as a public execution (p. 60).

Soon after its London opening, Nancy Sikes went to America, playing at two New York theatres in October and November 1878. Lazenby quotes American responses as mixed: one ridiculed the production, another regretted Searle's omission of Fagin's scene in the condemned cell because it detracted from his role and eclipsed him as the hero. Eytinge, a veteran as Nancy, always played the role sympathetically, though she insisted that she disliked the part. She did, however, count her London performance a success when she learned how she had communicated such lessons as Nancy's misery presents. See Eytinge (VI. 44).

15. Collingham, George Gervase. **Oliver Twist.** Olympic Theatre, London. 21 December 1891.

Fulkerson (VI. 48) and Pierce (VI. 57) both describe this adaptation as an American import, for which no printed version or manuscript appears to exist. Walter Rigdon in his **The Biographical Encyclopaedia: Who's Who of the American Theatre** (New York, 1966), notes G.G. Collingham as the pseudonym of Mary Helen White, a playwright who died on 20 June 1923. For details of the cast, see the **Daily Graphic,** 22 December 1891, whose reviewer calls this a new American version of **Oliver Twist** and a "very gloomy play."

16. Ford, Alexander Hume. **Oliver Twist.** Carnegie Lyceum, New York. 10 January 1903.

Noted by Coleman (VI. 42). Two unidentified clippings in the Harvard Theatre Collection (VI. 49) describe this as a version designed especially for children by the Children's Stock Company. Ford followed the text of the novel closely and accentuated the comedy in his four-act drama, wrote one of the reviewers.

17. Brand, Oswald. **Oliver Twist.** Grand Theatre, Islington, London. 30 March 1903.

Noted by Coleman (VI. 42) and Fitz-gerald (VI. 46). Ivan Berlyn, who played Fagin in this production, also performed **Fagin, an Episode** at the Empress Theatre, Brixton, London, on 28 October 1907. In an unidentified review in the Harvard Theatre Collection (VI. 49), the author of the notice remarks that Brand followed Dickens's plot closely but put less emphasis on the criminals by ignoring Fagin's trial and referring only briefly to Sikes's death. This notice provides full details about the cast and other aspects of the production, as does a second, undated review in **The Era.**

18. Carr, Joseph William Comyns. **Oliver Twist.** His Majesty's Theatre, London. 10 July 1905.

A popular and widely acclaimed new stage version of the novel, which, after a trial run on 10 July 1905, subsequently re-opened on 4 September 1905. See B.W. Matz (VI. 53). Carr's adaptation, produced by Herbert Beerbohm Tree, who also played Fagin, was twice revived at the same theatre, opening again on 11 June 1912 (VI. 25) and on 19 April 1915, earning favorable reviews. See, for example, **The Athenaeum,** 15 June 1912, p. 688, and 24 April 1915, p. 390. Coleman (VI. 42) records that Carr's play also appeared at the Fifth Avenue Theatre, New York, on 13 November 1905, with J.E. Dodson as Fagin, and he lists a revival, with Nat. C. Goodwin as Fagin, at the New Amsterdam Theatre, New York, on 26 February 1912 (VI. 24).

In an earlier review commenting on Tree's first production, the drama critic of **The Athenaeum** (15 July 1905, pp. 91-92) writes informatively about the history of London's main stage productions of **Oliver Twist**, reflecting that Dickens's propensity to employ the methods of melodrama in the novel and his setting himself out "to depict scenes of violence" and characters of "unmitigated ferocity" account for the work's "lasting popularity" on the stage. By contrast, the Carr-Tree production departed significantly from this theatrical tradition. Nancy's murder occurred off stage and Sikes's fate was narrated and not shown. As a result, the writer thought, Carr lightened the play and spared the feelings of the audience. Queen Alexandra, recalled Lyn Harding, the actor who played Bill Sikes, found the scene in which Nancy leaves the room, followed by Sikes picking up a club, so impressive that she came back to the theatre three times more, bringing Edward VII with her every time. See **The Dickensian**, 35 (1938-39), 48.

Among other changes introduced by Carr were effective economies designed to unify the action (he dropped the workhouse scenes and showed Fagin not Noah Claypole spying on Nancy as she talks to Mr. Brownlow and Rose), and the use of a young boy, in 1912, to play Oliver. When Tree revived his production three years later, he dropped the scene of Fagin in the condemned cell. But even without this, noted the critic in **The Athenaeum** on 24 April 1915, Fagin "remains one of the actor-manager's most notable impersonations" (p. 390). Cf. XIII. 90 for a dissenting view of Tree's depiction of Fagin. Fulkerson (VI. 47), in a letter to Paroissien, mentions the existence of a typescript of Carr's play (in four Acts and nine scenes) in the NYPL's Theatre Collection.

19. Whyte, Harold, and Rollo Balmain. **Oliver Twist.** King's Theatre, Walthamstow, Essex. 2 October 1905.

Noted by Coleman (VI. 42) and Fitz-gerald (VI. 46). Described in an unidentified review in the Harvard Theatre Collection (VI. 49) as a "new and original version, in four acts." The reviewer praised this adaptation "as one of the most successful attempts ever made" to place Dickens on the stage. He also noticed how the "chief interest" revolved around Nancy, Sikes, and Fagin, in which latter part Balmain distinguished himself as a red-haired, fiendishly malignant villain. A second clipping notes the revival of the Whyte-Balmain adaptation at the Euston Theatre, London (27 October 1906), while a third refers to Balmains's **Oliver Twist, or The Thief Maker,** a Sketch in Three Scenes, at the Queen's Theatre, Poplar, London, on 20 August 1906. This Sketch, a much abbreviated version of the whole play, appears to have been a vehicle for Balmain's virtuoso performance of Fagin as "the odious ... Jew."

20. Pink, Wal. **Oliver Twisted; or, Dickens up a Tree.** Pavilion Theatre, London. 13 November 1905.

Music by J.S. Baker. Noted by Coleman (VI. 42) and Fitz-gerald (VI. 46).

21. Roby, Bernard Soane. **Bill Sykes** [sic]. Palace Pier, Brighton. 4 October 1909.

A dramatic episode in one act noted by Coleman (VI. 42).

22. Dexter, Walter, and F.T. Harry. **Oliver Twist: A New Adapatation of Charles Dickens's Novel in Five Acts.** Broadway Theatre, New Cross, London. 13 December 1909.

Coleman notes that all reviewers highly commended this version of the play, which was later revived and performed at the King's Theatre, Hammersmith, on 4 September 1922. Dexter and Harry manage an effective economy by dropping the workhouse scenes and by opening their adaptation at the Three Cripples, where Monks, in league with Fagin, plots to take Oliver from the Maylies, with whom he is living, and make him into a thief. Dexter and Harry also drop the scene of Noah Claypole spying on Nancy as she talks to Mr. Brownlow. They retain the murder of Nancy, omit Sikes's fall, but conclude with Fagin in the condemned cell. The play ends with a Tableau showing Mrs. Maylie's house, Harry and Rose standing together, Oliver running out into the garden, and then back to Rose. A typescript of the play is in the Dickens House collection. For favorable reviews, see the **Daily Chronicle**, 14 December 1909, and **The Era**, 18 December 1909, (Harvard Theatre Collection).

23. Beckett, Dan. **The Thief Maker; a Protean Sketch.** The Rehearsal Theatre, London. 27 November 1910.

An adaptation of the novel by D. Beckett. Noted by Coleman (VI. 42).

24. **Oliver Twist.** New Amsterdam Theatre, New York. 26 February 1912.

An important, all-star revival of Carr's adaptation (VI. 18) by the Liebler Company of Boston variously described by clippings in the Harvard Theatre Collection. (VI. 49). Writing in **The New York Times** on 11 February 1912, one critic notes in his "Stage History of **Oliver Twist**" that the American adaptations of the novel have produced more than their share "of the great Nancys, Fagins, and Bills," many of whom he names. In a second, unidentified notice, Harriet Quimby comments approvingly on the decision of the producer, Hugh Ford, to make this version "Dickensy" and melodramatic "in the style of two generations back." See also "The Biggest Hits of the Old Days," in the **Boston Post**, 8 April 1934, which provides more comments on Ford's production in 1912.

25. **Oliver Twist.** His Majesty's Theatre, London. 11 June 1912.

A revival of Tree's production of Carr's adaptation (VI. 18). Leonard (VI. 52) lists the cast.

26. **Oliver Twist.** Lyceum Theatre, London. 25 November 1912.

Noted by Leonard (VI. 52). An unmarked clipping in the Harvard Theatre Collection (VI. 49) described this as a four-act drama produced by the Melville brothers (VI. 32). See also **The Dickensian**, 9 (January 1913), 15-16, for a brief review. A second newspaper notice at Harvard refers to a revival of this version at the Lyceum on 9 July 1913.

27.   Rosener, George M. **Under London: A Dramatization of Oliver In One Act.** New York: Wetzel, Rosener, and James, 1912. 14 pp.

Noted by Coleman (VI. 42).

28.   Doughty, G. Henry. **Oliver Twist.** Lyceum Theatre, Sheffield, 12 May 1913.

A new version in four acts. Noted by Coleman (VI. 42).

29.   Jones, James Edmund, comp. "Mr. Bumble's Proposal." In his **Scenes from Dickens: Trials, Sketches, and Plays.** Arranged by the Dickens Fellowship Players of Toronto. London: Cecil Palmer, 1923, pp. 175-85.

A dramatized version of Chapter 23 for two actors only, lasting about twenty-five minutes.

30.   Skeen, W.H. "Scenes from Dickens: **Oliver Twist.**" In French's **Scenes from Dickens.** London: Samuel French, [1926?]. 16 pp.

Adapts two scenes from the novel, showing one of the thieves' kitchen and one of Fagin's final appearance in the condemned cell. Fagin plays the principal part in both. Noted by Coleman (VI. 42).

31.   Suter, Henry Charles. "An Episode from Dickens's **Oliver Twist:** Fagin's Last Night Alive." In his **Dramatic Episodes from Dickens.** London: A.H. Stockwell, 1930, pp. 43-50.

Noted by Coleman (VI. 42).

32.   Melville, Walter, and Frederick Melville. **Oliver Twist.** Lyceum Theatre, London. 11 March 1933.

The revival of an earlier four-act drama by the Melville brothers (VI. 26) in which they deliberately played their version in the old melodramatic tradition and successfully resisted "the modern craze for burlesque." Writing thus in a notice in the **Times** on 12 March 1933, the reviewer made further points about the differences between "old-fashioned melodrama and modern plays." The writer also provides full details about the cast.

33.   Vance, Daisy Melville. **Short Plays from Dickens.** New York: Samuel French, 1935, pp. 41-45 and 89-90.

Includes two brief adaptations of scenes from **Oliver Twist:** "A Lamb among Wolves," and "Vengeance," both of which are set in Fagin's den. Noted by Coleman (VI. 42).

34.   Ravold, John. **Oliver Twist.** New York: Samuel French, 1936. 94 pp.

A three-act version of the novel. Noted by Miller (IV. 17) and Coleman (VI. 42).

35.   Robinson, Marvin G. **Oliver Twist. A Dramatization in Six Episodes.**
      Boston: Walter H. Baker, 1936. 31 pp.

One of a Junior high series, "Arranged expressly for boys and girls of the
junior and senior high school ages." Noted by Miller (IV. 17) and Coleman (VI.
42).

36.   Way, Brian. **Oliver Twist.** In his **Three Plays for the Open Stage.**
      London: Isaac Pitman, 1958, pp. 119-90.

An intelligently adapted version of the story condensed into two acts.
The first covers Oliver's introduction to Fagin and life with the thieves, his
meeting with Mr. Brownlow, who takes him in, and Oliver's subsequent
recapture while returning the latter's books. Way introduces Oliver's
workhouse past in the dialogue between him and the Dodger. Monks appears
at Fagin's malevolently intent upon ruining Oliver, and acting for the same
reasons as he does in the novel. In Act Two Sikes plans but bungles the
Chertsey robbery, fleeing from the scene and leaving Oliver shot. Way
follows the remaining events of the plot closely, staging Nancy's death out of
sight and using Noah Claypole to recount Sikes's fate. Rose Maylie appears as
the mistress of the house in Chertsey, but Way eliminates what he terms "the
romantic aspects" of her life. See also Preen (VI. 59).

37.   Williams, Guy. **Dramascripts: Oliver Twist.** London: Macmillan, 1969.
      86 pp.

A simplified and shortened version of the novel in two acts intended for
use in British secondary schools, theatrical groups, and youth clubs. Williams notes that he designed this adaptation with young actors in mind,
making sure that he arranged the parts so that they were within their
dramatic range.

38.   Bland, Joellen. **Oliver Twist.** Denver: Pioneer Drama Service, 1979.
      57 pp.

A two-act adaptation lasting about thirty-five minutes designed primarily
for young actors and audiences. In this simplified version, which opens with a
scene in the workhouse, Nancy delivers Oliver to Mr. Brownlow after the
thieves capture him while returning Brownlow's books. Thereupon Sikes
murders Nancy, the police shoot Sikes, and Fagin is arrested. Bland's
adaptation has been published on three other occasions in **Plays: The Drama
Magazine for Young People,** 30 (November 1970), 85-96; 34 (March 1975),
84-96; and 39 (March 1980), 67-79.

39.   Emson, Frank E. **Bumble's Courtship.** From Dickens's **Oliver Twist.**
      A Comic Interlude, in One Act. London: n.p., n.d. 11 pp.

Noted by Miller (IV. 17). Pierce (VI. 57) notes that the text is available in
French's Acting Drama no. 481.

40.   **Scenes from Dickens for Drawing-Room and Platform Acting.**
      Adapted by Guy Pertwee and edited by Ernest Pertwee. London:
      George Routledge, n.d., pp. 177-206.

Includes "Mrs. Corney's Tea Party for Two" and "Oliver Twist in Fagin's Den," a dramatization of Chapter 15 in which Oliver is returned to the thieves by Sikes and Nancy.

41.   Wallace, John, Jr. **Fallen Among Thieves.** In two scenes. Adapted from **Oliver Twist.** London: William Walker, n.d. 16 pp.

Number nine of the "Charles Dickens" series of character sketches. Noted by Miller (IV. 17).

COMMENTARY ON STAGE ADAPTATIONS

42.   Coleman, Edward D. "Dickens, Charles. **Oliver Twist.**" In his "The Jew in English Drama, Part VII." BNYPL, 44 (May 1940), 432- 34.

Includes a section on dramatic adaptations of **Oliver Twist** in his annotated list of printed plays of Jewish interest. Coleman's focus on Jews in English drama leads him to comment particularly on actors who played Fagin, although his authoritative and important bibliography provides a rich source of information about reviews of various adaptations of **Oliver Twist**, short quotations from reviewers reacting to how Fagin was portrayed, and information about opening nights and theatres where the plays were produced. Some disparity in factual details occurs among Fitz-gerald (VI. 46), Nicoll (VI. 56), and Coleman; the last frequently gives cross-references to these other two authorities. Coleman annotates adaptations of **Oliver Twist** by Almar (VI. 3), Barnett (VI. 2), Coyne (VI. 6), Greenwood (VI. 4), Johnstone (VI. 12), Mordaunt (VI. 9), Murray (VI. 8), Oxenford (VI. 11), and Stirling (VI. 5), all of whom wrote stage versions of the novel during Dickens's lifetime. He also provides separate entries on fourteen adapters of the novel active after 1870, as well as notes on many lesser-known and anonymous dramatic versions of **Oliver Twist** staged in London and New York between 1838 and 1912. The list includes dramatic versions of the novel which have been published but not necessarily performed by professional actors. Coleman bases his bibliography on materials in the New York Public Library, the Library of Congress, Harvard, and his own collection.

43.   Collier, Constance. **Harlequinade, The Story of My Life.** London: John Lane, 1929, pp. 157-61.

Collier provides anecdotes about Carr's production of **Oliver Twist** (VI. 18) and speaks of her work rehearsing and practicing for Nancy's death off stage. When this scene took place, Fagin, played by Tree, watched the murder

as he stared through a door, registering in his face his satisfied response to
Nancy's violent death.

44.   Eytinge, Rose. In her **The Memories of Rose Eytinge, Being Recollec-
      tions and Observations of Men, Women, and Events During Half a
      Century.** New York: Frederick A. Stokes, 1905, pp. 298-300.

Records the reaction of one member of the audience who saw this
American actress play Nancy in Searle's **Nancy Sikes** at the Olympic Theatre,
London, in July 1878 (VI. 14). As she returned to New York by ship, Eytinge
describes how she was approached on deck by a venerable Baptist, one brought
up never to read fiction, who had chanced to see her act in London. The play
and Nancy's fate, she writes, captivated the old man, who told the actress
that when the curtain fell at the end of the performance "he awakened to the
truth that he had received one of the deepest, most far-reaching lessons in
Christian charity of his life, and he felt profound gratitude to Charles Dickens
for having given the world the story, and to me for having revealed it to him."

45.   Fawcett, F. Dubrez. **Dickens the Dramatist: On Stage, Screen, and
      Radio.** London: W.H. Allen, 1952, passim.

The work of an enthusiastic amateur whose study provides a good deal of
information, some of which is inaccurate and frustrating to use. Fawcett
does not document his sources and he frequently omits pertinent facts.
Writing briefly about the first spate of **Oliver Twist** stage adaptations, he
attributes a Beckett's (VI. 1) to Coyne (VI. 6) and falsely describes the first
part of Barnett's version. See Fulkerson's comment in VI. 48. Later parts of
the book survey twentieth century stage adaptations of the novel (Carr's [VI.
18] and two by Russell Thorndyke), silent and sound films based on **Oliver
Twist,** and occasional BBC radio adaptations, one of which he devotes several
pages to, having witnessed a studio rehearsal. Fawcett gives no date for this
twelve-part serial, adapted by Giles Cooper and produced by Charles
Lefeaux.

46.   Fitz-gerald, S.J. Adair. "Oliver Twist." In his **Dickens and the Drama:
      Being an Account of Charles Dickens's Connection with the Stage and
      the Stage's Connection with Him.** London, 1910; rpt. New York:
      Benjamin Blom, 1969, pp. 97-116.

Supplements Fulkerson (VI. 48) by providing information about the cast of
various productions and by covering adaptations through 1909. Of interest is
an excerpt from a self-serving theatre bill advertising a production of Almar's
adaptation at the Surrey in November 1838. "The stage is never devoted to
more noble or better purpose," the bill proclaims, "than when it lends its
powerful aid to improve the morals and correct the vices of the age."
Following that pronouncement appears an extract from the **Times** of 13
November 1838 in which the paper laments the powerlessness of the police to
prevent crimes and to remove those who train thieves and pickpockets.
Fortunately, the management states, Dickens's novel raises "a beacon on the
basis of truth to warn the erring" and inculcates "the great moral lesson" that
vice will ultimately meet with punishment. Perhaps by such tactics the
Surrey hoped to counter the rising criticism of those who, soon afterwards,
convinced the Lord Chamberlain to ban further stage performances of **Oliver
Twist.** See VI. 60 and 61.

47. Fulkerson, Richard P. "The Dickens Novel on the Victorian Stage."
Diss. Ohio State 1970.

Two particular questions animate Fulkerson's study: what do the dramatic adaptations of Dickens's work tell us about the Victorian theatre and what do the plays reveal about the nature of his novels? Fulkerson confines his attention to the period from 1837 to 1870, examining over fifty plays and treating all Dickens's novels. The second chapter, devoted exclusively to **Oliver Twist**, discusses in detail the main features of the adaptations by a Beckett (VI. 1), Barnett (VI. 2), and Almar (VI. 3), whose play Fulkerson finds the best of the six early stage versions of the novel. Fulkerson argues that a Beckett and Barnett fail as adapters because they tend to simplify Dickens's characters, rely on implausible situations and improbable plots, and avoid any social criticism. Almar, who had the complete novel to work with, succeeded in several ways, presenting Oliver as a pathetic victim, using Nancy and Fagin effectively, and recreating, without exploiting, the sensational death of Nancy. (Almar's text specifically directs that she be killed off stage without her body being shown.) Contemporary sources quoted by Fulkerson called a Beckett's play an "execrable hotch-potch," but praised Almar's "great skill" in his adaptation and the care with which the piece was produced.

In his conclusion, Fulkerson notes that the adaptations played mainly in London's minor theatres, whose lower class patrons suggest an audience different from the public who bought and read his novels. Such generalizations, he cautions, are slippery; instead, he emphasizes that Dickens's works on stage were markedly different from those in print. The abundance of villains, murderers, and victims, especially children and women, in Dickens rendered him vulnerable to the "intellectual pickpocket[s]" who stole so freely from his works and adapted them to the prevailing Victorian taste for melodrama. What these thieves finally offered to the public, Fulkerson stresses, was a pale copy of the original, one lacking in subtlety, complexity, and seriousness.

48. _____. "**Oliver Twist** in the Victorian Theatre." **The Dickensian**, 70
(May 1974), 83-95.

Within one year of the serial commencement of **Oliver Twist** in Bentley's **Miscellany** in February 1837, dramatic adaptations of the novel began to appear before Dickens had completed the work. Gilbert A. a Beckett wrote the first version, which opened on 27 March 1838 at St. James's Theatre (VI. 1) and ran for only one night. Fulkerson summarizes the adaptation, provides information about the script, and supplies similar information about the following plays: Barnett's (VI. 2), which opened on 21 May 1838 (Pavilion Theatre); Almar's (VI. 3), the first to make use of the whole novel, which opened on 19 November 1838 (Surrey Theatre) and became quite popular; Stirling's, 3 December 1838, at the City of London Theatre (VI. 5); and Greenwood's at Sadler's Wells on the same date (VI. 4). No texts for these two appear to have survived. The last of these early adaptations is Coyne's on 25 February 1839 at the Adelphi (VI. 6).

After this initial interest, adapters appear to have ignored **Oliver Twist**, although Fulkerson believes that censorship by the Lord Chamberlain's office from about 1841 prevented performances, apparently in response to public opinion about the play. See further entries VI. 9, VI. 11, and VI. 60-61.

This ban was temporarily lifted in 1856, when Mordaunt produced an unsuccessful version of the novel at the Marylebone Theatre (VI. 9); further adaptations were revived in 1868. Oxenford's version appeared at the Queen's Theatre on 11 April (VI. 11), and Johnstone's opened at the Surrey on 18 May (VI. 12).

Fulkerson concludes his survey of the Victorian stage history of **Oliver Twist** with a reference to Searle's **Nancy Sikes** (VI. 14) on 9 July 1878 and to Collingham's adaptation (VI. 15) on 21 December 1891. He also comments on what these dramatizations share: each cuts the plot to the bone, simplifies Dickens's novel by dropping almost all his social criticism, and seizes from the text its key scenes and most vivid characters.

49.   Harvard Theatre Collection. Pusey Library, Cambridge, Mass. **Oliver Twist:** Playbills, Reviews of Dramatic Adaptations, Miscellaneous Newspaper Clippings, etc.

An extensive but uncatalogued collection of American and British playbills and newspaper clippings of reviews of Victorian and modern versions of Dickens's novels compiled by an industrious but unscholarly enthusiast. Cuttings from a variety of sources include reviews of the numerous adaptations which flourished on both sides of the Atlantic and useful articles on their stage history, making this collection an important resource for the stage historian interested in the adaptations of Dickens's novels. Materials are loosely grouped according to individual novels, but the contents of the folders lack specific and systematic arrangement within those categories. As a result, users must inspect the files in person. A further complication arises with the journal and newspaper clippings, many of which lack details about their source and date. Yet despite these inconveniences, the full potential of this collection has yet to be realized by scholars studying the stage history of **Oliver Twist** or any one of the other novels.

50.   Hollingshead, John. "Dickens's Readings." In his **My Lifetime.** 2 vols. London: Sampson Low, Marston & Co., 1895, I, 187-90.

Includes an account of an adaptation of **Oliver Twist** Hollingshead witnessed at the Victoria Theatre, Lambeth, which helps us understand why officials at the Lord Chamberlain's office banned performances of the play for several years (VI. 60). In the gallery of the Victoria--a huge amphitheatre holding about fifteen hundred spectators--men and women divided their time between watching the play and hauling up large stone bottles of beer from the pit. The audience, comments Hollingshead, was "a huge, rough, dangerous instrument" waiting to be roused into violent action. Unfailingly, the murder of Nancy provided "the great scene" as they saw Sikes drag her, smeared with red-ochre, twice round the stage by her hair. "[N]o explosion of dynamite ... no language ever dreamt of in Bedlam" could equal the outburst of a thousand enraged voices greeting "the smiling ruffian" as he came forward and bowed. In plain English, writes Hollingshead, the audience "expressed a fierce determination to tear [Sikes's] sanguinary entrails from his sanguinary body." The "Old Vic," as local inhabitants referred to this theatre, specialized in melodramas of the blood and thunder variety.

51.   Lazenby, Walter. **Stage Versions of Dickens's Novels in America to 1900.** Diss. Indiana University 1962.

The only full-length scholarly study of American dramatic adaptations of Dickens's novels and their staging and production between the summer of 1837 and 1900. In the chapter Lazenby devotes to **Oliver Twist,** for which "the American playgoer seems to have had a special liking," he comments briefly on Barnett's version (VI. 2) and analyzes Almar's (VI. 3) in great detail, distinguishing two distinct phases in the appeal of **Oliver Twist** to American theatrical audiences in the nineteenth century.

After opening in London in November 1838, Almar's adaptation of the novel quickly crossed the Atlantic, leading to the production of at least six versions throughout the United States in 1839. The first American dramatization of the novel opened on New Year's Day in Philadelphia at the Walnut Street Theatre and was followed by productions in New York (the Franklin Theatre on 7 January) and Boston (the National Theatre on 18 January). Within months, different productions also appeared in New Orleans, Chicago, and St. Louis. Almar, writes Lazenby, mixed "smiles and tears," retained much of Dickens's social criticism, and produced a slavish stage copy of the novel. During this first phase, which Lazenby dates from 1839 to the early 1850's, stage managers throughout America reworked Almar's text to suit the capabilities and strengths of different companies. Occasionally, some of the early scenes were cut and the action telescoped to shorten the play; but generally, states Lazenby, productions included melodrama, comedy, and social satire, making the play anything but a simple "progress" of Oliver's story.

The second phase of **Oliver Twist's** appeal, argues Lazenby, began in December 1851, when Fanny Wallack emerged as a "notable Nancy" at Burton's Tripler Hall, New York, and prepared the way for other actresses to star in this role. Several others repeated her success until in 1860 Matilda Heron played Nancy in "the most significant performance of the play since its premiere in 1839." Joseph Jefferson (VI. 10), apparently believing that Almar's old script needed some revising, produced "an entirely new version" of **Oliver Twist** at the Winter Garden Theatre, New York, in which Bumble's role was greatly reduced, much of the social satire removed, and the play's emphasis shifted from Oliver to Fagin, Sikes, and Nancy. This revision, notes Lazenby, henceforth "became the standard one played all over America to the end of the century."

Thereafter a succession of American actresses made names for themselves as Nancy, introducing into the role greater realism and greater emphasis on the story's horror and bloodshed. Among them, Lucille Western is said to have originated the practice of making Nancy's murder "a naturalistic one, with simulated blood flowing from her mouth," causing ladies to faint during the performance of this scene and driving "strong men from the theatre." Rose Eytinge (VI. 44), another well known Nancy, was featured in a revival of **Oliver Twist** at Wallack's Theatre, New York, which coincided with the interest in Dickens aroused by his reading tour of 1867-68 and ran so successfully as to bring in seven thousand dollars a week in late December and early January.

Well-known and obscure productions of **Oliver Twist** frequently recurred on the American stage for nearly another decade, until time relegated the play to "the lesser houses as a stock melodramatic piece" and first-rate actresses avoided the role of Nancy. Yet despite **Oliver Twist's** loss of prestige by the 1880's, its popularity and statistics remain impressive. In New York alone it played in thirty-one of the thirty-three seasons between 1851 and 1884; in the sixty-two years from its premiere in 1839 to 1900 it appeared in forty-one years, and it was adapted and presented more often than any other Dickens play. Unlike several of the other famous Dickens plays in America, Lazenby adds, **Oliver Twist** survived the deaths of the actors who first created its main roles, and its disappearance, he speculates, may have been due "to its reliance on the stage effects of the old melodrama which were to be entirely outmoded by the film's technique, rather than to diminution of its basic appeal, since it has been popular in movies since 1900." After 1900, only seven Dickens plays have had Broadway productions, and only two of them, **Oliver Twist** at the New Amsterdam Theatre (VI. 24) in 1912 (eighty performances) and **Pickwick** at the Empire Theatre in 1927 (seventy-two performances) "can be called successful," writes Lazenby.

52.   Leonard, William Torbet. **Theatre: Stage to Screen.** 2 vols. Metuchen, N.J.: The Scarecrow Press, 1981, II, 1137-50.

Provides selective information about various early American productions of **Oliver Twist** and lists six productions in New York between 29 April 1895 and 11 April 1898 not recorded by Coleman (VI. 42), Fitz-gerald (VI. 46), and Pierce (VI. 57). Leonard adds details to the novel's stage history in London too, giving infrequently recorded facts about the cast, number of performances, and dates of adaptations at the Olympic Theatre on 12 December 1891 and the Novelty Theatre on 31 August 1896. In addition, he notes two versions of the novel produced by Walter and Frederick Melville in 1912 and 1933 (VI. 32).

This book also supplies details about various road companies, travelling professionals who played versions of the novel in 1894-95, 1897, and 1912-13 in different cities throughout the United States. Useful information about early film versions of **Oliver Twist**, often with quotations from reviews, appears, together with well-documented notes about **Oliver!** and references to American television adaptations of the novel.

53.   Matz, B.W. "**Oliver Twist** Dramatised." **The Dickensian,** 1 (August 1905), 211-12.

Comments favorably on Herbert Beerbohm Tree's production of Carr's dramatized version of **Oliver Twist** (VI. 18) at His Majesty's Theatre, London. Matz adds in a later note that this adaptation played for one night only at the close of the season in July and reopened on 4 September 1905 at the same theatre for the new season. Tree (Fagin), Lyn Harding (Sikes), and Constance Collier (Nancy), writes Matz, were "as remarkable a trio of power in impersonation as has appeared in any one play of its kind for years."

54.   Morley, Malcolm. "Early Dickens Drama in America." **The Dickensian,** 44 (Summer 1948), 153-57.

Notes two anonymously adapted stage versions of **Oliver Twist** in New York. The first to reach America played on 7 January 1839 at the Franklin Theatre; a month later, a second opened at the Superior Park Theatre on 7 February. Coleman (VI. 42) confirms these two dates; Coleman also notes two other New York productions of **Oliver Twist**: 29 July 1844 at the Bowery Theater and 27 December 1851 at Burton's Theater. Cf. also Lazenby (VI. 51), whose study provides the fullest record available of American stage versions of Dickens's novels and notes early adaptations of **Oliver Twist** unrecorded by Morley.

55.   _____. "Early Dramas of **Oliver Twist**." **The Dickensian,** 43 (Spring 1947), 74-79.

Surveys early productions of **Oliver Twist**, beginning with the first adaptation of the St. James's Theatre on 27 March 1838 (VI. 1), about which little is known. Morley notes that a degree of secrecy surrounded the production (no advertisements were published in the daily papers), that apparently it had only two performances, and that reviewers responded negatively. No stage version has survived, but the names of the cast are known. So, too, is the name of the adapter, who, Morley agrees with others, was Gilbert Abbot a Beckett. Morley also comments on the other main adaptations which soon followed, noting that after the first batch of early stage versions **Oliver Twist** disappeared from the stage for about sixteen years until numerous versions reinvaded the theatre in the 1860's. Cf. Fulkerson (VI. 48).

56.   Nicoll, Allardyce. **A History of English Drama 1660-1900: Volume IV. Early Nineteenth Century Drama 1800-1850.** 2nd ed. Cambridge: Cambridge Univ. Press, 1963, passim; **Volume V. Late Nineteenth Century Drama 1850-1900.** Cambridge: Cambridge Univ. Press, 1962, passim.

A chronological survey of the century's theatrical activities and a hand-list of plays. Nicoll devotes a volume to each half of the century; and because dramatic adaptations of **Oliver Twist** run from 1838 to 1891, the interested reader needs to consult each. Within the division by volume, each hand-list follows the same arrangement, noting the nature of the play itself, the production date (and day of the week, where records permit verification), the theatre where it was produced, reference to the Lord Chamberlain's collection of manuscripts, where relevant, and existing published versions of the play. Nicoll comments, with justification, on the difficulty of accurate bibliographical research in Victorian drama because so little scholarly work has been done on this period when theatres multiplied decade by decade and because reliable guides to minor drama, including adaptations of novels, do not exist. Nicoll differs principally from other sources in crediting Stirling and not Coyne with the Adelphi production of **Oliver Twist** on 25 February 1839 (VI. 6) and in recording no version of the novel by Stirling at the City of London Theatre on 3 December 1838 (VI. 5). Nicoll also lists an adaptation of the novel by Thomas Henry Hazelwood submitted to the Lord Chamberlain in 1855 but probably not performed.

57.   Pierce, Dorothy. "Special Bibliography: The Stage Versions of Dickens's Novels." **Bulletin of Bibliography,** 16, No. 1 (September-December 1936), 10, and No. 2 (January-April 1937), 30.

Bases her lists on the plays noted by Fitz-gerald (VI. 46), but also supplements both him and Coleman (VI. 42) by adding information they do not record about an occasional American production. Pierce, whose work appears less accurate, and certainly less detailed than Coleman's, credits Stirling (VI. 5) with an adaptation of **Oliver Twist** at the City of London in March 1838, lists the later production at that theatre on 3 December 1838 (VI. 5) as anonymous, and provides a different version of productions of the novel at the Adelphi. She records a revised version of Almar's adaptation (VI. 3) on 15 February 1839, with **Nicholas Nickleby,** in which Mrs. Keeley played Oliver at the Adelphi, an anonymous adaptation at the same theatre in March, and she credits Thomas H. Lacy not Coyne (VI. 6) with the adaptation Yates produced there on 25 February 1839. Tentative confirmation of a version of **Oliver Twist** by Lacy at the Adelphi with Yates as Fagin and his wife as Nancy appears in the Introduction Charles Dickens, Jr., contributed to the Macmillan edition of the novel in 1892. See II. 18. For further comments about Lacy's adaptation, see VI. 2 and 7.

58. Podeschi, John B. "H. Dickensiana: Playbills." In his **Dickens and Dickensiana** (IV. 19), pp. 425-35.

A useful collection of British and American playbills of Dickens's work which includes several contributions to the stage history of **Oliver Twist** in both countries. A dramatization of the novel appeared at the Theatre Royal, Hereford, on 2 October 1855, some months before Fulkerson notes the temporary lifting of the ban in London on dramatic versions of **Oliver Twist** in 1855 (VI. 48); an adaptation of "the celebrated melo-drama, in two acts," was also performed at the Theatre Royal, Edinburgh, on 8 November 1849. American stage versions of the novel opened in Boston at the National Theatre on 18 January 1839 and on 6 March 1839, the first within less than two weeks of the earliest recorded adaptation in New York. See Morley (VI. 54) and Lazenby (VI. 51). The playbills, intriguing reading in themselves, testify both to the popularity of the novel among numerous anonymous adapters and to the manner in which the dramas appear to have been presented. The bills frequently provide an elaborate "Synopsis of Scenery and Events," which lists the major incidents of the play, summarizes each act, and promises various spectaculars to the audience. The 1863 version at the Walnut Street Theatre, Philadelphia, for example, elaborates on Dickens's novel by introducing a fire at Toby Crackit's hideaway which drives Sikes onto the roof, where he slips and falls to his death, so Nancy is "avenged without the aid of an executioner." With an equal emphasis on poetic justice, but unaided by pyrotechnics, the 1852 playbill of the National Theatre, Boston, summarized the drama's ending as follows: "Desparation [sic] of the Murderer and Horrid Death of Sykes [sic]: 20 guineas reward; the lost one restored; Virtue Rewarded. Tableau." The playbills also document the frequency with which actresses played the role of Oliver; none names an adapter or specifies a particular dramatic version of the text.

59. Preen, D.W. "Plays in Production: X, **Oliver Twist**." **The Use of English**, 17 (Spring 1966), 213-16.

Practical advice about producing Brian Way's version of **Oliver Twist** (VI. 36) based on Preen's experience putting on the play with a group of secondary students in England.

60. Stephens, J.R. "**Jack Sheppard** and the Licensers: The Case Against Newgate Plays." **Nineteenth Century Theatre Research**, 1 (Spring 1973), 1-13.

A detailed examination of the growth of opposition to the stage versions of **Jack Sheppard** which illuminates allied objections to the adaptations of **Oliver Twist** and shows how alarmed "magistrates, gaol-chaplains and 'respectable householders,'" forced the Lord Chamberlain to take a stand against both plays. Stephens cites several factors that fueled the "Sheppard craze" and convinced many of London's citizens that dramas with criminal heroes were "nothing short of a social menace." He notes that existing records do not indicate clearly whether **Jack Sheppard** was officially prohibited on stage or whether it was withdrawn by theatre managers on the basis of an "understanding" between them and the licensing authorities. At any rate, **Jack Sheppard**, together with **Oliver Twist**, both appear to have been under "some kind of interdiction, probably unofficial," from 1840 onwards.

The first formal record does not occur until 1848, when the Lord
Chamberlain stopped performances of **Jack Sheppard** scheduled at the Surrey
and Haymarket theatres. Thereafter this interdiction continued until W.B.
Donne's appointment as Examiner of Plays in 1857. See VI. 48 and 61.
Shortly after taking office, Donne argued for a wholesale prohibition of the
allegedly corrupting Newgate dramas following "a partial revival of Jack
Sheppard, Oliver Twist & Turpin's Ride-to-York" in the spring of 1859. "All
of these pieces," Donne wrote to his superior, "have long ago been licensed:
subsequently to their licence two of them, Jack Sheppard and Oliver Twist,
have been interdicted: the ban was taken off the Adelphi version of Jack
Sheppard; never, I believe, off Oliver Twist." (Public Record Office, London,
quoted by Stephens.)
   In response, the Lord Chamberlain wrote that he doubted the expediency
of banning "all the 'Highway Pieces,'" but agreed to interdict **Jack Sheppard**.
Donne, however, continued to oppose the performance of **Oliver Twist**,
arguing that its instructional examples of thieving, picking-pockets, and
housebreaking were equally as dangerous as those in **Jack Sheppard**. Dramatic
versions of Dickens's novel, he wrote, are "highly objectionable" in their
moral, more especially as **Oliver Twist** is performed "at Theatres where the
Gallery is the main resort, and the greater portion of its frequenters consists
of apprentices and young persons of either sex." This unofficial ban continued
until 1868, when the Lord Chamberlain overruled Donne's advice, removing
the ban on **Oliver Twist** after the stage-manager of the Queen's Theatre
submitted John Oxenford's adaptation (VI. 11) for approval.

61.   Stottlar, James F. "A Victorian Stage Censor: The Theory and Practice
      of William Bodham Donne." **VS**, 13 (March 1970), 253-82.

   An informative analysis of the rationale for Victorian stage censorship
which helps us understand the apparent contradiction between the ban on
dramatic versions of the novel extending from the 1840's to the 1860's and
Oliver Twist's continued success in print during the same period. Plays were
subject to censorship when books were not because Victorian censors
commonly ascribed greater influence to the stage, especially when
playwrights treated "immoral" subjects and exalted highwaymen and robbers.
Citing the Minutes of Evidence before the Select Committee on Theatrical
Licenses and Regulations, Stottlar notes how Donne in his testimony voiced a
common assumption when he argued that the representation of a story on
stage appeals "much more strongly" to the senses of an audience than merely
reading one in the pages of a book.
   The ban on **Oliver Twist** and other dramas depicting criminal activities
continued for well over twenty years and resulted in Donne's opposition to
these subjects on stage even in the 1860's, when, presumably, threats to the
public peace were less likely than they were in the 1840's. As Stottlar's
analysis of the **Daybooks Indexing the Lord Chamberlain's Plays 1824-1903**
shows, fear of appearing to encourage crime proved a strong motive for not
allowing its representation on stage. These manuscript volumes--seven in
all--record the details of Donne's actions and list words and scenes he found
offensive, including his instructions to the author of **The Young Girl from the
Country; or, A Peep at the Vices and Virtues of Rustic and City Life**. Omit
three scenes, Donne commanded J.B. Howe in 1862: the one in which the
picking of pockets occurs, the preparations for the burglary, and "the whole
chloroform business" (Quoted by Stottlar, p. 274). Such scruples about the
depiction of crime as Donne reveals here clearly account for the basis of his
longstanding opposition to the performance of adaptations of **Oliver Twist**.

62. Waugh, Arthur. "Oliver Twist at New Cross." The Dickensian, 6
     (January 1910), 10-14.

     Reviews the Dexter-Harry production (VI. 22), praising the cast and the
adaptation. Waugh provides photographs of the main characters in costume.

VII. FILM, MUSICAL, RADIO, AND TELEVISION ADAPTATIONS

FILM ADAPTATIONS

1. "A Dickens Galaxy." **The New York Times Magazine,** 23 November 1947, pp. 24-25.

    Two pages of stills from Lean's **Oliver Twist** (VII. 18) presented as "scenes from the forthcoming picture," whose appearance, in America, was delayed until 1951. See VII. 3.

2. Billington, Michael. "Dickens on the Screen." **Illustrated London News,** 28 November 1970, pp. 19-21.

    General observations about modern film versions of Dickens's novels noting the failure of directors to get away from a straightforward, chronological approach to adapting his works to the screen, with the exception of Delbert Mann's **David Copperfield** (1970). Billington admires the "verve, exuberance, and panache" of Reed's **Oliver!** (VII. 19) but regrets the way he toned down the menace and murderous passion of the novel, ignoring Dickens's dark side and "surrealistic strangeness," as have numerous other film directors.

3. Bodeen, DeWitt. "Oliver Twist." In **Magill's Survey of Cinema: English Language Films.** 1st ser. Ed. Frank N. Magill. Englewood Cliffs, N.J.: Salem Press, 1980, III, 1256-58.

    Provides factual details about the cast, plot, and American release of Lean's film (VII. 18), which was delayed in the United States until July 1951 because the Anti-Defamation League and various Jewish organizations successfully argued that Alec Guiness's conception of Fagin was anti-Semitic and that the film would "fan the flames of interracial bigotry." After a three-year battle, the Motion Picture Association of America reversed its decision in response to arguments from the National Board of Review, the American Council for Judaism, and other groups, who countered that a greater danger lay in "open or covert actions of intimidation, boycott, or arbitrary censorship" than in threats to Jews the film might pose. After the excision of eleven minutes of footage (mainly close-ups of Guiness in some of his more revolting expressions), **Oliver Twist** received the Production Code Administration seal for exhibition in American theatres. Bodeen speculates that Lean's version came too soon after the Holocaust and the infamous anti-Semitic propaganda spread by Hitler and his associates, the memory of which, he thinks, promoted widespread opposition to the film in America. Cf. VII. 10 and 29.

4. Butler, Ivan. "Dickens on the Screen (With a Glance at Other Victorian Novelists)." In **Film Review, 1972-73.** Ed. F. Maurice Speed. London: W.H. Allen, 1972, pp. 18-25.

    Surveys adaptations of Victorian novels from the earliest silent films to

1971. Butler includes brief details about the main versions of **Oliver Twist** and remarks on the novel's popularity, together with **A Christmas Carol**, among British and American filmmakers.

5.   Castelli, Louis P., and Caryn Lynn Cleeland. **David Lean: A Guide to References and Resources.** Boston: G.K. Hall, 1980. xiii + 134 pp.

The authors set out to promote the critical study of Lean's films by assembling a comprehensive account of all the materials necessary to that objective. They provide synopses, credits, and notes for each of Lean's fifteen films, including **Oliver Twist** (pp. 76-77), as well as a list of reviews, an annotated guide to writings about Lean, and useful information about Lean material in various archival sources. Castelli and Cleeland list seven reviews of **Oliver Twist** when it was first released (22 June 1948 at the Odeon, Leicester Square, London) and seventeen reviews of the American version after it was released in July 1951 (pp. 98-99), which was cut in deference to those opposing the film's alleged anti-Semitism. See VII. 3. Production files containing clippings from **Oliver Twist** are held by the Margaret Herrick Library, Beverly Hills, California; the Theater Arts Library at UCLA has the unpublished screenplay of **Oliver Twist,** and the Information and Documentation Department of the National Film Archive, Dean Street, London, holds the draft script of **Oliver Twist** (Castelli and Cleeland, pp. 121-24).

6.   Cohen, Joan L. "Oliver Twist." In **Magill's Survey of Cinema: Silent Films.** Ed. Frank N. Magill. Englewood Cliffs, N.J.: Salem Press, 1982, II, 825-27.

Provides factual information about the 1922 film of **Oliver Twist,** a popular successor in eight reels to the 1916 (VII. 17) adaptation of the novel, featuring child star Jackie Coogan in the title role. Frank Lloyd directed this version, which was released by Associated First National and produced by Sol Lesser for Jackie Coogan Productions. Lesser followed the novel's plot closely but put the emphasis of his selection of scenes on those best suited to Coogan, who played Oliver in the tough but vulnerable role he had established for himself in **The Kid** (1921) and **Peck's Bad Boy** (1921). Coogan received acclaim for his performance, as did Lon Chaney (Fagin) and several other supporting actors.

7.   Crabbe, Katharyn. "Lean's **Oliver Twist:** Novel into Film." **Film Criticism,** 2 (Fall 1977), 46-51.

Argues for a "three part taxonomy" to discuss the means by which Lean transforms Dickens's novel into a successful film: simplification, expansion, and substitution. All three modes, Crabbe continues, allow Lean to "capitalize on or compensate for the capabilities and limitations of film as a medium." The same means, she also notes, enable Lean to move Dickens's story closer to romance and soften the realistic and ironic aspects of the novel. By dropping the Rose Maylie sub-plot (simplification), for example, Lean shifts more attention to his protagonist and thereby increases Oliver's stature. Secondly, the film's opening storm sequence (expansion) associates the birth of the hero with cosmic events and adds further elements of romance in the brief shots of Oliver playing on a swing in Mr. Brownlow's sunlit garden. Thirdly, by transforming Mr. Brownlow from a friend to a grandfather (substitution), Lean provides Oliver with a family, making him an archetypal lost heir, the hero who proves himself after a series of trials and then claims his rightful place. Such changes, Crabbe concludes, demonstrate Lean's preference "for romance structures" and characterize his adaptations of other literary works.

8.   Crowther, Bosley. **"Oliver Twist."** New York Times, 1 August 1951, p. 17, col. 2.

Reviews the opening of Lean's film at the Park Theatre, New York, after its eventual release in the United States (VII. 3), pronouncing it "a superb piece of motion picture art and ... one of the finest screen translations of a literary classic ever made." Crowther regrets the film's delay occasioned by the controversy surrounding Guiness's portrayal of Fagin, but judges the trimming judicious and undetrimental to the work as a whole. Fagin, he writes, has not been "appreciably Bowdlerized," having only the duration of his appearance on screen reduced, not his impact on the story. "And that is both just to the purpose of the producers and considerate of those who might take reasonable exception to an excessive portrayal of a stereotyped Jew," he concludes.

9.   Eisenstein, Sergei. "Dickens, Griffith, and the Film Today" [1944]. In his **Film Form: Essays in Film Theory.** Ed. and trans. Jay Leyda. New York: Harcourt, Brace, and World, 1949, pp. 195-255.

A seminal discussion of the interrelationship between film and literature in which Eisenstein acknowledges his debt to D.W. Griffith and, in turn, traces connections between Griffith and Dickens. This link, he argues, demonstrates the fact that "our cinema is not altogether without parents and without pedigree, without a past, without the traditions and rich cultural heritage of the past epochs." Eisenstein illustrates the affinity he sees between Dickens and Griffith by commenting on the optical qualities of Dickens's fiction and by pointing out how Griffith frequently affirmed his debt to the novelist. But most persuasive, Eisenstein thinks, is Dickens's use of two kinds of montage: montage exposition to convey the atmosphere of a particular scene or the inner psychological traits of a character and a montage progression of parallel scenes, in which separate episodes of the plot intercut with each other. Turning to **Oliver Twist** to illustrate his argument, Eisenstein cites examples of both kinds of montage, pointing first to Chapter 21, with its opening panorama of Smithfield market, whose atmosphere, he thinks, Dickens conveys as if he were compiling a cinematic "shot list." Dickens's arrangement of the scene into its component parts and the way in which he interweaves visual and auditory details, Eisenstein continues, convey the dynamic tempo of the market place and give "the fullest cinematic sensation" of that particular early morning. **Oliver Twist** also provides examples of montage plot structure, that disjunctive method of narration shared by film and novels. Eisenstein illustrates this point by commenting on Chapter 14, where Dickens interweaves several story lines (Oliver returning Mr. Brownlow's books, the thieves at the Cripples, Oliver's recapture by Nancy and Sikes, and Brownlow and Grimwig awaiting the boy's return) and heightens the dramatic tension by cutting rapidly from one to the other. "Most curious of all," comments Eisenstein, is Dickens's "'interruption'" at the beginning of Chapter 17, a digression the filmmaker calls Dickens's own "'treatise'" on the principles of his montage construction of the story. A.L. Zambrano draws on Eisenstein's observations in her discussion of Dickens and Eisenstein, "Charles Dickens and Sergei Eisenstein: The Emergence of Cinema," **Style,** 9 (Fall 1975), 469-87. See also VII. 14.

10.   "Fagin in Berlin Provokes a Riot." **Life,** 26 (7 March 1949), 38-39.

Describes two nights of rioting at the Kurbel Theatre in West Berlin, Germany, where Jews, offended by Guiness's portrayal of Fagin, angrily protested the screening of Lean's **Oliver Twist.** British military authorities refused to intervene, but the exhibitors gave way and withdrew the film in deference to the protests. The article reports that Lean denied the charges of anti-Semitism and defended his position by saying that he modelled Fagin's appearance on Cruikshank's depiction of him. Comments **Life:** calling Fagin "a wily old Jew" in the novel might have been an unimportant matter in the nineteenth century, but between Dickens and Lean "history had interposed the ghost of six million murdered Jews and the specter of genocide." Further editorial comment in the article expressed puzzlement about Lean's insisting on such complete fidelity to Dickens and to Cruikshank and added that "it was harder still to guess why the authorities had not only permitted exhibition of the picture in Germany but refused to withdraw it immediately after the inevitable reaction came." Lean's film caused similar problems in the United States, where it was banned until 1951 until American censors approved an altered version. See VII. 3 and 29.

11.   Fawcett, F. Dubrez. "Dickens on the Screen." In his **Dickens the Dramatist** (VI. 45), pp. 193-208.

Provides a detailed summary of the 1909 Vitagraph **Oliver Twist,** which, with few sets and slick casting captured a remarkable amount of the novel's plot. Fawcett calls this film "the first home-made screen story" to show the classic simplicity of the early silent days, after which major advancements followed. The next landmark, he thinks, was the Hepworth-Bentley **Oliver Twist** in 1912, a three thousand foot version which took a whole hour to show. Perfunctory comments on other films follow, and include references to a sound version of **Oliver Twist** Fawcett attributes to American Pathe in 1933, the Monogram film of the same year with Dickie Moore as Oliver (also sound), and Lean's 1948 adaptation.

12.   Findlay, Ian F. "Dickens in the Cinema." **The Dickensian,** 54 (Spring 1958), 106-08.

A chronological list of film versions of Dickens's novels now superseded by Zambrano (VII. 33).

13.   Friedman, Lester D. Hollywood's Image of the Jew. New York: Frederick Ungar, 1982, pp. 16-18.

Readers should note that Hollywood's image of the Jew, in all its multiple perspectives, was often the product of Jews themselves, who maintained a significant degree of control over "America's largest propaganda machine," as the author describes the film industry. Friedman proceeds by decades, devoting a long chapter to "The Silent Stereotypes," where he notes how directors, looking for ready-made plots, turned to literary classics which featured Jewish figures. During the silent film era, **The Merchant of Venice** and **Oliver Twist** accounted for at least eleven adaptations, six of which were taken directly from Dickens's novel (1909, 1910, 1912, 1912, 1916, and 1922). In addition, there was one variation, **Oliver Twist, Junior** (1921). Made in England and widely distributed in the United States by Kineto Film Traders, the films ignored the workhouse scenes and concentrated on Oliver's story after he joined the thieves. Friedman sees a tendency to tone down Fagin's viciousness in performances by Nat Godwin (1912), Tully Marshall (1916), Irving Pichel (1933), and Ron Moody (1968), all of which portray him as a charming rogue rather than as a totally despicable villain. Yet despite these modifications, Friedman concludes that the silent adaptations essentially recycled presentations of Jews that today "we would label as racist stereotypes."

14.   Griffith, David Wark. "Griffith to Film History of World in Gigantic Serial." The [New York] Globe and Commercial Advertiser, 2 May 1922, p. 12.

Griffith's most explicit statement about the debt he owed Dickens, whose works, he claimed, directly inspired such major innovations of his in film method as the technique of montage or cross-cutting and his discovery that tragedy and comedy can, "with care, be mixed to make a homogeneous whole." Examples of the former, Griffith thought, can be found throughout Dickens's fiction, when he shifts the focus from one scene to another to heighten the tension. Dickens "introduces a multitude of characters and incidents, and breaks off abruptly to go from one to another, but at the end he cleverly gathers all the apparently loose threads together again and rounds off the whole." This method, Griffith thought, would suit him far better than the method in vogue at the beginning of the twentieth century, when directors generally held the camera steady, as if they were recording a play rather than making a motion picture. Petrie (VII. 21) questions whether Dickens was quite the vital influence on the development of film structure that Griffith maintains, suggesting that he and Eisenstein (VII. 9) "used the genuinely cinematic elements in Dickens's fiction to create a respectable literary precedent and to provide a theoretical justification for techniques Griffith probably absorbed largely unconsciously from his own early experiences as an actor and playwright and that Eisenstein in turn inherited from Griffith." Griffith's comments in The Globe were first recorded by A. B. Walkley, who interviewed Griffith for the Times shortly after his arrival in England. See "Switching Off: Mr. Griffith and Dickens: A Strange Literary Analogy," [London] Times, 26 April 1922, p. 12. Walkley notes that the technique of shifting the story from one group to another "is really common to fiction at large," citing examples from Thackeray, George Eliot, Meredith, Hardy, and others.

15.   Hunt, Peter. "Research for Films from Dickens." The Dickensian, 44 (Spring 1948), 94-97.

A short but interesting analysis of why Dickens "provides inexhaustible material for film research workers." In film language, Hunt writes, Dickens is "the perfect combination of Script-Writer, Art Director and Set Dresser, giving everything the final cohesion of a Director." Hunt illustrates this point by discussing how Dickens's description of the Three Cripples provided useful visual directions for those preparing Lean's version of Oliver Twist (VII. 18). The only difficulty members of the company had, he adds, was with Dickens's lack of specificity in dating the novel's action. Because the text supplied only indirect allusions, the film researchers had to look carefully at the period to find authentic visual means of dating the action. Among the sources Hunt found useful for visual information about the period, he notes Cruikshank, a collection of water colors of Saffron Hill, Field Lane, and Jacob's Island in the Library of London County Hall, and issues of the Illustrated London News.

16.   Huntley, John. "The Music of **Hamlet** and **Oliver Twist**." **The Penguin Film Review**, No. 8. London: Penguin Books, 1949, pp. 110-16.

Argues that a study of the music of Lean's adaptation of **Oliver Twist** reveals considerable craft, the credit for which goes largely to Sir Arnold Bax, a well-known composer who successfully followed the director's requirements. Huntley discusses several of these and, drawing on notes from Lean's files, quotes some of his suggestions. Lean wanted the music accompanying the titles to convey an ominous note and then gradually fade away. Bax obliged and worked in two other important motifs, the "locket theme"--the locket which holds the key to Oliver's identity--and the theme associated with the protagonist himself. Lean also had ideas for other sequences, suggesting the need for the music to "accent" the locket and music to convey the idea of a new, better day after the death of Oliver's mother. Further credit goes to Lean for "Fagin's Romp," a piece of music which transforms the lesson in picking pockets into a comic ballet but which retains a single angry note to suggest Fagin's viciousness. Huntley concludes that Bax's music "does full justice to Lean's requirements."

17.   Kelly, Tanita C. "**Oliver Twist**." In **Magill's Survey of Cinema: Silent Films** (VII. 6), II, 821-24.

Discusses James Young's 1916 version of **Oliver Twist**, a five-reel film produced for Jesse L. Lasky's Feature Play Company. Young assembled an all-star cast, which included Marie Doro (Oliver), Tully Marshall (Fagin), and Hobart Bosworth (Sikes). Young and the Company also made a sustained effort to portray the novel's Victorian milieu and capture the atmosphere of Cruikshank's illustrations. Kelly notes that much of the novel was cut in order to adapt Dickens's plot to five reels of film, yet despite complaints about its shortness, this filmed version remained popular until 1921. In that year, a modern version of Dickens's novel set in New York and starring Harold Goodwin was released (**Oliver Twist, Junior**), followed the next year by the popular 1922 version (VII. 6) with Jackie Coogan.

18.   **Oliver Twist**. Dir. David Lean. J. Arthur Rank/Cineguild, 1948.

Lean's highly acclaimed adaptation, starring Robert Newton (Bill Sikes), Alec Guiness (Fagin), Kay Walsh (Nancy), John Howard Davies (Oliver Twist), and Francis L. Sullivan (Bumble). Running time: 105 minutes. A 16mm print of Lean's film, now part of Janus Films "Classic Library," may be rented from Films Incorporated, 400 Park Avenue South, New York, NY, 10016. Tel. 212/889-7910; toll-free outside N.Y. 800/241-5530.

19.   **Oliver!** Dir. Carol Reád. Romulus Films, 1968.

Film version adapted from Lionel Bart's stage production **Oliver!** (VII. 37), starring Ron Moody (Fagin), Shani Wallis (Nancy), Oliver Reed (Bill Sikes), and Harry Secombe (Bumble). This adaptation collected many 1968 Academy Award Nominations and Awards. See VII. 24. Running time: 146 minutes. A 16mm print of Read's film may be rented from Audio Brandon Films, Adelphi Cinema Enterprises, Inc., Arcus Films, Inc., Cine-Craft Films, Clem Williams Films, Inc., Jensen's Cinema 16, ROA Films, Swank Motion Pictures, Twyman Films, Inc., Wholesome Film Center, Inc., and Westcoast Films.

20.   **Oliver Twist**. Dir. Clive Donner. 1982.

A full-length feature film first shown on CBS-TV on 23 March 1982. Adapted by James Goldman, this version follows the opening scenes of the novel fairly closely by relating the main events in Oliver's life before he arrives in London, where he falls in with Fagin and his gang. Thereafter, Goldman makes some necessary cuts, pruning Harry Maylie's romance with Rose and showing Oliver being taken in by the Maylies after the attempted robbery at Chertsey instead of first rescued by Mr. Brownlow and then recaptured by the thieves. Goldman relies on Monks to heighten the drama after Oliver is saved, depicting him actively plotting against the orphan and putting up money to have him killed. Nancy foils this plot by warning Oliver's protectors but is murdered by Sikes for revealing Monk's plan. Fagin's Jewishness is present but considerably muted in George C. Scott's interpretation and without the stereotypical attributes that caused so much trouble in Guiness's portrait (VII. 3 and 10). For reviews of the film, see Judith Crist, TV Guide, 30 (20 March 1982), A-5, and John J. O'Connor in the New York Times, 23 March 1982, p. C12.

21.   Petrie, Graham. "Dickens, Goddard, and the Film Today." YR, 64 (Winter 1975), 185-201.

Brief comments on Lean's adaptations in the context of a general essay remarking on various filmic aspects of Dickens's fiction. Petrie notes how the numerous adaptations of Dickens's novels have provided a bridge between the Victorian theatre and early silent films and how Eisenstein, Griffith, and Charles Chaplin all owe important aspects of their work as directors to Dickens. At the same time, Petrie contends, the later novels, in particular, still offer contemporary film directors useful clues for the means of solving such major preoccupations as creating a multi-dimensional world and fusing the experience of the individual with his social universe. Often, however, the advice Petrie sees implicit in Bleak House and Little Dorrit is ignored, and directors tend not to think of looking to Dickens for clues "as to how to solve technical or esthetic problems." Lean, for example, captured the atmosphere of Victorian London in his Oliver Twist (VII. 18) but fails to render the novel's dreamlike quality. He also ignores the affinity between Oliver and Fagin, making the film a simple episodic-pictorial composition "with none of the undertones that help to hold the original work together."

22.   Pointer, Michael. "A Dickens Garland." American Film, 1 (December 1975), 14-19.

Attributes Dickens's popularity among filmmakers to "the astonishing characterizations in his books," but notes how the omission of favorite individuals, inevitable in any film version, brings loud cries of lament. Pointer refers to a version of Oliver Twist unnoted by film historians--R.W. Paul's Mr. Bumble the Beadle in 1898--and praises the work of Edwin Thanhouser and Cecil Hepworth among the early producers to make silent versions of Dickens's novels.

23.   Prately, Gerald. "Oliver Twist (1948)." In his The Cinema of David Lean. South Brunswick, N.J.: A.S. Barnes, 1974, pp. 72-81.

Provides facts about the cast, film credits, a synopsis of the story, and comments by Lean about the preparation of his film version of the novel. Lean saw Great Expectations as a fairy tale, "just not quite true," and Oliver Twist as "a grimly realistic study of what poverty was like" in Victorian

times. Preparing the script for each film, Lean describes how he made "a
one-line summary of the actual incidents in each chapter, ignoring all
conversation and descriptive matter." From this summary Lean built actual
scenes, adding Dickens's dialogue--"perfect for the screen"--straight from the
books. Quoting Lean from the same source, Prately notes that Lean found
Oliver Twist more difficult to adapt for the screen than Great Expectations.
"The main problem," Lean explains, "was that of making fantastic, larger than
life characters fit into a starkly real setting." Prately calls Oliver Twist a
technical and artistic advance over Great Expectations, seeing a "restless
spirit of experimentation" in every sequence. Prately also praises the musical
score by Sir Arnold Bax for giving "splendid operatic tones to this very
operatic material." Cf. VII. 16.

24.   Roddick, Nick. "Oliver!" In Magill's Survey of Cinema (VII. 3), III,
       1252-55.

Comments on Read's 1968 film of the musical (VII. 37) as a "wholesome,
tuneful, and spectacular family entertainment" meeting with prodigious
success. After a Royal Premiere in London on 26 September 1968, the film
ran for thirty-six weeks in New York, Boston, and Chicago, and thirty-five
weeks in San Francisco and Washington, D.C., grossing by mid-1970
approximately fifty million dollars. The film also won Oscars for Best
Picture, Best Direction, and three other categories, besides receiving five
more nominations and various international awards, including two Golden
Globes from the Hollywood Foreign Press Association and a scroll for
"outstanding mastery" presented to Carol Reed by the jury at the Moscow
Sixth International Film Festival.

25.   Silver, Alain, and James Ursini. "The Dickens Adaptations: Great
       Expectations (1946); Oliver Twist (1948)." In their David Lean and His
       Films. London: Leslie Frewin, 1974, pp. 53-84.

The authors devote most of their attention to Great Expectations, but in
the pages they reserve for Oliver Twist (78-84), they make interesting
observations about Lean's focus and methods in his second adaptation of a
Dickens novel. Lean concentrates, they argue, on the themes of social
injustice and criminality, successfully portraying each in visual terms.
Low-key photography and careful attention to detail, they argue, capture the
novel's dark, claustrophobic atmosphere, while masterful editing, camera
angles, and montage shots embody the novel's social satire and convey
Dickens's emphasis on the sordid aspects of crime. Silver and Ursini examine
the film's opening in detail, demonstrate how Lean quickly establishes the
drudgery, starvation, and regimentation of workhouse life, and give instances
of Lean's interweaving of objective and subjective camera work. They also
comment on this last aspect of the film in their Introduction. See pp. 10-12.

26.   S[taples], L.C. "David Lean's Oliver Twist." The Dickensian, 44
       (Autumn 1948), 203-05.

An intelligent appraisal of the film, which Staples sees as an artistic
work in its own right, telling the story by the means of the camera and
sweeping along the viewer.

27.   Tharaud, Barry. "Two film versions of Oliver Twist: Moral Vision in
       Film and Literature." DSN, 11 (June 1980), 41-46.

After comparing the 1933 Monogram production of **Oliver Twist** with the 1947 Cineguild production (VII. 18), Tharaud concludes that both fail because they provide no searching moral vision and merely tell simplified versions of Dickens's novel. In 1933, William J. Cowen ignored Dickens's "radical message" about the destructiveness of industrial Victorian England and preached: "Don't rebel, don't turn to crime, there is nothing to be done: some folks are just born lucky." Forty-four years later, David Lean did little better. He portrays society as a brutal mob and appears to ignore the social conditions which create Fagin, Sikes, and the thieves. Tharaud finds evidence of visual subtlety in both films, but argues that successes such as Cowen's claustrophobic sets or Lean's use of clasped or outstretched hands to convey mercy or meanness cannot sustain films lacking an "intelligent, purposive moral vision." A 16mm print of Cowen's adaptation may be rented from Budget Films and Classic Film Museum, Inc.

28.　Thorndike, Russell. **Cineguild's Screen Version of Charles Dickens' Oliver Twist.** London: Raphael Tuck, n.d. 64 pp.

A condensed version of Lean's adaptation of **Oliver Twist** (VII. 18) illustrated with stills from the film. This publication and the edition of **Oliver Twist** noted in II. 36 represent two obvious attempts in Britain to cash in on the favorable reception of the 1948 film.

29.　Vermilye, Jerry. "Oliver Twist." In his **The Great British Films.** Seacaucas, N.J.: Citadel Press, 1978, pp. 117-20.

A synopsis of the plot of Lean's 1948 adaptation (VII. 18) with some stills and brief comments about the effective casting. Yet Guiness's very success with Fagin--his "lisping, rasping speech and oily, mincing mannerisms" Vermilye notes, proved its undoing in the United States, where the film lost considerable revenue by being banned until 1951. No completely unexpurgated print of **Oliver Twist** was shown, he writes, until October 1970, when the original version was screened at the Museum of Modern Art in New York during a David Lean retrospective. Vermilye comments: "It was almost as though America were retaliating, belatedly, for Britain's censorship of our 1922 silent **Oliver Twist**, with Lon Chaney as Fagin. The objection to that version: it was feared that the movie might encourage juvenile delinquency in England!"

30.　Young, Vernon. "Dickens Without Holly: David Lean's **Oliver Twist.**" **New Mexico Quarterly,** 22 (Winter 1952), 425-30.

Young writes enthusiastically of Lean's film version of the novel (VII. 18), praising it as a masterful translation of the book into a complex cinematic experience. The film works brilliantly, Young argues, because Lean not only rescued characteristic elements of the Dickens world from a weak novel--"untiring energy, eccentric profusion, and black-and-white brutality"--but found vivid and forceful visual equivalents for the novel's attack on industrial England. Lean managed this, he argues, by boldly adapting the story and by cutting out material peripheral to his vision of the film's focus on "the fight for existence in a chokingly inhuman world." From its dramatic opening, whose blasted heath and straining tree-boughs plunge viewers into a setting of agony, to its close, Lean conveys "a unity of helplessness" in the various auditory and visual images weaving the scenes together. Harsh voices, tramping feet, grasping hands, and ugly faces all become thematic tokens working to produce a memorable experience.

31.   Zambrano, Ana Laura. "Audio-Visual Teaching Materials: A Dickensian Checklist--Part II." DSN, 7 (December 1976), 110-13.

In the section on **Oliver Twist** (pp. 111-12), gives details of one filmstrip introducing characters from the novel and three records or cassettes by different companies featuring readings, dramatizations, and discussions of **Oliver Twist.** Anyone interested in 16mm films, videotapes, and filmstrips utilizing **Oliver Twist** in different ways should consult Part I of Zambrano's Checklist (June 1976), pp. 43-44, where she lists materials available in 1974-75 on Dickens's life and times. Many of these draw specifically on **Oliver Twist** and refer to some aspect of it. For further references to audio-visual aids, see **The Cumulated Dickens Checklist** (IV. 4), p. 271.

32.   ____. **Dickens and Film.** New York: Gordon Press, 1977. ii + 442 pp.

Begins by acknowledging Dickens's extensive debt to the early Victorian theatre but argues that for all the stage's formative influence Dickens's art lies closer to that of the film. Zambrano rehearses in detail the case Eisenstein made--see VII. 9--for the filmic qualities inherent in Dickens's narrative method and his descriptions of scenes; she also reviews aspects of Griffith's debt to Dickens (VII. 14). In Chapter 4, Zambrano surveys modern film adaptations of Dickens's novels, including Lean's **Oliver Twist** and Reed's **Oliver!** both of which she praises as imaginative and successful attempts to translate **Oliver Twist** into the film medium. While Lean captures much of the novel's realism through his camera work, she argues, **Oliver!** also provides a fine version of the novel by using the conventions of music, dance, and song, to draw attention to the suffering, hunger, and villainy present in the original. This stylization of the story works, Zambrano concludes, citing Pauline Kael's remarks on this same point with approval, because Reed combines musical entertainment with an imaginative version which treats the novel as "a lyrical, macabre fable." For Kael's review of **Oliver!** see "Current Cinema: The Concealed Art of Carol Reed," **New Yorker,** 44 (14 December 1968), 193-96. Also of interest are comments Zambrano cites by Ron Moody about how he softened his portrayal of Fagin and deliberately made him amusing. "I play him kind of mockingly," Moody explains in an interview, "because I think it's healthy for us to realize that what was once anti-Semitic is now best handled by a light approach. Sort of saying to people, 'isn't it rather amusing that things were once this way but now they're changed, Thank God.'" See Wayne Warga, "Oliver's Fagin Here Sightseeing," [Los Angeles] **Times,** 15 January 1969, Sec. 4, p. 9, cols. 1-2.

33.   ____. "Feature Motion Pictures Adapted from Dickens: A Checklist--Part II." DSN, 6 (March 1975), 9-13.

In the section on **Oliver Twist** (pp. 11-12), lists thirteen film versions of the novel made between 1906 and 1968 in America, Britain, Italy, Hungary, and France. The earliest American versions, silent one-reelers, include two films from Vitagraph (1906 and 1909), which were superseded by later five-reel versions, the General Public and Sales in 1912, based on Carr's stage adaptation (VI. 18) and Paramount's in 1916 (VII. 17). Thereafter, versions expanded to eight-reelers--Fox Film's **Oliver Twist, Jr.,** in 1921 and Jackie Coogan's 1922 version (VII. 6), before the first American sound production by Monogram Pictures in 1933. The first British **Oliver Twist** appeared in 1912 (Hepworth), followed by Cineguild's production in 1948, which David Lean directed, and Romulus Films' **Oliver!** in 1968 directed by Carol Reed.

Leonard (VI. 52) provides useful supplementary information about the early versions of 1909, the American and British films of 1912, and the versions of 1916 and 1922.

MUSICAL ADAPTATIONS

34. Cassidy, James. "The Artful Dodger Galop." Dublin: Piggott, n.d.

    Instrumental-dance music. In Dickens House collection.

35. Copeland, H. "Oliver Twist." From a Song by W.T. Townsend. n.d.

    Noted by James T. Lightwood in his **Charles Dickens and Music**: London, Charles H. Kelly, 1912, p. 173.

36. Leonard, William Torbet. "**Oliver Twist.**" In his **Theatre: Stage to Screen** (VI. 52), pp. 1138-39, and 1144-47.

    Full information about the American and British productions of **Oliver!** Leonard lists the members of the cast, the titles of the songs, and gives similar facts relating to the various companies performing the musical after its premiere in London on 30 June 1960.

37. **Oliver!** Dir. Robin Midgley and Larry Oaks. Words and music by Lionel Bart. New Theatre, London. 30 June 1960.

    Stage musical produced by Donald Albery which opened in London and later came to New York, where it started on 6 January 1963 and ran successfully on Broadway and on a national tour for nearly four seasons. On their first night in London, the cast received fourteen curtain calls. **Oliver!** continued in London for 2,618 performances, making this one of the most acclaimed musicals in the history of the London stage.

38. Sloman, Charles. "Sequel to the Artful Dodger, or the Dodger's Return." [A song]. n.p., n.p., 1856.

    For the text, see **The Dickensian,** 9 (June 1913), 157-58. See also T.W. Hill, "A Catalogue of the Miller Collection of Dickens Music at the Dickens House," **The Dickensian,** 37 (Winter 1940-41), 48-54, where Hill lists entries under **Oliver Twist.**

39. Sloman, Charles, and Sam Cowell. "The Artful Dodger."

    Music by Fred Bridgeman. Glasgow: Morison Kyle [c. 1850's]. For the words, see **The Dickensian,** 9 (August 1913), 217-19. Sung to the tune of "Botney [sic] Bay." In Dickens House collection.

40. S[taples], L[eslie] C. "**Oliver!** Dickens to Music." **The Dickensian,** 56 (September 1960), 174-75.

    Reviews favorably Lionel Bart's stage musical (VII. 37) and praises the spectacular production with its revolving stage and lively cast.

84   Text

RADIO AND TELEVISION ADAPTATIONS

41.   Butler, David, and Hugh Leonard. "The Further Adventures of Oliver
       Twist." [British] ATV.

A thirteen-part children's serial produced on Associated Television
(ATV), England. This version, which began on 2 March 1980, takes Dickens's
characters and invents an entirely new story line constructed around the life
of the Artful Dodger when he returns to London after serving time in
Australia, where he was transported.

42.   Fawcett, F. Dubrez. "Dickens on the Air." In his **Dickens the
       Dramatist: On Stage, Screen, and Radio** (VI. 45), pp. 209-23.

Describes the format for British radio adaptations of **Oliver Twist** as
weekly broadcasts lasting up to twelve or thirteen weeks. Fawcett gives a
detailed account of the production of an adaptation by Giles Cooper but omits
facts about the dates of the performances. He also refers to a 1941
production, adapted by Audrey Lucas and produced in eight parts by Moray
McLaren, and to a BBC version (undated) of **Oliver Twist,** one of six Dickens
novels prepared as part of a series for British schools.

43.   **Oliver Twist.** DuPont Show of the Month. 4 December 1959.

A ninety-minute version of the novel adapted for television by Michael
Dyne, televised by CBS, and directed by Dan Petrie. Leonard (VI. 52) supplies
details about the cast.

44.   **Oliver Twist.** Various British Radio and Television Adaptations.

Factual information about all the adaptations of **Oliver Twist** broadcast
in Britain is not easy to obtain. Fawcett (VI. 45) identifies some versions but
omits dates, while the BBC Data Enquiry Service inhibited this researcher by
stipulating a minimum time of two hours research at $120 an hour in response
to a request to supply details relating to the various radio and television
productions. Other sources, however, suggest the novel's continued popularity
in each medium. They also indicate that reservations about the dramatization
of the novel's more violent scenes have continued into the twentieth century.
Referring to the BBC's weekly serialization of **Oliver Twist** in 1962, Victor
Yates (MP for Birmingham) questioned the British Postmaster General,
Reginald Bevins, about the propriety of broadcasting a "most brutal and
bestial" depiction of Nancy's murder at five o'clock on a Sunday, a peak
viewing hour and one usually set aside for children. In response, Bevin noted
that he had been in consultation with the BBC about the episode, adding his
own objection to it as "brutal and quite inexcusable." See "Television
Programmes (Scenes of Brutality and Violence)," **Hansard,** 656 (27 March
1962), 987-92.

45.   Williams, Nigel. "The Parish Boy's Progress." **The Listener,** 94 (18
       December 1975), 819-20.

Comments on how adaptations of Dickens's frequently performed works
generally succumb to a box-office demand for happy endings. Williams, who
adapted **Oliver Twist** for 2nd House (BBC2), makes his case for keeping the
novel's political message by pointing to similarities between the Poor Law

Amendment Act of 1834 and Britain's present cuts in social services. He also argues that an adaptation emphasizing the novel's original political aims better represents Dickens's outlook than "the Christmas beanfeast view" of his writing apparent in the adaptations of his books frequently broadcast in England, often at Christmas.

VIII. PROSE ADAPTATIONS

PARODIES

1. "Bos," pseud. [Thomas Peckett Prest]. **The Life and Adventures of Oliver Twiss, The Workhouse Boy.** London: E. Lloyd, [1839]. 631 pp.

   Opens at the Mudanshush workhouse, run by Mumble, in a close parody of Oliver Twist, published originally in seventy-nine weekly installments, each with a crude woodcut on the first page, and then as a single volume. Prest follows the main outlines of Dickens's plot, but begins to depart with increasing frequency as he adds numerous picaresque episodes and adventures. For further comments on **Oliver Twiss,** see Louis James (XII. 118 and 119).

2. "Poz," pseud. **Oliver Twiss, the Workhouse Boy.** London: James Pattie and James Turner, the Starr Press, n.d.

   Published in penny parts, each consisting of eight pages and one illustration. Tillotson notes (II. 48) that this version, described as "an original satirical work, intended as an expose of the New Poor Law, etc," ended after four weekly parts, with Oliver returned to the workhouse after appearing before "Slang" the magistrate. See also Louis James (XII. 118), who notes that the only known surviving copy of the "Poz" plagiarism is in the Rochester Museum Dickens Collection Library.

UNAUTHORIZED PROSE VERSIONS (CHRONOLOGICAL LISTING)

3. **Oliver Twist; or, the Parish Boy's Progress.** Otley: William Walker, [c. 1839]. 10 pp.

   A summary, in the simplest form, of the outline of the plot followed by a piece of doggerel in couplets, "Description of a Parish Poor-House."

4. **Oliver Twist, or the Parish Boy's Progress.** London: L.L. Marks, [c. 1839]. 8 pp.

   Follows the text of the plot summary in (VIII. 3) but omits the verse.

5. **Oliver Twist.** Bradford: B. Walker, [c. 1839]. 12 pp.

   Noted by Tillotson (II. 48), who describes this as a "simplified, unsensational, and slightly inaccurate synopsis of the completed novel, with particular emphasis on the burglary."

6. **The Story of Oliver Twist** by Charles Dickens. The Penny Library of Popular Authors. Ed. Charles H. Ross. London: Henry Vickers, [c. 1881]. 16 pp.

A clumsy arrangement of extracts from the novel put together to reveal the main events of the plot. Ross omits the Maylies entirely and gives more attention to the criminals.

7.   **The Artful Dodger.** Complete. By Charles Dickens. British Standard Library. One Penny. London: J. and R. Maxwell, [c. 1882]. 32 pp.

This and the two following entries in the same series present scenes associated with the character of the title and attempt to round out the plot in a sketchy and simplified manner. Each appends a few sentences indicating the novel's ending in which the criminals are punished and Oliver is safety restored to Mr. Brownlow. For further reference to this series, see Suddaby (VIII. 14).

8.   **Bumble the Beadle.** Complete. By Charles Dickens. British Standard Library. One Penny. London: J. and R. Maxwell, [c. 1882]. 32 pp.

9.   **Nancy Sikes.** Complete. By Charles Dickens. British Standard Library. One Penny. London: J. and R. Maxwell, [c. 1882]. 32 pp.

10.   Dickens, Charles. **Oliver Twist.** Manchester and London: John Heywood, 1886. 112 pp.

A cheap (one penny) edition of the novel in very small print which provides the **Bentley's Miscellany** text unabridged and with illustrations.

11.   _____. **Oliver Twist.** London: Dean and Son, n.d. 32 pp.

A condensed version of the novel in Dean's Penny Tales for the Million series. This version of the text reduces the novel to forty-six chapters, setting them out in small print and double columns.

12.   _____. **Oliver Twist.** London: John Dicks, n.d. 123 pp.

An illustrated and cheap (sixpence) edition of the novel in Dicks' English Novels series.

13.   _____. **The Adventures of Oliver Twist.** London: Edward Lloyd, n.d. 204 pp.

A cheap version of the novel set in double columns with a small typeface and published as part of Lloyd's Sixpenny Dickens series by the proprietors of **The Daily Chronicle** and **Lloyd's Weekly News.** Illustrated by J. Mahoney.

14.   Suddaby, John. "Charles Dickens and Mary Elizabeth Braddon." **The Dickensian,** 11 (May 1915), 117-20.

Provides some useful background about Braddon's role in her husband's publishing business, J. and R. Maxwell, the London firm which put out penny tales from Britain's leading authors. Suddaby writes that Braddon (Mrs. Maxwell) took an active part in the establishment of the British Standard Library of Fiction, a series of abridgements of major authors designed to compete with the penny dreadfuls and offer poorer readers a greater choice of texts. Each booklet, thirty-two pages long, roughly folded and uncut and placed loosely in a terra cotta cover, sold for one penny and provided abridged versions of several of Dickens's novels, including **Oliver Twist.** See VIII. 7-9. Suddaby dates the origin of this enterprise to "about thirty years ago," i.e., the 1880's.

CHILDREN'S VERSIONS

15.   Braybrooke, Patrick. "Oliver Twist." In his **Great Children in Literature.** London: Alston Rivers, [1929], pp. 139-60.

An essay sketching Oliver's character, together with short extracts from the novel. Braybrooke admits that Oliver is "something of a symbol," but argues that he also has human qualities which affect some of the other characters.

16.   Cobb, Joyce. "Oliver Twist: the Boy Who Asked for More," and "Oliver Twist and the Artful Dodger." In her **Stories from Dickens.** London: Methuen, 1910, pp. 11-20, 20-30.

Retells in two separate episodes various aspects of Oliver's early history. In the first, Cobb condenses the story of Oliver's birth, apprenticeship to Mr. Sowerberry, and subsequent flight to London, where he meets the Dodger. In the second, she shows Oliver as an apprentice in the hands of Fagin and follows a simplified version of Dickens's narrative until Oliver is rescued from the court by Mr. Brownlow. The story ends with Oliver recounting his history and Mr. Brownlow adopting him.

17.   Dickens, Mary Angela. "Oliver Twist." In her **Children's Stories from Dickens.** London: Raphael Tuck, n.d., pp. 19-41.

A variation of Mary Angela Dickens's other versions of Oliver's history (VIII. 18). In this one, which retains some of the original dialogue, Oliver goes to London, where he lodges in a boy's home until Mr. Brownlow befriends him. Sikes steals the boy away, planning to train him as a thief, but the Maylies restore Oliver to Mr. Brownlow.

18.   _____. "Oliver Twist." In her **Trotty Veck and His Daughter Meg and Other Stories.** London: Raphael Tuck, n.d., pp. 13-43.

Retells in a simplified and incomplete version suitable for children the story of Oliver's birth, apprenticeship, and flight to London. The story ends soon after Oliver is shot in the attempted burglary at Chertsey, showing him taken in by the Maylies, who restore him to life and happiness.

19.   _____, and Edric Vredenburg. "Oliver Twist." In **Oliver Twist and The Blind Toymaker.** London: Raphael Tuck, n.d., pp. 5-48.

The same simplified version of Oliver's early life as in VIII. 18.

20.   _____, and others. "The Brave and Honest Boy, Oliver Twist." In **Charming Children of Dickens's Stories.** Chicago: Hertel, Jenkins, 1906, pp. 243-78.

A condensed version of the novel which ignores the criminals and ends with Oliver's rescue and rehabilitation by Mr. Brownlow. This summary of **Oliver Twist,** together with pieces adapted from **Hard Times** and **The Pickwick Papers,** also appeared in Mary Angela Dickens's **Charming Stories About Children** (Philadelphia: John C. Winston, 1906), in which "A Brave and Honest Boy, Oliver Twist" occupies pages 243-78.

21.   Jackson, Alice F. **Oliver Twist Retold for Boys and Girls.** London: T.C. and E. C. Jack, n.d. 180 pp.

A detailed version of the novel, which covers later events in the narrative often omitted from children's texts. Jackson includes Noah spying on Nancy, her murder, Sikes's death, and the last hours of Fagin in the condemned cell.

22.   **Oliver and the Jew Fagin.** From the **Oliver Twist** of Charles Dickens. New York: Redfield, [c. 1855]. 179 pp.

A simplified version of the plot in the series, "Dickens' Little Folk." Despite the book's title, the adapter cut Fagin's role considerably, omitting his trial and last hours in the condemned cell. He leaves out much of the novel's violence, too. A later impression of this adaptation (New York: Clark, Austin, Maynard, and Co., 1861) suggests that the book proved popular.

23.   **Oliver Twist.** The Bridge Series. Harlow, Essex: Longman, 1962. 137 pp.

A version of the story edited and abridged by Latif Doss. The Bridge Series provides reduced texts and a simplified vocabulary and syntax for use by students of English as a second or foreign language.

24.   **Oliver Twist.** Illustrated Now Age Books. West Haven, Conn.: Pendulum Press, 1979. 62 pp.

Adapted by Stella Houghton Alico and illustrated by Fred Carrillo. A list of eight questions and occasionally glossed words constitutes the extent of the editors' commitment to their professed purpose of preparing **Oliver Twist** as one of several classic texts designed for use in American schools.

25.   **Oliver Twist.** The Kennett Library. Glasgow: Blackie and Son, 1961. 122 pp.

The story retold by John Kennett in a graded series of classics prepared for school children.

26.   Reg, Uncle. "Oliver Twist." In his **Beautiful Bairns: Stories from Dickens.** London: Charles H. Kelley, 1914, pp. 125-71.

A radically altered version of Dickens's story, to which the author adds characters, alludes to figures in Beatrix Potter's stories, invents dialogue, and modernizes the setting to reflect early twentieth-century England.

27.   Rives, Hallie Erminie. "Oliver Twist." In her **Tales from Dickens.** Indianapolis: Bobbs-Merrill, 1905, pp. 49-74.

An altered and simplified version of the plot covering Oliver's early life, his adventures in London, and the attempted robbery in Chertsey. Rives divides her narrative into three parts, heading the last one "How Everything turned out Right for Oliver in the End."

28.   Robarts, Edith.   **The Story of Oliver Twist.**   London: Sisley's, n.d. 96
      pp.

Retells Oliver's early life for the Pixie-Book Series. This simplified version ends shortly after the Chertsey expedition, thus omitting Dickens's focus on the criminals in the latter part of his novel.

29.   Scott, Broughton, ed. "Oliver Twist." In his **Boys & Girls from Dickens.**
      New York: Macaulay, 1912, pp. 11-22.

Narrates briefly in very condensed form Oliver's major adventures.

30.   Smith, Jessie Willcox. "Oliver's First Meeting with the Artful Dodger."
      In her **Dickens's Children: Ten Drawings.** London: Chatto and
      Windus, 1912.

Illustrates Oliver's meeting with the Dodger in Chapter 8 of the novel.

31.   Sweetser, Kate Dickinson. "Oliver Twist." In her **Ten Boys from
      Dickens.** New York: R.H. Russell, 1901, pp. 11-41.

Sets out "to bring these sketches, with all their beauty and pathos, to the notice of the young people of to-day." Sweetser preserves some of Dickens's dialogue, adding connecting passages where necessary, in her condensed version of Oliver's life and history. Dickens, she tells her youthful readers, was "a loyal champion of all boys" who presented boy lives "as completely as possible."

32.   Weedon, L.L. "Oliver Twist." In his **Child Characters from Dickens.**
      London: Ernest Nistar, n.d., pp. 181-213.

A simple version of Oliver's life that ends after the attempted robbery in Chertsey, showing Oliver rescued by Rose and Mrs. Maylie.

33.   _____. "Oliver Twist." In his **The Children's Dickens: Stories Selected
      from Various Tales.** London: Henry Frowde and Hodder and
      Stoughton, n.d., pp. 30-36.

A shortened version of VIII. 32.

MISCELLANEOUS ADAPTATIONS

34.   **The Adventures of Oliver Twist.** Roermond, The Netherlands: Inter-
      national School Publications, 1978. 32 pp.

An introduction to Dickens's life, a plot summary of the novel, and the text of four early chapters from **Oliver Twist.** This publication, for use in Dutch schools, accompanies a record or cassette of the chapters from the novel, read in English, with a printed gloss of terms and historical references in Dutch.

35. Bill Sikes and the School Board. London: Stevens and Richardson, 1879. 32 pp.

Listed by Miller (IV. 17).

36. Clay, Mrs. Laurence. The Dickens Reciter: Recitations, Character-Sketches, Impersonations, and Dialogues. London: George Routledge, n.d., passim.

Includes the description of the murder of Nancy and extracts of dialogues involving the Artful Dodger, Sikes, and Fagin, each adapted and edited for recitation by Mrs. Clay.

37. The Comic Adventures of Oliver Twist and the Artful Dodger. Puck, [London], 30 July, and 6, 13, and 20 August 1904.

Listed by Miller (IV. 17).

38. [Dexter, Walter]. "Dickensian Peeps into Punch--IV." The Dickensian, 32 (June 1936), 181-84.

Shows how Oliver Twist became "a veritable gold mine" for both cartoonists and writers working for Punch in both the nineteenth and twentieth centuries as they adapted scenes and characters from the novel to comment ironically and humorously on various contemporary events. Dexter cites John Leech's cartoon of Henry Brougham as Oliver "asking for more" on 30 March 1844 as the first of Leech's frequent references in Punch to Oliver, Bumble, and the Artful Dodger. Subsequent contributions to this series document how Raven Hill and Sir John Tenniel made similar use of the novel. Tenniel caricatured Disraeli as Fagin, drew a series in which Bumble represents the indifference of London administrators to social problems, and also used Sikes twice in 1889. The following century Sikes appears on 4 November 1914 as "The Kaiser" addressing his dog "Turk," and other references to Oliver Twist continue regularly until 1928. For the subsequent articles in the series, see The Dickensian, 33 (December 1936), 27-29; 34 (1937-38), 27-28; and 35 (Spring 1939), 117-22.

39. "Mr. Bumble on Old-Age Pensions." In The Westminster Gazette, 9 January 1909. Rpt. in The Dickensian, 5 (February 1909), 46.

An imaginary dialogue between the writer of the piece and Mr. Bumble about old-age pensions, with the Beadle hotly dissenting at this example of state interference in the affairs of the poor.

40. Oliver Twist. In Best Loved Books. London: Readers' Digest Association, n.d., pp. 215-434.

Condensed by the Editors of the Readers' Digest, who provide a simplified version of the text by removing much of Dickens's satire. Cruikshank's illustrations are included; Treasure Island, The Call of the Wild, and The Diary of a Young Girl appear in the same volume with Dickens's novel.

41. Oliver Twist. In The Dickens Digest: Four Great Dickens Masterpieces Condensed for the Modern Reader. New York: McGraw-Hill, 1943, pp. 209-300.

Condensed by Mary Louise Aswell and also includes **The Pickwick Papers,**
David Copperfield, and **Martin Chuzzlewit.**

42. "Oliver Twist: Old Saffron Hill." In **A Charles Dickens Bazaar.**
     Programme. [Holborn, 1888], pp. 1-2.

Reprints Oliver's arrival with the Dodger in the Saffron Hill area. This
extract, together with illustrations and passages taken from other novels,
formed part of the program announcing a Bazaar in 1888 to raise money for
the Restoration of St. Peter's Church, Saffron Hill, London.

43. **Oliver Twist, or the Parish Boy's Progress.** A Drama in Three Acts.
     Adapted only for Redington's characters and scenes. London: n.p.,
     n.d. 16 pp.

Podeschi (IV. 19) assumes that Redington was Pollock's (VIII. 46)
predecessor, taking over from him the production of toy-theatre scenes.
Noted by Miller (IV. 17).

44. **Oliver Twist or the Parish Boy's Progress.** The Characters, Scenes,
     Book of Words. To Suit the Juvenile Stage. Being the only One
     Published in this Form of Any of the Works of Dickens. U.p., n.p., c.
     1870? 41 pp.

A short, dramatized version of **Oliver Twist** in three acts, together with
scenes and characters specially designed for a toy theatre. The text and the
plates--some from Pollock's (VIII. 46)--are carefully inlaid, making this an
elaborate and exceedingly rare piece of Dickensiana. "This Book is Privately
Printed," reads a note in the front, "and Only Twelve Copies To Be Had." The
book also contains some interesting reproductions of pen and ink drawings,
done from sketches made in 1840, of Fagin's London, a three-quarters portrait
of Fagin "from an old cut by J. Leech," and verses by an unidentified author,
"To Fagin." Copy in the Beinecke Library, Yale University.

45. Perugini, Kate, comp. **Oliver Twist.** In her **The Comedy of Charles**
     Dickens. A Book of Chapters and Extracts Taken from the Writer's
     Novels. By his daughter Kate (Mrs. Perugini). London: Chapman and
     Hall, 1906, pp. 82-98.

Includes excerpts from Oliver's first meeting with the Dodger, Fagin
training his pupils to pick pockets, and Bumble's courtship of Mrs. Corney.

46. Pollock's Juvenile Drama. **Oliver Twist, or the Parish Boy's Progress.**
     London: Pollock's, [1860]. 16 pp.

Provides a three-act version of the play, together with six plates of
characters, thirteen stage-sets, eighteen separate scenes, and one set piece
and three wings. All are hand-colored and are adapted only for Pollock's
characters and scenes; reading time of the text, about thirty minutes. Walter
Dexter, reviewing A.E. Wilson's **Penny Plain, Two Pence Coloured** (1932),
notes that **Oliver Twist** was the only one of Dickens's novels adapted for the
popular toy-theatre business. See The Dickensian, 29 (1932-33), 37-40.

47. "Scene from **Oliver Twist.**" In **Lloyd's Comic Reciter.** London: Printed
     for the Booksellers, [c. 1839], p. 3.

Reprints Oliver's first encounter with the Artful Dodger and their ensuing conversation as an exercise in dialogue and quick oral exchange.

48.   Schaffer, George J. "Oliver in Hollywood: A New Year's Fantasy." The Dickensian, 35 (Autumn 1939), 254-58.

An imaginary conversation between a present-day Oliver and Nancy in which the characters discuss the enlightened attitudes towards juvenile offenders now evident in Los Angeles, where they are housed, helped, and properly fed.

49.   Swan, Mabel Munson. "The Sculpture Gallery." In her The Athenaeum Gallery 1827-1873: The Boston Athenaeum as an Early Patron of Art. Boston: The Boston Athenaeum, 1940, pp. 151-52.

Provides a brief history of Robert Ball Hughes's statue of Oliver Twist (VIII. 51) prior to its apparent disappearance. Hughes's model was exhibited at the Athenaeum from 1842 to 1847, in return for a loan of $120 advanced to Hughes by the institution. Subsequently, one Edward Brinley bought the statue and by the wish of the artist withdrew the figure from public exhibition until second thoughts prompted Brinley to try and sell it back to the Athenaeum "at a very moderate price." The correspondence between Brinley and the Athenaeum cited by Swan reveals his wish to see the figure publically displayed in Boston, but despite Brinley's co-operativeness the statue was not disposed of to the Athenaeum and never again appeared there. Swan comments that it was probably placed in Brinley's loft and may have been destroyed. "[N]or has there been any other mention of it in connection with the work of Ball Hughes," she adds. Cf. VII. 51.

50.   Williams, Bransby. Fagin. Typescript 37 pp.

The typescript of a four-act monologue by Fagin, adapted for a reading by Bransby Williams, which ends with Fagin in the condemned cell. The typescript provides no information about the date or occasion of Williams' performance. Williams played Fagin in the 1909 Dexter-Harry adaptation of Oliver Twist (VI. 22) and his familiarity with the role may well have led to his arranging this monologue. Coleman (VI. 42) notes that Williams received special praise from reviewers favorably impressed with the play as a whole. In Dickens House collection.

51.   "The Work of [Robert] Ball Hughes." The Dickensian, 29 (Summer 1933), 229-30.

Describes Hughes's statue "Oliver Twist" and notes that no one seems to know the present whereabouts of the piece. See also Swan (VIII. 49).

PART II
STUDIES

IX.   CONTEMPORARY REVIEWS (CHRONOLOGICAL LISTING)

1.   [Forster, John]. "Bentley's Miscellany." In "The Literary Examiner. "
     The Examiner, 12 March 1837, pp. 165-66.

     Forster's first notice of Oliver Twist in The Examiner, commenting on
the great improvements he noted in the second number of the Miscellany and
on "an exquisite mingling of humour and pathos" in Oliver Twist. Forster
added that he regretted Dickens's employment of his talents "upon such false
points of sympathy," but did not elaborate on his criticism of the novel's
attack on the Poor Law of 1834 until his long review the following
September. See IX. 9. Some weeks later (?26 May 1837), Dickens wrote to
Forster: "Believe me that it affords me great pleasure to hear that you
continue to read my writings, and far greater gratification than I can well
describe to you to hear from your own lips that poor Oliver 'affects'
you--which I take to be the highest of all praise" (P, I, 262).

2.   ["Oliver Twist"]. The Carlton Chronicle, No. 40 (8 April 1837), 635, and
     No. 44 (6 May 1837), 698.

     After several brief but complimentary notices summarizing the contents
of the literary periodicals for April, the author of the magazines column
wrote: "The surface of the stream [of Oliver Twist] seems bright, and
cheerfully bubbling as it rushes on--but in its windings you come ever and
anon upon some place of depth, which is dark at top, and as you look into it,
... inscrutable to the vulgar many, and mysterious, because we know it hath
within it the voice of an oracle, to the singular few." The following month,
recording his increasing admiration for the serial, the writer added: Oliver,
transformed to Field Lane, "will soon make his debut in the great sink of sin
and sea-coal. We have little doubt he will prove a sort of London Ulysses--a
person of various and vast experience--of much suffering--of great practical
wisdom--and, therefore, no small left-handed wisdom, as Lord Bacon has
described cunning."

3.   "Tulrumble and Oliver Twist." The Southern Literary Messenger, 3
     (May 1837), 323-25. For a reprint of the text, see The Dickensian, 33
     (1937), 87-90.

     An abusive and unintelligent attack on Dickens's pen-name, Boz, his
motives for writing, and the opening chapters of Oliver Twist. The first
number consists only of sneers at the Poor Laws, the reviewer protests, and a
history of what Oliver did and did not eat. He concludes by saying that he can
only account for the phenomenon of writers putting their trash upon the
public solely in terms of commercialism and the apparent willingness of
booksellers to take anything they think will prove profitable. In a subsequent
review of The Pickwick Papers in the same journal, the author notes how
readers have responded angrily to the sweeping denunciations of Oliver
Twist. See The Southern Literary Messenger, 3 (September 1837), 525-27.

4.   "The Magazines." The Sun, 1 July 1837, p. 2; 1 May 1838, p. 2; 4 June
     1838, p. 3; and 1 August 1838, p. 3.

Notices in The Sun record the serial publication of **Oliver Twist** in **Bentley's Miscellany** from February 1837 to November 1838. Referring to the fifth number, the reviewer of 1 July 1837 wrote: "There is more careful finish about [these scenes], more lucid painting, more matter worthy to be remembered." The writer also praised Fagin, observing that the portrait showed how Dickens could "pierce beyond the surface, and search and drag into light the most hidden mysteries of the human heart." Further brief notices commented favorably on the novel's rural scenes (1 May 1838), and on Oliver surprised by Fagin and Monks at the Maylies' (4 June 1838), before the writer registered disapproval of the scene in which Monks meets Mr. and Mrs. Bumble at night. "We hope Boz will soon return with Oliver," wrote the reviewer on 1 August 1838, "to the green leaves and fields of the country, for he has really given us quite enough of low London flash life, which has scarcely one redeeming merit."

5.   "**Bentley's Miscellany**." In "Literary Memoranda." **The Atlas**, 12 (9 July 1837), 441; 12 (5 November 1837), 713; and 13 (6 October 1838), 634.

This writer quickly noted the originality of Dickens's work, saying of **Oliver Twist** in July 1837 that "There is that sort of **verisimilitude** in it which we detect in the consistent delineations of modes of existence with which we are unacquainted, but the propriety of which hangs well together." Returning to this point later, he wrote in November 1837 that **Oliver Twist** is assuredly "an invention" because "It bears no sort of resemblance to any other fiction, looking like truth, with which we are acquainted." While the reviewer stopped short of agreeing with Ainsworth, whom he cites as having suggested that **Oliver Twist** had done more for London than all the work of Paul de Kock for Paris, he admitted that Dickens "has developed an entirely new vein in this strangely ludicrous yet strangely affecting story of **Oliver Twist**." See also Ainsworth (XI. 1). In particular, the reviewer responded to the serial's "air of reality," which seized his imagination, despite its "unaccustomed scenes, and curious colloquies" by creating a sense of veracity impossible to doubt.

Almost a year later, the periodicals critic of The Atlas reflected about other aspects of **Oliver Twist**'s appeal, finding in its "core of pathos and tragic interest" qualities of lasting value which made him rethink Dickens's reputation as a comic writer. "[T]hose who look only for fun" in Dickens's writing, he notes, will probably be surprised. "Mere humour could not have so long sustained his reputation." Rather the secret of the novelist's "extraordinary success," this writer thought, lay in the "grain of truth" always present, whether in his most whimsical passages or in those "overdone" and "exaggerated," like the episode of Nancy in the current number (Chapters 39 to 41). Her story, **The Atlas** critic thought, "is neither probable nor artistical as a whole," but her figure rushing through the streets "on an errand of life and death" possesses "a fidelity that is equally powerful in the conception and treatment."

6.   [Buller, Charles]. "The Works of Dickens." **London and Westminster Review**, 29 (July 1837), 194-215. Extract in Collins's **Dickens: The Critical Heritage** (IX. 39), pp. 52-55.

Covers **Sketches by Boz, The Pickwick Papers,** and the first six installments of **Oliver Twist** to appear in the **Miscellany.** Buller offers reasons for Dickens's popularity--his humor and wit, his descriptive powers, and his ability to "catch the peculiarities" of all classes of Londoners--and comments briefly on **Oliver Twist.** He sees the novel revealing a greater seriousness than Dickens's previous works; at the same time, he finds **Oliver Twist** flawed by a tendency towards monotony. This occurs, Buller writes, when Dickens accumulates too many details of misery and discomfort, which, he thinks, harass the reader.

7. ["Oliver Twist"]. **Weekly Dispatch,** 13 August 1837, p. 394; 3 September 1837, p. 430; and 12 November 1837, p. 550.

One of the few dissenting voices, critical, in these notices, of the novel's serial publication. This reviewer found "continuations" "perfect nuisances to magazine readers," who, he thought, could not retain in their memories all the incidents from month to month. "[H]ow contemptible is this system of writing a novel, bit-by-bit, in a magazine," he exclaimed. Cf. **The Courier** for a similar criticism (IX. 13).

8. ["Oliver Twist"]. **Morning Chronicle,** 2 September 1837, p. 3.

In the column surveying the literary periodicals published in September, the writer commented on the apparent impact of Dickens's attack on the Poor Law in his serial. "Boz has produced so strong an impression in some quarters," he wrote, "in connection with the late changes in the laws relating to the management and maintenance of the poor, that in Chelsea, for instance, people have gone about lecturing for the purpose of counteracting the effect of his writings."

9. [Forster, John]. **"Bentley's Miscellany."** In "The Literary Examiner." **The Examiner,** 10 September 1837, pp. 581-82. Reprinted in **The Dickensian,** 34 (1937-1938), 29-32.

Treats fully the first seven installments of **Oliver Twist** published between February and September 1837. Forster calls the novel Dickens's "masterpiece," a work destined to take its place "among the higher prose fictions of the language." **Oliver Twist** deserves praise, Forster explains, because no writer before Dickens has so perfectly "copied from nature as it really exists in the common walks of life" and so powerfully demonstrated to readers how "the characteristics of humanity" are "pretty much the same" in kings and parish boys. In Dickens's writings, he asserts, "we find **reality.**"
     The deep pathos of Oliver's birth and his mother's death--both portrayed "with fine touches of the grotesque"--elicit further enthusiastic comment, as do the scenes set among London thieves. These, writes Forster, "are quite worthy of Fielding"; the sketch of Sikes and his dog, he adds, is executed in "the true Snarleyyow spirit." See XIII. 141.
     Forster's one disappointment proved to be Dickens's attack on the new Poor Law because the novel's criticism relied too heavily, he thought, on "certain bugbears of popular prejudice and vulgar cant." Elevating the pauper in our sympathies at the expense of the struggling laborer, he explained, "is a system of curious philanthropy" beyond his understanding.

10. [Hayward, Abraham]. **"Pickwick Papers and Sketches by Boz."** **Quarterly Review,** 59 (October 1837), 484-518. Extract in Collins's **Dickens: The Critical Heritage** (IX. 39), pp. 56-62.

Closes a long review discussing Dickens's talents and the reasons for his popularity by noting that **Oliver Twist** affords "much higher promise" of

Dickens's chances of sustaining himself in the prominent position his earlier works had won. Hayward finds Oliver Twist a more substantial book because it reveals "a sustained power, a range of observation, and a continuity of interest" far beyond its predecessors. At the same time, Hayward warned Dickens against writing "too often and too fast," saying that persistence on this course will surely confirm the following prophecy: "he has risen like a rocket, and he will come down like the stick." This remark clearly annoyed Dickens, who later countered Hayward's prediction with his own, saying that he would do "great things with Nancy" and "defy Mr. Hayward and all his works" (P, I, 328).

11. [Forster, John]. "Bentley's Miscellany." In "The Literary Examiner."
     The Examiner, 19 November 1837, pp. 740-41.

Expresses scorn for the Miscellany--"a very stupid magazine"--but one which, Forster continues, quoting Duke Senior, "Wears a precious jewel in its head" [sic] (As You Like It, II, i, 12). Reading Oliver Twist, Forster finds himself "in the midst of a real story," one less concerned with making "points" and more with "the management of a sustained plot." Forster also speaks of taking as deep an interest in the novel as in any of the "most masterly creations" of the great painters of real life.

12. [Lewes, G.H.?]. "Sketches by Boz, Pickwick Papers, and Oliver Twist."
     National Magazine and Monthly Critic, 1 (December 1837), 445-49.
     Extract in Collins's Dickens: The Critical Heritage (IX. 39), pp. 63-68.

Praises Dickens for his "startling fidelity of observation," his originality, and his remarkable ability, especially in Oliver Twist, to catch the idiom of "vagabond, thief, footman, ostler, and gentleman" without a single coarse word. At the same time, Lewes also notes the "positive absurdities" of Oliver's language and phrases. "These are sad blots in this otherwise surpassing work," writes Lewes, because Oliver's speech is entirely inappropriate for an "uneducated workhouse-boy."

13. ["Oliver Twist"]. The Courier, 5 February 1838, p. 3; 2 March 1838, p.
     3; and 3 April 1838, p. 4.

Like the writer in the Weekly Dispatch (IX. 7), this critic also complained about the "tiresome" effect of reading a novel published in "such exceedingly small portions." Later notices, however, found Oliver Twist taking deeper and deeper hold of the reviewer's sympathies. Chapters 26 and 27 drew the comment that Dickens's writing showed "a profound acquaintance with the human heart," and the writer went on to praise the novelist for portraying characters "not surpassed by any great prose-painter in our language." The following month, The Courier chided the plagiarists who eagerly grabbed Oliver Twist before Dickens had finished the novel and presumptuously concocted stage versions of an incomplete work. "We must express our hope," the reviewer wrote on 3 April 1838, "that the 'dramatists' will leave him [Oliver] alone, and not molest the parish-boy in his progress. It is a gratuitous cruelty for the playhouse to finish the ill-treatment which the workhouse began." See VI. 1-5 for information about the early unauthorized stage versions of Oliver Twist.

14. "Bentley's Miscellany." In "The Magazines for May." Bell's Weekly
     Messenger, 6 May 1838, p. 142.

This newspaper proved one of Dickens's most frequent and strongest supporters as a regular commentator on the publication of **Oliver Twist**. **Bell's Weekly Messenger** noted on 5 November 1837, p. 355, that **Oliver Twist** had "immensely enlarged" the **Miscellany's** circulation; it continued to praise Dickens in its successive notices, calling him "our modern Hogarth" (3 September 1837, p. 283), and delighting in his droll and excellent writing. On 6 May 1838 the reviewer spoke highly of Dickens's style--a blend of "very minute description of low manners and scenes" and humor--and his ability to provide astonishingly truthful figures and images "without exciting feelings of disgust or offense."

A month later, the reviewer returned to this point at greater length, declaring that the more he read **Oliver Twist** the more struck he was by Dickens's ability to paint scenes from low life without coarseness or vulgarity. "He has almost always the good taste to stop at the proper point, and to pass over all circumstance which ... though belonging to low life, and therefore natural to it, would be intolerable and offensive in narration." While other writers presenting similar material, he added, violate "this rule," Dickens exhibits tact and selects scenes that are not "totally insufferable" (3 June 1838, p. 174).

After an earlier column compared Dickens's art to David Tenniers's (6 May 1838), the author of the 8 July 1838 review of magazines called Dickens "the Wilkie of the cottage, the lodging-house, and the tavern club." In drawing scenes and images belonging to this sphere of life, he declared, Dickens "has no competitor." Because Dickens is so thoroughly acquainted with his subjects and has observed them "so closely and so minutely," he can present them to readers "with all the fidelity and freshness of nature." "This is his first excellence as a writer:--his talent of exact observation" and his habit of describing what he sees "strongly and picturesquely." And in his ability to convey sympathetically the character and feeling of the scenes before him, "he occasionally mounts very high towards the dignity of poetry," wrote the reviewer. By identifying with his characters and thus giving them "a further air of truth and nature," he exhibits "a higher talent than what belongs to any other novelist of the day" (p. 214).

15. [Lister, Thomas Henry]. "**Sketches** (1st and 2nd Series), **Pickwick, Nickleby,** and **Oliver Twist.**" **Edinburgh Review,** 68 (October 1838), 75-97. Extract in Collins's **Dickens: The Critical Heritage** (IX. 39), pp. 71-77.

A wide-ranging discussion of Dickens's characteristics as a writer, commenting on his remarkable powers of observation, exuberant humor, and closeness to Hogarth in his satire and "keen and practical view of life." Lister also considers Dickens's progress as a novelist, evidence of which he sees in **Oliver Twist,** even though the story remains incomplete at the time of the review. "There is more interest in the story," he writes, "a plot better arranged, characters more skilfully and carefully drawn, without any diminution of spirit, and without that tone of humorous exaggeration which, however amusing, sometimes detracts too much from the truthfulness of many portions of the **Pickwick Papers.**" After reading this review, Dickens wrote to Forster, "It is all even I could wish, and what more can I say!" (P, I, 438).

16. "**Oliver Twist.**" The Athenaeum (17 November 1838), pp. 824-25.

Reprints almost verbatim and without comments Sikes's arrival at Jacob's Island and Dickens's narrative of the events that lead to his death.

17.   "Oliver Twist." The Atlas, 17 November 1838, pp. 729-31.

    Recounts in some detail "the main features" of Oliver Twist and analyzes
at length the book's construction and the extent of its fidelity to nature. Of
the first, the reviewer argues that the demand of the serial for excitement
and incident inhibits the gradual development of character "in a natural
way." At the same time, he concedes, the book's melodramatic energy
releases a "wild flood of action and passion" capable of carrying along the
reader in a manner unparalleled since the romances of Victor
Hugo.
    Praise for the life-like reality of much of Oliver Twist follows this
criticism of the work's construction. The reviewer commends Dickens's
ability to portray the features of real life with "the minuteness and felicity of
Ostade," although he finds Dickens's departure from his opening focus on the
workhouse system unfortunate. The narrative, he objects, expands into "a
sort of thieves' romance," revealing a taste for the Newgate Calendar that
becomes at last "painful and oppressive," especially after Nancy's attempt to
help Mr. Brownlow find Monks. "What follows," he writes, "is revolting."
Curiously, the reviewer admits that the description of the murder, Sikes's
flight, and his consuming terror possesses more power than any similar
passages he knows "in the whole range of English fiction." But he finds one
paramount objection to the whole: "it introduces us to a description of life
which, however faithfully pourtrayed [sic], is indescribably repulsive and
demoralizing."

18.   "Oliver Twist." The Globe, 17 November 1838.

    Cited by Tillotson (IX. 40) but unavailable for annotation.

19.   "Oliver Twist." Naval and Military Gazette, 17 November 1838.

    Cited by Tillotson (IX. 40) but unavailable for annotation.

20.   [Forster, John]. "Oliver Twist." The Literary Examiner, The
      Examiner, 18 November 1838, pp. 723-25.

    Pending a critical examination of the entire novel next week (IX. 25),
Forster provides a long extract from the closing scenes of the third volume
and praises the murder of Nancy as a tragic picture of common life
"transcending anything of the sort with which we are acquainted throughout
the entire range of fiction." In these scenes, Forster continues, the reader
will find a fearful delineation of the terror and retribution implicit in the
novel, whose effect achieves "a nobler moral" than few other works have
done--"not simply the scorn of vice but the 'pity of it' too"--Forster explains,
adding: "Vice loses nothing of its grossness, and virtue nothing of her triumph."

21.   "Oliver Twist." Morning Advertiser, 20 November 1838.

    Cited by Tillotson (IX. 40), but unavailable for annotation.

22.   "Oliver Twist." The Sun, 20 November 1838.

    A short notice concentrating mainly on the events of the close of the
novel. The writer compares the "truly powerful piece of description" of Fagin
awaiting death with Hugo's "Last Days of a Condemned Criminal" and judges

Dickens's writing superior because he is "equally vigorous, and not half so exaggerated" as Hugo. The reviewer also notes that Dickens gives no reason for Fagin's execution, although all readers, he writes, agree "that he deserves it." Favorable comparisons with Fielding's Jonathan Wild follow, with praise given to Dickens for making his villains more impelling by leavening their wickedness with touches of "real humanity" and humor and feeling, the evidence of "a man of superior powers of mind," he concludes. For further comments on Hugo and Dickens, see XIII. 139.

23.   "Oliver Twist." Literary Gazette: Journal of the Belles Lettres, 24 November 1838, p. 741.

Extolls Dickens's ability in Oliver Twist to raise up and embody "a number of original human beings in so substantial a form" that they immediately become known to the reader, an achievement without parallel, the reviewer thinks, "if we except, perhaps, the mighty names of Shakespeare and Scott." By peopling "the regions of the imagination" with a crowd of new, palpable characters, he continues, Dickens sets himself far above all contemporary novelists, achieving in two or three years what Richardson, Fielding, and Smollett accomplished in a lifetime.

24.   ["Oliver Twist"]. Spectator, 11 (24 November 1838), 1114-16. Extract in Collins's Dickens: The Critical Heritage (IX. 39), pp. 42-43.

An intelligent response to the novel as a whole which attempts to specify some of the work's weaknesses and identify the reasons for its success and popularity. The author argues that despite Dickens's deficiencies in narrative, his reliance on improbabilities, and other structural flaws, the parts move readers and affect them profoundly because the descriptions are "often powerful" and the author's command of language "considerable." This reviewer ranks Dickens far above Hook, Ainsworth, and Bulwer, his immediate competitors, and attributes some of Dickens's success to "extrinsic factors." Among them, he notes the advantage of part publication, which gives the press something "to fasten upon," resulting in "a score of 'notices'" for Dickens, while other writers, "however taking, only receive one." Dickens's ability to avail himself of any temporary interest, he thinks, also accounts for some of his appeal. As examples, the reviewer cites how Dickens hit at Laing (XVI. 8 and 21) "whilst that functionary's pranks were full in the public mind," chimed in with the popular clamor against the new Poor Law, drew on public inquests for information about "scenes of pauper misery," and even flattered the opponents of capital punishment in some points "thrown out" by Fagin.

25.   [Forster, John]. "Oliver Twist." In "The Literary Examiner." The Examiner, 25 November 1838, pp. 740-41.

A confident expression of Dickens's genius and popularity based on a review of the three-volume edition of 1838. Forster states that the literati of England, America, France, and Germany all share this view, admiring, as he does, the enviable lot of one so young, popular, and prosperous who "[does] good." Who, like Dickens, he asks, "ever promised to bring reforms into the Augean stables of mercenary schools and prisons and workhouses, by the apparently light arms of humour and the gentle ones of pathos?"
    This full notice also comments on elements of Dickens's style, noting how he combines "solid, existing, every-day life" with wit and tenderness, and, as if superseding "the old petrifying process of the magician in the Arabian

tale," makes palpable England's prisons and parish government. After quoting passages illustrative of "the healthy wisdom" of Dickens's philosophy, Forster ends with a long extract from Chapter 50, in which Sikes seeks asylum with his hunted companions. The fear and horror his return inspires, and the sudden resistance of the naturally good-hearted Charley Bates to the murderer, writes Forster, constitute "some of the most beautiful reliefs and self-assertions of humanity even in scenes and among characters so debased."

26.   "Oliver Twist; or, The Parish Boy's Progress." Weekly Dispatch, 25 November 1838.

Random comments on the appearance of the novel in three volumes, a welcome alternative, the reviewer thinks, to its issue in "detached monthly parts." The reviewer faults Dickens for his monotonous depiction of lower-class life but praises his mastery of the tender and the terrible before quoting a long extract from the murder of Nancy. He finds this incomparable scene beyond the skill of any living author and notes how Dickens rendered the episode with "the pen of the Dutch or Flemish painter."

27.   "Oliver Twist." The Observer, 26 November 1838, p. 2.

A short notice of the novel, praising Dickens for his pathos and for the fidelity to nature evident in his characters. The writer also comments on the story's conclusion, finding in the winding up evidence of "great judgment." A generous summary of the last third of the novel follows, to which the reviewer adds his admiration for Fagin's trial and last night in the condemned cell, calling the episode "Perhaps ... one of the best scenes in the book."

28.   "Oliver Twist." Sunday Times, 2 December 1838, p. 3.

Calls Oliver Twist "unquestionably the best" of all Dickens's productions, a work whose scenes are portrayed "with the skill and discrimination of a master-hand" and whose characters are sketched with force and fidelity. The reviewer wishes that Dickens included less of the vices of mankind and more of the virtues, but lays aside these objections, ending his short notice with a generous extract from the murder of Nancy, Sikes's flight, and his final moments.

29.   "Oliver Twist." The Court Journal, 15 December 1838, p. 850.

A brief, enthusiastic catalogue of all the effects of the novel the reviewer finds pleasing. The writer comments on how Dickens's humor, pathos, portraits of striking characters, and "sympathies with everything" will never tire his readers, who can never have too much of such qualities in the books they read. The better we become acquainted with such characteristics, he suggests, "then the better are likely to be our hearts."

30.   "Oliver Twist." Dublin University Magazine, 12 (December 1838), 699-723.

Acknowledges Dickens's success in "laying hold of the public mind" but warns that his sovereignty may be short if he tempts fate "by too frequent demands upon the public favour." Putting works like Oliver Twist before readers "in disjointed form," warns the reviewer, may lead to the erosion of Dickens's popularity. Scenes in the novel, he thinks, are "carelessly thrown together" and "framed with little regard to mutual dependence or sequence," making the whole singularly unskillful and overdependent on improbable events.

Despite these defects, the writer finds ample evidence of Dickens's qualifications for a writer of fiction. Dickens possesses the ability to transcribe faithfully his own "close and accurate observations of nature"; he also displays to a remarkable extent the power of looking beyond the mere surface of characters, eliciting from "the thick darkness of the deepest human baseness and degradation faint sparkings of a better spirit." Lengthy quotations from Oliver Twist document the reviewer's contentions.

31. "Review of Books." Magazine of Domestic Economy and Family Review, December 1838, p. 185.

Listed by Tillotson in her Appendix on the reception of Oliver Twist in the Clarendon edition (IX. 40), this essay includes a single paragraph on Oliver Twist, in which the writer praises Dickens's ability to describe things "as they are" and also make "the soul and spirit which gave them character" as manifest as their outward forms. The life that is written of in Oliver Twist, the reviewer continues, "has a powerful spell for the heart; and while it provokes laughter at one time, and weeping another, teaches it no unimportant lesson and wisdom."

32. "Oliver Twist." Monthly Review, 3 (January 1839), 29-41. For a reprint of the text, see The Dickensian, 1 (February 1905), 35-40.

Finds many features and excellencies to admire in Oliver Twist, but in a determined effort to speak moderately about its merits the reviewer also gives equal weight to his sense of Dickens's failings. He finds the plot powerful but too sketchy, the style occasionally too labored, and the subjects and Dickens's manner of treating them such that they exclude him "from the highest rank of our moral fictionalists." Voicing skepticism about Oliver Twist's continuing appeal, the reviewer speculates that the vogue for the novel among Londoners will probably decline, so that the work will add little to the future reputation of England's fiction.

33. [Ford, Richard]. "Oliver Twist." Quarterly Review, 64 (June 1839), 83-102. Extract in Collins's Dickens: The Critical Heritage (IX. 39), pp. 81-86.

Sounds at length several negative notes about Oliver Twist. Ford remarks on the weakness of the descriptive writing once the action leaves London, the "unendurable" appearance of the novel's genteel folks, Dickens's particularity for slang, and his tendency to deal only with "the outcasts of humanity." Ford also pronounces the attacks against the Poor Law and workhouse system unfair, arguing that Dickens not only exaggerates but assaults non-existent abuses. On the literary side, Ford faults the story's many improbabilities, Dickens's lack of realism in his treatment of Oliver, and the book's negative effects. These, he explains, arise when an author exhibits "enormities" to the young, thus perverting their education and deadening and extinguishing "those pure feelings which form the best guides through life." Ford, however, finds great power in the depiction of Nancy and Sikes and praises the account of Sikes's flight as first-rate writing. Earlier, Ford also commended Dickens for opening up a new world to his readers by showing one half of London how the other half lives in "the regions about Saffron Hill."

34.   D[wight], J[ohn] S[ullivan]. "Oliver Twist." The Christian Examiner and
      General Review, 27 (18 November 1839), 161-74.

A long, sympathetic response to the novel which draws heavily on the
concepts of the English Romantic poets and critics and suggests, to some
extent, why Dickens appealed to American Transcendentalists. Dwight
praises Dickens's powers of observation and description, attributing the
novelist's ability to present "things as they are" to his gift of shutting out "the
dogging phantom of [his] own egotism" and of entering every little group or
corner, living in it "till it becomes a world to him." Although these pictures,
he concedes, "show more of fancy than of imagination," both faculties operate
in Dickens's mind, Fancy playing "over the surface of Fact" and Imagination
animating his materials "into a living whole, so that his work shall seem ... a
necessary product out of the Soul of all things."
     Dwight also sees Oliver Twist as "a romance which is purely modern," one
whose poetic materials come from "about our feet" instead of from the
classics, people of rank or genius, or "events world-renowned." Rather, we
have been led through "the labyrinths of a great city," he writes, "by "one who
dares to look into the rotten parts of the world" without forgetting "its beauty
as a whole" and his own faith in human nature, "whose meanness he knows so
well." Dickens's humor provides further evidence of this outlook, resting,
Dwight thinks, on the protection of a healthy Christian faith and an optimistic
view of life. These same convictions, he argues, also shape the novel's moral
tone and tendency, whose inference Dwight finds "inevitable." Oliver Twist
"shows us how much crime in England is a direct and necessary product of
their oppressive Poor-Law system, and how crime and depravity everywhere
come, more than we think, from our want of sympathy with the poor, our
small respect for man as man, our violation of the natural pledge of
brotherhood. This drives men into iniquity."

35.   [Thackeray, W. M.]. "Charles Dickens and His Works." Fraser's
      Magazine, 21 (April 1840), 381-400. Extract in Collins's Dickens: The
      Critical Heritage (IX. 39), pp. 86-90.

Thackeray turns an intelligent, perceptive eye on Dickens's novels up to
1840, expressing reservations about his art, especially his apparent lack of
power to support a character consistently through more than three or four
scenes. Thackeray offers a lengthy analysis of Mr. Pickwick to demonstrate
his point that the protagonist begins "like a fool, a butt, and a blockhead" and
ends by inspiring "general respect and gratitude." Such conversions, he thinks,
prove too abrupt, a far remove from the art of Cervantes, Fielding, and
Goldsmith, all of whom created good men buffeted by misfortune but never
ridiculed their characters and made them, like Pickwick, jackasses who
became heroes.
     This same defect, Thackeray argues, mars Oliver Twist. Mr. Brownlow
begins as a "dreamy and stupid old man," who later displays inconsistent
qualities. He not only acts with "great goodness of heart" but also reveals
"unwearied zeal" in unravelling the intricacies of a complicated plot and
"determined activity" in pursuing a murderer to his last refuge. His behavior
seems all the more incongruous, Thackeray adds, if, as the plates would lead
us to believe, he is the "half blind and half childish" magistrate who prevents
Oliver from being indentured to the master-sweep.
     The novel's protagonist also upsets Thackeray, who finds intense folly in
Dickens's use of the pupil of the beadle, the undertaker, and the fence "as a
model of virtue, elegance, and refinement." Similar absurdities occur in

Nancy, who enters volume one as a prostitute talking "the common slang of London" and exits two volumes later speaking "more picked and perfumed sentences of sentimentality" than any other heroine "that ever went mad in white satin."

Such criticisms accord well with the realistic theory of fiction Thackeray formulated before he wrote Vanity Fair in 1847-48 and come as no surprise, unlike his remark in this essay that "when Boz meddles with the law, he is always unfortunate." Taking an example from **Oliver Twist,** Thackeray analyses Kags's comment in Chapter 50 that the prosecution "can prove Fagin an accessory before the fact" and hang him for the murder of Nancy. Far from providing a legal justification for consigning Fagin to the gallows, this contention, Thackeray thinks, proves worthless in view of the facts. See also XVI. 3 and 4. All Fagin has done, any proper legal counsel would argue, is to report to Sikes what Noah Claypole told him. Furthermore, Fagin enjoins Sikes to be crafty and not too bold or too violent, prudent advice clearly suggesting no violence of any kind. As for the brief glance Fagin and Sikes exchange before the housebreaker leaves, it would be hard, Thackeray notes, "to make a villainous look matter of legal proof against a man." Yet even if the doctrine of looking murder while advising moderation constituted grounds for making one an accessory before the fact, Thackeray continues, the Crown would still have to prove its case against Fagin by finding a witness other than the defendant himself. "To the House of Commons alone," Thackeray points out, "does the power belong of examining prisoners for the purpose of eliciting evidence against themselves."

As a further instance of Dickens's apparent ignorance of Old Bailey practice, Thackeray cites the impropriety of permitting people to visit Fagin in the condemned cell shortly before his execution "to extort from him some document required in a legal investigation" by playing upon his fears.

Fagin goes to the gallows, Thackeray concludes, "to oblige tender-hearted students of the circulating libraries," who, reading Dickens's stories in parts, prove less demanding critics than fellow authors like Thackeray. The latter fully sympathizes with the difficulties imposed by the necessity of filling a certain quantity of pages a month, but thinks that "novel-writing by scraps against time" can never do Dickens or his readers justice.

36. [Forster, John]. "**Oliver Twist,** Third Edition, with Dickens's 1841 Preface." In "The Literary Examiner." **The Examiner,** 25 September 1841, p. 614.

Repeats an argument frequently urged by Forster in the pages of **The Examiner** that **Oliver Twist,** unlike some of its imitators and contrary to the opinions of its critics, has a strong moral purpose. "The intention of this book," writes Forster, "is vindicated, and its grave moral tone effectively asserted, in a new introduction by the author," most of which he cites. Forster also adds that whoever reads **Oliver Twist** "will find its moral in his own kinder heart, in his larger sympathy, in the new feeling of consideration and charity with which it will dispose him to regard the ignorance, the vices, and the sufferings, of a great class of his neglected and despised fellow-creatures in this immense city."

37. "Boz versus Dickens." **Parker's London Magazine,** 2 (February 1845), 122-28.

Uses "Boz" to signify Dickens's works up to **Nicholas Nickleby** and

"Dickens" to refer to everything he wrote since that novel. This classification serves also to indicate the writer's preference for the earlier fiction, whose subject matter and style he wholly approves of when "Boz" retains control and whose weaknesses after **Nicholas Nickleby** he attributes to "Dickens" gaining the upper hand. The earlier works, he explains, describe scenes and characters that existed and avoid the labored quality he perceives in "Dickens's" later style. The reviewer also points to several instances of how the creations of "Boz" are "adapted and altered by Dickens." Illegitimate boys like Oliver are found in **Nicholas Nickleby** and **Barnaby Rudge,** undertakers reappear in **Martin Chuzzlewit,** and Fagin's miserliness resurfaces in Quilp and his cowardice in Dennis the hangman. Perhaps the strongest likeness, he adds, can be seen in the resemblance of Sikes's flight to Jonas Chuzzlewit's, both murderers fleeing from their crimes. The reviewer concludes by arguing that these self "plagiarisms" mark a deterioration in "Dickens" and document his sense that the novelist has written "too fast ... and has written himself out."

38. "The Collected Works of Charles Dickens." **Quarterly Review,** 35 (1 January 1862), 135-59.

A retrospective view of Dickens's fiction to 1862, which reflects on the reasons for the popularity of his novels. Writing about **Oliver Twist,** the reviewer offers various conjectures for the story's wide circulation and the hold it took "on the popular mind." The merits of the work account for much of its success, particularly "the stern power of the scenes in Saffron Hill and Jacob's Island" and the pathos of the dying mother in the workhouse and Nancy's yielding "to gentler and better feelings." Other factors, the reviewer thinks, also played a significant role. Because the reading public was satisfied with "silly, fashionable novels," they turned with relief from silver forks to the toasting fork and frying pan in Fagin's den. Furthermore, when Dickens denounced the tyranny of parochial authorities public interest in the old and new Poor Laws "was at fever heat." Thus the novel, he concludes, came home to readers of all classes, while "the picture of the young thieves and their trainers" led the public mind further in the direction it had already taken: "that of inquiring into the education of the lowest orders."

39. Collins, Philip. "Oliver Twist (1837-9)." In his **Dickens:. The Critical Heritage.** London: Routledge and Kegan Paul, 1971, pp. 42-45, and passim.

An anthology of 168 items chosen mainly but not exclusively from Victorian periodical reviews of Dickens's works. Collins successfully illustrates a broad range of responses to all Dickens's novels, including also his Christmas books and non fiction. To achieve this, Collins reprints extracts rather than essays in their entirety, a procedure which increases the volume's range but inevitably misrepresents a reviewer's argument and omits details of significance to some readers.

The selections for **Oliver Twist** (only four) provide only partial coverage of this novel, although the careful inquirer into **Oliver Twist**'s reception needs to look at the reviews Collins includes that discuss the early novels as a group. Collins contributes a short but informative introductory essay about the history of Dickens's critical reputation, one which offers many useful hints for possible lines of inquiry and indicates deftly the complexity and range of critical comment evoked by Dickens's fiction. Where possible, Collins indentifies anonymous contributors; Robert Patten adds a brief

Appendix about the sales of Dickens's works during the nineteenth century.
For Patten's other work on this subject see also XII. 163.

40.   Tillotson, Kathleen. "The Reception of the Novel in 1837-1846."
      Appendix F. In the Clarendon edition of **Oliver Twist** (II. 48), pp.
      398-400.

Provides the most nearly definitive listing of reviews of **Oliver Twist** to
date, although the editor's claim in 1966 to have made "a complete survey of
English periodicals" represents an obvious exaggeration. Tillotson clearly
meant English literary periodicals, whose contents she had completely
examined, and not those read by "The Unknown Public," as Wilkie Collins later
characterized the readers of periodicals scholars have only recently begun to
acknowledge and to survey. Tillotson notes that she had not searched for
American reviews, for notices in foreign periodicals, and for reviews in
provincial newspapers. Instead, she concentrated on London newspapers,
general notices of Dickens's early works, reviews of various serial numbers of
Oliver Twist, and essays on the novel's three-volume edition of 1838.
Between February 1837 and November 1839 an average of five reviews a
month appeared in various London newspapers, commenting on **Oliver Twist**
and often reprinting long extracts. Repeated notices by a single periodical
naturally occurred less frequently, although Tillotson notes Forster's
extensive coverage of the novel in several numbers of the **Examiner.** Among
the other sections of the Appendix, one lists attacks on the Newgate novel,
with which several reviewers aligned **Oliver Twist,** and another gathers
informal comments on **Oliver Twist** in contemporary letters, diaries, and
speeches. **Oliver Twist,** as this Appendix documents, drew responses from
almost every quarter of the British public. In part, the proliferation
originates in the enormous increase in newspapers and periodicals early in the
nineteenth century and in the habit of listing, often in a perfunctory way, the
contents of the major literary periodicals as they were published at the
beginning of each month. Credit also falls to Dickens, who wrote a novel
many reviewers recognized as an advance on **The Pickwick Papers** in
constructional skill and as a work of greater earnestness and purpose than its
enormously successful predecessor.

41.   Wall, Stephen, ed. "Part One: Contemporaneous Criticism." In his
      Charles Dickens: A Critical Anthology. Harmondsworth: Penguin,
      1970, passim.

Critical responses to Dickens's works chronologically arranged and
interspersed with passages from Dickens's letters addressing critical issues.
Wall includes an extract from Lister (IX. 15), Thackeray's **Catherine** (X. 4),
and Horne (XII. 11).

X. OLIVER TWIST AND THE NEWGATE NOVEL (CHRONOLOGICAL LISTING)

1. Fielding, Henry. Preface to **Miscellanies** (1743). Ed. Henry Knight Miller. **Miscellanies,** Vol. I. The Wesleyan Edition of the Works of Henry Fielding. Oxford: Clarendon Press, 1972, pp. 8-10.

Fielding's Preface to the three volumes he published in 1743 as his **Miscellanies** discusses the various subjects he treated on that occasion, including his **Life of Mr. Jonathan Wild the Great** in the third volume. Introducing his satire of Sir Robert Walpole in the Preface, Fielding notes that while "some very Shameless Writers" have treated Newgate "as no other than Human Nature with its Mask off," the serious moralist, like himself, may be excused "for suspecting, that the Palaces of the Great are often no other than Newgate with the Mask on." Nothing is more likely, Fielding concludes, to raise an honest man's indignation higher than the realization that "the same Morals should be in one Place attended with all the imaginable Misery and Infamy, and in the other, with the highest Luxury and Honour." And yet, he adds, while "Cruelty, Lust, Avarice, Rapine, Insolence, Hypocrisy, Fraud, and Treachery" characterize both places, "all these Ingredients glossed over with Wealth and a Title, have been treated with the highest Respect and Veneration in the one, while one or two of them have been condemned to the Gallows in the other."

As a reader of Fielding, Dickens knew his **Miscellanies** and appears to draw either directly or less consciously on Fielding's comments on the design of **Jonathan Wild** when critics of the Newgate novel forced him to defend himself in 1841. "Nor did I doubt that there lay festering in Saint Giles's as good materials towards the truth as any flaunting in Saint James's," wrote Dickens in his first Preface to **Oliver Twist,** an aggressive counter attack which quotes Fielding directly and makes an argument recalling that of his predecessor. Unlike the writer in the **Athenaeum** (X. 5), anti-Newgate reviewers frequently overlooked the fact that stories about criminals could have a moral purpose, seeing merely dangerous sensationalism and ignoring the design Forster (XII. 7) saw in **Oliver Twist, Gil Blas, The Beggar's Opera,** and **Jonathan Wild.** "Familiar with the lowest kind of abasement of life," writes Forster, "the knowledge is used, by [Dickens and Le Sage, Gay, and Fielding], to teach what constitutes its essential elevation; and, by the very coarseness and vulgarity of the materials employed, we measure the gentlemanliness and beauty of the work that is done." Moral quacks and imposters, adds Forster, will always complain that such writing is immoral; but for the rest of the world "it will teach the still invaluable lesson of what men ought to be from what they are." For Dickens and Gay, see XIII. 136.

2. [Thackeray, W.M.]. "Hints for a History of Highwaymen." **Fraser's Magazine,** 9 (March 1834), 279-87.

An early statement by Thackeray about his sense of the danger of glamorizing highwaymen and criminals. Thackeray makes no objection in principle to using material from the records of the Old Bailey, which he grants may be striking, interesting, and affecting. "Man any where," he writes, "and under any circumstances, is an object of deep and appalling interest, and from erring man examples of the highest moment have been ever drawn." But writers who focus on criminals, cautions Thackeray, must proceed carefully, displaying the villain "as he really is in action and in principle," conducting his research cooly and skeptically, and taking care to discriminate "between individual guilt and the community of error." Thackeray's remarks, made in a sharp attack on Charles Whitehead's **Lives and Exploits of English Highwaymen, Pirates and Robbers** (1834), reveal him almost three years before the serial version of **Oliver Twist** began as an articulate and outspoken opponent of the vogue for "gallows literature."

3. _____. "Horae Catnachianae: A Dissertation on Ballads, with a Few Unnecessary Remarks on Jonathan Wild, John Sheppard, Paul Clifford, and ----Fagin, Esqrs." Fraser's Magazine, 19 (April 1839), 407-24.

This essay constitutes the first of Thackeray's sustained attacks on the "School of Criminal Romance," a genre literary historians trace to Bulwer Lytton's **Paul Clifford** (1830), Eugene Aram (1832), and **Ernest Maltravers** (1837) and follow through Harrison Ainsworth's Rookwood (1834) and **Jack Sheppard** (1839) and Dickens's **Oliver Twist**. In this spirited polemic, Thackeray states a position to which he remains loyal throughout the campaign he conducted in **Fraser's** against the literature of the gallows. Dickens and Bulwer, he writes, are "perfectly absurd and unreal" when they descend from their natural sphere to indulge the public with pictures of low life because their sympathetic portraits of criminals as good-hearted young men harassed by misfortune and persecuted by an uncomprehending society gravely mislead readers. If people really want to learn about "the ways of cut-throats, burglars, women of bad life, Jew oldsclothesmen, and others," writes Thackeray, they should avoid the "counterfeits" of the novelists and go to the real source: penny newspapers and popular ballads. Let readers try the cheap papers sold at Mr. Catnach's emporium in Monmouth Street, Seven Dials, he suggests. In them "there is more information about thieves, ruffians, swindlers of both sexes, more real vulgarity, more tremendous slang, more unconscious, honest, blackguard NATURE, in fact, than Mr. Dickens will ever give to the public."

Thackeray entertains no proposal to muzzle the expression of this depraved taste; but gentlemen and men of genius, he argues, should teach the public something better. Thackeray concludes by pointing out that "At one time the literary fashion ran entirely on Grosvenor Square; at present it has taken up its abode in St. Giles's." Both social extremes, he agrees, furnish examples of human nature, which does, to be sure, "sometimes form monsters, but the world is not peopled with such: nor should the world of fiction produce them, except in very small proportion, if it would aim at copying nature."

4. _____. Catherine: A Story. Fraser's Magazine, 19 (May 1839), 604-17, 694-709; 20 (July 1839), 98-112, 224-32, 531-48; and 21 (January 1840), 106-15, 200-12. Reprinted in The Oxford Thackeray, Vol. III. Ed. with an Introduction by George Saintsbury. London: Oxford Univ. Press, [1908].

Thackeray's "horrific" account of the life of Catherine Hayes, a real murderer whose history he took from the **Newgate Calendar**. Thackeray retells her story under the pseudonym "Ikey Solomons, Esqr., Junior," deliberately imitating "the bombastic fiction" of the day, whose injurious influences he tried to counteract by exposing Catherine Hayes for what she was: a wretched woman utterly devoid of heroic or romantic qualities.

Thackeray sets out to achieve this end by writing realistically about the exploits of his protagonist and by reminding readers in frequent asides that his rogues are real rogues, not honest men, contrary to the way a "clever class of novelists" often shows villains performing virtuous acts. Don't let us have "any juggling and thimblerigging with virtue and vice here," he counsels readers. His thieves are not "dandy, poetical, rose-water thieves," or "whitewashed saints, like poor 'Biss Dadsy' in 'Oliver Twist.'" Later, Thackeray returns to this point, expressing annoyance with Dickens and Ainsworth not so much because they glamorized criminals but because they failed to represent them as complete human beings. "As no writer can or dare tell the whole truth concerning them, and faithfully explain their vices, there is no need to give ex-parte statements of their virtues."

Thackeray may have had more than one reason for the ridicule he heaps on Dickens, Ainsworth, and Bulwer, but the basis of his quarrel remains clear. Public taste by 1840, "gorged with blood and foul Newgate garbage," needed a corrective, he argued, one which induced in readers "a wholesome nausea" for crime instead of sympathy. As part of this aim, Thackeray also tried to expose "the errors" of novelists who falsified crime and thereby endangered public safety by lulling readers into accepting thieves, murderers, and prostitutes instead of abominating "all peoples of this kidney." Jonathan Wild and The Beggar's Opera worked because each was based on a satirical purpose; but "in the sorrows of Nancy and the exploits of Sheppard" Thackeray found no such moral. Occasionally, however, he betrayed a "sneaking kindness" for Oliver Twist and Jack Sheppard and admitted to feeling a vicarious excitement when reading Dickens's novel. "The power of the writer is so amazing," he conceded, "that the reader at once becomes his captive, and must follow him whithersoever he leads." But the final result, concluded Thackeray, proved disturbing when all Dickens's heroes "stepped from the novel onto the stage," titillating the whole London public, "from peers to chimney-sweeps," with a set of ruffians "whose occupations are thieving, murder, and prostitution."

Readers wishing to sample the full weight of Thackeray's anti-Newgate remarks should read Catherine, especially "Another Last Chapter," in the Oxford or the Furness edition, both of which follow the text as it was published intermittently in Fraser's Magazine from May 1839 through February 1840. Virtually all other reprints follow the practice, established by the first book edition of Catherine in 1869, of omitting the most ghastly episodes and some of Thackeray's comments about contemporary writers. For additional comments on Catherine, see Lucas (XII. 142).

5.   "Jack Sheppard." The Athenaeum, 26 October 1839, pp. 803-05.

Makes a distinction between novelists who pander to a depraved taste for stories about criminals and those who use Newgate material for serious purposes. The reviewer attacks Jack Sheppard as an example of the first kind--a bad book got up for a bad public--and distinguishes Dickens's work from that of imitators like Ainsworth, arguing that Oliver Twist belongs to a tradition established by Fielding and Gay. While the novel depicts "scenes of hardened vice," Dickens, he suggests, is guided in Oliver Twist "by a high moral object." Like Fielding, he enlists our best feelings and leaves readers "wiser and better for the perusal of his tale."

6.   [Forster, John]. "Jack Sheppard." In "The Literary Examiner."
      The Examiner, 3 November 1839, pp. 691-93.

Sets forth in unmistakably blunt terms the basis of Forster's opposition to
Ainsworth's sensational use of Newgate material in fiction. What offends
Forster is not the subject of **Jack Sheppard** but the book's complete absence
of a moral perspective. Earlier writers like Le Sage, Gay, and Fielding, he
argues, drew on thieves and low life "only to pull down the false pretensions
of the high." Others--read Dickens--"sought to discover the soul of goodness
in things evil." Ainsworth, by contrast, thrusts crime--"bare, rascally,
unmitigated, ferocious crime"--constantly before readers, so that the interest
of the novel hangs solely on the gallows.

This review conspicuously ignores **Oliver Twist** by name. But by
demonstrating how bad **Jack Sheppard** was, Forster sought to separate the two
works. Although circumstantially linked in the public mind by their serial
publication in **Bentley's Miscellany** and by Cruikshank's illustrations, each is
quite distinct in moral intention. When Dickens wrote his 1841 Preface (X.
14) he made explicit what Forster only hints at here. For a possible
explanation of Forster's hostility to **Jack Sheppard**, see Ellis (X. 23).

7. "Mr. Jack Sheppard Ainsworth, and the Fair Companion of his Midnight
    Revels." In **Paul Pry, the Reformer of the Age,** 15 December 1839, p.
    673.

An angry attack on **Jack Sheppard** and other crime novels recently
published in **Bentley's Miscellany** and other journals. The reviewer
recommends censoring "the vicious tendency of periodical literature" as a
means of controlling works that venerate criminals. "But whilst such
atrocious libels upon decency as Jack Sheppard and Oliver Twist is [sic]
allowed to emanate from the press," without the slightest intention of the
powers responsible for the rectitude and morals of the state to control them,
England, he concludes, "will, and must be called the school of thieves."

8. L'Estrange, A.G., ed. **The Life of Mary Russell Mitford, Related in
    a Selection from her Letters to her Friends.** London: Richard
    Bentley, 1870, III, 105-06.

In a letter to Elizabeth Barrett, dated 3 January 1840, Mitford wrote how
when reading **Jack Sheppard** she had been struck by the great danger, "in
those times," of representing authority "so constantly and fearfully in the
wrong," as Ainsworth and other novelists had done recently. Ainsworth, she
agreed, wrote with no such design, but the effect of his work, she thought, "on
the millions who see it represented at the minor theatres" is dangerous
because they cannot distinguish between "now and a hundred years back."
"Seriously," she continued,"what things are these--the Jack Sheppards, and
Squeers, and Oliver Twists, and Michael Armstrongs--all the worse for the
power which, except for the last, the others contain! Grieviously the worse!"

9. "Jack Sheppard." **Dearden's Miscellany,** 3 (January 1840), 66.

Describes Ainsworth's novel as the climax "of what we may call the
gallows-school of novelists," amongst whom the reviewer includes Dickens.
While he concedes that the latter is "a man of decided genius," capable of
"masterly strokes of pathos and contrast," he nevertheless objects strenuously
to **Oliver Twist.** In that clever tale, he writes, "we were introduced to the
very lowest characters in their most revolting state." For the reviewer, **Jack
Sheppard** represents an even greater excess, which, if it proves popular, he
adds, will justify the publication of a new edition of the Newgate Calendar

"as the historical basis of all that shall in future be written, and a convenient book of reference for every reading room."

10.   "Novel Writing and Newspaper Criticism." **The Monthly Chronicle,** 5 (January-June 1840), 33-38.

Criticizes the role of newspapers for puffing novels and failing, in their brief reviews, to do more than simply quote a few striking passages, thereby conferring transitory popularity on works that should be ignored. "The tawdry sentiment ... of the fashionable novel, or the glaring situations and exaggerated horrors of the Newgate school, are as well fitted to catch the eye as the advertisements of Morrison's pills or Warren's blacking," the author argues. The writer also states his belief that the novelists themselves pander to a debased public taste, choosing either the charmed circles of Mayfair or "the murky dens of Field Lane and Mutton Hill" as settings for their novels. One consequence, he maintains, is that the "middle ground" is neglected, a failing, he writes, true even of Dickens.

11.   [Thackeray, W.M.]. "William Ainsworth and Jack Sheppard." **Fraser's Magazine,** 21 (February 1840), 227-45.

Chides Ainsworth for "'pampering the vanity which perpetuates the determination to crime,' by investing the low ruffians of the **Newgate Calendar,** and their profligate companions, with all the interest and the graces of romance," a charge Thackeray made several years earlier in a different context (X. 2 and 3). Thackeray argues that by metamorphosing Jack Sheppard and his likes and endowing them with "melodramatic virtues and splendors," novelists ran the risk of filling "many a juvenile aspirant" with the idea that housebreaking was an ennobling profession. No reference to **Oliver Twist** appears but Thackeray's concerns about the danger of glamorizing scoundrels in print who later turn up as heroes of the London stage were shared by others, as we know from the censorship of **Oliver Twist** and **Jack Sheppard** by the Lord Chamberlain. See VI. 60 and 61. Gay and Fielding, Thackeray argues, both used similar figures but never failed to present them critically. "We must insist upon it," Thackeray declares, "that our thieves are nothing more than thieves, whom it is hopeless to attempt gilding over with the graces and glories of chivalry."

12.   [Forster, John]. "Mr. Phillip's Defence of Courvoisier." The Examiner, 28 June 1840, p. 402.

A long article attacking Francois Benjamin Courvoisier's defense attorney for pleading for a man who had already confessed to murder--see X. 13--in which Forster continues to exonerate **Oliver Twist** indirectly by disassociating it from Newgate novels like **Jack Sheppard.** Forster cites Ainsworth's work in support of his point about the dangers of portraying criminals without moral seriousness by arguing that **Jack Sheppard** inspired Courvoisier to murder his employer. "In Courvoisier's second confession," Forster contends, "he ascribes his crimes to the perusal of that detestable book, 'Jack Sheppard;' and it certainly is a publication calculated to familiarise the mind with cruelties and to serve as the cut-throat's manual, or the midnight assassin's **vade-mecum.**" Curious it is, continues Forster, "that the very words used by Courvoisier, in describing the way in which he committed the murder--'I drew the knife across his throat'--are to be found in the horrid book alluded to, in Blueskin's murder of Mrs. Wood." Concludes

Forster: "If ever there was a publication that deserved to be burnt by the hands of the common hangman it is 'Jack Sheppard.'"

13.   [Thackeray, W. M.]. "Going to See a Man Hanged." **Fraser's Magazine,** 22 (August 1840), 150-58. Extract in Collins's **Dickens: The Critical Heritage** (IX. 39), pp. 45-46.

Thackeray's effective protest against public executions based on his own observation of the killing of Francois Benjamin Courvoisier, the Swiss valet convicted of the murder of his master, Lord William Russell. Thackeray witnessed the hanging on 6 July 1840, together with an estimated crowd of 40,000, whose unruly behavior and lust for blood lead him to reflect on the difference between the reality of the young men and women about him and the way "late fashionable novels" have presented "such personages." Noting a number of young girls in the mob whom Cruikshank and Dickens might have taken as a study for Nancy, Thackeray fulminates against the "fig- ments" novelists tell the public. "Boz, who knows life well, knows that his Miss Nancy is the most unreal fantastical personage possible," writes Thackeray.
        Dickens's artistic crime, Thackeray thought, lay in his refusing to show thieves' mistresses as they really are, a point Thackeray developed at greater length in his other attacks on the Newgate genre. Because propriety and decency do not allow an honest painter of human nature to tell the whole truth, Thackeray reasoned, he should, therefore, "leave the picture alone altogether." Omission, he thought, remained preferable to presenting "one or two favourable points as characterising the whole" when the whole, in reality, was rotten.

14.   Dickens, Charles. Preface to the Third Edition of **Oliver Twist.** See II. 10.

The fact that Ainsworth's **Jack Sheppard** appeared serially in **Bentley's Miscellany** with illustrations by Cruikshank, took crime for its subject, and was advertised with **Oliver Twist** by Richard Bentley, the publisher of both works, encouraged readers and perhaps reviewers to link the two. In private, Dickens complained bitterly to his solicitors, Smithson and Mitton, that Bentley had used his name and the names of some of his works "in an unwarrantable manner, dragging them before the public ... and hawking them about in a manner calculated to do me serious prejudice," as he wrote on 16 December 1839 (P, I, 617). In public, nearly a year and a half later, Dickens tried in his 1841 Preface to **Oliver Twist** to put as much distance as he could between his own "higher aims" and those of authors who threw around criminals "certain allurements and fascinations." In the same document, Dickens pointedly exonerated **Paul Clifford,** trying, at the same time, to dissociate himself from Ainsworth without naming his friend, whose **Jack Sheppard,** Dickens wrote, invested the road with crimson coats and ruffles and all the dash and freedom of "time out of mind."
        To further Dickens's aim, Forster began a campaign against **Jack Sheppard** in **The Examiner,** reviewing the book critically on 3 November 1839 and later coming to the defense of **Paul Clifford** on 20 November 1841 in the same journal. See X. 6 and 12 and X. 17. Comments by Thackeray, several reviewers noted in this section, and other contemporaries of Dickens qualify Forster's success in attempting to separate the two novels. To many people at the time **Oliver Twist** and **Jack Sheppard** formed a pair, whose success on stage was presumed sufficiently dangerous as to justify the Lord

Chamberlain's banning both plays, despite having licensed them, when public pressure on his office forced him to reconsider his judgment. See VI. 60 and 61.

15. Gaultier, Bon [pseud. Theodore Martin]. "Illustrations of the Thieves' Literature--No. 1, Flowers of Hemp; or, The Newgate Garland." Tait's Edinburgh Magazine, 8 (April 1841), 215-23.

A group of mildly satirical poems addressed to Bulwer, Ainsworth, and Dickens, authors whom the poet emulated in "twining a few poetic garlands" around "the mighty names that flash upon us from the squalor of the Chronicles of Newgate." Their purpose, the author quotes from a spurious Preface, is to "secure for the boozing ken and the gin palace that hold upon the general sympathies which has been too long monopolized by the cottage and the drawing room."

16. [Thackeray, W.M.]. "Literary Recipes: A Startling Romance." Punch, 1 (7 August 1841), 39. Extract in Collins's Dickens: The Critical Heritage (IX. 39), p. 46.

Thackeray's series deftly satirizing various currents in Victorian fiction, including what he sees as Dickens's variation of the Newgate theme in which "a small boy" is taken, stewed well down with vice, garnished with oaths and flash songs, and boiled in "a cauldron of crime and improbabilities." Served up with a couple of murders and a hanging, this same formula can also accommodate a beadle and a workhouse, the effect of which is to lose "the whole flavour of vice" by making the boy "turn out a perfect pattern." Altered thus, Thackeray pronounces the ingredients "Strongly recommended for weak stomachs." For the attribution of this piece to Thackeray, see Ellis (XI. 5), 1, 361.

17. [Forster, John]. "Sir Edward Bulwer and the 'Times.'" The Examiner, 20 November 1841, pp. 738-39.

Defends Bulwer against a recent attack on his work in the Times, whose reviewer had accused him of spreading "false moral principles" and demoralizing the country by advocating in Paul Clifford and Eugene Aram a marked sympathy for criminals. Forster supports Bulwer by distinguishing between novels like Jack Sheppard, which hold up cutthroats to admiration "for the qualities belonging to their throat-cutting, and to them only," and those which treat crime seriously in the manner of Fielding and Gay. Forster makes no reference to Oliver Twist; but by defending Paul Clifford in terms similar to those used by Dickens in his 1841 Preface to Oliver Twist, he extends Dickens's attack against those of his "jolter-headed enemies" who failed to distinguish between serious and trivial examinations of crime.

18. "Anti-Conningsby; or, The New Generation Grown Old. By an Embryo M.P." Fraser's Magazine, 31 (February 1845), 211-22.

The reviewer ends his long attack on this burlesque of Disraeli's Conningsby (1844) with his observations on the importance of reviving the old relation between the landlord and the poor in the country and some censorous remarks about humanity-mongering novelists. The latter, he believes, appeal "to the brutal passions of the rabble of towns in melodramas, and snobbish scriblements in the shape of journals and novels." In such works, he continues,

"Every effort is made to excite sympathy for the wrong-doer, for the violator of the law, for the offender against society. Thieves, and prostitutes, and poachers, and murderers, are elevated into heroes and heroines." No specific references to Oliver Twist occur, but one can infer from his catalogue of villains that he probably included Dickens among those "advocates of debauchery, filthiness, and crime," writers who appear to have forgotten that the law punishes for example's sake, and not from anger or vengeance.

19.   "The Writings of Charles Dickens." The North British Review, 3 (May 1845), 65-87.

Despite the writer's main focus on Martin Chuzzlewit and the Christmas Books of 1843 and 1844, he comments at length on various aspects of Oliver Twist. He praises the book as Dickens's most compact novel to date, pointing with approval to the narrative's rapid progress, to the way Dickens groups and contrasts his characters, and to the affinity between the novel and Sketches by Boz, from which Dickens has drawn "the material for all his best characters." The remaining comments, however, sound familiar alarms about the supposedly dangerous consequences of depicting villains and criminals. "Our moral health is dependent on the moral atmosphere we breathe," he declares, worrying that Dickens, an incipient Eugene Sue, will corrupt English readers and blunt their "perceptions of moral purity." The fact that Dickens's works were so widely performed throughout the country added to his concerns because "the better and more sober parts [of the novels] necessarily disappear" when they are adapted for the stage.

20.   "The Historical Romance." Blackwood's, 58 (September 1845), 341-56.

A long essay about the genre which laments how Ainsworth's novels and "the Jack Sheppard school of writing" have warped the noble tradition of historical writing Scott began. The writer makes no specific reference to Oliver Twist, but clearly he has the novel in mind when he laments the vogue for stories set amidst "the lowest walks of life," whose effects the author fears as contagious and corrupting. The writer concedes that able works about criminals can amuse but concludes that they do not "elevate and purify" the minds of their readers, that the slang of thieves and prostitutes, the flash words of receivers of stolen goods, and scenes depicting the haunts of murderers and burglars are far from edifying. "It might as well be said," he writes, "that the refuse of the common-sewers should be raked up and mixed with the garbage of the streets to form our daily food."

21.   [Aytoun, W.E.]. "Advice to an Intending Serialist." Blackwood's, 60 (November 1846), 590-605.

Humorous advice to an imaginary friend offering suggestions for successful serial composition. Among the hints Aytoun gives, he exhorts his friend to make money, to shift the scene frequently, and to ignore the old practice of rewarding virtue and punishing vice. But don't step so low, he warns, as to look to the Newgate Calendar for subjects or search St. Giles's for possible characters. "However fond I may be of female society, Miss Nancy is not quite the sort of person I should fancy to look in upon of an evening about tea-time." Similarly, he writes, "The fetid den of the Jew, the stinking cellar of the thief, the squalid attic of the prostitute, are not haunts for honest men, and the less that we know of them the better."

22. "Middle-Class Education in England." **The Cornhill Magazine,**
     10 (October 1864), 411.

The writer comments briefly on how **Oliver Twist** taught middle-class
readers about the great range of class differences "between the gentleman's
butler and the city Arab." Until we read **Oliver Twist,** the author continues,
"some of us were too like the grand folks who confound all below themselves
under one denomination."

23. Ellis, S.M. "Jack Sheppard in Literature and Drama." Epilogue in **Jack**
     Sheppard. Ed. Horace Bleackley. Notable British Trials Series.
     Edinburgh: William Hodge, 1933, pp. 64-126.

Ascribes Forster's hostility to **Jack Sheppard** to the jealousy he felt when
the sales of Ainsworth's novel surpassed and eclipsed those of **Oliver Twist,**
the work of Forster's "idol." Ellis writes that Ainsworth remained untroubled
and unharmed by the articles in **The Examiner** (X. 6, 12, and 17) because stage
versions of his novel were filling half the theatres in London; he also
comments on the illogicality of Forster's pieces since Dickens was "one of the
band of the Newgate Novelists" and clearly had written the Fagin and Sikes
portions of **Oliver Twist** "in emulation of the earlier criminal romances" of
Bulwer and Ainsworth. Referring to the early intimacy between Dickens and
Ainsworth, Ellis speculates that "in the course of their conversations, around
the library fire at Kensel Lodge," Ainsworth provided Dickens with the name
for his Bill Sikes. In discussions about the figures in the **Newgate Calendar,**
Ellis explains, Ainsworth spoke of his research on eighteenth-century
criminals and mention was made of an actual James Sykes, "a violent ruffian
known as 'Hell and Fury,' a friend of Blueskin and Jack Sheppard, the same
who by his treacherous impeachment of the latter caused Jack's arrest and
imprisonment in St. Giles's Round House." Cf. Rushton (XVI. 24).

XI. RECEPTION BY DICKENS'S CONTEMPORARIES

1. Ainsworth, William Harrison. **Rookwood: A Romance.** Revised and corrected with a new Preface. London: R. Bentley, 1837.

    Refers in the Preface, dated 18 October 1837, to Sam Weller's ballad "Bold Turpin vunce on Hounslow Heath" in a footnote and adds the following tribute to Dickens: "MR. DICKENS, with his wonderful knowledge of London life and character, and unequalled powers of delineation, has done more for this metropolis in 'The Pickwick Papers,' and in 'Oliver Twist,' than Paul de Kock, in all his works, has done for Paris." See also XI. 5.

2. Barham, R.H.D. **The Life and Letters of the Rev. Richard Harris Barham.** London: Richard Bentley, 1870, II, 24.

    Comments in a letter to Mrs. Hughes that "By the way, there is a sort of Radicalish tone about **Oliver Twist** which I don't altogether like. I think it will not be long before it is remedied, for Bentley is loyal to the backbone himself."

3. Burdett, Sir Francis. Manuscript letter 27 November 1838. Bodleian MS Eng. letters, d. 98. Quoted by K.J. Fielding in XI. 7.

    "... I have finish'd the first vol of Oliver Twist, it is very interesting, very painful, very disgusting, & as the Old Woman at Edinburgh, on hearing a preacher on the sufferings of Jesus Christ, said Oh dear I hope it isn't true. Whether anything like it exists or no I mean to make enquiry for it is quite dreadful, &, to society in this country, most disgraceful."

4. Dickens, Charles. To G.H. Lewes. [? 9 June 1838]. In the **Pilgrim Letters,** (I. 1), I, 402-04.

    We can infer from Dickens's phrase "reference to that question of yours concerning Oliver Twist" in his letter to Lewes that the latter had written earlier to ask Dickens what authorities he had drawn upon for his description of the mental phenomenon he describes in the June 1838 installment of **Oliver Twist** in the **Miscellany.** In Chapter 34, Dickens describes the state Oliver passes through between sleep and waking, the passage the Pilgrim editors note as "most likely to have attracted Lewes." Responding, Dickens notes that "It came like all my other ideas, such as they are, ready made to the point of the pen--and down it went. Draw your conclusion and hug the theory closely." For Lewes' subsequent review of **Oliver Twist** see IX. 12 and for his final estimate of Dickens, see XII. 14.

5. Ellis, S.M. **William Harrison Ainsworth and His Friends.** London: John Lane, 1911, II, 344.

    Quotes Ainsworth's letter of 14 November 1838 to James Crossley telling his friend that if he had not read **Oliver Twist** he "had a treat in store." For Ainsworth's other comment on **Oliver Twist,** see XI. 1.

6.   Esher, Viscount, ed. **The Girlhood of Queen Victoria: A Selection from Her Majesty's Diaries between the years 1832 and 1840.** New York: Longman's, Green, 1912, II, 86-144.

Queen Victoria began reading **Oliver Twist** in September 1838 noting on the 30th that she found the novel "excessively interesting." Although the Queen's mother admonished her for reading "light books," she continued with the work, successfully persuading Lord Melbourne, her Prime Minister, to try it. Melbourne began the novel but quickly took a dislike to it, attacking **Oliver Twist** for its "low debasing view of mankind" set amidst "Workhouses, and Coffin Makers, and Pickpockets." Queen Victoria attempted vainly to defend Dickens against Melbourne's criticism but he stuck to his view that things he did not like "in **reality**" should not be represented in literature because "everything one reads should be pure and elevating." Melbourne's views on **Oliver Twist** may also be found in **The Greville Diary,** ed. P.W. Wilson (1927), I, 567.

7.   Fielding, K.J. "Sir Francis Burdett and **Oliver Twist**." RES, NS 2 (1951), 154-57.

Glosses Dickens's query in a letter to Forster dated 20 December 1838 about a reference Sir Francis had made to **Oliver Twist** during a speech in Birmingham. Fielding notes how editors and scholars, apparently unwilling to check the circumstances of the speech, have used the reference for exaggerated claims about Sir Francis's having spoken approvingly of Dickens as "the advocate of the poor." All he did, Fielding demonstrates, was to refer to the novel, remarking in his address on 19 December 1838 that he had occupied his intersessional hours reading **Oliver Twist.** For Sir Francis Burdett's other comment on **Oliver Twist,** see XI. 3.

8.   Frith, W.P. **My Autobiography and Reminiscences.** London: Richard Bentley, 1889, I, 60-61.

Notes how John Landseer, painter, engraver, and author, once rebuked his son, Edwin, then visiting teacher at the Royal Academy life school, for reading **Oliver Twist**--"some of Dickens's nonsense"--in front of his pupils.

9.   Hood, Thomas. **Memorials of Thomas Hood Collected, Arranged, and Edited by his Daughter.** London: Edward Moxon, 1860, II, 41.

Praises **Oliver Twist** as "wholesome" reading," a book whose drift he found "natural, along with the great currents, and not against them." Hood also commended Dickens's purpose as "sound" and admired the honest independence of an author who recognized "good in low places, and evil in high ones." These merits alone, Hood concluded, distinguished **Oliver Twist** from **Jack Sheppard,** a novel whose weakness was clearly implicit, he thought, in the way "thieves and blackguards" yelled their applause at its slang songs when a dramatic version of Ainsworth's novel played at the Adelphi.

10.   Hudson, Derek, ed. **The Diary of Henry Crabb Robinson: An Abridgement.** London: Oxford Univ. Press, 1967, pp. 185-91.

Praise for **Oliver Twist** as an able and original work mixed with some criticism. Dickens showed the sufferings of the very poor "very pathetically," Robinson noted, and added "but repulsively sometimes." Occasionally, he continues, Dickens almost exceeds "the allowable measure of human suffering and the temporary success of villainy." Robinson admired Nancy, Sikes, and Fagin as powerfully conceived figures but found Oliver without character and unrealistically helped to his property by "most romantic incidents."

11.   Ilchester, Earl of. **Chronicles of Holland House 1820-1900.** London: J. Murray, 1937, p. 245.

Quotes Henry Fox repeating in a letter Lady Carlisle's response to **Oliver Twist:** "I know there are such unfortunate beings as pickpockets and street walkers. I am very sorry for it and very much shocked at their mode of life, but I own I do not much wish to hear what they say to one another." Fox shared these sentiments, adding that he found the monthly numbers "painful and revolting" and the humor in various scenes forced.

12.   Knapp, William I. **Life, Writings and Correspondence of George Borrow.** New York: G.P. Putnams, 1889, II, 274-75.

Records how in the autumn of 1838 "every body was in raptures over ... Oliver Twist." Borrow notes his own personal delight, too, commenting that he found Fagin "truly a frightful character--the most diabolical creation ever engendered by the human brain."

13.   Pierpont, Robert. "Talfourd's Sonnet on **Oliver Twist."** The Dickensian, 16 (April 1920), 89.

Provides the text of the sonnet Thomas Noon Talfourd wrote and dedicated to Dickens on Christmas Day 1838 and which he first published in **Ainsworth's Magazine,** 2 (1842), 507. A handwritten version of the poem, dated 12 October 1850, also appears in a series of sonnets Talfourd appended to his **Tragedies.** See **The Dickensian,** 5 (1909), 130. For a different version of the text of the sonnet on **Oliver Twist,** see **The Dickensian,** 1 (1905), 15.

14.   Thackeray, W. M. "In Which Lady Kew Leaves his Lordship Quite Convalescent." Chapter 38. **The Newcomes.** London: Bradbury and Evans, 1855.

George Barnes suggests that the injured Lord Kew might like a novel, so he mentions **Oliver Twist,** which he had read to his family and which Lady Walham had read on the sly in her bedroom, hidden under Blatterwick's **Voices from Mesopotamia.** When Barnes receives permission, he summons up Miss Nancy and Fagin "to frighten and delight" the company and makes Kew laugh so immensely "as to endanger the re-opening of his wound."

15.   ____. Preface. 26 November 1850. **The History of Pendennis.** London: Bradbury and Evans, 1849-50.

Alludes to Dickens and refers directly to Eugene Sue in the Preface he wrote for the first book edition of **Pendennis,** stating that he originally intended to bring in a ruffian from St. Giles's, thieves' slang, escapes, murders, and an execution. But Thackeray explains that he laid his "exciting" plan aside because, on attempting it, "never having been intimate with any convict in my life, and the manners of ruffians and gaol-birds being quite unfamiliar to me," he realized that he could not compete with those who

wrote such novels. "To describe a real rascal, you must make him so horrible
that he would be too hideous to show," he stated, "and unless the painter
paints him fairly, I hold he has no right to show him at all." Thackeray
probably omitted Dickens's name as a matter of tact, but the criticism he
made of Sue resembles his earlier polemics against the Newgate novel. See
X. 2, 3, 4, 11, 13, and 16.

16.   Toynbee, William, ed. **The Diaries of William Charles Macready.** New
       York: G.P. Putnam's, 1912, I, 475.

Comments on Dickens's offer, made on his behalf by Forster, to
dramatize **Oliver Twist** and engage Macready's professional service. "Nothing
can be kinder than this generous intention of Dickens," Macready wrote on 8
November 1838, "but I fear it is not acceptable." After spending the whole of
the next day "skimming over **Oliver Twist,**" he told Dickens and Forster when
they called on him on 10 November that the novel was utterly impractical
"for any dramatic purpose." The subsequent popularity of **Oliver Twist** on
stage contradicts Macready's cautious advice. See section VI.

XII. CRITICISM

CRITICISM TO 1900

1. Bagehot, Walter. "Charles Dickens." **National Review,** 7 (July and October 1858), 475-76. Rpt. in his **Literary Studies.** Vol. 2. London: Longmans, Green, and Co., 1879, pp. 205-07.

Points to Sikes as one of the few instances of Dickens's ability to portray a fully realized character rather than a caricature. Sikes, argues Bagehot, "is the skulking ruffian who may be seen any day at the police-courts." Bagehot does not deny that even here "there is not some undue heightening admixture of caricature," but this effect, he thinks, "is scarcely thought of amid the general coherence of the picture, the painful subject, and the wonderful command of strange accessories." Bagehot extends his praise to Nancy as well, "a still more delicate artistic effort." She is "an idealization of the girl who may also be seen at the police-courts and St. Giles's," he adds, a compound of badness and compassion which Dickens delineates most successfully.

2. Bayne, Peter. "The Modern Novel: Dickens, Bulwer, Thackeray." In his **Essays in Biography and Criticism.** 1857; rpt. Boston: Gould and Lincoln, 1860, pp. 363-92.

Praises Dickens for his range of characters and argues that his power with them is based less on realism than on "a peculiar, delicate, and most captivating idealization." Bayne calls Rose Maylie and Esther Summerson "breathing epitomes of the tenderness, the sweetness, the beauties of life," while Oliver, in his view, concentrates "the single good qualities of a hundred children."

3. _____. "Studies of English Authors. No. V: Charles Dickens--the Second Half of Pickwick--M. Taine Reprimanding Dickens--Oliver Twist." **The Literary World,** 4 April 1879, pp. 216-18.

Defends Dickens against Taine's charge that he wanted light-hearted happiness and that he wrote thinking too relentlessly about a moral purpose. Bayne answers the first criticism by referring to **The Pickwick Papers** and the second by affirming the validity of writing to make a point, praising **Oliver Twist** for the vehemence with which Dickens attacked those who argued that introducing comforts into workhouses would make people flock to them. Bayne also suggests that despite the unpromising material Dickens had to work with in the workhouse officials, he made much of them, creating in Bumble a figure "superior in its kind" to any in the whole range of fiction.

4. Canning, Hon. Albert S.G. "Oliver Twist." In his **Philosophy of Charles Dickens.** London: Smith, Elder, 1880, pp. 54-96.

A leisurely chapter commenting on various aspects of the novel. Canning sees as significant Dickens's omission of the clergy as individuals engaged in alleviating the abuses and evils he attacks, concluding that their conspicuous absence in **Oliver Twist** implies criticism of their apparent inaction. Nancy's character development meets with Canning's approval, but he cannot easily credit Sikes--a mere brute--with the remorse that afflicts him after the murder. The last portion of the essay contrasts Scott and Dickens as popular authors, notes similarities and differences between the villains each depicts, and concludes that Dickens's greater emotional involvement with his characters served him better than Scott's "invincible calmness and self-control." While these qualities prevent exaggeration or inconsistency, writes Canning, Dickens's "intense earnestness" was probably "better suited to many readers of the lower classes in England. For certainly his success among them, especially in 'Oliver Twist,' was unprecedented in the annals of fiction."

5.   [Collins, Wilkie]. "Wilkie Collins about Charles Dickens." **The Pall Mall Gazette**, 50 (20 January 1890), 3.

In these marginal notes in Collins's copy of Forster's **Life** (XII. 7) printed shortly before the book's sale at an auction, an unidentified transcriber makes available comments by Collins on several of Dickens's novels. Responding to Forster's praise of **Oliver Twist** as "simply but well constructed," Collins writes "Nonsense," saying that the book's one defect was its "helplessly bad" construction. Nancy, however, impressed Collins as "the finest thing" Dickens ever did. "He never afterwards saw all sides of a woman's character--saw all round her. That the same man who could create 'Nancy' created the second Mrs. Dombey is the most incomprehensible anomaly that I know of in literature."

6.   Dickens, Charles, Jr. "Introduction." In 1892 Macmillan Edition (II. 18), pp. xiii-xxxii.

Contains minor factual errors about Dickens's agreements with Bentley (I. 6) relating to the origin of **Oliver Twist** and about the number of times the serial publication of the novel was interrupted in the **Miscellany** (II. 1). For the main part, Charles Dickens, Jr., confines his comments to a narrative of the book's composition, his father's hard work and efforts to finish the novel, and the publishing history of **Oliver Twist**. He also refers briefly to its stage adaptations and plagiarisms and rehearses in detail Cruikshank's inflated claim to have invented the story. See XIII. 9-11. Dickens's son sensibly refrains from attributing his father's breakdown in April 1869 directly to the strain of performing the murder of Nancy, but he adds: "it is certain that the tremendous exertion and the subsequent prostration which this grim and extraordinarily dramatic performance involved, did much to bring about the threatening of paralysis which then stopped the Readings, if it did not actually hasten the premature end which came in the following year." From the first to last, he concludes, **Oliver Twist** was associated with "overwork and excessive strain."

7.   Forster, John. "First Five Years of Fame." In his **The Life of Charles Dickens**. Vol. I. London: Chapman and Hall, 1872; ed. J.W.T. Ley, London: Palmer, 1928; ed. A.J. Hoppe, 2 vols., London: Dent, 1966, I, 65-94.

Forster recounts in a useful and informative section of his biography his growing intimacy with Dickens, noting how from February 1837 Dickens wrote nothing which Forster did not see before the world did. This part also includes Forster's account of Dickens's working habits while writing **Oliver Twist**, the interaction between Dickens and Forster and others about the text--Talfourd, writes Forster, pleaded as earnestly for Charley Bates "in mitigation of judgment as ever at the bar for any client"--and Dickens's conflicts with Richard Bentley. In an extended comment on the novel, Forster summarizes views he gave earlier in the reviews of **Oliver Twist** he wrote for **The Examiner** (IX. 1, 9, 11, 20, 25, and 36) and states his own judgment about the novel. **Oliver Twist**, he writes, has held its ground "in the first class" of Dickens's writings, occupying a place among them Forster thinks it fully deserves. For a reference to Dickens's Autobiographical Fragment as it appears in Forster's **Life**, see XIII. 83.

8.   Friswell, J. Hain. "Mr. Charles Dickens." In his **Modern Men of Letters "Honestly Criticised."** London: Hodder and Stoughton, 1870, pp. 1-45.

A chronologically arranged survey of Dickens's life and work, with emphasis on the early period. Friswell calls **Oliver Twist** "one of the best [novels] Dickens has ever written," praising it for a combination of realism and moral purpose. Friswell sees in Nancy's murder and Sikes's flight "the true intuition of genius," as the author also treads firmly and cleanly "amidst vice, depravity, cunning, theft, and murder" to teach us the best of lessons: "to pity the guilty while we hate the guilt." Later in the essay, Friswell accounts for Dickens's success in terms of his ability to supply readers with an alternative to novels that were either vicious or snobbish. "He arose at a time when ... one set of writers was producing the Satanic school of literature ... and another ... was cultivating ... the silver-fork school." Kitton (IV. 15) notes that the main part of this essay originally appeared in **The London Review**.

9.   Garnett, Richard. "**Oliver Twist:** The Editor's Estimate." In 1900 Autograph Edition (II. 21), pp. 1-2.

Offers a few slight words about the contrast between **The Pickwick Papers** and **Oliver Twist** together with dated opinions about Dickens's apparent artistic ineptitude. Garnett declares that **Oliver Twist** illustrates "as strongly as any" of Dickens's books the "fundamental fact" that he is "not really a novelist." Instead, Garnett sees him as "a fountain head of intellectual energy" responding to everything in the world around him. To make the characters and scenes he depicts work together harmoniously in a well wrought fiction is beyond him, writes Garnett, but he can throw each character "singly upon the stage."

10.   Gissing, George. "Introduction." In 1900 Rochester Edition (II. 22), pp. ix-xxi.

Sees the "profound seriousness" of Dickens's genius "fully declared" in Oliver Twist, whose twofold moral purpose hangs well together. This occurs, writes Gissing, because the novel's attack on the evil working of the Poor Law Act and its "faithful picture of the life of thieves in London" originate in Dickens's view that the pauper system was directly responsible for a great deal of crime. Gissing comments sensibly that Dickens's error in confusing the legislation of the old Poor Law with that of the new Act mattered little because the novelist's partisanship engages our sympathies and makes us realize that the proceedings of the law, whatever their cause, are "invalid in the court of conscience." Gissing likens the 1841 Preface to a statement

appropriate to "some representative of a daring school of 'naturalism'"
asserting, some fifty years after Dickens, "his right to deal with the most
painful facts of life." Dickens's scenes of the thieves and criminal London, he
concludes, are some of the best Dickens ever wrote, original contributions
which taught "English people a certain way of regarding the huge city." Of
the book's blemishes Gissing writes with equal conviction, rejecting the
"insufferable rant" of Monks and the "feeble idyllicism" of the Maylie group.
Overall, he finds the story weak. "There is no coherency in the structure of
the thing; the plotting is utterly without ingenuity, the mysteries are so
artificial as to be altogether uninteresting." This essay and Gissing's other
contributions to the Rochester Edition were later collected and published as
Critical Studies of the Works of Charles Dickens in 1924 (New York: Temple
Scott) and as **The Immortal Dickens** in 1925 (London: Palmer).

11.   Horne, Richard Hengist. "Charles Dickens." In his **A New Spirit of the
       Age.** London, 1844; rpt. London: Oxford, 1907, pp. 2-52.

A sympathetic and wide-ranging assessment of Dickens's early work, with
frequent examples drawn from **Oliver Twist** to illustrate Horne's sense of the
novelist's individual strengths and characteristics. Horne writes informatively about the extent of Dickens's affinity with William Hogarth, an
artist similarly interested in exploring "the constant tragedy of private life,"
especially among the poor, one who mixes the ideal and the real, and who
combines humor, tragedy, and a moral vision. At the same time, Horne notes
how Dickens, unlike Hogarth, stops short of offending, drawing back from
repelling readers with revolting details and lightening potentially disgusting
figures with humor. As an instance, Horne refers to such "evasive
appellation[s]" as "this young lady" for Nancy and "the merry old gentleman!"
for Fagin, whose humorous effects detract nothing from the true
circumstances of the prostitute and the fence. Rather, he continues, the
epithets illustrate a subtle instinct and good taste, qualities which allow
Dickens to treat frankly the circumstances of Nancy and Fagin without
alienating readers. In a similar vein, Horne comments that the scenes of
pathos and the purest tenderness in **Oliver Twist,** "the work which is most full
of crimes and atrocities and the lowest characters, of all its author's
productions," enlarge the reader's sympathy and do not degrade him.
Horne also writes sensibly about Dickens's method of characterization,
defending him against the charges of mere caricature on the grounds that he
combines "the roundness of individual reality" with generalizations about
class. Extended comments on Rose Maylie and Bill Sikes follow. Horne faults
Dickens's portrait of Rose because he thinks she defers too readily to a sense
of unworthiness in her willingness to sacrifice her love for Harry Maylie on
the false altar of respectability. He also criticizes the last scenes depicting
Sikes because they contradict Dickens's own aim by encouraging our sympathy
for the criminal as "one worn and haggard man with all the world against
him." If the reader responds by wanting Sikes to escape, a likely reaction,
according to Horne, Dickens erred by hunting the man with such ferocity.
The overstrained terror of the intended moral, he concludes, "has thus an
immoral tendency."

12.   Lang, Andrew. "Introduction." In the 1897 Gadshill Edition (II. 19), pp.
       v-x.

Comments briefly on the multiplicity of Dickens's literary commitments
at the time he began **Oliver Twist,** musing that Dickens stands as a warning

to successful beginners not to mortgage their talents too hastily. Familiar comments about the novel's strengths (the thieves) and its weaknesses (an exaggerated use of coincidence) follow, after which Lang appends brief notes about the novel's publishing history.

13. Lester, Charles Edwards. **The Glory and the Shame of England.** New York: Harper, 1841, I, 152-53; II, 3-16.

Enthusiasm for Dickens as a social reformer and sustained criticism of England's "shame," the poor, cruelly abused children who work in her factories, mills, and mines only to end up in the workhouse. That prospect, comments Lester, "is a dark cloud, that hangs on the vision of every poor man in England when he looks into the future." Lester adds that the descriptions of the workhouse in **Oliver Twist** "will not do, we all know, for the majority of them; but ... will do for many." Later in the narrative about his visit, Lester describes a two-hour interview he had with Dickens in which the novelist talked freely of his attempts to focus public attention on the lives of the poor and of the days and nights he spent "in the most wretched districts of the metropolis, studying the history of the human heart."

14. Lewes, George Henry. "Dickens in Relation to Criticism." **The Fortnightly Review,** 17 (February 1872), 141-54.

An important early essay without specific reference to **Oliver Twist** but one whose general observations bear upon the novel. Lewes writes with conviction about the source of Dickens's popular appeal, which he locates in his hallucinatory vividness, and combines with praise his well-known criticism of Dickens's characters. While they embody true observations, Lewes contends, they also have "nothing fluctuating and incalculable in them." The essay mingles admiration with condescension and admits a baffled respect for a writer who assumed that it was his duty to "make the lot of the miserable Many a little less miserable." Dickens quickly learned that his genius gave him "great power" this way, Lewes notes, and he lived determined to use that power effectively.

15. Ruskin, John. "Fiction, Fair and Foul. I." **Nineteenth Century,** 7 (June 1880), 941-63. Reprinted in **The Works of John Ruskin.** Ed. E.T. Cook and Alexander Wedderburn. London: George Allen, 1908, XXXIV, 265-302.

Attacks **Bleak House** as an example of how modern stories typically obtain funereal excitement by inflicting violent or disgusting deaths on the characters but separates **Oliver Twist,** "with honour," from the loathsome mass of fiction to which it belongs. Ruskin calls **Oliver Twist** Dickens's "greatest work," an earnest, uncaricatured record of criminal life "written with didactic purpose, full of the gravest instruction."

16. Sala, George Augustus. **Charles Dickens.** London, 1870; rpt. Westmead, Hampshire: Gregg International Publishers, 1970, passim.

Sala's obituary essay on Dickens originally published in the **Daily Telegraph** and later expanded to a pamphlet. Sala speculates that **Oliver Twist** was the one work for which Dickens showed a preference over the others, citing as evidence the "forcible and eloquent language" Dickens used to vindicate the intent and scheme of the work in the 1841 Preface. He also

finds further support for his contention in the public readings of the murder of
Nancy by Sikes. Dickens introduced this episode, Sala writes, "half with the
preoccupying wish to vindicate 'Oliver,' [and] half, perhaps, in unconscious
gratification of that melodramatic penchant in his mind."

17.   Whipple, Edwin Percy. "Introduction." In 1876 New Illustrated Library
      Edition (II. 17), pp. ix-xxix. Rpt. as "Oliver Twist." Atlantic Monthly,
      28 (October 1876), 474-79, and in his Charles Dickens: The Man and
      His Work. Boston and New York, 1912; rpt. New York: AMS Press,
      Inc., 1975, I, 47-71.

An inconsequential essay in which Whipple censures Dickens for regarding
his legal contracts with Richard Bentley as not absolutely binding and
expresses his exasperation with Dickens's use of colons for commas in the
novel. Whipple dismisses the plot as "improbable and melodramatic" but finds
much to hold the reader's attention in the story's pathos, humor, and
successful treatment of the criminals. He admires the psychology of Fagin's
character and finds the other thieves realistically presented.

18.   Williams, S.F. "Dickens's Work: A Series of Criticisms. No. 6 "Oliver
      Twist." The Rose, The Shamrock, and The Thistle, 20 (December
      1863), 145-57.

A superficial, impressionistic essay which attempts to explore various
affinities between Dickens and Crabbe. The two resemble each other,
Williams argues, in their subject matter, in their warmth and sympathy for
the poor, and in the accuracy with which they depicted scenes of wretched
criminal life. This point engages Williams at some length, as he develops his
contention that both showed the misery, selfishness, and sin associated with
low life "not in contempt but in compassion." Crabbe maintained, moreover,
that contemplating "the evils and miseries of our nature" served a useful
exercise, a point Dickens also made in his 1841 Preface to Oliver Twist.
Lengthy quotations support Williams's view that satire, "severe and forcible
paintings" of thieves, and pathos constitute the main ingredients of Oliver
Twist. For parallels between Dickens and Crabbe, see also Crabbe (XIII. 134),
Baker (XII. 25), and Lindsay (XII. 138).

CRITICISM 1900-1983

19.   Altick, Richard D. Victorian Studies in Scarlet. New York: W.W.
      Norton, 1970, passim.

Briefly links Dickens's early work with the Newgate novel and the latter
with "the taste of the masses" which the genre reflected on "a higher level of
literary interest." Altick cites Oliver Twist as one of the prominent examples
of the genre, revealing a typical Newgate preoccupation with a narrative of
crime and punishment. Contemporary attacks on the novel, Altick thinks, put
Dickens on the defensive, although his "many-sided interest in crime and
punishment" made certain the reappearance of criminals in Dickens's fiction
long after Oliver Twist.

20.   Auden, W.H. "Huck and Oliver." The Listener, 50 (1 October 1953),
      540-41.

Auden, in some extempore remarks made during a visit to Britain in 1953, uses **Huckleberry Finn** and **Oliver Twist** to illustrate what he argues are representative differences in American and British attitudes to nature, society, and life. Of the first, Auden writes that nature in **Huckleberry Finn** is "very big, very formidable, very inhuman," a view of the countryside quite at odds with Dickens's description of Mrs. Maylie's rural retreat. Huck's conduct--amazingly stoical and lonely as he improvises his moral decisions--strikes Auden as quite different from life in **Oliver Twist**, where characters appear to act according to the dictates of natural law. Auden also sees in **Huckleberry Finn** "a kind of sadness," an emotion not evoked in his response to **Oliver Twist**. When Twain's novel ends, comments Auden, one knows that Huck and Jim will part and never see each other again, "as if freedom and love were incompatible." Huck lights out "for the Territory," but Oliver remains snug, the adopted and loved son of a secure and domestic family.

21.   Austen, Zelda. **"Oliver Twist:** A Divided View." DSN, 7 (March 1976), 8-11.

Austen sees **Oliver Twist** as two novels. On the one hand, Dickens tells the story of Oliver tempted by the wicked, rescued by the good, and subsequently restored to his heritage and place in society. From this melodramatic plot emerge the novel's central conflict and "a cautionary tale" with a simple message: under the New Poor Law, the poor will either starve or turn to crime.
Revealing some of the nastiness beneath "the respectable skin" of Victorian society, Dickens also found himself facing something more profound: a divided and complex view of crime, the expression of which occupies "the other **Oliver Twist**." Dickens's understanding of the relationship between poverty and crime, his sympathy for Fagin and Sikes, and his attacks on the corrupt representative of "the world of officialdom" make **Oliver Twist**, Austen argues, "the dark novel of Dickens's immaturity."

22.   _____. "'Poverty and Villainy in **Oliver Twist**': A Response." DSN, 13 (December 1982), 113-14.

Argues that Brueck's reading of **Oliver Twist** (XII. 41) ignores the emphasis that she, Austen, put on the novel's cautionary aspect (XII. 21). Austen also restates her conviction that the novel demonstrates an undercurrent of sympathy "with both the poor and the criminal poor," but denies that hers is the position typical of a "bleeding heart."

23.   Axton, William. "'Keystone' Structure in Dickens's Serial Novels." UTQ, 37 (October 1967), 31-50.

Argues that Dickens regarded the mid-point of his works as "an especially significant place in their structure," by which he had to establish a novel's coherence in order that serial readers could grasp "the pattern of action and idea" developing through the monthly numbers. Axton suggests that Dickens attempts to impose his desire for organizational control by placing "a crucial action or symbolic event" at the center of the narrative in order to "[lock] into place the thematic and aesthetic concerns" which the rest of the book exploits.
In the case of **Oliver Twist**, installments eleven through thirteen appear to be the "keystone" episodes introducing the cause of Oliver's difficulties

during the first half of the story (Monk's machinations) and setting in motion the plot machinery which will defeat those ranged against the child hero. These same chapters, Axton argues, also serve to connect the workhouse and the underworld, two interests which he sees as symbolically linked by Monks, who represents "self-interested evil." Once Dickens establishes these larger themes, Axton thinks, the second half of the novel serves to work out the downfall of Oliver's enemies and reveal the hero's true identity. Axton uses examples from **The Pickwick Papers, Dombey and Son, Bleak House,** and **Great Expectations** to support his "keystone" thesis.

24. _____. "Oliver Twist and Grotesquerie." In his **Circle of Stage Fire: Dickens's Vision & Style & the Popular Victorian Theater.** Lexington: Univ. of Kentucky Press, 1966, pp. 84-109.

Axton limits the discussion of **Oliver Twist** to his exclusive interest in Dickens's stylistic voices and an analysis of the theatrical idioms Dickens employs. This chapter in particular focuses on what Axton considers the outstanding feature of Victorian popular theatre: its balance of opposing or discordant qualities, summed up for him by the term "grotesquerie." Axton defines this concept as a style associated with the strain of "dark" grotesque running from Breughel to Kafka, and as a quality that subverts the familiar, emphasizes the incongruity in life, and tries through satire, burlesque, farce, humor, and irony to turn the established world upside down.

Axton sees evidence of such qualities in **Oliver Twist** but argues that they appear more obviously in the novel's serialized form in **Bentley's Miscellany,** where Dickens also published "The Mudfog Papers" in the place of installments of **Oliver Twist.** See II. 1. Axton views these three papers as part of the novel, chiefly on the basis of their theatrical qualities and because they were originally "closely integrated into [the novel's] structure and texture." By exposing the heartlessness of philosophical radicalism and by satirizing scientific objectivity with its reliance on statistical inquiry, the three papers join "with a comparable strain of grotesque and macabre burlesque" in the novel, the effect of which is to make **Oliver Twist** "a world in which pathos and melodrama are juxtaposed with the broadest kind of pantomime burlesquerie." Axton implies that the omission of "The Mudfog Papers" weakens **Oliver Twist,** a point one can only take seriously if one accepts the claim he makes for the importance of Dickens's grotesque mode.

25. Baker, Ernest A. **The Age of Dickens and Thackeray.** Vol. 7 of **The History of the English Novel.** London: H.F. and G. Witherby, 1936, pp. 254-56.

Examines briefly some of the circumstances that helped "mould the handiwork of [Dickens's] genius" and surveys all the novels and most of the short fiction. Baker sees "the veracity" of Dickens's study of Sikes and Nancy and the "stern realism" with which he treats crime as **Oliver Twist's** principal strengths. The book's weakness, he thinks, lies in its "pious romancing" about Oliver and that part of the work Baker dismisses as "the novel of sentiment." Baker's general assessment of Dickens illustrates markedly dated assumptions. He condescends to Dickens as "the man in the street raised to the power of genius," who equals Shakespeare in his extraordinary range of characters but who falls below him because he could not portray them with depth. Baker concedes that Dickens rarely went wrong when he read the dial-plate of a watch but laments his inability to expose its "inner mechanism."

26. Basch, Francoise. "Dickens's Sinners." In her **Relative Creatures: Victorian Women in Society and the Novel.** Trans. Anthony Rudolf. New York: Schocken Books, 1974, pp. 210-28.

Argues that Dickens deserts his original social and psychological interest in Nancy after finding himself "in the dead-end" of all Victorian novelists wishing to write candidly about prostitution and underworld life. With reticence forced upon him by the demands of his reading public, Dickens moves in the later part of the novel from observer to preacher. As a result, Basch believes, Nancy turns into a typical "impure woman," the representative female sinner from the underworld who reappears, with variations, in subsequent novels. Basch also comments that Dickens uses a theatrical style to describe this type, making Nancy and her fallen sisters inherently melodramatic. That genre, she concludes, best expresses "a manichaean and anti-intellectual vision of the world" in which good and evil confront each other "without nuance."

27. Bayley, John. **"Oliver Twist: 'Things as they Really Are.'"** In **Dickens and the Twentieth Century.** Ed. John Gross and Gabriel Pearson. London: Routledge and Kegan Paul, 1962, pp. 49-64. Reprinted in **Dickens: A Collection of Critical Essays.** Ed. Martin Price. Englewood Cliffs, N.J.: Prentice-Hall, 1967, pp. 83-96.

Bayley argues that two main features account for the novel's impressive power and its ability to upset us by touching "a raw nerve." First, he cites the dream atmosphere as the book's imaginative principle, whose power and terror prove so compelling that we renounce realistic assessments. Grotesque scenes and characters appear true because we accept the novel's imaginative certainty that "the child is **right**" and that the system is monstrous.
Dickens combines this "Gothic nightmare" with a "terrifying imaginative indictment" of the secrecy of private life in the laissez-faire society of early Victorian England. Criminals, representatives of the social order, and even the good people, he argues, exhibit "an almost neurotic antipathy to external influence" in their desire to be let alone and feel no pressure "of social or national existence." One of the book's sinister ironies, Bayley contends, is that "Murder transforms all this," changing animals back into men and bringing even Sikes to life as he finds "the form and conscience of a man" after killing Nancy. By making murder "a kind of social revelation" Dickens effectively combines "social denunciation" with "Gothic nightmare" and achieves a feat "surely unique in the history of the novel."

28. Benson, A.C. "Introduction to **Oliver Twist.**" In the Waverley Dickens (II. 28), pp. x-xiv.

Notes how Dickens avoided the temptation of repeating the formula that made **The Pickwick Papers** so successful, choosing instead a totally different kind of novel, a melodramatic work with a fantastic, sensational plot and direct social purpose. Sketchy comments follow about Dickens's professed aims, his lack of realism, dependence on the "intricate coincidences" of melodrama, and use of defective good figures, whom Benson calls "intolerably uninteresting." Despite these failures, Benson admits that **Oliver Twist** possesses deep appeal, not least of which, he thinks, is its ability to stir people from complacency and quicken "the moral temperature" of society, the result of which leads to the gradual amelioration of the ills the novel addresses.

134 Studies

29. Bicanic, Sonia. "The Function of Language in our Experience of Oliver Twist and Nancy." SRAZ, 37 (July 1974), 277-86.

Compares two methods Dickens uses to convey two markedly different characters. Nancy, Bicanic notes, consistently appears in scenes where she interacts with other characters, using real and colloquial language and simple short statements to convey her attitudes and views. Oliver, by contrast, seldom speaks; when he does, he relies extensively on "if" and "perhaps" clauses, and other ways of expressing conjecture and uncertainty. But because Dickens also uses context and background to describe Oliver's plight Oliver nevertheless remains vivid and a figure to whom we respond. Nancy, concludes Bicanic, occupies a realistic role in the novel; Oliver's appeal rests in the force of his symbolic presence through which Dickens appeals directly to the conscience of his readers.

30. Bishop, Jonathan. "The Hero-Villain of **Oliver Twist**." **Victorian Newsletter**, 15 (Spring 1959), 14-16.

Argues for "an imaginative statement" in the false identifications of Oliver as a villain by the gentleman in the white waistcoat, Charlotte, and Mrs. Sowerberry, all of whom speak of Oliver as a potential or actual murderer. Can there be "another meaning," wonders Bishop, if we disregard the comic exaggeration of the woman's language, ignore Noah's coarse jest about Oliver's mother being a "bad 'un," and recall that Oliver is "actually, though not morally, responsible [for a death]; for by merely being born, he killed his mother."

Other aspects of the novel, Bishop thinks, reinforce Oliver's false identity "as a villain and a murderer." While Fagin tries to corrupt Oliver by making him "one of us," events link Oliver with the death, potential or actual, of young women and shadow in the idea of retribution "for sexual looseness." After the burglary, Rose almost dies, two incidents which Bishop connects, reading the first symbolically, particularly since the house into which Oliver forces an entry (through an aperture "too narrow to admit an adult") is inhabited by Oliver's female relatives. "The burglary is ... a rape, an act of violence in which Sikes and Oliver act as a single being," he comments, adding that the murder of Nancy, rich "in sexual undertones," in effect "dramatizes the motives symbolized by the lesser crime."

Speculating, therefore, that Sikes and Oliver "are counterparts," Bishop arrives at the center of his thesis: the structure of **Oliver Twist** "expresses the coexistence of the motive of aggression against the young virgin-mother and the counter-motive of guilt and self-repudiation by separating the wish to kill and the wish for innocence into distinct characters with contrasting fates." The conviction that Oliver willfully destroyed his mother finds a vicarious re-expression in Sikes's murder of Nancy, while the counter-wish "to have the mother back" manifests itself in the recovery of Rose and the establishment of Oliver as the "son" in Brownlow's household. From this point of view, Bishop concludes, the burglary may be read as a reversal of the act of birth: "Oliver is forced back into the 'house' from which he came." Because Oliver sinned in seizing his life at the expense of his mother's, he is punished for his "criminal" experiences, until he can find an adult male, Sikes, to act out his crime. "When Sikes fulfills the prophecy [of the gentleman in the white waistcoat], the interior drama is ended, and Oliver is free to escape into the idyll of his new family."

31. Blount, Trevor. **Dickens: The Early Novels**. Writers and their Work: No. 204. London: Longman, Green, 1968, pp. 15-18.

Discusses all works between **Sketches by Boz** and **David Copperfield** in just over thirty pages. Blount contrasts the Victorian preference for humor in Dickens's early works with the modern emphasis on his disillusion and alienation from society, noting briefly that neither of these stereotypes "comprehends the whole truth." Blount does not explore this issue further but provides instead a modest introduction to each of the works included in his survey. He comments briefly on the structure of **Oliver Twist,** refers to the contradictions inherent in Oliver's role as both a victim of the workhouse and a symbol of good, and indicates a preference for the criminals, whom he sees as realistic and artistically vivid figures.

32.   Bodenheimer, Rosemarie. "Dickens and the Art of the Pastoral."
       Centennial Review, 23 (Fall 1979), 452-67.

Discusses the relationship between pastoral language and characterization in **Oliver Twist, David Copperfield,** and **Great Expectations** and argues for a more complex use of landscape in the latter, where Dickens uses the rural environment as "a metaphor for psychological configurations and their changes." Bodenheimer also sees a rhetorical strategy in the passages describing the countryside in **Oliver Twist,** which she declines to dismiss as romantic sentiment. On the contrary, she argues, Dickens works in allusions to "Lines Written above Tintern Abbey" and "Intimations of Immortality" to prompt in the reader reflections upon our "sad mortality" and the universality of death. A further strategic value of these passages lies in the powerful but ambiguous role Dickens assigns to nature. By stressing Oliver's natural goodness, she suggests, Dickens makes Oliver "an all-purpose middle-class child" without quite acknowledging that his transformation really represents his absorption into the values of the Maylies. At the same time, Bodenheimer thinks that Dickens unconsciously corrects the claim of the pastoral passages to promote a generalized, classless condition for mankind by shattering his vision with the sudden intrusion of Fagin and Monks into the pastoral world in Chapter 34.

33.   Boll, Ernest. "Charles Dickens in **Oliver Twist.**" **The Psychoanalytic Review,** 27 (April 1940), 133-43.

A naively reductive biographical reading of the novel, some sense of which the following assertion conveys. Harry Maylie, writes Boll, "is a symbolic self-projection, of Dickens the man. The name may have been unconsciously assumed as an autograph through the influence of the common association of Tom, **Dick, and** Harry. Harry and Rose live in the same household, as did Dickens and Mary Hogarth. Both couples are related: the first as cousins, the latter as brother- and sister-in-law. The close relationship between Dickens the youth and Dickens the man is not contradicted by the use of the same family name for both Rose and Harry."

34.   Boll, Theophilus E. "**Oliver Twist,** Centenarian." **General Magazine and Historical Chronicle** (Univ. of Pennsylvania), 40 (1938), 156-63.

Listed by Gold (IV. 13) but unavailable for annotation.

35.   Brantlinger, Patrick. "Benthamite and Anti-Benthamite Fiction." In his **The Spirit of Reform: British Literature and Politics, 1832-1867.** Cambridge: Harvard Univ. Press, 1977, pp. 35-59. Originally published as "Bluebooks, the Social Organism, and the Victorian Novel." **Criticism,** 14 (Fall 1972), 328-44.

Analyses **Oliver Twist** as an expression of "the broadly Benthamite, reformist culture of the 1830's," citing Dickens's desire to improve society and to warn readers about the ruinous effects of a bad environment on individuals as those aspects of the novel most closely associated with the reformist spirit of the period. The novel's thesis, Brantlinger argues, insists that institutions determine conduct, a point Dickens expresses symbolically by opening the novel in the workhouse and by ending it "with the helpless villain trapped in the condemned cell." Cf. XII. 58. Brantlinger also discusses how Dickens's penology differs from Bentham's, points to the reformist similarities between **Oliver Twist** and Bulwer Lytton's **Paul Clifford,** and suggests that Oliver's unchanging innocence serves the book's thesis by dramatizing the child's helplessness. The novel, however, contains several inconsistencies, the most significant, Brantlinger thinks, being Dickens's belief that "Benevolent middle-class individualism" can counter the ills he exposes.

36.   Brier, Peter A. "Lamb, Dickens and the Theatrical Vision." CLS
        Bulletin, NS 10-11 (April-July 1975), 65-70.

Discusses aspects of a theatrical vision common to both Dickens and Lamb, noting also how they differ in their use of theatrical conventions. Brier cites as one instance Lamb's "The Praise of Chimney Sweeps," whose concluding scene of sausage eating and revelry he contrasts with Oliver's first appearance before Fagin in Chapter 8. While Dickens's scene "very much evokes James White and his chimney sweepers," Brier notes, the tone in the former differs markedly in its stress on the ominous and the grotesque. Dickens begins by presenting Fagin as a clown-like figure, making his readers accept him, as Oliver does, because the setting evokes entertainment and pantomime. Later, however, Fagin's satanic spirit dominates, sweeping the pantomime and farce into melodrama and terror. The resulting "medley," Brier thinks, resembles Thomas Hood's **Tylney Hall,** a comic, experimental novel much to Lamb's taste. **Oliver Twist,** he concludes, is simply a "more advanced version" of Hood's mixture of melodrama, pantomime, comedy, and tragedy.

37.   Briggs, Katharine M. "The Folklore of Charles Dickens." **JFI,** 7 (June
        1970), 3-20.

Examines specific instances of folklore in Dickens's fiction and touches briefly on **Oliver Twist** and **The Old Curiosity Shop,** two works full of "the very stuff of folklore." **Oliver Twist** presents innocence hunted by evil, reveals a mystical belief in heredity, and takes Oliver, "the princeling in disguise," to the Ogre's castle, where he meets a compassionate woman who, as often happens in fairy tales, is killed.

38.   Brody, Benjamin. "Brainwashing and **Oliver Twist.**" HSL, 14 (1982),
        61-66.

Comments on the similarities between Fagin's method of subduing Oliver and trying to turn him into a thief and the techniques used by various contemporary governments engaged in thought reform and forceful indoctrination. Russian and Chinese Communists, for example, Brody argues, isolate their victims, remove their personal clothing and possessions, ration basic necessities, and bewilder them by alternating harsh and relatively lenient treatment. Employing such means, especially after Oliver is recaptured, Fagin attempts to corrupt Oliver and bring him up as a criminal. But he fails, Brody speculates, because Dickens believes, unlike modern psychologists, that character is destiny no matter how it is formed.

39. Brogan, Colm. "Oliver Twist Re-examined: Charles Dickens's Short-comings as a Novelist." The Listener, 40 (26 August 1948), 310-11.

If Brogan's article bore a recent date, one might jokingly label it a parodic attack on the novelist based on long-discredited assumptions. Dickens, writes Brogan, is long on sentiment but short on intelligence, so much so that he cannot draw consistent characters, distinguish between the old and new Poor Laws, formulate a coherent blueprint for social reform, or resist the "censorship of demand" imposed by a narrow-minded reading public averse to books treating sex but happy with those portraying comic types. Brogan also comments briefly on Fagin, arguing that his stereotypical Jewish qualities are not anti-Semitic because Dickens was "simply following the accepted conventions of melodrama."

40. Brown, Ivor. "Dickens as Social Reformer." In Charles Dickens 1812-1870, ed. E.W.F. Tomlin. London: Weidenfeld and Nicholson, 1969, pp. 142-66.

Brown divides reformers into those who "expose evils and rouse public indignation ... [by putting] thunder in the air" and those who collect evidence and draft reports from which new laws evolve. Clearly Dickens belonged to the first group, as is evident in Oliver Twist, which indicted "a whole system of workhouse incarceration," attacked prevailing attitudes to poverty, and denounced as inhuman the treatment of apprentices. Brown's section "Poverty and the Poor Law" provides an introductory view of the treatment of paupers and asserts that Dickens did not toil in vain, although no major change in the New Poor Law occurred until the appointment of the Royal Commission of 1905.

41. Brueck, Katherine T. "Poverty and Villainy in Oliver Twist: Unravel-ling the Paradox." DSN, 12 (September 1981), 66-69.

Takes issue with recent critics of Oliver Twist like Austen (XII. 21), who present Dickens as a man with twentieth-century views intent upon presenting criminals sympathetically as victims of disadvantaged circumstances. Brueck emphasizes that poverty plays an important part in the novel, but its two-fold purpose, she writes, exists not to arouse compassion for criminals but to underscore the moral ugliness of Fagin and his gang. Citing Dickens's descriptions of Fagin's vile milieu, Brueck argues that the material deprivation he and the others experience serves as "a metaphorical representation of an ethical decline," underscoring the moral ugliness of the pursuits of thieves, murderers, and prostitutes. By contrast, Dickens uses humor and irony to express his indignation when he treats the poor inhabitants of the workhouse. Brueck also sees a "doleful melody" interwoven with this "jocular song of compassion for the poor," suffusing Dickens's treatment of Oliver with deep pathos.

42. _____. "'Poverty and Villainy in Oliver Twist': A Further Comment." DSN, 13 (December 1982), 114-15.

Brueck restates her contention that Dickens reserves his sympathy for the orphan Oliver and his opprobrium for Fagin and his fellow malefactors.

43.   Burton, S.H. "Introduction." In 1961 Longman Edition (II. 42), pp. vii-lii.

A brief but serviceable summary of Dickens's life with some minor inaccuracies followed by a sound discussion of the novel's social and historical background. Burton comments effectively on the conditions the Poor Law Amendment Act was designed to address, setting forth briefly the reformers' assumptions, their ideological outlook, and the nature of Dickens's response. Burton also writes helpfully about Dickens's language, emphasizing the tension in his description of the slums between his wish to reveal through realistic detail and the restraints he observed in deference to his readers. In an analysis of Oliver as the novel's hero, Burton draws attention to the significance of the protagonist's allegorical role. This paperback includes an intelligent summary of the plot by chapters, twenty-two pages of notes glossing slang and unfamiliar expressions, and the 1867 Preface.

44.   Busch, Frederick. "Dickens: The Smile on the Face of the Dead." **Mosaic**, 9 (Summer 1976), 149-56.

Posits some general assumptions about the novel as a genre broad enough to accommodate **Oliver Twist** and any other work that begins with birth and ends with death. The prevalence of this pattern in fiction, Busch argues, indicates how novelists ritualistically celebrate life and affirm light over darkness. But while Busch sees Dickens as no exception in this respect, he also presents him as a writer whose imagination responds more vividly to scenes of death and violence than to images of happiness and marriage. For Busch, Dickens's "greatest moments" occur when, "working apparently in a near manic, near-hallucinatory, state, his characters are driven to murder." Headstone, Jonas Chuzzlewit, and Sikes provide examples of characters whose guilt-ridden psyches "(and, presumably, his own)" Dickens explores, debating not the moral question of **whether** to kill but **how** to kill. Busch also sees in Dickens's dramatic performances of Sikes's brutal act "Dickens' own sense of drama, and his own involvement in the emotions of murder." Busch concludes: "It is as though Dickens never can stay away from violence and death," finding in them a dark knowledge which he craves but which is available only on the other side of death.

45.   Calder-Marshall, Arthur. "Introduction" and "Appreciation." In 1970 Heron Books Series (II. 50), pp. xiv-vi and 513-39.

Makes several thoughtful points in the Introduction to Dickens's life, referring briefly to Dickens's class mobility, moderate social views, and conviction that there was nothing wrong in making one's readers feel good. Calder-Marshall also notes how Dickens inspired Dostoevski and showed Kafka the potentialities of impressionist art, especially by transforming the London he knew so well "into a battleground between the forces of Heaven and Hell." Concluding, Calder-Marshall suggests that Dickens's popularity in Russia owes much to the official party line that his novels "prove to the ill-housed millions of Russia ... how much luckier they are than the masses of workers in contemporary Britain." But because Dickens emphasizes that good and evil exist in all classes of society, reading his novels may prove a counter-revolutionary activity. In such a climate as that of the Soviet Union, writes Calder-Marshall, Dickens "may turn out to be as subversive as Pasternak, Solzhenitsyn, Yevtushenko and all those other subversive writers who have cared more about people than about politics."

The Appreciation raises critical and biographical issues in greater detail, treating various topics under several subheadings. Calder-Marshall sees Dickens combining elements in **Oliver Twist** drawn from real life (the criminals) with others from fairy tales, allegory, and the popular theatre, whose impact on the novel he characterizes as mainly harmful. Calder-Marshall argues that Dickens held the political views of a pacifier, who sought to build bridges between classes rather than advocate warfare and revolution. Speculating about the later impact of Ellen Ternan on Dickens's life, he suggests that the actress may have turned Dickens towards the public readings because, "as the older lover," he wanted to prove his superiority in her profession, even though he was an amateur. Calder-Marshall argues against blaming the readings from **Oliver Twist** for shortening Dickens's life, but his death, he thinks, "was hastened by his discovery that at the end of life he was perhaps closer to Bill Sikes the murderer and hunted man than he was to Oliver Twist, the parish boy who by natural grace came into a fortune."

46.   Cameron, J.M. "Dickens and the Angels." UTQ, 50 (Winter 1980/81), 159-76.

A general study of Dickens's treatment of angels in his fiction set against a scholarly discussion of the imaginative concept of angels in British literature. Cameron concludes that "unintellectual moralism" and scorn for dogma and ritual characterize Dickens's "central religious position." But Dickens, he notes, did expound one dogma: "that children when they die are turned into angels." No Christian body endorsed this view, states Cameron, although frequent references to it appear in Dickens's fiction. Among the instances Cameron refers to, several variations of the idea occur in **Oliver Twist**. Some young people, writes Cameron, like Oliver and Rose "are as near being angels as makes no matter." Little Dick, facing certain death, dreams "of Heaven and Angels" in Chapter 7, and even Fagin is so moved by Oliver's immanent spirituality as he lies asleep that he refrains from waking him to discuss his part in the robbery he plans with Sikes (ch. 19). Identifying virginal girls as angels, Cameron adds, represents another Dickensian unorthodoxy, one "purely sentimental and picturesque [and] religiously vacuous."

47.   Canning, Hon. Albert S.G. "**Oliver Twist**." In his **Dickens Studied in Six Novels**. London: T. Fisher Unwin, 1912, pp. 3-52.

A revised and enlarged version of his earlier work, **Philosophy of Charles Dickens** (1880). See XII. 4. This chapter generously summarizes the plot and abstains from critical commentary.

48.   Carey, John. "Dickens' Children." In his **The Violent Effigy: A Study of Dickens' Imagination**. London, 1973; rpt. London: Faber and Faber, 1979, pp. 131-53. Retitled in the U.S. as **Here Comes Dickens: The Imagination of a Novelist**. New York: Schocken Books, 1974.

Comments briefly in a discussion of Dickens's fictional treatment of childhood on the apparent oddness of rewarding Bob Fagin's fidelity to young Charles by later using his name for the villain of **Oliver Twist**. See Forster (XIII. 83). Carey speculates that Dickens's choice was "really quite logical." While Paul Green's hostility properly acknowledged the social gulf between Dickens and his fellow workers in the blacking warehouse, Fagin's offer of friendship threatened to drag the young boy down to his own level. Carey also suggests that Oliver's virtuous uncontamination represents another reassertion of "the purity of the middle-class soul," which miraculously survived life in the rotting warehouse and then imprisonment in Fagin's den when Dickens treated this experience in fictional guise. The readable and entertaining chapters comprising the rest of the book examine aspects of Dickens's imagination obviously fascinating to Carey. He writes well about corpses, coffins, waxworks, portraits, clothes, sex, and wooden legs, but presents a distorted view of the workings of Dickens's mind by restricting his focus to Dickens's apparent fondness for detachable parts and by ignoring how moral and social issues also shape the writer's imaginative outlook.

49.   Cassid, Donna. "Dickens: A Feminist View." **Woman: A Journal of Liberation**, 2 (Fall 1970), 21-22.

Notes two conflicting responses to women in Dickens's novels: his realism and his romantic idealism. Cassid praises the first because it allows Dickens to express his sympathy for victimized and oppressed women in Victorian England; the second, predictably, she damns as the view of a reactionary male, whose "wooden figures" like Agnes Wickfield embody the values of "a male-dominated society." Cassid takes comfort in Dickens's willingness to satirize romantic love, citing the way Noah orders Charlotte around in Chapter 42 as an example. She also praises Dickens's honest admission in Sikes's murder of Nancy that violence is always a potential threat to the non-submissive female, a truth Dickens "lay[s] bare" in that fearful scene.

50.   Cawelti, John G. "The Best-Selling Social Melodrama." In his **Adventure, Mystery, and Romance: Formula Stories as Art and Popular Culture.** Chicago: Univ. of Chicago Press, 1976, pp. 260-95.

A taxonomy of popular-story formulas, amongst which Cawelti includes "social melodrama," a term he uses to describe novels like **Oliver Twist,** which combine melodramatic structure with a realistic social or historical setting. Such works typically examine aspects of a social problem (crime, in Dickens's case) and reinforce conventional social values by "showing forth the essential 'rightness' of the world order." If Dickens did not invent this genre, writes Cawelti of social melodrama, he developed the formula for it "into one of the most successful fictional genres of the nineteenth and twentieth centuries." By synthesizing social criticism with "the archetype of melodrama," Cawelti concludes, Dickens gave his readers "the pleasure of seeing the follies of men and institutions combined with the satisfaction of witnessing the triumph of virtue and the punishment of vice."

51.   Cecil, David. "Charles Dickens." In his **Early Victorian Novelists: Essays in Revaluation.** Indianapolis and New York: Bobbs-Merrill, 1935, pp. 36-74.

Cecil sets out to rescue the Victorian novelists from the dust and oblivion they had gathered, at least on the shelves of gentlemen, who kept Dickens and company in **"Editions de luxe"** or in standard reprints. These essays in "revaluation," originally lectures Cecil delivered at Oxford in the 1930's, represent perhaps the **locus classicus** of a kind of criticism to which none aspires today. Cecil relies on such fuzzy criteria as "those profounder feelings to which the very greatest art appeals" for assessing works and delights in the grandiose paradox. In one sentence he calls Dickens "a fantastic genius" and in the next writes that he "had no special insight into the qualities which are characteristic of man as man."

The essays also illustrate Cecil's formula that these "lawful and undisputed monarchs of literature" cannot be appreciated without first exploring their weaknesses, a task he appears to relish with Dickens, whom Cecil thinks has more than a representative share. Dickens errs because he is "vulgar" and because he was "unintellectual and uneducated," a man of the middle class who shared their instincts and wrote as "a semi-educated Cockney" for readers with neither taste nor brains. Cecil says little about **Oliver Twist** but his essay is worth reading as an example of the condescension, ignorance, and snobbery that characterizes a response to Dickens once fashionable among some British intellectuals. Cecil professes to admire Dickens for his humor, his poetry, and his imaginative vitality, qualities which raise this crude and vulgar Cockney to greatness but nevertheless limit him because he could not portray "complex, educated or aristocratic types" and wrote only of charwomen, schoolmasters, shopkeepers, and tramps. When Cecil reconsidered his judgments twenty-three years later, in **Victorian Novelists** (Chicago and London: Univ. of Chicago Press, 1958), he found his opinions substantially unchanged. But he did note that the more Dickens is studied, "the richer and deeper" does the symbolic and imaginative strain of his genius appear.

52.   Chakravarty, Sudeshna. "The City in the Novels of Dickens and Dostoevsky." **Bulletin of the Department of English Calcutta University,** 12 (1976-77), 65-84.

Briefly traces the image of the city through Dickens's works, arguing that each novel illustrates a recurring pattern. Chakravarty defines this as an individual confronting the city ("modern mass society") and concerning himself with finding "a meaningful life within this environment." This essay draws on Miller (XII. 153), Fanger (XII. 77), and others, and offers predictable responses to familiar city passages in **Oliver Twist** and other Dickens novels.

53.   Chandler, Frank Wadleigh. "The Rogue in his Social Environment." In his **The Literature of Roguery.** Vol. 2. Boston: Houghton Mifflin, 1907, pp. 415-20.

Attributes Dickens's interest in rogues partially to his familiarity with the picaresque tradition, where rogues are presented as individuals, and partially to the reform tradition of Godwin and Bulwer, which studies rogues as "social phenomena." Chandler emphasizes **Oliver Twist's** strong moral purpose, notes that Dickens stresses the social environment of the criminals, and comments briefly on the major and minor representatives of villainy.

54.   Chesterton, G.K. "Oliver Twist." In 1907 Everyman Edition (II. 25), pp. v-xiii. Rpt. in his **Appreciations and Criticisms of the Works of Charles Dickens.** London, 1911; rpt. New York: Haskell House, 1966, pp. 38-49.

Calls **Oliver Twist** "by far the most depressing" of all Dickens's books, an illustration of the fact that the man who conceived "the humane hospitalities of Pickwick" could also imagine "the inhuman laughter of Fagin's den." To the readers of **The Pickwick Papers,** the difference between the two may come as a surprise, although the disturbing elements in **Oliver Twist,** Chesterton argues, typify "another kind of energy" which infuses Dickens's work and exists "alongside of his happy laughter." Chesterton praises the book's nightmare qualities and writes approvingly of the anger Dickens directed at social oppression and of the sterner side of his character **Oliver Twist** reveals. "Dickens attacks the modern workhouse," he writes, "with a sort of inspired simplicity as a boy in a fairy tale who wandered about, sword in hand, looking for ogres and who has found an indisputable ogre." Whereas a modern realist, Chesterton thinks, would have made all the children in the workhouse "utterly crushed" and fearful of speaking at all, Dickens gains immeasurably by making Oliver ask for more. The tragedy of the incident lies in Oliver's assumption that the universe will be kind to him and that he lives in a just world. "Oliver Twist is pathetic because he is an optimist," Chesterton concludes.

55.   Christian, Mildred G. "Carlyle's Influence upon the Social Theory of Dickens. (Part Two: Their Literary Relationship)." **The Trollopian,** 2 (June 1947), 11-26.

Notes the difficulty of determining when identity of view between Carlyle and Dickens means "influence of the former upon the latter, and when it means merely coincidence." Christian finds evidence of Carlyle's completed social theory most easily discernible in **Bleak House, Hard Times, Little Dorrit,** and **A Tale of Two Cities** and presents her case persuasively in a discussion of those novels. "[S]pecific, though less extensive," evidence of Carlyle may also be found in **Oliver Twist** and **The Chimes,** she writes, but she ignores these works in the essay.

56.   Churchill, R.C. "Charles Dickens." In **From Dickens to Hardy.** Ed. Boris Ford. Vol. VI of the Pelican Guide to English Literature. Harmondsworth: Penguin, 1958, pp. 119-43.

A chronological survey of Dickens's canon prefaced by a dated estimate of his genius, which Churchill damns as heartily as he praises. Dickens, he notes, produced more rubbish than any other writer of distinction, the rubbish in this case being the ridiculous sentiment and melodrama Churchill finds in all Dickens's novels. **Oliver Twist** provides no exception, although Churchill admires its opening chapters as "among the best things that Dickens ever wrote" because they remain free from melodrama and sentiment and pillory institutions and forms of social evil "still very much with us."

57.   _____. "Dickens, Drama and Tradition." **Scrutiny,** 10 (April 1942), 358-75.

A general essay which bestows high praise on Dickens's comic characters but finds him inferior compared with George Eliot and other novelists. Churchill observes that Dickens has "no sustained piece of writing" where his virtues appear without faults and that he has therefore "no masterpiece." But he does find brilliant patches, such as the opening of **Oliver Twist,** a section of the novel sustained by "refreshingly cool irony" and Dickens's "particular genius." This quality Churchill defines as Dickens's unique ability "to put his finger on the social evil which hurts the sufferer most." Churchill appears to draw heavily on this essay for his contribution to volume VI of the Pelican Guide to English Literature (XII. 56).

58.   Cockshut, A.O.J. "The Expanding Prison." In his **The Imagination of Charles Dickens.** London, 1961; rpt. London: Methuen, 1965, pp. 29-32.

Cockshut uses **Oliver Twist** to support his thesis that "the prison is a dominating image" in Dickens's fiction, whose urgency arises not simply from its frequency but from its presentation from the inside as an experience "which we are all compelled to share." **Oliver Twist** opens in an institution richly suggestive of prison and "ends with Fagin's condemned cell," as if to suggest "that there is ultimately no escape." Towards his "intractable preoccupation" with prisons the narrator reveals two attitudes, whose origin, Cockshut argues, spring from "a too close personal identification with his hero." In some descriptions of the lonely boy self-pity breaks through as Dickens recalls his own childhood; in others, the narrator's facetious tone distances him from the protagonist in an attempt by the author "to keep up respectable appearances" by separating his own troubles from Oliver's.

59. Colby, Robert A. "Oliver Twist: The Fortunate Foundling." In his **Fiction with a Purpose: Major and Minor Nineteenth-Century Novels.** Bloomington: Indiana Univ. Press, 1967, pp. 105-37.

Studies seven important British novels published between 1814 and 1872 and relates each to its original literary background. Colby's erudite analysis of **Oliver Twist** provides the most thoroughly researched examination of the book's literary context available and authoritatively surveys the way Dickens apparently wove into the novel a variety of popular elements long since forgotten and now ignored by most twentieth-century readers.

Four principal threads occupy Colby's attention. Part of the book's didactic concerns he traces to the work of Hannah More, Laetitia Matilda Hawkins, and Elizabeth Hamilton, "bluestockings ... who dedicated their pens to the cause of the education of the poor," an issue which Dickens takes up in **Oliver Twist**'s skeptical portrait of parochial voluntaryism as a means of providing schooling for infants. Colby also stresses the novel's affinity with serious Newgate fiction--novels that sought to connect low and high life and reveal to the inhabitants of St. James's their own reflections in the cesspools of Saffron Hill. Colby makes this point by showing how Dickens comments ironically on the way the humbler classes ape the manners of those above them, including the peacocks and dandies who strut through the "Silver Fork" novels. Dickens's fictitious slum dwellers, Colby concludes, "could just as well be the inhabitants of St. James in masquerade," for both groups pursue identical occupations: "drinking, gambling, idling, and whoring."

The rest of the essay Colby devotes to a persuasive analysis of "the foundling literature of the 1830's," whose range and variety he demonstrates in an illuminating discussion of works by Agnes Maria Bennett, Mrs. Barbara Hofland, John Brownlow, and Carlyle. Colby traces in works by each author such genre conventions as the mixing of philanthropy and picaresque adventure, outcast waifs saved from the parish by benevolent gentlemen, flights to the city which bring together different classes, sentimental pastoral scenes, and orphans who establish their identity by amulets and by demonstrating their innate virtue and innocence. For specific links between **Oliver Twist** and Bennett, Brownlow, Carlyle, and Hofland, see respectively XIII. 130, 132, 133, and 138. For a discussion of the Newgate elements in **Oliver Twist**, see section X. 1-23 and Hollingsworth (XII. 107).

60. Collins, Philip. "Murder: From Bill Sikes to Bradley Headstone." In his **Dickens and Crime.** London, 1962; rpt. Bloomington: Indiana Univ. Press, 1968, pp. 256-89.

Collins's first chapter (pp. 1-26) provides an indispensible introduction to anyone interested in Dickens's fictional treatment of criminals and his penal and social philosophy. Two broad assumptions inform his approach: a conviction that Dickens's attitudes to crime can best be understood by placing them within their historical context, and disagreement with those who discard cultural history and interpret Dickens's apparent obsession with "prisons, executions, thieves, murderers and rebels" according to modern psychological theory. This approach, which originates with Edmund Wilson (V. 24), appears to value only the later, "dark" novels and to concentrate exclusively upon the "morally ambiguous elements" in Dickens's personality and writings. Collins does not wish to deny Dickens's complexity--particularly as it manifests itself in ideas about crime--but he attempts to counter those who conjecture about Dickens's identification with his criminals. Collins grants Dickens's "ever-increasing intimacy with the criminal mind" but denies that his fictional ability means that he sympathized with murderers and wicked men or that he could write about them because he himself was an outcast denouncing society.

The discussion of Bill Sikes illustrates these issues. Dickens's interest in the social and economic origins of crime apparent in the 1841 Preface to **Oliver Twist** (X. 14) clearly implies sympathy for young offenders, whom he believed society should help by providing them with schools and practical training. But towards Sikes and other "men of vicious temperament" Dickens felt no such compassion, preferring instead to see them removed from society for the protection of lawful citizens. Collins praises the verisimilitude with which Dickens depicts criminals in **Oliver Twist**--he states that Dickens based Fagin on Ikey Solomons--cf. XIII. 123. He argues persuasively that Sikes is no tragic Macbeth--cf. Senelick (XII. 182) and Macready (V. 5)--and he comments on the **Sikes and Nancy** public reading. In particular, he takes issue with the hypothesis that the strain of the performances hastened Dickens's death--see W. Collins (V. 22) and cf. W.H. Bowen (V. 1)--and with the argument advanced by Wilson (V. 24) and endorsed by House (XII. 111), Johnson (V. 18), and others (V. 17) that Dickens's motive for these readings was suicidal. Collins sees them as "the climax of a long process," not something unique, and as the expression of histrionic zest and "an emotional self-indulgence" which provided, like the other readings, an outlet for disappointment in his later personal life.

61. _____. "The Rights of Childhood." In his **Dickens and Education.** London, 1963; rpt. London: Macmillan, 1965, pp. 172-208, and passim.

Discusses **Oliver Twist** and other novels as they illustrate Collins's sense of "the pattern of Dickensian child-victim": "the child unloved and lonely, thrown prematurely into the unsympathetic adult world." Cf. Coveney (XII. 62). Collins reads **Oliver Twist** as a realistic criticism of the times--"society is more to blame for [Oliver's] sufferings than any individual"--and faults Dickens for "obvious weaknesses" in his argument. Among them he cites the characterization of Oliver, whose allegorical role leaves the protagonist "impossibly untouched in soul and in speech by his vicious companions."

62. Coveney, Peter. "The Child in Dickens." In his **Poor Monkey: The Child in Literature.** London: Rockliff, 1957, pp. 86-92. Revised and republished as **The Image of the Child. The Individual and Society: A Study of the Theme in English Literature.** Harmondsworth: Penguin, 1967.

Coveney calls **Oliver Twist** the first novel in English "with its true centre of focus on a child." This **"roman a these"** works when Dickens attacks the harsh logic of the Poor Law Amendment Act and insists on the helplessness and isolation of children in the new age of Malthusian economics and Benthamite reform. The novel proves less successful when Dickens's personal feelings obtrude, as they do in the country scenes and the ending, where the author allows his emotions about "The lost Chatham days" to undermine his art. But overall, Coveney finds the novel a remarkable account of "the world seen through the eyes of a child."

63. Crawford, Iain. "Time and Structure in Oliver Twist." The Dickensian, 77 (Spring 1981), 23-31.

Discusses three aspects of the novel's chronological structure: Dickens's attempt to use the seasons and the natural world to mirror the novel's actions; his use of time in the Monks plot to sharpen the parallels between good and bad characters by emphasizing their similarities in ages; and the novel's historical setting. With respect to the first, Crawford argues that Dickens probably set out with no conscious, pre-meditated design, but became more aware of the need for a consistent time-scheme as the novel progressed. As evidence of Dickens's design, Crawford cites Dickens's use of seasons to evoke mood, as winter, cold, and mist provide the background for trying and threatening events and as spring and summer reflect the novel's sense of pastoral security. These alternations, Crawford agrees, coincide, to some extent, with the seasons of the novel's publication in serial parts, but the treatment of time in Oliver Twist, he argues, "is far more relevant" to its internal structure than is true of The Pickwick Papers. In Dickens's first novel, he tended to subordinate subject matter to the time of its serial publication.

Crawford's examination of the Monks plot reveals the difficulties Dickens experienced in making Oliver's age coincide with the events of the novel's past history. To fit with Mr. Brownlow's remark to Monks, "I speak of fifteen years ago when you were not more than eleven years old" (ch. 49), Oliver should be at least thirteen, while the action of the novel renders him no more than eleven or twelve. Mr. Brownlow's comment, however, helps date the ages of Monks and Rose, who at twenty-six and seventeen reinforce the contrast between their respective coevals, Harry Maylie and Nancy. This "series of closely paralleled contrasts between the good and evil characters through reference to their ages," argues Crawford, helps create the effect of the different generations of two opposing families within the novel and may owe something to Fielding's Tom Jones. In a brief word about Oliver Twist's historical setting, Crawford suggests that Dickens tried to combine events "around or before 1830" with those that had immediate topical relevance. Cf. Hollingsworth (XII. 106).

64. Crotch, W. Walter. "The Criminals." The Pageant of Dickens. London, 1915; rpt. New York: Haskell House, 1972, pp. 85-105.

Selects from among Dickens's "veritable Chamber of Horrors!" his more prominent criminal figures, whom Crotch values for their psychological realism and for the insight with which Dickens treats them. Beginning with Oliver Twist, Crotch praises Sikes and Fagin as two of Dickens's greatest accomplishments in a novel that offers a range of criminal characters. The portraits succeed, Crotch argues, because Dickens presents his criminals sympathetically and yet without false allure. Dickens insists, for example, that the gallows instigate rather than deter criminals, and he shows that retribution inevitably awaits those who break moral laws.

65. _____. "The Interpreter of Childhood." In his **Charles Dickens Social Reformer: The Social Teachings of England's Greatest Novelist.** London: Chapman and Hall, 1913, pp. 38-64.

Calls Dickens England's greatest interpreter of childhood and praises the novelist for his ability to depict "all sorts and conditions of children." Crotch credits Dickens with correcting the conditions that caused so much misery to children in Victorian England and applauds the "courage and insight" Dickens showed in presenting characters from "the worst class of children," the child thief, the boy criminal, and the juvenile robber. "From the moment that Dickens published **Oliver Twist**," writes Crotch, "the reaction against this brutality and neglect set in" as Dickens rendered "immense service" to the English by "liberating their frozen sympathies and revivifying their lost confidence in childhood."

66. Dabney, Ross H. **Love and Property in the Novels of Dickens.** Berkeley: Univ. of California Press, 1967, passim.

Unlike critics who dismiss the story of Oliver's suppressed identity and stolen rights as extraneous pieces of "melodramatic machinery," Dabney argues that the forced marriage of Oliver's father "is the original sin in the story" and the mainspring by which Oliver is set apart from other parish orphans. Mercenary marriages, he suggests, repeatedly occur in Dickens's fiction and form the basis of **Oliver Twist** and other novels, illustrating Dickens's interest in "the special, extraordinary position and rights of a particular child" and the consequences of violating them. This thematic concern, he believes, binds the mechanism of "conspiracy, forged wills, suppressed identity, etc." to the novel as a whole and accounts for the insertion of the story of Harry Maylie and Rose Fleming. By dropping his powerful friends, abandoning his prospects, and taking a wife without wealth or high status, Harry makes a thematic statement: "the trouble started with a marriage made to satisfy family pride and ambition; the book ends with a marriage conceived as a deliberate rejection of these."

67. Daleski, H.M. "Oliver Twist." In his **Dickens and the Art of Analogy.** London: Faber and Faber, 1970, pp. 49-78.

Sees **Oliver Twist** as a confused work because it incorporates "two novels": the imaginative evocation of a social problem posed by the existence of the poor, and an affirmation of Dickens's moral belief in "Virtue Triumphant." Daleski develops each point at length, providing multiple quotations to support his analysis of the "bifurcated structure" evident in the juxtaposition of the streets, poverty, and crime with homes, civilization, and goodness. Daleski finds Dickens's social criticism "effective" but not subversive, unlike Kettle (XII. 125), whose essay, he thinks, blurs "the fundamental distinction between the poor and the criminal." **Oliver Twist**, he counters, is not concerned with what the poor should do against the oppressive state, but with "what the well-housed and the well-fed should do to ensure that the poor do not opt for the criminal."
Dickens pursues this end, Daleski argues, by presenting two simple prescriptions: he shows those in power things as they really are (Dickens's "own kind of realism"), and he advocates responsible public action to ensure that the poor do not drift into crime. At the same time, he works against his own intention by portraying Oliver as virtue incarnate. A similar problem manifests itself for Daleski in the novel's divided view of criminals: its

"spiritual drama" requires a protagonist who personifies "the principle of Evil," while its social criticism treats Fagin and his companions as products of the environment.

68. Devonshire, M.G. "Dickens." In her **The English Novel in France 1830-1870.** 1929; rpt. London: Frank Cass, 1967, pp. 289-97; 312-29.

Provides some information about Dickens's French translators and publishers between 1838 and 1848, observing of that period that Dickens's success in France cannot be compared to that of Scott, Cooper, or Maryatt. Devonshire summarizes the responses of early French reviewers and notes how opinion turned in Dickens's favor around 1850. Between 1830 and 1870, she observes, Oliver Twist, with eight editions, stood second to David Copperfield, with thirteen, in apparent popularity in France.

69. Dexter, Walter. "The Villain of the Piece." In his **Some Rogues and Vagabonds of Dickens.** London: Cecil Palmer, 1927, pp. 48-59.

Describes Monk's role in the novel, introducing him with quotations from the text and linking commentary between the extracts. Dexter argues that while Monk's character may travel on conventional lines, savoring much of the theatre, "we must not condemn either the character or the story as they are both true to type." He writes that at the time Dickens wrote Oliver Twist he was obsessed with his love for the stage and adds that "of all the stage figures he drew, none was truer to the type beloved of the dramatist of the day, than that of Monks, the villain of the piece."

70. Dilnot, A.F. "Dickens's Early Fiction and the Idea of Practical Utility." SoR, 8 (June 1975), 141-51.

Cautions against the assumption, conditioned in part by excessive enthusiasm for F.R. Leavis's view of **Hard Times** as an attack on Utilitarianism, that Dickens persistently saw himself as the enemy of those who valued human activities in terms of their social utility. To support this point, Dilnot examines Dickens's portrayal of work in the early novels, citing in particular his condemnation of the workhouse. The importance of Dickens's attack, Dilnot argues, lies less in his objection to specific social theories than in the way workhouses denigrate work by forcing paupers to pick oakum, crush bones, and break stones. Thus rather than read Oliver Twist as one of Dickens's first attacks on Utilitarian theory, Dilnot prefers to stress that the novel's main point constitutes its opposition to a society that makes work useless. And as long as such an attitude predominates, he argues, the corruption which flows from people feeling useless will flourish "at all levels," a warning the early novels repeat and elaborate.

71. Donovan, Frank. "Children of Good and Evil." In his **The Children of Charles Dickens.** London: Leslie Frewin, 1969, pp. 61-68. Published in the U.S. as **Dickens and Youth.** New York: Dodd, Mead, 1968.

Donovan puts Dickens's juvenile characters into various categories--"saintly maidens," servant girls, children at school, and so on--after a sketchy chapter on how Dickens saw childhood. The section on Oliver Twist presents a detailed summary, in chronological order, of the episodes Dickens devotes to Oliver's career and history. Donovan quotes extensively from the text but provides no analysis or comment.

72.   Duffy, Joseph M., Jr. "Another Version of Pastoral: **Oliver Twist.**"
       ELH, 35 (September 1968), 403-21.

       Detailed commentary on Dickens's juxtaposition of the contaminating
effects of city life with the restorative virtues of country living. Duffy
examines aspects of this familiar theme in other writers, alluding briefly to
Wordsworth, Arnold, and Hardy. He finds Dickens's ideas similar to theirs,
but implies that his "version" of the pastoral differs in its apparently
pessimistic sense that social good "is without meaning" in a society as
unprincipled, hostile, and exploitative as that of Victorian England. Personal
love can triumph and personal evil can be defeated, he admits, but society
remains "enduringly blank and corrupt," except for those who retreat and
form small groups in the country. "A bad world is depicted" in **Oliver Twist,**
writes Duffy, not only for the economically poor "but for all men
impoverished in their hearts by the false pieties of society." This view, he
believes, links Dickens with the gloomy questions of the Stranger in T.S.
Eliot's "Choruses from 'The Rock'" and **The Secret Agent,** that "most
Dickensian" of Conrad's novels.

73.   Edgerton, Larry. "Dickens's **Oliver Twist.**" **Explicator,** 40 (Fall
       1981), 28-30.

       Comments on Oliver's appearance in court before Mr. Fang (ch. 11) as a
metaphor for the incidents that befall the protagonist in the other chapters.
The ensuing confrontation between the magistrate and Oliver's protector,
Mr. Brownlow, Edgerton argues, represents the juxtaposition of two realms:
"Fang's dingy hell, populated by whores, mendicants, thieves, and beleaguered
orphans" and Brownlow's "airy corner of the world," where compassion and
memory operate. In the course of the novel, Oliver makes the hero's journey
from the streets to the gentleman's world. He initiates the first step himself
as he flees from Sowerberry's but remains incapable of continuing his
geographical progress across the land and his upward social journey until he is
"borne from court to carriage" at the end of Chapter 11, after which he is
supported by Brownlow and others for the rest of the novel.

74.   Empson, William. "The Symbolism of Dickens." In **Dickens and the
       Twentieth Century.** Ed. John Gross and Gabriel Pearson (XII. 27), pp.
       13-15.

       Empson touches briefly on the novel, arguing that Dickens invests
Oliver's goodness with the symbolic meaning that "all the little boys in the
orphanage were being robbed of their English heritage." By making readers
feel that one of their own boys was in Oliver's place, he adds, Dickens
impressed his audience, although the novel turns out to be less than alarming
for Empson, to whom the work offers a practical and soothing reflection: "All
you need do, really, is go through these workhouses and pick out the little
gentlemen, because all the other little boys are just pigs."

75.   Engel, Monroe. "Oliver Twist." In his **The Maturity of Dickens.**
       Cambridge, Mass.: Harvard Univ. Press, 1959, pp. 85-94.

       Finds **Oliver Twist,** with the possible exception of **Hard Times,** Dickens's
most "purposeful work." In part, Engel argues, the novel derives its
concentration from the magazine serial form, which imposed on Dickens "a
radically different pace of narration" from that of **The Pickwick Papers,**

whose publication in twenty parts almost twice the length of the installments of Oliver Twist allowed leisurely discourse and a less exacting use of plot. A second reason for the novel's economy, Engel suggests, lies in Dickens's confident exposition of the connection between crime and poverty and his concrete presentation of what poverty means. Misery and poverty appear in the novel as "a terrible presence," whose consequences in the form of deprivation of food, shelter, and medical care Dickens rarely allows us to forget. Engel also comments on the rational and controlled depiction of criminals, whom Dickens treats with deliberate ambiguity by mixing sympathy for them with the view that they are also responsible for their depravity. Dickens's interest in the thieves' world, he adds, "is at least as much political as neurotic, part of the subversive view of English society that he seems to have held always."

76. Eoff, Sherman. "Oliver Twist and the Spanish Picaresque Novel." Studies in Philology, 54 (July 1957), 440-47.

Argues for the affinity between Dickens's early works, particularly Oliver Twist, and the loose narrative structure, comic adventures, and low life of the Spanish picaresque tradition. Eoff adds that interest in the picaro, a human being entangled in adverse circumstances, also informs Oliver Twist, whose first fifteen chapters evoke parallels with the anonymous Lazarillo de Tormes and Quevedo's El Buscon, each of which depicts a homeless child launched into a cruel world and forced to follow a life of roguery rather than one of honesty and goodness. But, as Eoff points out, Dickens departs sharply from the picaresque tradition by showing Oliver as incorruptible and by making his temporary criminal companions unattractive. In this respect, Eoff concludes, Dickens wrote "an anti-picaresque novel," transforming the Spanish picaresque pattern, which was his starting point, "into something entirely different."

77. Fanger, Donald. "Dickens: Realism, Subjunctive and Indicative." In his Dostoevsky and Romantic Realism: A Study of Dostoevsky in Relation to Balzac, Dickens, and Gogol. Cambridge, Mass.: Harvard Univ. Press, 1965, pp. 65-100.

Fanger uses the phrase "Romantic realism" not as a paradox but as a hybrid term to characterize a stage in the evolution of the novel as it developed during the period marked by a fusion of romance and realism. The four writers of his study, he argues, can best be understood not as "deviationists" from a familiar canon of realism but as exemplars of "a particular attitude toward the art of fiction." Fanger defines this as a concerted effort to render the actual life of a given time and place through "a highly and openly personal vision." In each case, the writer's vision centered on the observed or observable reality of a great modern city--Paris, London, or St. Petersburg--whose low life the novels convey, shaped or distorted by the novelist's imagination. Focusing on urban social history, the works also reveal a startling similarity in subject matter--"strangeness, alienation, crime"--and in technique--"a carefully fostered sense of mystery ... of grotesquerie, a penchant for stark contrasts, for the improbable, the sensational, the dramatic."

After these preliminaries, Fanger devotes individual chapters to the novelists, exploring how each achieves his effects through heightening, intensification, and a Manichaean world view in which innocent victims battle with demonic predators. The chapter on Dickens ranges widely and analyzes how he uses atmosphere and myth to expose the extraordinary reality behind London's official face. Fanger discusses Dickens's use of diabolism in **Oliver Twist** (Fagin), which marks one of the novel's moral poles, with angels enthroned at the other (Rose Maylie). He also comments on how Dickens's criminals, unlike those of Balzac and Dostoevsky, never "stand against society on principle," seeing in this evidence that Dickens's opposition to Victorian society, though strong, was fundamentally loyal. A section of the chapter, "Representing London," traces the growing complexity of Dickens's portrayal of urban life. In **Sketches by Boz**, Fanger writes, the picturesque description of London neighborhoods tends to be "a sufficient value in itself"; in **Oliver Twist**, Oliver moves in a world whose picturesqueness "carries the ballast of constant moral preoccupation."

78. Ferns, John. "**Oliver Twist**: Destruction of Love." QQ, 79 (Spring 1972), 87-92.

Calls **Oliver Twist** an important novel despite its literary unevenness. The source of its power, Ferns contends, lies in its powerful criticism of materialism and its advancement of a theme that "extends the scope of the English novel" by showing how communities based on love are destroyed and how human affections are replaced by monetary values. Ferns looks on the novel as "Dickens's own search for a true sense of community," one which leads him to the "bleak recognition" that events have torn asunder England's social fabric. Nancy's fidelity to Sikes, he writes, represents the book's "most moving idea"; in Sikes Dickens locates "a symbol of a man torn from any nourishing environment and set adrift in a chaotic and meaningless universe."

79. Fielding, K.J. "**Oliver Twist**." In his **Charles Dickens: A Critical Introduction**. London, 1958; rpt. Boston: Houghton Mifflin, 1965, pp. 32-46.

This chapter explores Dickens's treatment of the criminal world and discusses Forster's "somewhat cryptic ... remarks" about how upper and lower classes would be startled if they understood the connection between them implied by the novel (XII. 7). Dickens's "close approximation" of criminals and law-abiding citizens, Fielding argues, indicates **Oliver Twist's** affinity with serious Newgate fiction, where writers frequently linked "fictional crime with radical views of society." Thus part of the novel's purpose, he suggests, was to show the law as "utterly contemptible" and to expose national institutions, where brutality and stupidity predominated, as instruments designed "merely to keep the lower classes from bothering those above them." Attacks on the law "as the destructive instrument of the rich" belong to an earlier tradition with which Dickens was familiar. What distinguishes **Oliver Twist**, Fielding believes, is the combination of social criticism with a "powerful expression of a nightmare sense of evil." Fielding cites the responses of Chesterton (XII. 54) and Greene (XII. 97) to corroborate his impression of the book's disturbing portrayal of "how evil mankind may become." At the same time, he backs away from interpreting **Oliver Twist** as one of Dickens's "dark" novels in which despair is "rounded off with forced pessimism" and argues for its affirmative outlook. Circumstances cause crime; goodness cannot be destroyed; and people can live "purposefully and happily" together if they will look, in the words of the narrator, to "The real hues" of nature instead of to "the sombre colours ... [reflected from] their own jaundiced eyes and hearts." This "is the teaching of Henry Fielding," comments the critic, "imaginatively concentrated with the intensity of fable in the figure of the child."

80. Finkel, Robert J. "Another Boy Brought Up 'By Hand.'" NCF, 20 (March 1966), 389-90.

Notes Dickens's use of this phrase, meant as an alternative to breast feeding, in the first chapter of **Oliver Twist**. Finkel cites the passage describing how Oliver was raised as an early instance of its use, rebutting the assertion of a previous contributor to NCF, who turned to a letter written by Captain Marryat in 1838 as an example of the phrase's currency. Finkel also denies that the Victorian connotation has slipped out of use, citing several English and American dictionaries recording the phrase as Dickens used it. Cf. Phillips (XII. 165).

81. Flynn, T. Edward. "Dickens and the Pathos of Freedom." Humanitas, 15 (May 1979), 209-25.

A wide ranging, occasionally provocative essay which tends to choke on its terminology when the author tries too hard to align **Oliver Twist** with the theological tradition of Kierkegaard and his philosophical allies. Flynn sees the novel, particularly Dickens's study of Sikes's psychological state after the murder of Nancy, partially as a reflection of nineteenth-century libertarian views of human nature, in which freedom is valued as an end in itself, and partially as a religious meditation on the negative aspects of freedom. Flynn argues that Dickens defines these by presenting Sikes as self-divided, prone to self-destruction, and prey to fierce, libidinal and anti-social urges.

Dickens responds critically to Sikes, Flynn suggests, when he judges him by the ethical values of the middle class; but Flynn also sees, in Dickens's insight into Sikes, evidence of the author's fascination with and sympathy for his character's self-tormenting destructive nature. Freedom, argues Flynn, means that we must choose between ethical alternatives, a dilemma which usually brings with it a sense of guilt, all the more intense to those with deeply religious personalities. Dickens, in Flynn's view, fits this pattern and reveals his religious outlook in the novel's presentation of a gradually evolving sense of dread, guilt, and gloomy self-destruction. This probing of man's spiritual distress and pain, he concludes, resembles Dostoevsky's portraits of "criminal-rebel[s]," whose inner agonies and guilt reflect the emotions and responses that figure so prominently in the work of Kafka, Kierkegaard, and Sartre.

82. Ford, George H. "Skyrocket and Stick." In his **Dickens and his Readers: Aspects of Novel Criticism Since 1836.** Princeton: Princeton Univ. Press, 1955, pp. 38-43.

Summarizes briefly the mixed responses of several early commentators on the novel. **Oliver Twist** occupies little of Ford's attention, which focuses primarily on a broader matter of Dickens's general reputation among English readers and critics.

83. Forster, E.M. **Aspects of the Novel.** New York: Harcourt, Brace, 1927, passim.

An influential discussion of the main parts of a work of fiction, whose taxonomy of characters as "flat" and "round" gave many of Dickens's detractors powerful terms to use against him. Although Forster makes only passing (and pejorative) reference to Dickens, he tried to overcome his own bias against "mere caricature" and conceded that Dickens's immense success

152

with types "suggests that there may be more in flatness than the severer critics admit." Forster writes about novels with an enduring clarity and charm, despite his dated judgments about British writers, whom he finds deficient in greatness and incapable of giving as complete a picture of either domestic or heroic life as Tolstoy or Dostoevsky.

84. Frederick, Kenneth C. "The Cold, Cold Hearth: Domestic Strife in **Oliver Twist.**" CE, 27 (March 1966), 465-70.

Examines the novel's presentation of family life, discovering in the domestic scenes "a vast emptiness where the center of affirmation might be expected to be." Frederick extends this argument even to the Brownlow and Maylie households, which for all their importance as symbolic havens, he nevertheless finds "disquietingly empty" and dominated by "an uneasy silence." Dickens presents these domestic centers in hushed tones, describing first Oliver's illness and then Rose's. Brownlow is a bachelor and Mrs. Maylie a widow, each presiding over a retreat or hospital rather than a home filled with a complete, happy family. And if we consider the households of the Bumbles, the Sowerberrys, and the Leefords, argues Frederick, we see "a panorama" of "marital blight" indicative of how the family unit is "crumbling from within."

The purpose of these scenes, Frederick suggests, is to indicate Dickens's sense of how far "respectable" society is corrupt and implicated in the evil "that is frankly practised by the likes of Fagin." But reversing conventional values in this way also poses problems for outcasts like Oliver. If society itself is corrupt, asks Frederick, where is Oliver to turn "in his quest for a fixed place?" The answer, he thinks, lies in an escape from society, the destruction of old family relationships, and the creation of "a family on the basis of the bonds of love rather than law or blood." By withdrawing from the world, the good people affirm this new order and overturn the world's judgment by defying the stigma of illegitimacy and by renouncing conventional values.

85. Frye, Northrop. "Dickens and the Comedy of Humors." In **Experience in the Novel.** Ed. Roy Harvey Pearce. New York: Columbia Univ. Press, 1968, pp. 49-81. Also pub. in Frye's **Essays on Criticism and Society.** Ithaca: Cornell Univ. Press, 1970, pp. 218-40.

Offers a taxonomy of Dickens's novels that allies them with "the New Comedy Structure," whose form Frye traces back to Plautus and Greek Romances. Frye defines works in this category as "fairy tales in the low mimetic displacement," that is as stories that employ stock devices, stress the triumph of the young over the old, end with festivities, and ignore the restrictions of realistic fiction by violently manipulating events. The main action of such plots, writes Frye, usually centers on the love of the hero for the heroine. They constitute the "congenial society," whose lives are thwarted by members of the "obstructing society." Through a series of twists, plot reversals, and discoveries, the novels typically end with members of the congenial society in the ascendancy, virtue vindicated, and vice baffled, as in **Oliver Twist.**

86. Gardner, Lyett I. "The Endocrinology of Abuse Dwarfism, with a Note on Charles Dickens as Child Advocate." **American Journal of Diseases of Children,** 131 (May 1977), 505-07.

Draws briefly on **Oliver Twist, The Old Curiosity Shop, A Christmas Carol,** and other works referring to abused, crippled, and abandoned children to document how Dickens was "especially attuned to the need for child protection." Gardner locates the source of Dickens's sympathy in his own childhood, citing the "abuse and maternal deprivation" Dickens suffered at twelve when he went to the blacking warehouse as the principal reason for his imaginative insight into how psychosocial deprivation and dwarfism are often linked.

87.   Garis, Robert. **The Dickens Theatre: A Reassessment of the Novels.**
      Oxford: Clarendon Press, 1965, passim.

A spirited and polemical rebuttal of what Garis calls the new Dickens orthodoxy, the view that his works represent complex organic structures infused with a symbolic coherence. Garis proposes instead an artist whose "self-delighting fancy" never fails to exhibit its own dazzling brilliance by perpetually reminding readers of his presence through "a highly artificial speaking style." Garis likens Dickens to a superb illusionist or magician whose displays of talent delight but prove inimical to high art because showing off one's style flouts the tasteful writer's "code of literary manners." Verbal tricks and dazzle also conflict with the presentation of characters' inner lives when the author insists on occupying the spotlight instead of turning it on his creations. One notable exception to this tendency Garis finds in the description of Fagin in Chapter 52, where, in "a brilliant passage of an irresistible truthfulness," Dickens wonders what it is like to be another person. Garis thinks that this scene works because Dickens subordinates his own characteristically "energetic and emphatic voice" to that of his character, whose center of self comes not from the author but from Fagin.

88.   Gelphi, Barbara Charlesworth. "The Innocent I: Dickens' Influence on
      Victorian Autobiography." In **The Worlds of Victorian Fiction.** Ed.
      Jerome H. Buckley. Harvard English Studies, 6. Cambridge: Harvard
      Univ. Press, 1975, pp. 57-71.

A speculative and thoughtful essay which discusses the rise in the number and quality of Victorian autobiographies and the link between them and the new emphasis in early Victorian fiction on "the mystery of the individual's growth and change through the interaction of all those things that make up his or her character and circumstances." Gelpi ranges widely, considering the contribution of Goethe, Rousseau, and Wordsworth to the novel and the influence of Dickens's "heart-wringing fantasies" of Oliver, Little Nell, Paul Dombey, and David Copperfield on the autobiographies of Mill, Ruskin, and Pater. Variants of the "typical Dickensian waif-children"--lonely, observant, loveless, motherless, and filled with a sense of their own inadequacy--appear in the autobiographies of each, she suggests.

Gelpi's second focus concerns the significance of this motif in Victorian autobiography, especially the self-pity she sees dominating the presentation of childhood in Mill, Ruskin, and Pater. Turning to Jung, she uses his theory about the archetype of the child to explain qualities she sees common to Dickens's fictional children and those the autobiographers evidently remember. On the one hand, Jung suggests that the archetype of the child embodies the motifs of "'insignificance,' exposure, abandonment, danger"; on the other, the child can symbolize a move "toward greater consciousness" and an understanding that such consciousness is necessarily **"all alone in the world."** When Dickens and the autobiographers reveal self-pity, she concludes, one may see it as "arising from their failure to dissociate the archetypal symbol of the child from the memory's image of their childhood selves." Cf. Marshall (XII. 147).

89.   Gerson, Stanley. "Name-Creation in Dickens." **Moderna Sprak,** 69 (1975), 299-315.

Calls attention to Dickens's method of naming characters as one developing from the humorous, allegorical tradition going back via Smollett, Bunyan, and Ben Jonson to Langland. Gerson divides his study into several categories and draws on **Oliver Twist** for some of his examples. Noah Claypole's alias, "Morris Bolter," suggests flight in both words--**Morris** carries the slang meaning of moving away, decamping, while **Bolter** obviously refers to the verb **bolt.** Similarly, Toby Crackit's occupation appears self-evidently in his surname and less obviously in his first, where **toby** refers to "the highway as a resort for robbers." Gerson also notes the double associations with Bumble and speculates about Dickens's possible indebtedness to **She Stoops to Conquer** for Oliver Twist's name. One of Tony Lumpkin's friends, he notes, is Tom Twist, while Oliver may derive from the play's author, Oliver Goldsmith.

90.   Gibson, Frank A. "Dogs in Dickens." **The Dickensian,** 53 (September 1957), 145-52.

Discusses Bull's-eye as an example of one of Dickens's "leading fictional dogs," whose characteristics reflect his master. Cf. Whitlow (XII. 211). Gibson also notes that Dickens describes Bull's-eye's coat as "shaggy," although Cruikshank portrays him as a short-tailed, almost hairless dog like a bulldog or bull-terrier.

91.   Gold, Joseph. "Dickens' Exemplary Aliens: Bumble the Beadle and Fagin the Fence." **Mosaic,** 2 (Fall 1968), 77-89.

Gold's contribution to a special issue on Literature and Alienation in which he uses his essay to argue that Dickens presents with precision "characters who embody for us states of alienation which perhaps only now we can recognize and describe." Gold defines the term as "a condition of separateness in the midst of a potential harmony" and discusses two versions of the concept in **Oliver Twist.** Active alienation, Gold suggests, deliberately avoids self-knowledge and self-questioning, allowing a character like Bumble (his exemplar) to flourish in a society that esteems false values and hollow men because its members put too much value on "codes, forms, rituals, and rules." A passive alien such as Fagin, by contrast, might well retain his personal integrity and a greater degree of psychological wholeness than his opposite. But he can only flourish underground because society rejects him. Gold suggests that these two types originate in societies which put the values of the marketplace before those of the cross and he argues that the good people in the novel provide "exemplars of integration" to counter the alternative images of the horrors of the workhouse and the den of thieves. This thesis, in slightly altered form, also appears in Gold's chapter on **Oliver Twist** in XII. 92.

92.   _____. "'An Item of Mortality:' **Oliver Twist.**" In his **Charles Dickens: Radical Moralist.** Minneapolis: Univ. of Minnesota Press, 1972, pp. 25-65.

Advances Gold's general thesis that Dickens's early works provide an "Anatomy of Society" and his later ones a focus on the "Autonomy of the Self." In the former, Gold sees characters attempting to integrate themselves into "a hostile and destructive society," whereas in the latter, he argues, Dickens concentrates on individuals who search for freedom and find answers within themselves "regardless of how society swirls around [them]."

Gold's analysis of **Oliver Twist** makes straightforward points about the varieties of evil that beset Oliver--middle class cruelty and indifference, the sordid world of Fagin, and so on--and describes at length how Oliver progresses from "an item of mortality" to an apprentice, a foster-child, a nephew, a brother, and finally a son. Gold rehearses the stages of Oliver's journey leading to his eventual inheritance of food, warmth, and love in laborious detail, thus boring the reader familiar with the text and obscuring the thesis he states in his introduction.

93. Goldberg, Michael. **Carlyle and Dickens.** Athens: Univ. of Georgia Press, 1972, passim.

Notes the difficulty of ascertaining the extent of Dickens's knowledge of Carlyle's works before they met in March 1840. The repeated references to clothes in **Oliver Twist,** for example, and the way in which Oliver's social position fluctuates as he is alternately garbed by institutions and individuals and then stripped by the thieves exemplifies "the main point" of Carlyle's "clothes philosophy." Nevertheless, Goldberg sticks to his cautious estimate that it was not until the fifties that Dickens had familiarized himself with a large selection of Carlyle's major writings.

Goldberg also discusses how both writers use the contrast between pastoral and urban worlds but suggests that Dickens soon lost his belief "in the efficacy of the idyll." While Oliver retains a brief memory of a happier existence, "This elusive Edenic condition," writes Goldberg, "is not anything Oliver has directly known himself." Rather a nostalgic sense of an idyll remains in his mind "somewhat like Jung's description of the operation of the collective unconsciousness." It is something he responds to but is "unrealizable in the world."

94. Goldknopf, David. "Coincidence in the Victorian Novel: The Trajectory of a Narrative Device." CE, 31 (October 1969), 41-50.

Makes no specific reference to **Oliver Twist** but helpfully discusses the use of coincidence by different Victorian novelists. Goldknopf presents coincidence as a device for making "a tacit metaphysical statement" about God's "therapeutic intervention" in the novels of Charlotte Bronte and Dickens, while for George Eliot the device served to illustrate "the historical connectedness" of members of a society. For Hardy, coincidence suggested either a sense of malevolence in the universe or of "God's moral neutrality."

95. Gomme, A.H. "Mystery, Coincidence, and Melodrama." In his **Dickens.** London: Evans, 1971, pp. 93-98.

Writes about coincidence from a realistic point of view, accepting novels that do not make the reader stretch his eyes too far, and rejecting those in which Dickens fits extravagant coincidences on situations that will not bear them. Gomme cites **Oliver Twist** as an extreme example of this fault, arguing that the book's moral pattern depends on coincidences foreign to the nature of the material of the story. Gomme also thinks that the novel fails because Dickens tries to make Oliver perform two contradictory functions: he must serve as an example of how middle class authorities abuse the poor and also illustrate how criminals attempt to corrupt the godly.

96.   Gordon, Elizabeth Hope. **The Naming of Characters in the Works of Charles Dickens.** Lincoln: Univ. of Nebraska Press, 1917. 35 pp.

Discusses the affinity evident between the names of many of Dickens's fictional people and their characters, and divides her analysis of Dickens's naming techniques into several categories. Among them, Gordon notes characters whose original names have been identified (Laing/Fang), names that are directly descriptive (grim-faced Mr. Grimwig), and those that are neutral (Brownlow).

97.   Greene, Graham. "The Young Dickens." In his **The Lost Childhood and Other Essays.** London: Eyre and Spottiswode, 1951, pp. 51-57.

A brilliant and deliberately subjective response to the novel, which Greene originally published as an Introduction to **Oliver Twist** (II. 39). The story's power, for Greene, lies not in its social realism but in Dickens's "secret prose" in which he detects "delicate and exact poetic cadences" of a truth creeping into the novel unrecognized even by the author. Greene finds himself lost, not around Saffron Hill like Oliver, but in "the interstices of one young, angry, gloomy brain," whose power to conjure up "oppressive images" Greene exalts.

In this "Fagin darkness," he writes, Dickens's hand seldom fumbles, unlike those passages describing the daylight world, which Greene finds peopled with "inadequate ghosts of goodness." These figures finally triumph over the villains, but Greene remains unconvinced by their victory wrought by "the complex narrative of illegitimacy and burnt wills and destroyed evidence," believing instead in the evil-doing of Monks, Sikes, and Fagin. Dickens, he concludes, deals out his happy endings and his unreal retributions, but he can "never ruin the validity and dignity of our realization that not only London but the whole world belongs to Monks and Fagin "after dark." Is it too fantastic to imagine that in this novel, asks Greene, the author hints that the world was made by Satan and not by God, as he tells us "with the music of despair?" For Pritchett's response to Greene's essay, see XII. 168.

98.   Grylls, David. **Guardians and Angels: Parents and Children in Nineteenth-Century Literature.** London: Faber and Faber, 1978, pp. 132-52.

Contains no separate analysis of **Oliver Twist** but skilfully explores Dickens's attitudes towards children as they evolved from "conventional jollity" at their expense in his apprenticeship fiction to a profound identification with and sympathy for the offspring of cruel and ineffective parents in subsequent novels. Grylls's strengths include his intelligent awareness of the advantages and limitations of his consistent but not exclusive focus on imaginative literature and his ability to place Dickens's concern for children within a broad context. Grylls presents Evangelical Puritanism and Rousseauism as the two dominant ideologies informing the Victorian debate about children and usefully juxtaposes Dickens with Jane Austen. Both novelists, he argues, deal with education and upbringing and reveal attitudes that derive from both "the climate of their age" and from their own unique sensibilities. Cf. also Pattison (XII. 164).

99. Gummer, Ellis N. Dickens' Works in Germany 1837-1937. Oxford: Clarendon Press, 1940, passim.

Provides factual information about the responses of German critics to Oliver Twist and notes on some of the novel's translators. By 1915, thirty-five editions of Oliver Twist had been published since its first appearance in Germany, one scholar reported, thus making Oliver Twist the most popular of Dickens's works to that date.

100. Hannaford, Richard. "The Fairy World of Oliver Twist." DSN, 8 (June 1977), 33-36.

Hannaford argues that as an archetypal story of a youngster succeeding against all misfortunes, Oliver Twist makes repeated use of "fairy-tale motifs." In particular, Dickens draws on the hero Dick Whittington, whose journey to London to seek his fortune, testing by severe trials, and unexpected but welcome befriending by a benefactor run parallel to the experiences of Oliver. Dickens also alludes to other familiar folk motifs: the power of dress to cloak or reveal identity; mysterious parents; a refusal to minimize the power of evil; and the eventual victory over enormous odds, all the more poignant because triumph cannot be expected.

101. Hardy, Barbara. "Dickens and the Passions." In Dickens Centennial Essays. Ed. Ada Nisbet and Blake Nevius. Berkeley: Univ. of California Press, 1971, pp. 67-84.

In a brief discussion of some of the methods Dickens uses to portray passion in his characters, Hardy examines the account of Sikes's flight in Chapter 48 to show how Dickens shifts from an emphasis on conduct and gesture to a depiction of inner feelings. Part of the chapter's appeal, Hardy suggests, lies in the histrionic and exciting events of the pursuit, flight, and fire, and part in Dickens's success in capturing "the inner register" of Sikes's mind as he tries to escape. By keeping Sikes in touch "with certain common features of human feeling," Dickens manages to evoke compassion for this brutal but hunted man.

102. Hayens, Kenneth. "Introduction." In 1954 Collins Edition (II. 40), pp. 5-7.

Provides a brief biographical introduction to the professional and personal highlights of Dickens's life.

103. Henkle, Roger B. "Early Dickens: Metamorphosis, Psychic Disorientation, and the Small Fry." In his Comedy and Culture England 1820-1900. Princeton: Princeton Univ. Press, 1980, pp. 111-44.

Discusses the various elements Henkle sees in Dickens's early comic vision. The Pickwick Papers, he argues, puts "the whole unnerving upheaval of social change in comforting, controlled perspective" by suggesting how eccentricity is acceptable as long as the individual's behavior is socially harmless. Oliver Twist, by contrast, serves a different purpose because Dickens's fascination with "the wild side of life" pushes aside the narrative of Oliver, allowing the novelist's "real interests" in the fortunes of the streets and the vitality of London's underworld inhabitants to predominate. The book's loyalties, Henkle concludes, are divided between "a little boy's [middle-class] nightmare of being kidnapped and held prisoner" and delight in the bizarre, comic phenomenal world of the Artful Dodger, who exclaims to Oliver: "Here's a jolly life!" as he draws forth a handful of shillings and halfpence, "Here, catch hold."

104. Hill, T.W. "Notes on **Oliver Twist.**" **The Dickensian,** 46 (Summer 1950), 146-56.

A useful but by no means comprehensive attempt to annotate **Oliver Twist.** Hill provides a number of literary, topographical, social, and historical allusions, but he ignores thieves' slang where the context suggests the meaning and makes no reference to manuscript cancellations or textual changes by Dickens in later editions.

105. Hobsbaum, Philip. "Oliver Twist (1837-38)." In his **A Reader's Guide to Charles Dickens.** London: Thames and Hudson, 1972, pp. 37-47.

A brief survey of the novel illustrating Hobsbaum's determination to provide "a structural survey of Dickens's fiction" as a counter to the modern tendency to ignore the shape and function of his plots in favor of more specialized studies. By looking at plot--"the main line of action"--and theme--the common end to which the plots or strands of the plot tend--Hobsbaum sets out "to help people understand Dickens."
Applying this approach to **Oliver Twist,** Hobsbaum focuses on how plot and theme only marginally coincide. The latter emerges clearly in the first eleven chapters, where Oliver appears as an emblematic waif whose wanderings illustrate how "impersonal officialdom" and dehumanizing bureaucracy grind down people and rule with systematic oppression. Unfortunately, Dickens fails to sustain this powerful moral fable and turns Oliver into "a smug young bourgeois" once he is rescued by Mr. Brownlow. Hobsbaum thinks that this collapse occurs because Dickens found more comfort in allaying his own childhood fears by turning the novel into a Victorian success story than in facing the implications of asking what happens to all the boys Oliver left behind in the workhouse. Only after he "got rid of a good deal of autobiography" did Dickens write novels in which the theme stands out clear: "the fight of the individual against the System."

106. Hollingsworth, Keith. "Date of the Action of **Oliver Twist.**" B. Appendix B. In his **The Newgate Novel 1830-1847** (V. 17), pp. 232-33.

Argues that "Certain events of the decade before Dickens wrote **Oliver Twist**" suggest "terminal dates" for the London part of the story, whose years 1828 to 1832 appear to cause several inconsistencies and anachronisms in the novel as a whole. Hollingsworth's evidence, however, reveals flaws in his case, especially in the contention that the action in London closes no later than the first half of 1831, a date he calculates by assuming that the phrase "the ancient bridge" in Chapter 46 refers to the one where Nancy meets Mr. Brownlow and Rose. Since old London Bridge was demolished soon after the new bridge opened in August 1831, Hollingsworth reasons that the phrase must fix the action before that date. Two facts contradict his claim: (1) reading the phrase in context, we see that it occurs as part of a reference to two churches long "giant-wardens of the ancient bridge" rather than as a description of the place where Nancy waits; (2) Dickens's description of the steps and Cruikshank's illustration portraying Noah Claypole spying from behind a stone wall clearly refer to the new not the old, wooden bridge.

Hollingsworth proves more successful when he cites Oliver's arrest by "a police-officer" in Chapter 10 as a means of dating the London scenes from 1828 or after (i.e., after Peel's Metropolitan Police Act of 1829). He also notes that Fagin could not plausibly threaten Noah in Chapter 43 with hanging after 1833. In addition, Hollingsworth points to a minor inconsistency apparent in Mr. Losborne's fictitious explanation of Oliver's wound to Blathers and Duff--spring-guns were made illegal in 1827--and to a problem with the procedure used by the judge to sentence Fagin. Pronouncing the sentence of death immediately after the jury's verdict, Hollingsworth argues, represents an innovation introduced with the establishment of the Central Criminal Court in 1834, whereas prior to that date Old Bailey prisoners received their sentence in groups at the end of the session. (Readers should note that this criticism retains its validity only if one accepts that the action ends before 1831.)

Although Hollingsworth mistakenly limits the close of the book to about 1832, he successfully illustrates how Dickens's satire against the workhouse in the opening chapters suggests conditions after the Poor Law Amendment Act of 1834, whereas Oliver's age--he was about ten when he was arrested--would place those scenes in the 1820's. Either Dickens failed to plan his chronology, he concludes, or he decided to attack "new-poor-law injustice through the device of an economy-minded parish of slightly earlier date."

107. ____. "The 'Real' World of **Oliver Twist.**" In his **The Newgate Novel 1830-1847** (V. 17), pp. 111-31.

Argues for **Oliver Twist** as a quintessentially Newgate work whose degree of attachment "to the contemporary [criminal] scene" exceeds that of other Newgate novels. Hollingsworth documents how the book's interest in juvenile crime reflects concerns of the press, stresses how Dickens drew on current information for his picture of the trade in stolen goods, and suggests that the years Dickens spent as a parliamentary reporter gave him a detailed knowledge of criminal law as he listened to speakers discussing revisions to the penal code. Hollingsworth also refers to some of Dickens's early sketches reflecting an interest in criminal behavior--"The Hospital Patient" (XIV. 1) provides, he thinks, "the tangible beginning of **Oliver Twist**"--and mentions **Snarleyyow** (XIII. 141) and **Le Dernier Jour d'un condamne** (XIII. 139) as two books which possibly influenced Dickens. Readers interested in **Oliver Twist's** contemporary reception will find more details here than they will in Ford's book (XII. 82). In a later discussion of Thackeray's **Catherine** (X. 4)--see pp. 148-65--Hollingsworth examines the opposition to **Oliver Twist** and the Newgate genre Thackeray's parody generated.

108. Holloway, John. "Dickens and the Symbol." In **Dickens 1979.** Ed. Michael Slater. London: Chapman and Hall, 1970, pp. 53-74.

Holloway's opening remarks convey his belief that recent critics of Dickens tend to overlook what is "mysterious, enigmatic and contradictory" about his symbolism in their eagerness to count symbols or look for their origin in folklore or the unconsciousness. In a muddled and confusing demonstration of his assertion, Holloway compares **Oliver Twist** and **The Old Curiosity Shop,** two narratives into which Dickens weaves mythic stories about the Enemies of the Child. Yet to treat both "as if they consisted of a core or mythic narrative" would do violence to each novel. Both contain examples of symbolism (Holloway discusses several from **The Old Curiosity Shop** but none from **Oliver Twist**), but neither has an overall symbolic purpose.

109. Hornback, Bert G. "The Early Novels." "Noah's Arkitecture": A Study of Dickens's Mythology. Athens, Ohio: Ohio Univ. Press, 1972, pp. 14-21.

Contends that all Dickens's novels focus on "the initiation of children into the ways of life" and explore how to make the best of the world and "make new beginnings in it." The preponderance of "a Genesis mythology" and Dickens's use of such recurring mythic symbols as the days of Creation, Eden, the Flood, Noah's Ark, and the tower of Babel, Hornback explains, led him to this conclusion. As an early novel, **Oliver Twist** illustrates Hornback's thesis that Edens or retreats constitute Dickens's primary response to the chaos he saw in the world around him. His discussion of the text, however, provides little evidence of Genesis mythology and fails to note that Noah--"the mythic model for all [Dickens's] benevolent men"--bears no relation to Noah Claypole, a figure singularly devoid of any shred of kindness or decency.

110. House, Humphry. "Economy: Domestic and Political (II)." In his **The Dickens World**. London, 1941; rpt. London: Oxford Univ. Press, 1965, pp. 92-105.

House sets his examination of Dickens reformism against a broad discussion of what the adjective "Dickens" means and then relates what the novelist wrote to the times in which he worked. A Dickens novel, he argues, typically combines the novelist's "habitual retrospection" about his own past with anger at various abuses in the immediate present. **Oliver Twist** fits this pattern, although House's interest in the text focuses exclusively on his analysis of the point of Dickens's satire in the early part of the novel.

House distinguishes between two targets in Dickens's treatment of the New Poor Law of 1834. First, Dickens resisted "with all his might" the Law's Malthusian attempt to apply the theory of deterrence to charity and relief. By deliberately making the workhouse diet sparse, reformers hoped to prod the able-bodied unemployed to return to work and live more comfortably on their wages than they could on charity. Second, Dickens abhorred the Benthamite preoccupation with efficiency apparent in the Commissioners' reorganization of parishes into unions, their introduction of uniform standards for paupers throughout the country, and their replacement of Justices with Boards, to whom all local administrative matters were entrusted.

House argues that "as a criticism of administrative methods," the opening chapters of **Oliver Twist** were "almost prophetic." Reports about the inadequacy of the official diet reached the House of Lords a year after Oliver "asked for more"; and the failure of board members to distinguish among the needs of various classes of paupers aroused criticism not long after Dickens had made that very point. To the educated middle classes, the Law represented an inhuman response to poverty; to the working classes, the 'house' became a "horrible reproach," which they tried to avoid at all cost. Dickens makes this point later through Betty Higden in **Our Mutual Friend**--see XIV. 4, and he treated other aspects of the Law's destructiveness in Old Nandy in **Little Dorrit** and the articles he wrote for **The Examiner** about the baby-farm at Tooting (XIV. 2). House calls the latter "the proper historical appendix to **Oliver Twist**."

111. ____. "Introduction." In 1949 Oxford Illustrated Dickens (II. 38),
        pp. v-xix. Rpt. in **All in Our Time: The Collected Essays and
        Broadcast Talks of Humphry House.** London: Rupert Hart-Davis,
        1955, pp. 190-200.

A short essay critical of much of the novel. House faults Dickens's
tendency to solve plot complications off-stage and then explain the
"conundrums" in "hurried, uneasy dialogue." He also takes issue with Richard
Ford's assessment (IX. 33) that the novel expands the scope of prose fiction by
examining "the regions about Saffron Hill," and criticizes the novel's apparent
lack of a serious moral lesson. Instead of Oliver becoming the monster that
starvation and cruelty would make him, he remains, argues House, "a paragon
of sweet gratitude." House, however, responds positively to the book's
"different" qualities, which, for him, lie in Dickens's sympathy for the
criminals and the "infinite pains" Dickens took to follow the workings of the
minds of Fagin, Sikes, and Nancy. House considers the fact that Dickens
became so fond of the Sikes and Nancy reading "revealing" because Dickens
developed for it an "obsessive passion" which "in fact [was] a main cause of
his death." House explains the conjunction of "the earnest moralities" of
Dickens's Preface with his sympathy for Sikes by borrowing heavily from
Edmund Wilson's "rebel-reformer" thesis (V. 24), which he restates with no
apparent qualification.

112. Howe, Irving. "Introduction." In 1982 Signet Edition (II. 54), pp. ix-
        xix. Also published as "Reconsideration: **Oliver Twist.** The Spell of
        Fagin." **The New Republic,** 20 June 1983, pp. 27-32.

A brief essay covering various aspects of the novel's appeal comparable
in its brilliance and originality to Greene's (XII. 97). Howe argues for **Oliver
Twist** as a classic, placing Dickens's second novel in a European tradition
worthy of Gogol, Balzac, and Dostoevsky, a work which blends the voice of a
splendid comic writer with that of "a mordant social critic" expert in the uses
of "the symbolic grotesque." Useful comments about Oliver and Fagin
follow. Howe warns readers against the mistake of reacting to the
protagonist as if he were a particular small boy rather than an allegorical
figure like Bunyan's Christian and argues that Dickens reveals in Oliver's
powerlessness an enormous power: "the world cannot destroy him." At the
same time, Howe grants the difficulties and weaknesses inherent in the
passive protagonist, especially one ranged against an antagonist like Fagin, in
whom Howe locates the "living core" of the novel. Howe sensibly qualifies his
perception of Dickens's "subterranean kinship" for the criminals and writes
powerfully about Fagin, the problem of Dickens's alleged anti-Semitism, and
the novel's weak ending. Just as **Huckleberry Finn** lacks a plausible resolution
to the problems Huck and Jim transcend on the raft but return to when they
come back to the shore, so Dickens, argues Howe, fails to solve the
difficulties his imagination leads him to having launched his child-hero "on a
terrifying journey through the city." Falling back on Mr. Brownlow, Howe
notes, Dickens could not confront the obvious truth that "the individual
benevolence of a kindly gentleman ... is utterly unequipped to deal with the
problem of Oliver."

113. Humpherys, Anne. "Dickens and Mayhew on the London Poor." DSA,
        4 (1975), 78-90.

Compares, together with other aspects of their work, Dickens's and Mayhew's descriptions of Jacob's Island. The effectiveness of Dickens's passage relies on the rhythm of his prose and the use of sound patterns to build up a climactic sense of the vileness of the place. Mayhew, by contrast, presents a more sharply visualized sense of place, using particularities and sensory details to make the reader respond to the scene's repulsiveness. These opposing but complementary styles, Humpherys thinks, appear throughout their work and characterize their attempts to portray lower-class life. Humpherys also discusses how Mayhew and Dickens differed in their contacts with the poor and examines their attitudes towards the destitute as they emerge in various essays and interviews. For Dickens and Mayhew, see also XII. 133 and XVI. 2 and 16.

114. Hutter, Albert. "The Crimes of Oliver Twist." The Dickens Society, Annual Meeting MLA Convention, Chicago, 29 Dec. 1977. See DSN, 9 (March 1978), 3.

Linking Oliver Twist to the sensational narratives of the Newgate calendars, Hutter argues that the dominant activity of the book becomes one of storytelling. The first of these criminal narratives belongs to Oliver, a boy who is apparently destined to tread the familiar path of the rogue who ends his life on the scaffold. Tales are told of others too. At the novel's center stands Fagin, the arch fabulist, who dramatizes the Artful Dodger's trial for Charlie Bates, weaves a "plot" in which Nancy will poison Sikes, and later creates a sensational tale of Nancy's treacheries for Sikes.

115. Ingham, Patricia. "The Name of the Hero in Oliver Twist." RES, 33 (May 1982), 188-89.

Notes how nineteenth-century thieves used oliver as a slang term to refer to the moon or moonlight, as in the clause "Oliver is in Town" to signify an unsuitable night for a robbery. Ingham speculates that Dickens probably knew the expression since it was current in books by Bulwer Lytton and Ainsworth but argues that Dickens deliberately used "oliver" as a name only. For example, when Sikes and Fagin refer to the house they intend to rob in Chertsey, Fagin observes approvingly, "There's no moon" that night (ch. 19) and makes no use of the cant phrase. By taking care to avoid introducing any ambiguity into the hero's name, she concludes, Dickens restricts the word to a name only, making Oliver his representative of "Good surviving through every adverse circumstance," whose name remains uncontaminated by slang.

116. James, Henry. The Middle Years. London: W. Collins Sons, 1917, pp. 56-58.

Notes his response on his first visit to Craven Street, the Strand, London, the place where Mr. Brownlow lived after he returned from the West Indies. James marvelled at the "queer, quite sinister windows" and the look of that "inscrutable riverward street, packed to blackness with accumulations of suffered experience." To James the whole "absolutely reeked" to his fond fancy "with associations born of the particular ancient piety embodied in one's private altar to Dickens."

117. ____. A Small Boy and Others. 1913; rpt. New York: Charles Scribner's, 1914, pp. 102-20.

Writes of Dickens's impact on the James family and refers to how the
novelist's presence entered early "into the blood and bone" of Henry James's
intelligence. James found himself powerfully affected by **Oliver Twist,** a
work which perhaps even seemed to him "more Cruikshank's than Dickens's."
The novel, he comments, "was a thing of such vividly terrible images, and all
marked with that peculiarity of Cruikshank that the offered flowers of
goodness, the scenes and figures intended to comfort and cheer, present
themselves under his hand as but more subtly sinister, or more suggestively
queer, than the frank badness and horrors. The nice people and the happy
moments, in the plates, frightened me almost as much as the low and the
awkward."

118. James, Louis. **Fiction for the Working Man 1830-1850: A Study of
the Literature Produced for the Working Classes in Early Victorian
Urban England.** London: Oxford Univ. Press, 1963, passim.

Describes two plagiarized versions of **Oliver Twist, Oliver Twiss** by 'Bos'
and **Oliver Twiss** by 'Poz'--see VIII. 1 and VIII. 2--and comments briefly on
how Dickens's work in turn illustrates affinities with at least two identifiable
elements of the popular literature of the 1830's. James cites T.P. Prest's **Ela,
the Outcast** (1838), to which Dickens was "indebted ... on several counts." **Ela**
opens with the introduction of a mysterious child, makes use of a benevolent
protector, and includes a romantic sub-plot about two lovers, a staple of the
domestic novel which James thinks influenced Dickens's presentation of Harry
and Rose Maylie. James also links **Oliver Twist** to "such criminal literature as
The Newgate Calendar, and **Dick Turpin,**" where felons were either
glamorized as dashing highwaymen or portrayed as London apprentices who
fell into bad company and led exciting lives.

119. ———. "The View from Brick Lane: Contrasting Perspectives in
Working-Class and Middle-Class Fiction of the Early Victorian
Period." YES, 11 (1981), 87-101.

Uses T.P. Prest's **Oliver Twiss** (VIII. 1), together with other works, to
illustrate how books address themselves to particular audiences and reveal
through their style, appearance, and content the assumed readers authors
wrote for. James notes that while Dickens appealed to a broader
cross-section of Victorian readers than any other nineteenth-century author,
working-class readers often reached him through dramatizations and
"penny-issue plagiarisms" of his novels. James makes this assumption after
comparing **Oliver Twist** with T.P. Prest's imitation, **Oliver Twiss,** and by
noting how perspectives differ in the two. Dickens, he writes, criticizes the
middle classes, presents a complex social viewpoint, and combines concern
over social justice with a fascination for the romantic and the violent. **Oliver
Twiss,** on the contrary, offers a less complicated view of reality, with its
crude woodcuts and simple text reflecting the outlook of those who read
broadsides and frequented popular melodramas. Prest, he notes, also portrays
working-class life with greater realism than Dickens did because he did not
fear offending the "respectable" reader. James cites Prest's treatment of
sex, violence, and life in the workhouse as examples, concluding that the
short, entertaining weekly installments of **Oliver Twiss** appealed to people
with little training in reading and with tastes formed by the contemporary
popular theatre and broadsheets.

120. Jarmuth, Sylvia. **Dickens' Use of Women in his Novels.** New York:
Excelsior Publishing Company, 1967, pp. 38-46.

Comments briefly on the novel's minor women characters, dividing them into opposing categories of hags and saints, and laments Dickens's inability, even in the case of Nancy, to create a psychologically complex woman in **Oliver Twist.** Jarmuth compares Nancy with Emma Bovary, finding in Dickens's early female characters none of Flaubert's subtlety or the sensitivity and psychological insight that the mature Dickens revealed in his portrait of Betty Higden in **Our Mutual Friend.**

121. Johnson, Edgar. "The Thieves' Den and the World." In his **Charles Dickens: His Tragedy and Triumph** (I. 9), I, 273-83.

Johnson sees the power of **Oliver Twist** in the combination of indignation and anger at the awful harvest of cold-hearted cruelty driving paupers from the workhouse to the criminal underworld with the "dreadful concrete reality" which Dickens imparts to "the stews of Whitechapel and Saffron Hill." The bullying Mrs. Corney, the training of boys to pick pockets, the "sodden ferocity" of Sikes, and Fagin's willingness to betray others so that he might live, Johnson argues, were all based on "observed reality."

In no sense, however, can one call Dickens an "uncompromising naturalist" because he always aimed to move the heart rather than turn the stomach. To that end, he used generalized epithets to describe the midnight streets, toned down the language and the degree of vulgarity, infused the workhouse scenes with bitter comedy, and treated Fagin with "sinister hilarity." Dickens's strategy was "to fuse drama, pathos, and laughter with a realism pleading for humane feeling." Although Johnson finds the plot "luridly melodramatic" and one which poses problems of belief, he thinks that Dickens's own faith in his fictional world and the story's speed compel us "to intense emotional participation."

122. Keating, P.J. **The Working Classes in Victorian Fiction.** London: Routledge and Kegan Paul, 1971, passim.

Comments on the growth of Victorian interest in the working classes from its first appearance in the "Newgate-novel-Dickens-Kingsley-early-Gissing Tradition" to a more sustained examination of working-class life and values later in the century. Keating notes how a focus on London dominates the attention of writers and refers to **Oliver Twist** as "the father of the slum novel," citing Dickens's influence on Arthur Morrison's fiction as an example of the impact **Oliver Twist** had. Dickens's shadow, Keating thinks, appears in Morrison's **A Child of the Jago** (1896) in several ways: Aaron Weech, a Jewish fence, trains young boys to become thieves; Josh Perrott, a tradesman turned robber, flees from the police in a scene reminiscent of Sikes's pursuit and death, and Perrott's subsequent trial Keating calls "virtually a plagiarism of Fagin's." Where Morrison differs, he adds, is in his treatment of the slum child: Dick Perrott, unlike Oliver, could never be mistaken for a lost aristocrat. See also Morrison (XIII. 143).

123. Kennedy, G.W. "Dickens' Endings." SNNTS, 6 (Fall 1974), 280-87.

A general essay with only passing reference to **Oliver Twist.** Kennedy argues that in the later novels Dickens progressed steadily towards more subtle and varied endings, avoiding the simple summaries that often characterized his first works.

124. Kennedy, George E., IL "Women Redeemed: Dickens's Fallen Women." **The Dickensian,** 74 (January 1978), 42-47.

This article attempts, in part, to suggest reasons for Nancy's death, offering several possible explanations without fully illuminating the issues implicit in her fate. Does Nancy die because sexual offense must be wiped out entirely, requiring her to break completely with Sikes, which she cannot do, before a God-fearing society can grant the sinner absolution? Or because Nancy appears to Victorians an unsettling figure, inspired by her "loyalty, love, and devotion" to Sikes, virtues normally the provenance of only good women? In the end, writes Kennedy, "since Dickens puts so much emphasis upon the order that must be maintained in the human community, Nancy's death is the only possible result of her transgression." Yet another interpretation suggests that Dickens drew upon "his own practical knowledge of fallen women," which taught that individuals such as Nancy would falter, unable to turn completely from their old lives. Kennedy also notes that Dickens wanted to make Nancy "a sympathetic figure" who, decisive and heroic in life, attains almost tragic stature in her violent and bloody end.

Kennedy's sense that these questions presume the larger ones of redemption and atonement in Dickens's fiction indicates a thoughtful response to the problem of fallen women; but as a study of Nancy and her ilk this essay raises more issue than it resolves.

125. Kettle, Arnold. "Dickens: **Oliver Twist** (1837-8)." In his **An Introduction to the English Novel**. Vol. I. 1951; rpt. London: Arrow Books, 1962, pp. 133-51.

Kettle calls Oliver's rescue by Mr. Brownlow "a central situation in the book" and asks why Dickens returned here and throughout his novels to the motif of "emergence out of squalor into comfort and kindness." This pattern occurs in **Oliver Twist**, Kettle argues, because the plot--a wronged woman, an illegitimate baby, a destroyed will, and so on--asserts and reasserts itself until it completely transforms "the organization of the novel" as it seeks to twist and negate the book's moral vision. The latter Kettle sees in Dickens's evocation of "a world of the most appalling poverty and ugliness" in the first eleven chapters and their central theme: "what are the poor to do against the oppressive state?"

Summing up his response to the novel, Kettle concludes that the book's total artistic effect "is not one of disaster." The truth and depth of Dickens's central vision survive despite even the novel's anti-climax, in which the poor boy who struggles against the inhumanity of the state becomes "a young bourgeois ... done out of his property." Kettle's claim that the plots of Dickens's novels "are their weakest feature" and his praise for **Oliver Twist's** theme provide the starting point of Hobsbaum's essay (XII. 105).

126. Kincaid, James R. "**Oliver Twist:** Laughter and the Rhetoric of Attack." In his **Dickens and the Rhetoric of Laughter**. Oxford: Clarendon Press, 1971, pp. 50-75. Originally published as "Laughter and **Oliver Twist**." PMLA, 83 (March 1968), 63-70.

Argues that the laughter in which this novel abounds serves a fundamentally serious, non-comic purpose, principally by "dislocating" the reader and undercutting the usual aloofness or distance implicit in comedy. Dickens achieves this effect, Kincaid suggests, by continually shifting the narrator's voice, parodying at the opening the reader's refined and delicate sensibilities, inviting him on other occasions to share the ironical comments about "the tender laws of England!" and working generally to upset the comfortable assumptions and ease laughing at others typically generates.

Kincaid also applies his thesis to Mr. Bumble, whom he sees as a complex figure, somehow different from the hated institution he represents and an object of pity after he is symbolically castrated and "virtually annihilated" by his marriage to Mrs. Corney. Cf. Schlicke (XII. 180) and Sucksmith (XII. 190).

Kincaid accounts for this interpretation by calling Bumble "a victim," thus aligning him with the novel's other victims and its central conflict between the individual and threatening institutions. Because there are no victims in the Brownlow-Maylie good world (and therefore no one with whom readers can sympathize), he reasons, and because the thieves' world ultimately decays, we are left "with no social possibilities." The novel thus pushes "towards a position which it finally refuses to countenance." Yet by isolating the reader just as he isolated Oliver at the beginning, Dickens writes a thoroughly "subversive" novel by providing "a kind of home" in the "one isolated pocket of spontaneity" shown by Dickens: Fagin's den. Kincaid admits that this result startles the reader, but suggests that the novelty of this unexpected alliance demonstrates the rhetorical power of laughter: one hates the villains and institutions oppressing the poor and therefore sympathizes with all those who suffer. By the time of Fagin's execution, he concludes, "we have been encouraged to cast aside altogether our normal social identification by means of the most solid of all social gestures, laughter, and we are left without a society."

127. Knoepflmacher, U.C. "The Counterworld of Victorian Fiction and The Woman in White." In The Worlds of Victorian Fiction (XII. 88), pp. 351-69.

A provocative essay tracing an important theme in Victorian fiction: the novelists' tendency to delight in a deliberately concealed anarchic "intelligence" but also to protect themselves and their readers "from impulses antagonistic to society" by stressing moralism and "the collective ethic of love." Knoepflmacher concedes that critics correctly stress "the communal emphasis of Victorian fiction," but he finds the persistence of alienated outsiders--figures one associates with European and American fiction--significant. Scott's Ivanhoe, he suggests, serves as a paradigm of a work drawn to the anarchic yet emphatic on the need for law. The novel also reflects a "tentative fascination" with the counterworld which soon reappeared in the Newgate fiction of Ainsworth and Bulwer.

Before examining Wilkie Collins's "fascination with the amorality of the counterworld," Knoepflmacher adds the example of Oliver Twist to illustrate Dickens's "powerful empathy with the defiance of the social outcast." The writer admits that Sikes's death and Fagin's trial represent Dickens's "great authorial investment" in trying to "purge himself" of his fascination with the criminal and the rebel. At the same time, Knoepflmacher argues, Dickens allows his "engagement with a lawless counterworld to dominate the novel." Virtue triumphs in Oliver Twist through "the machinery of respectability and goodness," but that victory, he states, "cannot detract from Dickens' real empathy with the defiance of the criminal at bay."

128. Kotzin, Michael C. Dickens and the Fairy Tale. Bowling Green, Ohio: Bowling Green Univ. Popular Press, 1972, passim.

Passing references to Oliver Twist as illustrative of certain character-istics of the world of "Fairie." Events happen in the novel as if by magic, the central character belongs to the innocent victim-hero type, Oliver is helped by a benevolent old man, and he is confronted by supernatural adversaries and beset by "fairy-tale-like incidents." Kotzin cites the "little, ugly humped-backed man" who threatens Oliver in Chapter 32 as a typical fairy encounter, disagreeing with Williamson's thematic interpretation of this episode. Cf. XII. 213. For an earlier version of Kotzin's remarks, see his essay, "The Fairy Business in **Oliver Twist** and **Great Expectations**," in Univ. Teachers of English: Proceedings of the Conference Held at Bar Ilan University, April 1970, ed. Ruth Nevo (Ramat Gan, Israel: Bar Ilan Univ. Press, 1970), pp. 21-33.

129. Kreutz, Irving W. "Sly of Manner, Sharp of Tooth: A Study of Dickens's Villains." NCF, 22 (March 1968), 331-48.

Offers some generalizations about Dickens's evil characters and comments briefly on the criminals in **Oliver Twist**. Kreutz finds Sikes "dull" and lacking in complexity, Fagin funny in a grotesque way, and Monks an animal trained to seek revenge. Unlike the two former characters--men with no moral sense--Monks, Kreutz thinks, should know better, calling him the first of Dickens's "educated" villains.

130. Kucich, John. **Excess and Restraint in the Novels of Charles Dickens.** Athens: Univ. of Georgia Press, 1981, passim.

The desire to find a new way to talk about what Kucich calls "a special concentration of energy in Dickens' prose" motivates this sometimes opaque yet frequently rewarding study. Kucich achieves his goal of finding a fresh perspective by drawing on Georges Bataille's theory of the human demand for "expenditure," a theory of life that posits a tension between limitations and the innate human desire to transcend our physical, social, and psychological boundaries through various enactments of excess. **Oliver Twist** occupies no special place in Kucich's general scheme, although his provocative analysis of a species of Dickens villains--those devoted to excess for its own sake--includes useful comments on Fagin and Sikes. And in his penultimate chapter on Dickens's style, based on Nabokov's distinction between satire and parody, he provides a close analysis of the opening of **Oliver Twist** which convincingly demonstrates Dickens's stylistic excesses, manifestations of energy for their own linguistic (and parodic) sake rather than for a moral (and satiric) purpose.

131. Lankford, William T. "'The Parish Boy's Progress': The Evolving Form of **Oliver Twist**." PMLA, 93 (January 1978), 20-32.

Argues that Dickens's difficulties with the form of **Oliver Twist** originate in the two kinds of truth the novel explores: a thematic study of the consequences of social injustice and a symbolic representation of the beneficent role Providence plays by protecting the good. Lankford suggests that Dickens became aware of the inherent contradiction between his faith in the Principle of Good and his realization that innocents like Oliver could be corrupted once Oliver reached London. Faced with the complexities city life presented, Dickens recognized a new issue: are the criminals corrupt or are they corrupted by the social order that systematically represses and bullies Oliver?

Oliver's rescue and later arrival at the Maylies' residence introduces the novel's second element: a belief in the existence of unconditionally good characters, which, Lankford thinks, polarizes the novel's values and causes confusion. He portrays Dickens at this stage of the novel as "forced to build an entirely new system of symbols" to make Rose Maylie plausible. Once she falls ill, however, Dickens questions his own faith in Providence, underlining the change in his position by juxtaposing Oliver's naive trust in Heaven with Mrs. Maylie's experience of "illness and death" and by introducing "a symbolically dogmatic event," the country funeral of a child. See Chapter 33.

The originality of Lankford's essay lies in an emphasis on Dickens's own awareness of the problems caused by the book's lack of coherence. By analyzing the developments in the novel's narrative voice, Lankford demonstrates how Dickens sought to modify his position and reorient **Oliver Twist** along its original axis as a progress. While Dickens asserts the novel's symbolic triumph of good, he also succeeds, by controlling the point of view, in moving Oliver towards a closer identification with Noah Claypole, the Artful Dodger, Sikes, and Fagin. In the compressed and humanized account of the criminals in the last third of the novel, Dickens manages to suggest, Lankford concludes, the course of life the parish boy might have led.

132. _____. "Mr. Lankford replies." PMLA, 93 (October 1978), 1010-11.

Replying to his critics, Lund (XII. 143) and Thomas (XII. 194), Lankford notes that while serialization may externally justify his emphasis on the process of the novel, the issue is not necessarily relevant to his investigation of Dickens's adaptations and redirections of narrative form, as Lund maintains. To Thomas, he reasserts his contention that Dickens discovered moral complexities in his story while writing it but could not explore them without upsetting the novel's moral equilibrium. He argues that Dickens intended no analogy between Harry Maylie and Monks but thinks that a pattern of analogies between the two young men establishes a connection between them by the sequence of events. As Oliver's innocence is endangered by the thieves, so is Rose's purity by Harry's proposal.

133. Leavis, Q.D. "**Bleak House:** A Chancery World. Appendix B: Mayhew and Dickens." In F.R. Leavis and Q.D. Leavis. **Dickens the Novelist.** London: Chatto and Windus, 1970, pp. 184-86.

Argues that Mayhew's main interest for readers of Dickens rests in the way **London Labour and The London Poor** (1851-62) "incidentally furnishes collateral evidence" for many aspects of Dickens's novels. His interviews with the poor from London's streets, she suggests, document the actuality of Artful Dodgers, Noah Claypoles, and Fagins and confirm aspects of Dickens's work we might otherwise disbelieve. For further discussions of Dickens and Mayhew, see XII. 113 and XVI. 2 and 16.

134. _____. "Dickens and Tolstoy: The Case for a Serious View of **David Copperfield**. Appendix B: **Oliver Twist, Jane Eyre** and **David Cooperfield**." In F.R. Leavis and Q.D. Leavis. **Dickens the Novelist** (XII. 133), pp. 108-11.

Notes that while **David Copperfield** and **Oliver Twist** share "the underlying myth [of] the orphan's tale," David, she argues, "is recognizably a 'real' child and boy, with specific sufferings" in a realistic and not merely symbolic setting. Oliver, by contrast, Dickens uses "almost entirely [as] an object" for satiric diatribe against the Poor Laws and the society that produced them. Oliver hardly exists, Leavis thinks, "as more than an innocent anonymous consciousness to register suffering and bewilderment engendered by these conditions."

135. Leck, Simpson A. "Some Weaknesses of Oliver Twist." The Dickensian,
      34 (Summer 1938), 194-98.

Objects to the book's lack of realism and its involved, elaborate plot with
too many characters and too many confusing details. These flaws, Leck
asserts, blot the novel's landscape.

136. Le Comte, Edward. "Afterword." In 1961 Signet Classic Edition (II.
      41), pp. 482-94.

Le Comte occasionally appears to write for effect, aiming at a
cleverness that flattens the text and reduces the Victorians to laughable
stereotypes. Referring to Dickens's readings of the murder of Nancy, for
example, he states that the performances before "semihysterical audiences"
were never a success unless women screamed or fainted and that the readings
may literally have killed the novelist. That "murder" took for Dickens the
place of central excitement "that sex takes for others" is, for Le Comte, an
"inescapable fact."
By contrast, Le Comte raises useful questions about the fairy tale
elements in Oliver Twist and faces, unlike the authors of most Introductions,
the implications of Dickens's habitual references to Fagin as "the Jew."
Using the epithet "almost exactly three hundred times," comments Le Comte,
represents poor taste for those of us reading the novel after Hitler and
Eichmann; but Dickens's usage, he thinks, represents a matter-of-fact
identification and not a reproach. "They go further than they can
demonstrate," he argues, "those who shout that Dickens is here being
anti-Semitic. This is not anti-Semitism, this is the phantom of
anti-Semitism--others provided the reality." Connections between Bunyan
and Dickens and some helpful remarks about Dickens's use of coincidence
conclude Le Comte's essay.

137. Levin, Harry. "The Uncles of Dickens." In The Worlds of Victorian
      Fiction (XII. 88), pp. 1-35.

Attributes the memorable quality of Dickens's works to the intensity
with which he presents his world through the eyes of waifs, children who are
either orphans or "demi-orphans." Levin refers to how, in Dickens's life, this
"cutting-off" was a psychological process, which biographers attribute to the
breakup of his family through his father's imprisonment. As a result, Levin
argues, mixed responses towards fathers reoccur in Dickens's fiction. On one
hand, Dickens appears iconoclastic towards authorities, heads of houses,
schoolmasters, and so on; on the other, he acknowledges that children need
someone to whom they can turn for protection and guidance. Thus when blood
relatives playing this role turn up in Dickens's fiction, Levin continues, they
are uncles, occasionally aunts, or "quasi-avuncular" figures, who stand in as
parents. In the survey that follows, Levin traces what he calls "a series of
individual conflicts in a continuous psychomachia" in which the spiritual
struggle between good and evil becomes less certain and more complex as the
novelist develops. Levin finds Oliver Twist "closest to explicit allegory" of all
the novels; in it the child is shunted back and forth between malefactors and
benefactors until he is finally restored to his inherent goodness by Mr.
Brownlow. This "old-fashioned Pickwickian bachelor," Levin notes, is almost
Oliver's uncle, "having once been engaged to Oliver's father's sister long
defunct."

138. Lindsay, Jack. "At Closer Grips." In his **Charles Dickens: A Biographical and Critical Study.** New York: Philosophical Library, 1950, pp. 167-72.

The pages Lindsay devotes to **Oliver Twist** yield a degree of speculation quite disproportionate to the brevity with which he treats the novel. The attacks on **Oliver Twist** by Victorian critics, he tells us, forced Dickens "for the first time" to think about his public and realize that if he were to succeed as a novelist "give-and-take between himself and his public" would be necessary. Hence Dickens's life-long devotion to the serial novel, a form "which did not survive him." Lindsay also guesses that "Probably there is much truth" in the story that Cruikshank "originated" **Oliver Twist** (XIII. 10 and 11), although he offers several other sources: "Peter Grimes" in Crabbe's **The Borough** (XIII. 134), Marryat's **Snarleyyow, or the Dog Fiend** (XIII. 141), and Lytton's **Paul Clifford.**

Lindsay's most striking claim, however, emerges from the connection he sees between "the demented guilt-progress" of Sikes after murdering Nancy and the author's "deeply interwoven" fantasies about Mary Hogarth, his young sister-in-law, who died suddenly on 7 May 1837. Lindsay notes that Sikes's route after the murder goes over the familiar ground "of Charles's own walks" and that Sikes sinks exhausted "at the very spot" in Hampstead where Dickens went after Mary's death. From this coincidence Lindsay draws a startling conclusion: the guilt Sikes feels after clubbing Nancy "is the same as that of Charles after he had 'killed off' Mary with his all-too-strong death-wish!"

Readers curious to know why Dickens should want to "work off" Mary, whose death left him unable to write for a month, must look to Lindsay's interpretation of the "single nexus of relationships" in Dickens's unconscious mind involving himself, his wife, and Mary. Lindsay sees child-bearing Kate as representing Dickens's sense of the adult world and the virginal, innocent Mary as "the magical restorer of the dream of Eden," the sister who recreates "an other-half of the wife." Finding in this arrangement "maximum harmony, maximum unity," Dickens wanted to arrest life and therefore unconsciously wished for Mary's death as a way of keeping her "irredeemably" and "all his." With such stuff Lindsay rounds out Dickens and finds in his psychic life the "complicated tangle of fantasies" that drives the novelist forward "into new dimensions of creative realization."

139. Lucas, Alec. "Oliver Twist and the Newgate Novel." **The Dalhousie Review,** 34 (Spring 1954), 381-87.

Defines the Newgate formula and discusses Dickens's literary debts to Bulwer and the genre with snappy and sometimes inaccurate judgments. Newgate authors, Lucas states, produced "the improbably good" criminals, and novelists of the sensation school "the improbably bad." Lucas sees in Dickens's 1841 Preface a version of Bulwer's introduction to **Eugene Aram** (1831), where Bulwer asserted the need for philosophers to investigate the criminal intellect, but thinks that Dickens, like Bulwer, did not succeed especially well in revealing the truth about the criminal character. Dickens fails, he argues, because **Oliver Twist** is "too obviously contrived" and because sentiment and pathos intrude and obscure the fact that Fagin and Sikes are Oliver's worst enemies and two evil men. Fagin's trial, Lucas states, illustrates the point well, "for Dickens fails in it to make the old Jew as repulsive in dying as in living," while Sikes, after murdering Nancy, is placed so as to make him "simply a poor persecuted man." Lucas grants that **Oliver Twist** found responsive readers among the naive and uneducated, but stresses that it was soon recognized as a Newgate novel by R.H. Horne (XII. 11) and Thackeray (X. 3 and 4).

140. Lucas, Audrey. "Some Dickens Women." **Yale Review,** NS 29 (1940), 706-28.

Arranges Dickens's female characters in groups--innocent, fallen, "borderline," and comic--and illustrates each with plentiful examples. Nancy merits only a single reference as "gunman's moll."

141. Lucas, John. "Dickens and **Dombey and Son:** Past and Present Imperfect." In **Tradition and Tolerance in Nineteenth-century Fiction: Critical Essays on some English and American Novels.** Ed. David Howard, John Lucas, and John Goode. London: Routledge and Kegan Paul, 1966, pp. 99-140.

Draws on **Oliver Twist** to illustrate his contention that Dickens reverses in Dombey and Son "the pattern of allegiances" evident in the earlier novel by putting individuals with genuine vitality and regard for each other outside the mercantile values of respectable society and by portraying a criminal like Carker as one who naturally inhabits the Dombey world of business. Lucas considers this an advance because it suggests Dickens's preference for vitality over "the characteristic frigid indifference" of the middle class. In **Oliver Twist,** he argues, Dickens attacked the middle class on these grounds but showed himself "greviously confused" by making Fagin and his band attractive, thereby undercutting his condemnation of them as criminals.

142. _____. "Oliver Twist." In his **The Melancholy Man: A Study of Dickens's Novels.** London, 1970; rev. and rpt. Brighton and Totowa: Harvester Press and Barnes and Noble, 1980, pp. 21-54.

Two principal reasons support Lucas's contention that **Oliver Twist** is "the finest of all the early works." He begins by praising the novel as Dickens's "first sustained effort at realism," whose measure he takes from the book's attack on Newgate fiction. Instead of romanticizing criminals, Dickens portrays them with "shocking realism," a fact which even Thackeray admitted, despite his criticism of **Oliver Twist** in **Catherine** (X. 4). Thackeray, Lucas argues, expresses a disturbed sense that Dickens is "too realistic for comfort" rather than the opinion that he is not realistic enough. In Lucas's view, Thackeray's ambiguous response to the novel resembles that of other readers, who regarded with horror Dickens's attempt to force them to collide with the truth that criminals, especially young offenders, were the products of society forced into crime, for which they were brutally punished when they were caught.
Lucas finds the second of Dickens's "deepest interests" in his taking seriously Oliver as "a Rousseauistic child of nature," whose goodness the author "somehow makes believable" through Oliver's contact "with the world of nature" and life away from the city. Lucas admits that Oliver's role can thwart the novel's realism, but he finds in Dickens's recognition of Oliver's "terrible vulnerability" an adequate defense of the sort of innocence he wanted his protagonist to embody. In the world that **Oliver Twist** presents "humanity must ... prey on itself, and the natural child is threatened" by Fagin, Monks, and Sikes. The essay also remarks on Fagin, in whose unnecessary death (receiving stolen goods was no longer a capital offense) Lucas sees the complicity of the middle class. By offering prayers for the

condemned man and withholding systematic help to the criminals their own laws create, respectable citizens, Lucas argues, deny all responsibility for the injustice they perpetrate.

143. Lund, Michael. "To the Editor: Oliver Twist." PMLA, 93 (October 1978), 1009.

Responds to Lankford's analysis of the stages in the development of the novel's narrative form (XII. 131) by noting that he pays no attention to the novel's original serial publication. This alone, Lund thinks, could more easily account for the shifts in the nature of Dickens's narrative than the expectations of formal unity to which Lankford assumes Dickens aspired. The true form of Oliver Twist, Lund suggests, may be found by looking at the novel as an evolving structure, one which presented a complex vision of the inter-relationship between good and evil and placed less emphasis on aesthetic consistency than modern critics generally do. See also Thomas (XII. 194).

144. Manheim, Leonard. "Dickens' Fools and Madmen." DSA, 2 (1972), 69-97.

Examines Dickens's major neurotics and psychotics in relation to his extensive knowledge of Victorian theories of psychopathology and psychiatry and refers briefly to Nancy, Sikes, Fagin, and Monks. Manheim notes that despite Dickens's "alleged sympathy with the underdog," he appears to have adhered to the view that punishment should deter. Nancy, he thinks, represents the closest Dickens came to comprehending the criminal psychopath in Oliver Twist, where melodrama spoils the accuracy of "the general clinical picture" of the other major villains.

145. Manning, Sylvia. "Masking and Self-Revelation: Dickens's Three Autobiographies." DSN, 7 (September 1976), 69-75.

The autobiographies to which Manning refers are Oliver Twist, David Copperfield, and Great Expectations, all three of which treat an orphan given over to cruel authorities early in life who later seeks compensatory relationships with other adults, and who travels from his rural birthplace to the city. This pattern crudely represents Dickens's own "abandonment" by his parents, his youthful trials in London, and his later economic security and maturity. Organized around these "skeletal events," Oliver Twist expresses a child's dream in which wishes are fulfilled by a miraculous rescue. David Copperfield reworks this "fantasy" by realistically ascribing success to hard work and not to a fairy godfather. Great Expectations represents Dickens's most complex and mature attempt to understand himself by turning upside down the two earlier stories and by revealing the hollowness of the Victorian dream of gentility.

Manning also argues that while David Copperfield bears the closest resemblance to Dickens's life, the thicker masks of fiction in the other two novels allow the author to reveal more about himself. To demonstrate this claim she proposes biographical analogues for fictional scenes possibly reflecting the author's concern with mother substitutes, sibling rivalry, "low" homes, and substitute fathers. Manning concludes her catalogue by positing the existence of some other "buried causation" whose traumatic impact arising from an unspecified event accounts for Dickens and his heroes' "sense of their own evil." "The violence and criminality that suffuse Oliver Twist and Great Expectations ... derive ... from Dickens's inmost sense of himself." That boy should have been hanged!

Criticism   173

146. Marcus, Stephen. "The Wise Child." In his **Dickens: From Pickwick to Dombey.** London: Chatto & Windus, 1965, pp. 54-91.

An eclectic chapter in which Marcus touches on cultural, biographical, and artistic questions pertinent to his examination of Dickens's thought and art in the first seven novels. Dickens's satire in the opening chapters of **Oliver Twist** appears effective because it is intense, devoid of partisan allegiances, and full of moral energy directed against all those enemies of life who violate humanity by denying the problems of the poor. Marcus also argues that **Oliver Twist** works because it dramatizes and symbolizes "abstract ideas" by taking its cue from **Pilgrim's Progress,** whose influence on the novel he traces.

Dickens and Bunyan resemble each other, Marcus shows, in their use of parable and reliance on the homiletic tale, in which two adventurers flee from their place of origin and set off on a series of wanderings. Both protagonists shuttle "back and forth between the forces of good and the forces of evil," and both meet figures out of a morality play. But while Christian's final bourne is a supernatural one, paradise for Oliver remains middle class and temporal, true to the nineteenth-century conviction that the quality of one's social life mattered.

The novel nevertheless reveals "substantial pressure" of Christian sentiment in its reliance on "cosmic coincidences" and its faith that the meek shall inherit the earth.

Why does grace descend upon Oliver? Marcus thinks that the explanation is biographical to the extent that Oliver's experiences record "without doubt" Dickens's memory of his own unhappy childhood and his own miraculous escape from the blacking factory. The fable can also be read as "a consummate expression" of Victorian social mobility and belief that "the absolute test of character" depends on what a person is not where he begins. "For the style of the gentleman, **Oliver Twist** asserts, rests, not on birth but on behavior, not on legal privilege but on incorruptibility of character."

147. Marshall, William H. **The World of the Victorian Novel.** South Brunswick and New York: A.S. Barnes, 1967, passim.

Refers occasionally to **Oliver Twist** in his discussion of how the Victorian novelists tried to found an ontology upon values derived from experiences of the self. Cf. Gelphi (XII. 88). Marshall sees this search as a direct response to the disintegration of medieval certitude the Victorians experienced. He also comments on devices the novelists used, citing, for example, Dickens's symbolic use of clothes and houses in **Oliver Twist.** He calls the bridge where Nancy meets Rose and Mr. Brownlow "emblematic of the wretched girl's passage to a point between two worlds, from both of which she remains essentially an alien" until she is released by death. He also refers briefly to Dickens's use of parallelism to reflect Oliver's course in the actions of others.

148. McMaster, Juliet. "Diabolic Trinity in **Oliver Twist.**" Dalhousie Review, 61 (Summer 1981), 263-77.

Argues that Dickens presents Fagin, Sikes, and Monks as an evil triumvirate based on "a tight theological pattern" in which the criminals invert the three qualities Christians traditionally associate with God-- knowledge, power, and love. Fagin, the informer, represents a perversion of knowledge, the brutal and violent Sikes provides a demonic inversion of omnipotence, and Monks, gratuitously malignant, reverses benevolence and love. McMaster emphasizes the tentative nature of her thesis but notes that the demonic parody of the Trinity seems to be "too fully developed in the novel to be accidental." While the analogies are not made explicit and are not worked out with equal consistency, she concludes, "echoes at least are traceable."

149. Michaelson, L.I. "Defoe and Dickens: Two London Journeys." The Dickensian, 74 (May 1978), 103-07.

Compares the passage in **Moll Flanders** where Moll meets "a pretty little Child" near Smithfield whose gold necklace she steals with Dickens's description of the journey of Sikes and Oliver through similar terrain in Chapter 22. Both novelists refer to street names, describe the background, and set their characters against a crowd of figures. But although the routes taken by Moll and Sikes overlap, Michaelson notes, they are "unlike in reality." Moll's, he shows, by referring to a map, "backtracks and twists," providing a correlative of her state of mind as she sinks deeper into a life of crime, while Sikes's route, an almost straight course from east to west, could be taken as "a correlative to the bold, vigorous criminality and certainty" of his mind. Defoe and Dickens, he concludes, use London as a realistic setting but also shape their descriptions to an imaginative reality.

150. Miller, D.A. "The Novel and the Police." **Glyph: Johns Hopkins Textual Studies**, 8 (1981), 127-47.

Miller's essay assumes the validity of Michel Foucault's hypothesis about the rapid spread of punitive institutions in Western society during the nineteenth century and carries Foucault's views further by discussing the meaning of the "literary hegemony" of the traditional novel "in the age of discipline." In **Discipline and Punish** (Paris, 1975; trans. Alan Sheridan, 1977; rpt. New York: Random House, 1979), Foucault argues that seemingly humane institutions contributed to a massive system of surveillance in the hands of the middle class, who used prisons, schools, factories, barracks, and hospitals to gain control over social deviants. Characteristically, the ruling elite remained "invisible" as they imposed their "mechanisms of normalization" on the "prisoners" through timetables, regulations, exercises, and other instruments of coercion set up to influence and monitor behavior. For Foucault, Jeremy Bentham's plan for the Panopticon, a circular prison set around a central watchtower, serves as the chief symbol of this sinister development.

Miller believes that the ideology of this movement extended itself into the nineteenth-century novel. By placing their fictional protagonists under "social surveillance," he argues, the novelists reveal an "explicit coerciveness" typical of the elite, especially when they show how those who try to escape social control are ultimately reclaimed by the forces they resist. For literary evidence of this "somber tradition," Miller turns to French and British novels, citing **Oliver Twist**, among examples also taken from Trollope and George Eliot, as a story of "active regulation." **Oliver Twist**, he argues, achieves this through its double plot, in which the police regulate "the world of delinquency" while their vigilant amateur counterparts get rid of Monks. Both groups come together "in the connivance of class rule." Even more disturbing--and more interesting to Miller--are "the quasi-legal procedures" Mr. Brownlow uses to impose his respectable values on Oliver. Miller notes that Brownlow sets out to "inquire" into Oliver, "confirm" his "statement," and produce "a **full account**" of his life, an undertaking also implicit in the book's form. For by conceiving narrative as a **genesis**--"a linear, cumulative time of evolution"--Dickens and his fellow novelists economically fuse form and purpose. By literally bringing the plot "into line" and by discarding "dispersive tendencies" in the narrative, the writers also place and evaluate their protagonists according to the values the novelists share with society. "Structured as genesis," comments Miller, the narrative "forwards a story of social discipline" and simultaneously "advances the novel's omniscient word." He concedes that Dickens and the other writers neither glorify the police nor show their novels embracing power. At the same time, they make over power "**into** the world," literally secularizing it and reminding us that we too inhabit a "novelistic panopticon."

151. Miller, J. Hillis. "Introduction." In his 1962 Holt, Rinehart and Winston Edition (II. 43), pp. v-xxiv.

For the purposes of this essay, Miller subordinates his interest in Dickens's "imaginative universe" (XII. 153) to a discussion of **Oliver Twist** as an objective plea for reform, as a recreation of the author's childhood experiences, and as a fiction whose meaning and form transcend their historical and biographical sources.

Miller begins with the contention that **Oliver Twist** is "rooted in the reality of the eighteen-thirties." The book's topicality, decor, and urban landscape, he argues, all spring "from the reality of the time," a fact which Dickens also emphasized when he defended **Oliver Twist** on the basis of its verisimilitude in the 1841 Preface. Miller accepts Dickens's claim of factual accuracy to the extent that he agrees that the novel serves as "a piece of literary journalism" protesting against the abstract theories of economists and "the actual experiences" of someone born into the workhouse system.

Other elements, however, indicate that **Oliver Twist** represents more than "a fictional transposition of real conditions for the purposes of preaching reform." The novel shadows forth "Dickens' own experiences as a child" when he was abandoned to the blacking factory and deserted by his parents after his father's imprisonment for debt. A study of the book also reveals significant differences between the hero and Dickens's own situation. The novel's dramatic contrast between evil and good, its fairy-tale elements, and its portrayal of the whole world as "a kind of collective wicked stepmother bent on destroying the helpless foundling" all suggest how Dickens universalized his own particular experience. Making these changes, Dickens refitted the central events of his own childhood, elements of a traditional fairy tale, and realistic reporting "to the conditions of life in industrialized England." Oliver's sufferings thereby become "a notable expression of the spiritual anguish and sense of alienation" generated by the changes which have produced the modern world.

152. _____. "The Narrator as General Consciousness." In his The Form of Victorian Fiction. Notre Dame: Univ. of Notre Dame Press, 1968, pp. 76-78.

Commenting briefly on **Oliver Twist**, Miller cites the novel's "juxtaposition of two minds" as an example of the tendency of authors to express the mind of narrator and that of the protagonist. The mind of the narrator of **Oliver Twist** reflects through his formal syntax and diction both his own security as a "member of genteel society" and his detachment from the events he describes. By contrast, Dickens uses the mind of the protagonist to project dramatically the child's experience from the inside in those passages

where the reader "relives from within Oliver's terror as the prisoner of Fagin."
The narrator's ironic detachment, which enables him to make arch jokes
about the hero's experiences, initially serves to generate the outraged
sympathy of the reader. By the end of the novel, Oliver has become so
identified with the language of the educated middle class that his awareness
of himself as a separate person disappears after he is adopted by Mr.
Brownlow and absorbed into "the collective consciousness" of the narrator.

153. ____. "Oliver Twist." In his **Charles Dickens: The World of His**
        Novels. Cambridge, Mass., 1958; rpt. Bloomington, Indiana: Indiana
        Univ. Press, 1969, pp. 36-84.

This essay concisely illustrates Miller's theoretical position that a novel
should be approached as an autonomous work of art beyond whose
"self-sufficient reality" the critic need not go. By ignoring social reality,
literary history, and the author's pre-existent psychological condition, Miller
isolates what he considers his most important goal: "the exploration of the
imaginative universe" Dickens constructs as he apprehends and creates
himself in his fiction. The test of the critic therefore becomes his ability to
reveal the contours of that mind as it evolves and as it defines its unique
personality during a search "for a true and viable identity."
Approaching **Oliver Twist** in this manner, Miller focuses on the novel's
concern with self awareness, as he sees this issue explored from the point of
view of Oliver. Hostility, aggression, and almost certain destruction threaten
the protagonist, whose implicit annihilation Miller documents by examining
the book's imagery. Suffocation, hanging, and enclosure provide major
variations of the forces seeking relentlessly to draw Oliver down into an urban
hell.
Although Miller agrees that Oliver searches actively to explore the
meaning of the external world, he finds the novel's resolution unsatisfactory
because it is "based on self deception" and on the narrator's unwillingness "to
face fully his apprehension of the world." Miller points to the fact that Oliver
sinks into unconsciousness each time he is suddenly extricated from the dark
world as evidence of Oliver's helplessness and the inability of his mind to
perceive its own reality and create its own authentic identity. Selfhood can
only come to Oliver as a package: he cannot derive his identity from anything
he has done "but only from what his parents were."
Miller's study presupposes that each sentence or paragraph of the novel
"defines a certain relationship between an imagining mind and its objects."
The world the mind imagines in **Oliver Twist** holds, for the greater part,
terror, although the mind also knows something of paradise or happiness.
Watching how the mind struggles to be born and define itself gives Miller a
sense of the book's true interest, to which concern with the conventions of
the plot and its attendant sensation, mystery, and melodrama are secondary.
So, too, are "The given conditions of a writer's life," whose psychological and
cultural nature provide "merely the obstacles or materials" which the writer
"transforms and vanquishes." Creating a novel or a poem, Miller contends,
gives the materials "a different meaning from the one they had in themselves."

154. Monod, Sylvere. "A Novel Tailored to the Time: **Oliver Twist**
        (1837-39)." In his **Dickens the Novelist.** Norman: Univ. of Oklahoma
        Press, 1968, pp. 115-39. Expanded translation of his **Dickens**
        Romancier (Paris, 1953).

The metaphor Monod uses in his chapter title operates in two principle senses, both of which characterize the novel as a work hastily put together under "many vicissitudes and accidents." Foremost among the obstacles attending the book's composition and publication was its appearance in Bentley's Miscellany, whose monthly installments Dickens had to share with others. With about half of the space allotted to him as he had had for The Pickwick Papers, Dickens found the sixteen pages of the Miscellany a difficult medium in which to develop a well-constructed novel with multiple strands. The way Oliver Twist overlapped nine issues of The Pickwick Papers added further difficulties, which in turn were complicated by the death of Mary Hogarth in May 1837 (Dickens suspended both Oliver Twist and The Pickwick Papers for one month), and by Dickens's impatience to publish Oliver Twist in three volumes six months before he was scheduled to finish its serial publication. These circumstances, Monod argues, account for the book's awkward transitions between one incident and the next, its digressions, uncertainties, and "many hesitations."

Monod cites the book's kinship with Newgate fiction as the second example of how external factors affected the narrative. If readers thirsted for blood, violence, mystery, and horror, Dickens was ready to cater to a "taste for every kind of sensation." Yet combining these effects with comic scenes adds to the novel's complexity. For despite the book's "lavish" use of coincidence and sudden shiftings of the scene, Monod detects "firmness" in the plot and finds in Oliver Twist not only better construction but "more construction" than in the other novels of Dickens's first period.

155. Nalecz-Wojtczak, Jolanta. "Mystery in the Composition of Dickens' Novels." KN, 17 (March 1970), 239-51.

An unconvincing taxonomy of mystery--structural and textual--and an analysis of early and late novels in these terms which purports to show Dickens's experiments with mystery and his movement from novels with a simple pattern (Oliver Twist) to those with more varied plots. Nalecz-Wojtczak calls Great Expectations and The Mystery of Edwin Drood the perfection in Dickens's handling of mystery.

156. Newman, S.J. "Nature in Oliver Twist and Nicholas Nickleby." In his Dickens at Play. New York: St. Martin's Press, 1981, pp. 39-61.

The book's thesis that Dickens makes "imaginative capital out of an increasingly disordered sense of life" dominates the discussion of Oliver Twist, which Newman examines together with Dickens's fiction up to Martin Chuzzlewit for evidence of "the development of Dickens's imagination." He selects the early novels because in them, he thinks, Dickens was least hampered by the need to provide a recognizable moral and social framework.

This chapter contends that Dickens chose the subject matter of Oliver Twist "as an antidote to the alarming beneficence of Pickwick," whose innocent optimism provided nurturing soil for the continuation of such Romantic principles as the child of nature. In its first two chapters Oliver Twist violently attacks this idea by showing how Wordsworth's primary laws are not "great and simple affections" but laws of self-preservation and cunning survival.

Discovering in his attack on the Romantic idea of the child of nature a similarity between his own position and that of Malthus causes Dickens to make "a massive dislocation of the book's impetus and trajectory." Dickens must do so because if he is to discredit the Malthusian premises of the new Poor Law of 1834, he must show Oliver as "the principle of Good surviving through every adverse circumstance." This switch, Newman argues, requires Dickens to purify "nature;" by doing so, he loses contact with "depravity and deprivation" and imposes on the novel an extended use of melodrama with its attendant happy ending and triumphant "Decency." "It is this sort of stuff that makes Dickens so hard to swallow, let alone digest," Newman concludes.

Fortunately this fall into orthodoxy generates its own radical imaginative growth. While lending moral support to the laws that repressed the unruly elements of Victorian life, Dickens realizes that he can use the underworld as "a theatre of the mind where the outlawed imaginative impulses act out their secrets." Newman cites Noah Claypole's conversation with Charlotte about oysters--an aphrodisiac and slang for vagina--as an instance of Dickens's being "on the side of life," despite the book's respectable credentials flaunted in the Preface. Even so, he concludes, **Oliver Twist** is cramped compared with the possibilities Dickens discovered in **Sketches by Boz.**

Newman's disappointment with the novel appears to stem from his wish to "decode" Dickens's performances and show them as "wildly unVictorian." Newman sees Dickens as a "master of the absurd" who celebrates the Nietzschean forces of disorder his contemporaries tried to field and restrain by upholding religious absolutes. For Dickens, "God is only a pious wish." Newman aligns himself with John Bayley (XII. 27), John Carey (XII. 48), and Gabriel Pearson, "who tend to be suspicious of Dickens the eminent Victorian," and militantly states his own position. Dickens's art, writes Newman, "testifies to a post-rationalist God of relativity and nonsense; to appreciate it we need to be prepared for the possibility of comic sublimity and a religiously subversive imagination."

157. Oddie, William. **Dickens and Carlyle: The Question of Influence.**
      London: Centenary Press, 1972, passim.

A cautious assessment of a problem Oddie clearly defines by saying that critics can more easily assert that Carlyle "influenced" Dickens than they can effectively demonstrate their claims. For example, Marcus (XII. 146) surmises that the clothes references in **Oliver Twist** suggest that Dickens may have recently read **Sartor Resartus** (p. 80n), to which Oddie responds by pointing out that Carlyle was virtually unknown to the general public at the time. **Sartor Resartus** was first serialized in Fraser's Magazine in 1833-34, and it was not republished in book form until 1838, making it unlikely that Dickens had read Carlyle before he began **Oliver Twist** in 1837 or before he met him in 1839. Oddie also differs from Marcus in his willingness to attribute Dickens's references to clothes in **Oliver Twist** to the writer's "'stage business'" rather than seeing in the novel, as Marcus does, a real affinity with the symbolism of Carlyle's philosophy of clothes. In a later chapter (7), Oddie contrasts Carlyle's greater sympathy for those who championed force as a means of redressing wrongs with Dickens's opposition not only to violent proletarian movements but to the more peaceful trades unions. Oddie does not speculate what the scenes of crowd violence in the novels meant to Dickens but comments that such descriptions as the mob hounding Sikes seem to occur to the novelist with "more than usual readiness."

158. Orwell, George. "Charles Dickens." In his **Inside the Whale.** London:
      Victor Gollancz, 1940, pp. 9-85. Rpt. in **Dickens, Dali and Others.**
      New York: Reynal and Hitchcock, 1946, pp. 1-75.

A memorable response to Orwell's own question: "Where exactly does [Dickens] stand, socially, morally and politically?" Providing a full answer requires Orwell to examine how Dickens's popularity and veneration as an English fixture coexist with his fierce attacks on British institutions and to discuss the significance of his middle class origins. Essentially, Orwell sees Dickens as a revolutionary writer of a particular kind: not the theorist with a blueprint for rebuilding society but the moralist who exhorts people to change their hearts and act decently. Orwell comments perceptively on the reason for Dickens's hatred of mob violence, his concern with those who abuse power, and his preoccupations with childhood. The essay refers to many of the novels, places Dickens among his contemporaries, and comments, in the final section, on Dickens's artistry. Orwell admires Dickens for his generous anger, for his hatred of "smelly little orthodoxies," and for his lack of "vulgar nationalism." The latter, Orwell argues, indicates "a real largeness of mind" apparent, for example, in Dickens's refusal to make fun of national types and indulge in "Jew jokes."

159. Ousby, Ian. "Introduction." In 1980 Pan Edition (II. 52), pp. 7-18.

A concise essay in which Ousby notes the novel's origin in the practical concerns of the author's need to earn a living, remind the public of the strengths he demonstrated in The Pickwick Papers, and reveal new aspects of his talent. Oliver Twist's humorous touches, Ousby suggests, connect it with The Pickwick Papers; its focus on social injustice and psychological horror demonstrates a mastery of two interests Dickens's first novel only hinted at. Ousby also notes how this novel satisfied Dickens's private experiences as a story expressing a personal yearning for security and comfort. At the same time, its affinity with the fairy-tale world, the eighteenth-century novel, and the Evangelical literature of the age demonstrate how Dickens's private myth intersects with the familiar and established culture in which he and his audience grew up. Ousby comments helpfully on the book's successes and accounts for the power of the criminals and the failure of the good characters. Dickens presents the world of evil as "particular, vivid, [and] persuasive," he writes, while the representatives of good lack authenticity and fail to engage Dickens's "best energies."

160. Page, Norman. "'A Language fit for heroes': Speech in Oliver Twist and Our Mutual Friend." The Dickensian, 65 (May 1969), 100-07.

Page argues that Dickens deliberately uses a convention of dialogue in Oliver Twist which sacrifices realism to moral appropriateness in the case of Oliver, who speaks standard English in spite of his workhouse origins. Dickens made this decision because he wanted readers to approve of Oliver and because he faced perhaps an impossible task as a novelist to create an impression of "dignity and worth" in a character speaking an idiom different from standard usage. Later in his career, Dickens challenged that assumption in his presentation of Lizzie Hexam, whose homely speech gradually changes as she herself develops from the daughter of a waterside character to a respectable middle-class heroine.

161. ____. Speech in the English Novel. London: Longman, 1973, passim.

Contains the discussion of Oliver's speech in slightly different form from XII. 160, together with comments in a later chapter on the care Dickens took polishing the reading from Oliver Twist. Page notes that Dickens revised primarily to exploit the spoken qualities of the reading version by introducing bolder rhetorical patterns, a greater dramatic antithesis between Nancy and

Rose, and a sustained theatrical quality. These characteristics Page also
traces to Dickens's later style in his chapter "Dickens and Speech," an
analysis of Dickens's linguistic mannerisms well worth reading, as is the whole
of this persuasive and stimulating study of fictional dialogue. Page draws
heavily on Dickens for examples and comments perceptively on the multiple
aspects of his style with special focus on the interplay of dialogue, narration,
and description.

162. Patten, Robert. "Capitalism and Compassion in **Oliver Twist.**"
     SNNTS, 1 (Summer 1969), 207-21.

A thematic study focusing on the novel's main conflict between
"benthamite calculus of self-interest" and "instinctive compassion and selfless
benevolence." Patten sees the former as the ruling passion of early Victorian
society and the ideology that unites the respectable world of the parish
authorities with the criminal underworld of Fagin and his associates through a
common bond of belief in calculation and self-interest. Left to survive in
these conditions without help, Oliver would obviously succumb to Fagin, his
principal enemy, "at once stereotype Jew, nighttime or underworld capitalist,
and devil." Fortunately, Patten argues, compassion replaces capitalism in the
form of Mr. Brownlow, who rescues and transforms Oliver. Dickens's use of
"the motif of the handkerchief," Patten adds, reinforces this movement.
Nancy accepts Rose's handkerchief as a token of God's grace and mercy,
while the parish authorities and the thieves take handkerchiefs away, for
different purposes, but reveal a similar acquisitiveness in their actions.

163. ____. **Charles Dickens and His Publishers** (I. 10), passim.

An authoritative and detailed account based on all the available evidence
of the sales of Dickens's works and his relationship with his publishers. Patten
also comments on foreign sales in countries without reciprocal copyright
agreements with England, discusses recent developments in the paperback
industry, and provides tables of sales and profits for various editions and
works. For **Oliver Twist,** see Appendix A, pp. 399-404; Appendix B, pp.
443-45, gives the printing history of Bradbury and Evans's 1846 edition of
Oliver Twist in ten parts. Between **Oliver Twist's** first appearance as a serial
in the **Miscellany,** Patten notes, and 1867, the novel went through thirteen
editions or variant issues.

164. Pattison, Robert. **The Child Figure in English Literature.** Athens:
     Univ. of Georgia Press, 1978, passim.

Examines the "bleak consistency" of the solitary, isolated children
apparent in Victorian literature, a phenomenon Pattison accounts for by
revealing how extensively the concepts of the Fall of Man and of Original Sin
affected many writers' views and informed their presentation of children.
Pattison also provides a lucid survey of the challenge to Augustine's doctrine
by Pelagius' belief in man's perfectability, Locke's rejection of innate ideas,
and the affirmation of goodness by Rousseau and Wordsworth. Cf. Grylls (XII.
98).
     In a chapter focusing on Dickens, Eliot, and James, Pattison traces
Dickens's use of the connection between the child and the old man, a motif he
sees everywhere in Dickens. **The Old Curiosity Shop** serves as his central
example of how Dickens uses the child as the precursor of a new way of life;
Nell dies but redeems her grandfather from "outright condemnation."

Variants of these pairs frequently appear--Oliver and Fagin, Tiny Tim and Scrooge, Jenny Wren and Riah--none with complete uniformity but each suggesting the possibilities of goodness in a corrupt world and each working to a similar conclusion: salvation can be found if one follows the child's example. Pattison connects Dickens's old man with the Christian image of the **vetus homo**, a figure of exigetical theology representing sin and the Old Laws of the Jews, a system replaced by Christ's redemption of man from this Law and from sin too. Pattison sees, therefore, an essentially Christian vision characterizing Dickens's fiction, which, from **Dombey and Son** onwards, treats these ideas "in an epic framework."

165. Phillips, Virginia. "'Brought up by Hand': Dickens's Pip, Little Paul Dombey, and Oliver Twist." **The Dickensian**, 74 (September 1978), 144-47.

Glosses the usual meaning of bringing up "by hand" as "to hand-feed" and notes how Dickens's use of the phrase elsewhere in his fiction reflects his middle class, moralistic attitude in favor of breast-feeding and dislike of any substitutes, whether hand-feeding or wet-nursing. Dickens's objections to these alternatives, Phillips points out, also mirror contemporary medical opinion, which argued that most mothers could and should breast-feed their infants and which endorsed the use of a wet-nurse only if the mother died or was totally unable to afford sufficient or proper nourishment to her child. Cf. Finkel (XII. 80).

166. Phillips, Walter C. **Dickens, Reade, and Collins Sensation Novelists: A Study in the Conditions and Theories of Novel Writing in Victorian England.** New York: Columbia Univ. Press, 1919, passim.

An early study of the literary ancestry of the sensation novel, whose simplified argument may be gauged by Phillips's claim that "In general terms the Dickensian recipe from **Oliver Twist** to **Edwin Drood** was melodrama plus grotesque and humorous character elaboration." Phillips defines the genre as one that traffics in villainy, violence, and crime and accounts for its popularity primarily in terms of the rise of a new democratic audience. With a taste for blood and melodrama nurtured by the popular theatre, these readers, he argues, constituted a new public whom Dickens, Collins, and Reade brilliantly exploited. Phillips also traces the "lineal descendant[s]" of the sensationalists' "picturesque ruffian[s]" back to Bulwer Lytton, Byron, and Mrs. Radcliffe, whence they originated in eighteenth-century Gothicism.

167. Pine, Frank W. "Introduction." In 1918 Macmillan's Pocket American and English Classics (II. 29), pp. xv-xxvii.

Prepared as part of a former series of English texts for use in American elementary and secondary schools, each with an introduction and notes. Pine comments on attitudes towards the poor in Victorian England, presents the main facts of Dickens's life in seven chronological periods, and writes briefly about the external facts of the composition and publication of **Oliver Twist**. The text provides the 1841 Preface and brief notes (pp. 467-72), most of which gloss unusual words and provide perfunctory information.

168. Pritchett, V.S. "Books in General." **The New Statesman and Nation**, 39 (25 March 1950), 344-45. Rpt. in his **Books in General.** London: Chatto and Windus, 1953, pp. 191-96.

A review of Graham Greene's Introduction to **Oliver Twist** (XII. 97) in which Pritchett responds skeptically to Greene's suggestion that "the eternal and alluring taint of the Manichee" may have crept into Dickens's novel. Instead, Pritchett proposes that the book's terror lies in its literary sources, which Dickens married to his personal hysteria. The Manichee, Pritchett adds, is also "good theatre," a point he develops by suggesting that we take seriously the emissaries of light as well as those of darkness, for in the end, the novel convinces us, "even though by the long arm of coincidence," that the long arm of humanity and justice also exist. "Hence--we may be tempted to think--not the absence of God or the taint of the Manichee, but the author's lingering assumption that the belief in justice, the knowledge of retribution and passion of mercy are self-evident in human nature, and that a good dose of terror ... will bring them out."

Although Pritchett takes issue with Greene on this one matter, he finds the Introduction "a really brilliant, melancholy and subtle appreciation" of the novel, about which Pritchett himself writes with spirit and obvious enjoyment.

169. Pugh, Edwin. "Oliver Twist." In his **Charles Dickens: The Apostle of the People.** London, 1908; rpt. New York: AMS Press, 1975, pp. 89-103.

Discusses briefly Dickens's youthful trials before devoting single chapters to the main novels. Each chapter illustrates Pugh's thesis that Dickens developed instinctively and unconsciously as "a Socialist." If Dickens, in **Oliver Twist,** Pugh argues, "had done nothing but give us this ugly, gaudy, repulsive symbol of corruption and bribery, toadyism and sycophancy, vested interest and high chicane and foul privilege, he had done enough ... to further the cause of Socialism and to entitle him to a niche in our temple of heroes that is even now a-building."

This passage typifies Pugh's charged language and his unsystematic exposition of Dickens's political philosophy in the third section of the book. A passionate defense of the poor and contempt for the privileged serve as the main qualifications for admitting Dickens to Pugh's definition of Socialism, although he does recognize some complicating factors. Pugh sees, for example, that Dickens set forth his views without system and lacked a theoretical base for his criticism. He also grants that Dickens was "All for palliatives" and the devoted champion of "private benevolence and charitable enterprise." Yet he insists that Dickens's instincts "were dead right for Socialism" and that "He was a Socialist without knowing it."

170. Punter, David. "Gothic and the Sensation Novel: Dickens, Wilkie Collins, Sheridan LeFanu." In his **The Literature of Terror: A History of Gothic Fictions from 1765 to the Present Day.** London: Longman, 1980, pp. 214-23.

Demonstrates briefly "the Gothic element" in Dickens's work by selecting examples from **Oliver Twist,** "a particularly blatant instance of fictional terror" which Punter thinks still retains an extraordinary hold over the popular imagination, whose tears Dickens, G.W.M. Reynolds, and others exploited as they competed "for a single crown of yew." Punter believes, however, that Dickens went far beyond the boundaries established by earlier writers of Gothic fiction. **Oliver Twist,** he argues, is "a hideously violent book," one in which sordid and brutal crimes are committed because they reflect a society so constituted rather than the grandeur or even "justifiable vengeance" characteristic of the actions of previous Gothic villains. While the theatrical and melodramatic aspects of the book are rooted in the Gothic tradition, the novel, concludes Punter, departs from the genre both in the degree of its terror and in Dickens's use of contemporary London for a background as he transforms the face of the Metropolis "into an evil grin."

171. Reeves, William J. "Chimney Sweeps and Charter'd Streets: The Teachings of Oliver Twist, with an Assist from William Blake." JETT, 7 (Spring 1974), 32-35.

Discusses affinities between Blake and Dickens and the strategy Reeves used to make his students aware of the implications of the opening chapters of Oliver Twist. Reeves employed "A Little Boy Lost," "The Chimney Sweep," and "London" to illustrate how Blake saw children treated in an urban, industrialized world and combined a discussion of the poems with Dickens's presentation of Oliver's near sale to Gamfield and his picture of the child as victim. This narrow focus, Reeves found, proved useful to his students, open admissions freshmen at Brooklyn College.

172. Rice, Thomas J. "Oliver Twist and the Genesis of Barnaby Rudge." DSN, 4 (March 1973), 10-14.

Two questionable assumptions underlie Rice's analysis of the "inverted" relationship he posits between Oliver Twist and Barnaby Rudge. First, that the novels occupy opposite ends of the political spectrum; second, that Dickens writes more conservatively in the latter as "an act of political atonement" for Oliver Twist, whose Radical views allied him with "the extreme left-wing English political faction."
Accepting that "ultra-Radicals" exploited Dickens's criticism of the New Poor Law presents no difficulty to the reader. Less convincingly, Rice argues that Dickens sought to disassociate himself from the highly emotional agitation militants directed against the second Melbourne ministry (1835-41) by "revers[ing] his apparent political alignments of four years before." Thus into Barnaby Rudge Dickens introduced "some of the peculiarly un-Dickensian elements" that characterize the later work: the innately depraved Hugh replaces the innately good Oliver, emphasis upon the sins of the father pushes aside the earlier Rousseauistic optimism, and a stern warning against agitators prevails in Barnaby Rudge instead of the sympathy Dickens showed for the lower classes in Oliver Twist. These changes signify, Rice contends, Dickens's "conscious inversion" of the earlier novel, so that Barnaby Rudge reads, in its political context, as "a plea for political moderation." Dickens's "partisan efforts" did not avert the fall of the government in August 1841, but the novel was "an intended service for the rapidly failing Melbourne ministry."

173. Riddell, William Renwick. "A Lawyer Reads Oliver Twist." The Dickensian, 30 (Winter 1933-34), 27-30.

Praises the novel as a graphic presentation of period life, selecting details which date the action of the plot. The characters ride in hackney-cabriolets and not hansoms, the thieves play whist rather than bridge, robbery and other crimes are capital offenses, and the treadmill exists as a common punishment. By these and other references, Riddell concludes, Dickens conveys "an accurate picture" of early nineteenth-century life.

174. Robison, Roselee. "Dickens's Everlastingly Green Garden." ES, 59 (October 1978), 409-24.

Makes only passing reference to **Oliver Twist** but usefully discusses how Dickens expands and develops his idea of the pastoral in his late fiction. "In essence," Robison argues, "he takes the garden out of rural England and brings it to the very heart of grimy and noisy London."

175. Rohrberger, Mary. "The Daydream and the Nightmare: Surreality in **Oliver Twist.**" **Studies in the Humanities,** 6 (March 1978), 21-28.

Argues against those who present the thieves and the brownlow-Maylie group as two sets of characters from separate worlds, preferring instead to see the two as part of an apparent duality of dark and light structuring the novel and providing "inner consistency." Rohrberger draws heavily on impenetrable surrealist theory to support her view of **Oliver Twist's** surrealistic nature. What makes it so, she thinks, is the presence of nightmares and daydreams, two "necessary pieces of [the novel's] symbolic action."

176. Romano, John. "The Sentimental Criticism of Philosophy in **Oliver Twist.**" In his **Dickens and Reality.** New York: Columbia Univ. Press, 1978, pp. 117-40.

Focuses principally on Dickens's use of sentimentalism to refute the assumptions of the Philosophical Radicals, who, according to the narrator in Chapter 13, characterize self-interest as one of nature's first laws. Romano admits that Dickens's use of "heart, or generous impulse and feeling" appears shadowy and even ambiguous, although these values, successfully realized in Nancy, provide an arresting counter to Fagin's exposition of "number one" philosophy in Chapter 43. Nancy's power to see, to feel, and to act, Romano argues, makes her "the sentimental hero of the novel" because she admits that she is not a fit model to Oliver and makes no pretence about her origin and criminal life. Romano sees evidence of Nancy's superiority in her recognition of Oliver's goodness and in her determination to help him, even at the expense of turning against herself and against those upon whom she depends. This "self-revulsion," Romano notes, runs "exactly contrary to Fagin's elaborate theory of self-interest." Nancy moved by Oliver's plight also serves a second role: her response may be taken as a metaphor for how Dickens wants his readers to feel about the scenes he has shown them, hoping to arouse in them similar indignation and action.

177. Sackville-West, Edward (Lionel Cranfield, pseud.). "Books in General." **New Statesman and Nation,** 29 (10 February 1945), 95-96. Rpt. as part of "Dickens and the World of Childhood." In his **Inclinations.** London: Secker and Warburg, 1949, pp. 13-26.

Defends **Oliver Twist,** and other early Dickens novels, against charges of exaggeration and excessiveness in their appeals to pity, tenderness, and other emotions. Such rhetorical strategies proved necessary, Sackville-West argues, because Dickens attempted to open the hearts of men callous to "the sordid tragedy of Peterloo," unreassured by Sir Robert Peel's invention of the Metropolitan Police, and inclined to view the new industrial proletariat with terror. "It was essential, if pity was to be aroused," Sackville-West contends, "to write in terms of the strongest pathos"; only rhetoric persuades, "not the naked report, [or] the prim blue book."

Accepting this premise, Sackville-West points out, implies that behind the figures of rhetoric lie real human beings "of vivid reality," extremes born of a chiaroscuro world characterized by violent opposition between the Gentle and the Unkind. This observation, he notes, should be all the more apparent in 1945, another period of "entire ruthlessness" that provides an interesting perspective on how Dickens's early creations were intended to be seen in 1837, once we retrieve his characters from the distance that lends them safety and disguises them with humor. "Fagin is really no funnier than Al Capone, Squeers and Sikes than S.S. men; Nell no more unreal or less pathetic than a starving Polish child, Nancy than some Czech girl hauled off to a German soldiers' brothel."

178. Saintsbury, George. "Dickens." In The Cambridge History of English Literature. Ed. A.W. Ward and A.R. Waller. Vol. XIII. Cambridge: Cambridge Univ. Press, 1916, pp. 316-17.

Comments on his difficulty placing Oliver Twist, suggesting that the revival of "a fancy for grime novels" twenty years ago should have been "in its favour," but also admitting that "in good judgments" it is doubtful if the novel "has ever been, or ever will be, put in the first class of Dickens's work." Saintsbury ascribes some of the book's unsatisfactory nature to Dickens's overconcern with "neglected or persecuted children," a personal sympathy, he thinks, which laid a rather cramping hand on his creative powers. He also finds the book too short and too unvaried to engage Dickens's full comic powers and laments how sentiment and melodrama "both have the reins flung on their backs." Saintsbury pronounces Oliver "totally uninteresting," and Monks a scarecrow scoundrel, whose presence is relieved by Nancy and Sikes. Of Sikes, one cannot say that he is "an impossible ruffian," but Fagin, Saintsbury finds, "is some way further from reality," adding his endorsement to an observation attributed to one G.S. Venables, that "Dickens hanged Fagin for being the villain of a novel."

179. Schachterle, Lance. "Oliver Twist and Its Serial Predecessors." DSA, 3 (1980), 1-13.

Comments on the differences in form of the magazine serialization of Oliver Twist and the monthly parts publication of The Pickwick Papers. While both share a common need to divide the narrative into segments, the first imposed tighter space restrictions on the author and forced him to limit the number of his characters. The Pickwick Papers, which averaged about 18,500 words a part, compared to about half the number for Oliver Twist, allowed Dickens to be digressive and panoramic.

Schachterle then examines Dickens's magazine serial predecessors and makes some useful generalizations about their work, providing a literary context and a set of criteria by which to measure Oliver Twist. Early writers of serial prose fiction such as George R. Gleig and David Stewart met the demands of serialization by providing a series of separate tales joined by a common narrator, as in the Canterbury Tales. As the form developed, others like Michael Scott and Frederick Marryat developed the serial adventure with a single hero, whose growth from youth to maturity gave their stories some coherence. Nevertheless, their reliance on episodic construction and their tendency to pile incident upon incident make The Cruise of the Midge, Peter Simple, Jacob Faithful, Japhet in Search of a Father, and Snarleyyow (XIV. 141) crude in comparison with Oliver Twist. Dickens surpassed his early masters, Schachterle argues, by stressing causality in his plot, by making the installment stand by itself and yet advance the plot, and by introducing into the novel an elaborate puzzle whose mystery readers are challenged to solve. Schachterle also examines the pattern of Dickens's installments and notes Dickens's contempt for the cliff-hanger ending as a means of retaining the serial reader's curiosity.

180. Schlicke, Paul. "Bumble and the Poor Law Satire of **Oliver Twist.**" **The Dickensian,** 71 (September 1975), 149-56.

Schlicke presents Bumble as Dickens's "most significant early satiric achievement" and argues that the novelist's success arises from the identification of the man with his role as a parish functionary, thereby focusing on the flaws of the office rather than on the officeholder's lack of personal integrity. Dickens achieves this result through "specific narrative techniques." By selecting a comic figure already familiar in Victorian theatre and in popular song, Dickens makes clear his interest in a type rather than an individual. Dickens further generalizes his portrait by withholding personal information about Bumble and by directing attention to his uniform. Comments on the clothing, Schlicke argues, stress the office as Dickens's target, wherein lies Bumble's power.

Later, when the beadle loses his hat, cane, cape, breeches, and "elegant button" bearing "the porochial seal" of the Good Samaritan, Dickens's satire "is drained of its source of power." This happens, Schlicke contends, because Dickens portrays Bumble as "a personally responsible agent" in the later chapters, thus contradicting his earlier view that Bumble's misdeeds derive from his role as beadle rather than his personality. Yet despite this "damaging ambiguity," Schlicke believes that the satiric strength of the opening chapters prevails. **Oliver Twist** demonstrates, he concludes, "most emphatically" how the inhumanity of the Poor Laws "derives from forces larger than individual wrongdoing." For different responses to Bumble, see Kincaid (XII. 126) and Sucksmith (XII. 190).

181. Schwarzbach, F.S. "**Pickwick Papers, Oliver Twist,** and **Nicholas Nickleby.**" In his **Dickens and the City.** London: The Athlone Press, 1979, pp. 43-68.

In a brief discussion of **Oliver Twist,** Schwarzbach suggests that Oliver finds London the negation of hope and opportunity, a dark world so powerful that he can escape only by entering into its opposite by supernatural means. Dickens evokes in the novel London's horrifying and labyrinthine qualities by describing the details of actual things, places, and people; he also, Schwarzbach adds, blurs specifics and makes the details abstract. These comments on **Oliver Twist** form part of Schwarzbach's broader thesis about the impact of urbanization on people and how Dickens's individual story provides a paradigm of a fall from pastoral innocence, the experience of urban misery, and an eventual compromise which permits, in some measure, acceptance of the city.

182. Senelick, Laurence. "Traces of Othello in **Oliver Twist.**" The Dickensian, 70 (May 1974), 97-102.

What gives the murder of Nancy "such an epic resonance" and raises to the level of Shakespearian tragedy the slaying of a street-walker by a brutal burglar? Certainly "the glare of the footlights" helps, argues Senelick, but more to the point are the echoes of Othello, which are "too numerous and too close to be merely coincidental." Consider: Fagin goading on Sikes and Iago's "Do it not with poison. Strangle her in her bed" (**Othello,** IV, i, 203);

Nancy's exclamation of pleasure when Sikes draws the curtain of her bed and
Desdemona's "Will you come to bed, my lord" (V, ii, 24); and the verbal
similarities in the exchange between Sikes and Nancy and Desdemona's "I
never did/ Offend you in life" (V, ii, 59). Furthermore, both women appeal to
God before they are slain; in both cases a handkerchief is the token of
misunderstanding; and the crime for which they are executed "is treachery,
infidelity to their mates, transgressing the unwritten law."
      Senelick supports his case with the conjecture that "Dickens's
consciousness" could not have avoided the fact that two successful
productions of the play strove to outdo each other (Charles Kean played
Othello at Drury Lane, W.C. Macready acted the same part at Covent Garden)
while he was creating Nancy's murder. On the basis of this evidence--textual
and circumstantial--Senelick concludes that "We may be justified in glimpsing
a reflection of Othello, then, in the rugged power of that bloody scene in
Oliver." Cf. Collins (XII. 60), p. 182, who argues that the verbal echoes of
Macbeth in Oliver Twist do not guarantee tragic stature for Sikes, and
Macready (V. 5).

183. Sitwell, Osbert. Dickens. The Dolphin Books Series. London: Chatto
      and Windus, 1932, passim.

      A brief essay reflecting on Dickens's changing literary reputation and an
appreciation of some of the notable aspects of his art. Sitwell does not place
Oliver Twist among Dickens's "best books," but he finds much about it worthy
of comment. Sitwell admires the novel's "continuous and elaborate" action,
which never allows one's interest to flag; he finds Dickens's combination of
the improbable with the "startlingly real" effective; and he respects the
author's invocation to humanitarian feeling. Rereading Oliver Twist, Sitwell
also argues that he should enter "fresh claims" for Dickens in two respects: (1)
"as the originator of the modern 'thriller,' the father ... to Sherlock Holmes"
and tales of crime detected through coincidence or "consummate ability"; (2)
as an artist who equipped himself with "an extraordinary and personal
technique."
      Sitwell makes original observations about Dickens's artistry. He credits
Dickens as the first English novelist to understand the romance of great
nineteenth-century cities, admiring Dickens's ability to probe London's
"secret spots" and reflect London "at every angle." After defending Dickens
against the charge of exaggerating his characters, Sitwell points to Charley
Bates as an example of Dickens's ability to "rise on the wings of his genius" by
accomplishing "one of the most difficult feats known to the writer of fiction."
In the scene in which Bates throws himself on Nancy's murderer, Dickens
causes a character, hitherto essentially comic, "to be transmuted to the
heights of heroism without a seeming flaw or any break in its apparent
continuity." Concluding, Sitwell makes two connections between Dickens and
continental writers critics now treat as commonplace. He finds the
treatment of Fagin towards the end of the novel "Russian" in that Fagin is
transformed into a "more pitiable and less repellant character" as Dickens
wins us over to the very side against which he had previously prejudiced us.
And he detects "something a little Proustian" in the phrasing and conception
of Mr. Brownlow searching his memory for the person of whom Oliver reminds
him after meeting the child for the first time (ch. 11).

184. Slater, Michael. Dickens and Women. London: Dent; Stanford:
      Stanford Univ. Press, 1983, passim.

Comments briefly on the minor female characters in **Oliver Twist** and
more extensively on Rose Maylie and Nancy. Slater finds much to admire in
the latter, a self-assertive, complete, and paradoxical character despite her
occasional melodramatic language and lack of social verisimilitude. Rose
Maylie, by contrast, appears a less significant achievement, a character,
Slater remarks, all too likely to disappear from the text and leave in her place
the shade of Mary Hogarth, about whom Dickens writes directly, as if
treasuring the memory of an ideal. Rose's main business, he continues, is to
fall ill and allow Dickens to "re-live in fiction that devastating May night of
the previous year" when Mary Hogarth suddenly collapsed and died (II. 1).
Because Dickens recasts this painful incident in the novel he can play God and
"save" Mary-Rose, adding as further balm to his own feelings the satisfaction
of making Rose and Oliver blood-relations just as, in an ideal world, Mary and
Dickens would appear similarly related. Such are the limitations of "pure
wish-fulfillment   art,"   Slater   comments,   referring   to   the   novel's
antepenultimate paragraph in which the narrator recalls Rose's looks, smiles,
and turns of thought and speech.

185. ____. "On Reading **Oliver Twist.**" The **Dickensian,** 70 (May
        1974), 75-81.

In a fresh and unpretentious essay, Slater comments on the qualities of
Oliver Twist that have haunted and fascinated him since he first read the
book as an eleven-year old. The novel's power, he believes, lies in its
"extraordinary mixture" of satire, documentary realism, fable, didacticism,
melodrama, and "near-tragedy."
Swiftian satire dominates the first seven chapters, in which Dickens
chronicles the devastating failure of the Government, the Law, and the
Church to treat people as human beings, seeing the poor instead as Malthusian
abstractions such as "the surplus population" or "paupers." After leaving the
parish, Oliver journeys directly to London's underworld, thus allowing Dickens
to suggest a direct connection between social injustice and neglect and
crimes. Aspects of Fagin's and Sikes's characters reinforce this documentary
message, although Slater finds that once Oliver arrives in the city, Dickens
the fabulist takes over. We watch a symbolic struggle between Good and Evil
as Fagin tries to destroy Oliver "as inevitably as Melville's Claggart must
seek to destroy Billy Budd."
Into this drama obtrude melodrama, "near-tragedy" as Dickens raises
Sikes "to a Shakespearian level" after the murder of Nancy, and the voice of
the moralist, who dramatizes Dickens's belief in the healing power of memory
to awaken our minds to past wrongs and sorrows. "Just as Scrooge's heart is
unfrozen by being shown a vision of himself as a forlorn and lonely child so
Nancy's humanity and goodness is aroused by witnessing a re-enactment [in
Oliver] of her own undoing." Slater concludes by stating that Dickens
provides continuity between the novel's two main centers--the institutions
satirized in the opening and Fagin's London--by linking them through the
common theme of selfishness. Among the former, each group and individual
is out for his own interests; among the latter, the same concern for "Number
One" prevails but without the hypocritical pretenses of those who represent
"respectable" society.

186. Smith, Graham. "The Early Novels: From **Pickwick** to **Barnaby
        Rudge.**" In his **Dickens, Money, and Society.** Berkeley: Univ. of
        California Press, 1968, pp. 11-52.

Argues that the early novels illustrate an obvious dichotomy between "didacticism and creative autonomy," two qualities generally fused in Dickens's later style but only occasionally joined before **Dombey and Son.** Smith cites the workhouse section of **Oliver Twist** and the scenes in the thieves' kitchen as exceptions to his generalization, praising the former for its powerful irony and commenting on how Dickens presents Fagin's world as an "ironic inversion" of bourgeois conventionality." These scenes succeed, he suggests, because Dickens conveys the sense that "there is no real difference" in the way Oliver is treated in the workhouse or exploited by the thieves. Didacticism breaks in, however, as Dickens exhorts his readers to respond to the poor with the same benevolence Mr. Brownlow shows Oliver.

187. Squires, Paul Chatham. "Charles Dickens as Criminologist." **Journal of the American Institute of Criminal Law and Criminology,** 29 (May-June 1938), 170-201.

Discusses Dickens's views about the nature of crime and criminals, contrasting **Great Expectations** and **Our Mutual Friend** with **Oliver Twist,** where he sees the youthful reformer at work "in all the white heat of his enthusiasm." Squires presents Dickens's position on crime in **Oliver Twist** as a balanced one that pays equal weight to social conditions and to heredity as factors explaining crime. Oliver's drift to London and induction into Fagin's gang, he argues, show how hunger and ill treatment supply "the underworld with its pawns," and how harsh social conditions force juveniles to steal in order to survive. At the same time, the novel also presents individuals like Sikes and Monks, who are both bad by nature rather than corrupted by the environment. Squires quickly disposes of Sikes as an "unadulterated beast of the lowest mental order," but finds much to admire in Monks, "a paranoid epileptic, rotted out with syphilis," whose clinical portrait suggests Dickens's belief that improved living conditions alone will not solve "the criminological enigma."

The remaining part of the section on **Oliver Twist** comments on the legal technicalities of Fang's intention in Chapter 11 to commit Oliver for three months of hard labor. Disagreeing with A.L., who cites Fang's response as "A classic instance of 'gerrymandering'" (XVI. 15), Squires argues that while Fang may have been prepared to alter the law so that he could prosecute Oliver, no such felony charge was brought and that, with respect to the matter of jurisdiction, Fang acted within his authority. Oliver's case, Squires notes, came under the Vagrancy Act of 1824 (5 Geo. 4, c. 83, s. 4), which specified that anyone frequenting a public street "with intent to commit a felony" is liable to the penalties of the Act, even though no opportunity should arise, if the justices find evidence that the individual frequented the street and did so with intent to commit a felony. This Act permitted commitment for not more than three months at hard labor; thus, Squires concludes, Fang was not guilty of gerrymandering, but he was guilty of sheer inhumanness. Against such legal obduracy Dickens set himself, evidently not without success, Squires thinks, for in 1840 the new Infant Felon Act (3 & 4 Vict., c. 90) provided for the care and education of infants convicted of stealing.

188. Stevenson, Lionel. **The English Novel: A Panorama.** Boston: Houghton Mifflin, 1960, pp. 244-45.

This survey proceeds chronologically and avoids sweeping assessments of a writer's canon by focusing on the literary context in which individual works appeared. Stevenson finds **Oliver Twist** handicapped by its sentimentality, melodrama, and pretentious speechmaking borrowed "from the cheap theater." But Dickens's observations on crime, informed by the reporter's familiarity with the subject, and his attacks on the Poor Laws confer authenticity on the novel and save it from "sentimental propaganda." Stevenson also praises Dickens's ability to render vividly the solitude felt by an individual like Oliver, "who has no place within the framework of society."

189. Stone, Harry. "From Pickwick to Chuzzlewit: Fairy Tales and the Apprentice Novels." In his Dickens and the Invisible World: Fairy Tales, Fantasy, and Novel-Making. Bloomington, Indiana: Indiana Univ. Press, 1979, pp. 71-118.

Stone's concern with fairy tales in Oliver Twist arises from his interest in how Dickens attempts to fuse a heightened and fantastic world with a fundamental realism. His chapter excludes a detailed study of the sources of folk elements in Oliver Twist but assumes Dickens's awareness of archetypal figures--Satanic fathers, innocent children, wicked half-brothers, fairy god-fathers, and so on--in order to address two issues: the origin of Oliver Twist's "haunted atmosphere" and the aesthetic consequences of "unalloyed evil" and "unalloyed good" in a realistic novel.

Stone responds to the first by conjecturing that the "blacking-warehouse months" provided a source for both the horrors Dickens expresses in the novel and the joy he takes in Oliver's escape. So intense was Dickens's perception of his own fall into disgrace and subsequent release, Stone argues, that the novelist involuntarily "enlarged" his fictional "wild nightmare fears" and "soft radiant hopes" with "monstrous story-book shapes."

These "antipodal fairy-tale intensities" define for Stone the novel's "innermost character," providing both its central strengths and weaknesses. Flaws arise, Stone argues in answer to his second interest, because Dickens fails to accommodate the book's supernatural elements with its workhouse scenes. If we accept Oliver's purity and miraculous immunity, how can we take seriously "the life-destroying threats that surround him?" Versions of Stone's thesis also appear in his "Dickens and Fairy Tales," DSN, 9 (March 1978), 2-3 and in his "Oliver Twist and Fairy Tales," DSN, 10 (June-September 1979), 34-39.

190. Sucksmith, Harvey Peter. The Narrative Art of Charles Dickens: The Rhetoric of Sympathy and Irony in his Novels. Oxford: Clarendon Press, 1970, passim.

Because Sucksmith's study proceeds topically references to Oliver Twist appear only when passages from the text provide examples of those aspects of Dickens's narrative art under discussion. Sucksmith begins with Dickens's conviction that novels should make an impact upon the reader, after which he analyzes how Dickens uses the rhetoric of fiction--"the technical means whereby, through structure, effects are created and vision focused." He also suggests how Dickens's preoccupation with "strongly emotive effects" owes something to Edgar Allen Poe, Bulwer Lytton, and Edward Mangin, whose Essays on the Sources of the Pleasures Received from Literary Composition (1809) scholars have overlooked.

Discussions of Oliver Twist include: Dickens's tendency to combine obtrusive but not irrelevant ironic language about "the petty world of Bumbledon" with other figures of speech also contributing to the book's generally ironic tone, the heightened pathos evident in the revisions Dickens made in the passage describing Oliver after the attempted robbery, and the novel's failure to arouse genuine emotion in the idyllic description of Oliver's sojourn in the country. This section fails because the cliches of pastoral convention and the idealized characters and scenes weaken the feelings of relief Dickens wishes to convey. Sucksmith also shows how Dickens's hints of potential violence in his first description of Sikes work far more effectively than G.W.M. Reynold's technique with Magsman in The Mysteries of the Courts of London (1848-56), where the latter clumsily forces on the reader epithets designed to signify what Dickens conveys indirectly. In his last extended comment on Oliver Twist, Sucksmith analyzes how Dickens takes a stock comic situation--the man with great matrimonial expectations suddenly discovering that marriage is a trap--and gives Bumble's public humiliation general significance by treating him as "a comic cipher for the England which bases its authority on fancy dress." Cf. Kincaid (XII. 126) and Schlicke (XII. 180).

191. Swinburne, Algernon Charles. Charles Dickens. Ed. T. Watts-Dunton. London, 1913; rpt. New York: Folcroft Library Editions, 1976. 77 pp.

Combines two separate essays Swinburne wrote on Dickens in 1902, the longer of which first appeared in the Quarterly Review of July 1902 (pp. 20-39). This essay treats generally most of Dickens's works but omits any reference to Oliver Twist, about which Swinburne had already written elsewhere, in an Introduction to the novel for George D. Sproul's "Autograph Edition" of Dickens's works. Sproul, however, subsequently abandoned that undertaking, publishing (1902-05) only fifteen of the projected fifty-six volumes after F.G. Kitton, his general editor, died in 1904. Thus Swinburne's essay on Oliver Twist remained unpublished until Watts-Dunton added it to the Quarterly Review piece and published both in 1913.

Swinburne notes that in Oliver Twist Dickens combined for the first time "the quality of a great tragic and comic poet" with the already famous qualities of a great humorist and a born master "in the arts of narrative and dialogue." Swinburne finds Oliver's innocence exasperating and holds little sympathy for his "morally malodorous half-brother," Monks, reserving his delight for the novel's more vibrant characters, whom he enjoys both as "life-long friends" and as figures "more fully and happily developed in later books." As examples of minor characters who later reappear, Swinburne cites Mr. Brownlow, Blathers and Duff, and Rose Maylie, rough sketches, he suggests, for Mr. Jarndyce, Inspector Bucket, and Agnes Wickfield and Esther Summerson. This slight essay closes with appreciative remarks on Cruikshank's illustrations.

192. Symons, Arthur. "Oliver Twist." In Essays of the Year (1929-1930). Comp. Frederick J.H. Darton. London: Argonaut Press, 1930, 252-67.

Despite the essay's ostensible focus on a single novel, Symons ranges widely and impressionistically over Dickens's works. He agrees with Swinburne's verdict on Oliver Twist (XII. 191), praises Dickens's treatment of the Thames in his novels, and commends the varied rhythm of Dickens's prose, citing examples from Oliver Twist. Symons also speaks highly of Cruikshank's contribution to Oliver Twist and comments on Dickens's preference for characters from "the lowest classes," criminals and assassins who evoke an extraordinary fascination, despite their vile lives and lack of redeeming qualities. On the debit side, Symons calls Dickens ignorant as a social satirist when compared with Fielding, laments his inability to create tragic female characters, and finds in the protagonists of Fielding and Austen a vitality never displayed in the powerful and lurid figures in Oliver Twist.

193. Tewari, R.P.   "The Treatment of Fallen Women in the Novels of
     Dickens and Mrs. Gaskell." **Agra Univ. Journal of Research (Letters)**,
     19 (January 1971), 43-52.

Examples of prostitution from **Oliver Twist, Dombey and Son,** and David
Copperfield presented at a general and descriptive level. Tewari refers to the
social conditions that promoted the spread of prostitution but offers no
particular thesis or literary analysis in this essay.

194. Thomas, Sidney.   "To the Editor: **Oliver Twist.**"   PMLA, 93
     (October 1978), 1009-10.

Takes issue with a particular aspect of Lankford's contention that
Dickens explores the relationship between genteel society and the criminal
world by exposing some of the underlying similarities between them (XII. 131
and 132). When Lankford sees Harry Maylie's proposal to Rose as a threat
analogous to Monk's desire to seduce Oliver into crime, he misreads a crucial
episode in the novel, writes Thomas. Harry proposes marriage not seduction,
a point explicit in his conversation with his mother, which shows that there is
nothing "criminal" about his intentions. Dickens presents Monks and Harry as
opposites, Thomas stresses, one depraved and vicious, the other generous and
good. See also Lund (XII. 143).

195. Thro, A. Brooker.   "An Approach to Melodramatic Fiction: Goodness
     and Energy in the Novels of Dickens, Collins and Reade." **Genre,** 11
     (Fall 1978), 359-74.

Why did the Victorian novelists adhere to melodrama despite their
admission that the conventions of the genre contradicted their sense of the
real world? Thro insists on the importance of this question because he thinks
that too many critics ignore the novelists' concern with "moralism" and
"emotional affect," assuming that Victorian fiction investigates only social
problems. Accordingly, Thro proposes a new perspective on melodrama whose
main features stress the genre's origin in "psychic phenomenon" and the
novelists' wish to "gratify their impulses toward extremes" by abandoning
themselves "to an amoral violence" and also revering "a morally perfect
gentleness."
To illustrate his theory, Thro examines **Oliver Twist, The Woman in
White,** and **Griffith Gaunt,** three representative novels in which he sees a
conflict between the "unmixed opposites ... [of] ideal goodness and pure
energy." Seeing life in these terms, the writers, Thro argues, prefer to
present exemplary, static figures like Oliver rather than portray morally
complex wrongdoers like Thackeray's Becky Sharp. Yet while Dickens, for
example, presents Monks' violence abstractly in order to insulate Oliver
"from opprobrious energy," forceful, energetic figures like Sikes and Fagin
flare up and command our admiration. Thro assumes that Dickens admires
them too but quickly reasserts his control over them by emphasizing the
novel's moral intent. He uses Sikes "to help exhibit Nancy's decisive turning
to goodness" and he dutifully gives his support to those who advocate love and
mercy. This movement, Thro thinks, reminds us that while melodramatic
fiction shares the strong romantic impulse we see in Gothic novelists like
Charles Maturin and M.G. Lewis, the Victorians reveal themselves to be "far
more inhibited" than their predecessors. While admiring boldness and wanting
to gratify feelings of self-release, melodramatic novelists, Thro argues, also
seek "a purifying self-control." As a result, they veer continually back and

forth between these two extremes but end by moralizing. Their novels deny
the validity of wild and terrible energy and stress ideal communities and
merciful love.

196. Thurley, Geoffrey. "Oliver Twist." In his The Dickens Myth: Its
     Genesis and Structure. London: Routledge and Kegan Paul, 1976, pp.
     34-50.

In an ambitious and stimulating Introductory chapter, Thurley challenges
"the heresies of the realist hegemony," which have ruled from Henry James to
even contemporary critics, whose praise for Dickens Thurley often sees as
"riddled with doubts." Thurley also puts to his sword the "Dickens monster[s]"
created by Taylor Stoehr, Garis (XII. 87), and Sucksmith (XII. 190), all of
whom offer provocative readings of the novels but err either in trying to align
Dickens with other novelists (to his detriment) or fail to define "the nature of
his vision." Who, therefore, is the Charles Dickens Thurley seeks, the writer
whom American critics, he argues, generally fail to see because they take too
facile a view of Dickens's preoccupation with snobbery?
     Thurley's answer, as he admits, proves vulnerable to the mistake he
accuses others of: by insisting on the primacy of one "real pulse" in Dickens's
art, Thurley tends to flatten the canon to make it fit his version of "the
Dickens myth." This phrase, Thurley explains, "designate[s] the narrative
pattern which underlies Dickens's works," whose elements he summarizes as
the abandoned child who climbs out of the abyss of poverty and who seeks
"security, peace, and light." As Dickens developed his myth beyond this "most
naive stage," he turned in his later fiction to a hypersensitive exploration of
"modern man's peculiar uncertainties, his fears, his debilitating hopes, and his
absense of identity."
     Although Dickens's treatment of the myth in Oliver Twist lacks the
critical self-awareness Thurley values in the later novels, he finds much to
praise in this almost embarrassingly complete "fantasy" of the Victorian
success story. Thurley recognizes the coincidences governing Oliver's journey
from the workhouse to security not as "an affront to decent realism" but as a
phenomenon "governed from within by a different logic," whose power resides
in the novel's moral vision. That vision, Thurley adds, presents itself in
Dickens's rhythmic pattern of evil leading to good, and vice versa, and in the
dexterity with which Dickens interweaves the novel's public tone (the
outraged observer recording England's hostility to her poor) with the work's
inner narrative, whose real issue is Oliver's safety. Thurley also comments
usefully on Dickens's juxtaposition of Rose and Nancy and provides a
convincing defense of Monks, whom he calls a minor study of "the satanic
personality." Rather than reject Monks as cardboard figure, Thurley analyzes
the source of his power and presents a case for taking seriously a villain who
desires not Oliver's death but his corruption. If one reads Oliver Twist
biographically, Thurley concludes, the story re-enacts and reaffirms Dickens's
emergence from "the abyss of penury and degradation"; reading the novel as
an expression of cultural preoccupations, Thurley sees it as "a universal
Victorian fear of falling down from one class to the one beneath."

197. Tick, Stanley. "Oliver Twist: 'A stronger hand than chance'"
     Renascence, 33 (Summer 1981), 225-39.

     Tick describes his essay as a psychobiographical approach to the novel in
which he aligns Oliver Twist with his sense of Dickens's overriding
preoccupation with child heroes, preserving the secrets of his early life, and a

recurring theme of confession in all the novels. The essay's main thesis constitutes Tick's claim that fiction allowed the adult Dickens to displace the guilt he felt in continuing to suppress his secret childhood misfortunes and that **Oliver Twist** reveals this phenomenon for the first time. As proof, Tick cites the passivity of the protagonist and the confessions by Oliver that punctuate the text. By making Oliver an explicit victim of "appalling adult neglect," Dickens recreates his own exploited self, and by deliberately introducing into the story occasions when Oliver tries to recount the facts about his past and tell "all his simple history" (ch. 30), Dickens disguises and satisfies a personal urge to reveal the truth about his own miserable childhood. This projection of his plight into that of an idealized child, Tick concludes, privately compensates Dickens "for his own adult cowardice" about revealing the truth about his background of poverty and manual labor at the blacking factory.

198. Tillotson, Kathleen. "Introduction." In 1966 Clarendon Edition (II. 48), pp. xv-xlvii.

Restates Tillotson's "long incubation" theory (XII. 201) in her detailed account of the novel's genesis and composition set against Dickens's relationship with Bentley and his involvement with the **Miscellany.** Tillotson also refers briefly to the novel's reception and the plagiarized dramatic versions performed before Dickens finished **Oliver Twist,** but devotes the main thrust of the Introduction to marshalling facts and arguments to support her decision to use the 1846 edition of the novel (II. 12) as her copy-text. For further discussion of her textual policy, see II. 48 and III. 1-7, 14, and 16-18. Tillotson appends her Descriptive List of Editions 1838-1867 (pp. xlviii-lvi) to the Introduction and also includes the 1965 Preface (II. 48) in which she and John Butt discuss the general aims of the Clarendon Edition of Dickens's novels (pp. v-vii). Four of Tillotson's seven Appendices are annotated separately and may be found under Commentary on the Text (III. 18), Dickens's Reading Adaptations: **Sikes and Nancy** (V. 23), Contemporary Reviews, and Dickens, Cruikshank, and the Illustrations (XIII. 57).

199. ———. "Introduction." In 1982 World's Classics Edition (II. 55), pp. vi-xiv.

A succinct essay commenting on the novel's genesis, the levels of reality Dickens drew upon for his narrative, and the work's topicality. Tillotson writes informatively about the novel's contemporary social context, pointing out that Dickens's alleged confusion between the old and new Poor Laws reflects "conditions themselves confused" rather than a lack of clarity in the author's mind. In a brief comment about the novel's originality, Tillotson notes how **Oliver Twist** differs from the popular narratives about foundlings. She also refers to the contemporary responses to Dickens's presentation of the realities of criminal life, commenting on both the tributes and attacks his pictures of the thieves evoked.

200. ———. **Novels of the Eighteen-Forties.** Oxford: Clarendon Press, 1954, passim.

A brief discussion of **Oliver Twist** opening "the door to a new kind of novel of low life" and notes on Thackeray's critical response to Dickens's Newgate interests. For Thackeray's criticism of **Oliver Twist,** see X. 3, 4, 13, and 16.

Criticism   195

201. ____. "Oliver Twist." Essays and Studies, 12 (1959), 87-105.

An important discussion of **Oliver Twist** as a coherent and planned work, whose principal objective appears to be the modification of Humphry House's statement that the unity of the novel derives "from impulse and from the energy of its imagination, not from its construction" (XII. 111). Rebutting House, Tillotson argues that the design of **Oliver Twist** is evident in its long incubation, which she traces to Dickens's statement to Kolle in 1833 (I. 1) and to similarities between the sketches of "low" life Dickens first published between 1834 and 1836 (XIV. 1) and those parts of the novel treating the London of Fagin and Sikes. Tillotson also notes how Dickens outlined the central features of his plan for the novel in his 1841 Preface, where he spoke of his intention to write a moral fairy tale about the London underworld and expose the sham romantic glamor with which other novelists had falsified criminals' lives. Interpreting the imaginative force with which Dickens conveyed their loneliness and terror "as a shift of moral sympathy" for Fagin and Sikes and a corresponding divergence from the book's stated focus on the triumph of "the principle of Good," asserts Tillotson, represents a misreading of **Oliver Twist**.

202. Tomkins, A.R. "Introduction." In 1965 Blackie Edition (II. 46), pp. v-vi.

Cursory comments about the novel's strengths and weaknesses. Tomkins finds the narrative "brilliant" up to the attempted burglary at Chertsey, after which "things begin to go rather awry." Tomkins pronounces the Maylies "boring," the deaths of the principal villains "strained," and Oliver unrealistic.

203. Vann, J. Don. "Dickens and Charley Bates." In **Of Edsels and Marauders.** Ed. Fred Tarpley and Anne Mosley. South-Central Names Institute. Publication 1. Commerce, Texas: Names Institute Press, 1970, pp. 117-21.

Takes issue with Le Comte's observation (XII. 136) that Dickens's references to Master Bates are merely an unfortunate accident belonging "apparently to the humor of the unconscious." Dickens, counters Vann, frequently used names to designate his characters' personal habits, and to suggest, therefore, that he did not recognize the word **masturbates** in Charley's name is "inconceivable." As proof, Vann notes that of the ninety-five references to Charley in the novel, forty-five address him as Master Bates, as opposed to Charley Bates (twenty-three), Charley (eighteen), Master Charley Bates (five), and Mr. Charles Bates (four). Vann also adds that as one frequently given to uncontrolled fits of laughter, impulsive behavior, and occasional incoherence, Bates illustrates some of the lesser evils to which Victorians thought self-abusers were prey. In 1857, for example, William Acton warned his readers of the "awful risk[s]" of self-stimulation, amongst which he numbered "early death" in his **The Function and Disorders of the Reproductive Organs.** "Master Bates," concludes Vann, "is a deliberate charactonym."

204. Wagenknecht, Edward. "White Magic." In his **Cavalcade of the Novel.** New York: Henry Holt, 1943, pp. 213-33.

Brief words about **Oliver Twist** combining the melodramatic, the impossible, and "tremendous faithfulness" in the treatment of Sikes and Nancy juxtaposed with sweeping and dated judgments about Dickens's lack of art and abundance of genius.

205. Walder, Dennis. **"Oliver Twist** and Charity." In his **Dickens and Religion.** London: George Allen and Unwin, 1981, pp. 42-65.

Walder's study focuses on Dickens's "fundamental outlook" and scrutinizes different aspects of his religion as they emerge at various stages of his career. Dickens's principal assumptions, Walder argues, include those of "a liberal Protestant with Radical, Romantic leanings," all of which reflect both personal impulses and prevailing currents of belief.

In **Oliver Twist** Dickens opposes the well meaning but cold and inhuman orthodoxies of Malthus and Bentham with a pronounced emphasis on charity, the social and Christian virtue Walder sees as the novel's central theme. Dickens wants to move us "into sympathy and charity for the poor," Walder argues, because the secular authorities now responsible for paupers since the Amendment of 1834 fail to show any mercy and persist in seeing the workhouse as an institution for correcting depraved criminals rather than as a refuge for the needy and infirm. Walder also sees in the opening of the novel evidence of Dickens's "growing distrust of the religious establishment," a special criticism he attributes to the influence of the **Times's** editorials early in 1837. "Even if Dickens did attend some of the early [parliamentary] debates on the new law, most of his information, as well as a confirmation of his basic position, was probably derived from **The Times."**

Seeing little evidence of mercy and charity among public and religious institutions, Dickens shows alternatives he admires in the behavior of private individuals, who offer Oliver not just alms but the sympathy and "Christian love" he needs to survive. The "overtly 'good' characters," Walder argues, also represent Christian forgiveness, which, linked with the power of providence in the novel, affirm a key theme. Instead of receiving "the condemnation of a vengeful God," fallen creatures like Nancy are given an opportunity to be tempted to virtue. "Dickens seems bent on exposing the difference between the more hopeful and optimistic form of Christianity he believes in, and the evangelical stress upon the innate depravity of sinners which calls down retribution on their heads," Walder affirms. But he adds that to call Dickens "a man who believed in charity" needs qualification. Dickens's belief "crossed sectarian lines" and was also based on "strong affection," "humanity of heart," and gratitude to a Being whose "great attribute," in the words of Chapter 53 of the novel, is Benevolence.

206. Wallins, Roger P. "Victorian Periodicals and the Emerging Social Conscience." VPN, 8 (June 1975), 47-59.

Argues that the periodicals of the 1830's and 1840's provided middle-class readers with the same basic information about social conditions as they got from Parliamentary blue-books, if they ever read them, and from the social novels of Dickens, Disraeli, and Mrs. Trollope. For example, the description of Oliver and Sowerberry walking through filthy streets (ch. 5) or of Jacob's Island (ch. 50) "would have been no great surprise," Wallins thinks, to those readers of **Bentley's Miscellany** who had seen "The Dregs of London" in the June 1833 issue of **New Monthly Magazine.** For details, see XVI. 17.

207. W[augh], [Arthur]. "Biographical Introduction." In 1906 Biographical Edition (II. 24), pp. vii-xv.

Focuses on the circumstances that led Dickens to contract with Bentley to write **Oliver Twist**, stating, incorrectly, that the Agreement of 22 August 1836 represents the date when Dickens arranged with the publisher to begin **Oliver Twist** as a monthly serial in the **Miscellany**. Cf. I. 6. Waugh stresses the extent to which Dickens overextended himself during these early years, presenting him as "desperately harassed and overworked." Yet despite these pressures, Dickens, Waugh notes, became more deeply involved with his characters than he had done during the composition of **The Pickwick Papers**. In that novel, he suggests, Dickens worked with his characters "from outside," whereas in **Oliver Twist** the main figures became living beings who even ran away with their creator. "This sentiment of personal relation with his characters grew so greatly," writes Waugh, "that later in life it was only with great difficulty that he was able to bring his stories to an end, and to part with the companions of so many pleasant months."

208. Westburg, Barry. "Oliver Twist: A Predevelopmental Fiction." In his **The Confessional Fictions of Charles Dickens.** Dekalb, Illinois, Northern Illinois Univ. Press, 1977, pp. 1-31.

Westburg's introductory chapter sets before us four principal assumptions upon which his study rests. First, he posits a Kierkegaardian notion that what distinguishes human beings from other animals is their attempt to "understand time as growth" and in turn to see growth as "a system of stages which ... comprise a whole course of life." Next, we are told that fiction typically involves writing self-conscious narratives of personal development, a genre Westburg labels "confessional" and defines as narratives that focus on a fictional protagonist's psychic growth and identity. Westburg also contends that Dickens would have agreed with Kierkegaard's idea "of the need for seeking unity in individual life" because Dickens showed great interest in a personal truth of this kind rather than in "inherited cultural truths." Finally, we confront Westburg's structuralist preference for "an art of pure construction." Such a predisposition typically disregards a fiction's mimetic role in favor of works which make artificiality their message, an achievement Dickens accomplished, Westburg thinks, in **Great Expectations,** which stands out as "an aesthetic confession" about art by the means of art supporting an "ethically neutral, messageless [view] about life." Explaining how Dickens arrived at this position occupies much of Westburg's attention, as he traces the evolution of Dickens's "three major confessional novels"--**Oliver Twist, David Copperfield,** and **Great Expectations**--a "Confessional Trilogy" in which he sees "radical probes into growth, time, and life-structure."

Oliver Twist plays a small but important part in Westburg's unfolding scheme, for while not a genuinely developmental novel (unlike its successors), the text provides him with evidence to support the view that the three are "systematically related." No fictional treatment of time, growth, and identity can ignore childhood, Westburg argues, a fact which makes **Oliver Twist** relevant to his thesis because he sees it as the first English novel "to take the child as its protagonist." Doing so provides Dickens with "evolutionary, temporal possibilities" such as the occasion when we see Oliver "at least momentarily" beginning to tie his experiences together when he goes back to the town of his birth with Mr. Brownlow. Westburg also attaches significance to Dickens's use of Oliver's "identity crisis" to transform "the narrative of adventure" into the confessional novel's existentialist interest in self-identity. The "crisis" Westburg refers to occurs in Chapter 20, where Dickens begins to explore the role of solitude "in the whole process of psychic growth" when Oliver is left alone to look at the book of Newgate histories

Fagin has given him. As Oliver's terror mounts upon reading the lives of the criminals, Dickens hints at the existence of a divided self, showing Oliver wondering if he will follow suit or remain worthy of his heritage. However, Dickens's reliance on "the discovery plot," which uncovers what was there but hidden, expresses "a definitely static notion of human existence" and undercuts these gains. This occurs, Westburg explains, because Dickens committed himself to representing Oliver as "the principle of Good," a decision that restricted his confessional possibilities.

209. ____. "Confidence Game: **Oliver Twist, A Child's History** and the Failure of Autobiography." Appendix in Westburg XII. 208, pp. 189-205. Originally published as "'His Allegorical Way of Expressing It': Civil War and Psychic Conflict in **Oliver Twist** and A Child's History." SNNTS, 6 (Spring 1974), 27-37.

Documents the claim that Dickens could not treat the facts of his life simply or directly but resorted to "veritable perversity" by embedding fragments of autobiography in an elaborate code, whose ingenuity Westburg professes to decipher. He rests his case on a fanciful attempt to explicate the "complex pattern of allusion to personages and events in seventeenth-century Parliamentary politics" in **Oliver Twist** and in what he calls "the 'King Charles situation'" in Dickens's work.

Two historical sequences--each, conveniently, the apparent mirror image of the other--strike Westburg as revealing in A Child's History of England (1853). In the first, Westburg attributes particular meaning to three beheadings--that of Charles I (actual), Oliver Cromwell (posthumously), and Charles II (imaginatively, by Dickens)--which form for Dickens "an historical triad" indicating "a basic ambivalence about lying and truth-telling." In the second, Dickens's rapid and compressed account of Cromwell's death, which links the death of Cromwell with that of his young grandson and his daughter's death too, suggests to Westburg "a strongly implied causality." The sequence also appears important, he thinks, because the given names of Cromwell's son-in-law and daughter--John and Elizabeth Claypole--coincide with those of Dickens's parents, thus prompting Westburg to read "national history as personal history" and ascribe to the second death sequence "the psychic disruption associated with betrayal, particularly betrayal of one sex by another within the same family."

No brief summary can do justice to the intellectual legerdemain Westburg displays in the course of this discussion, which terminates lamely in the modest conclusion that the "personal fantasies" Dickens projected into **Oliver Twist** represent "only a twisted fragment of a confession whose remarkable indirection asks for much more thoroughgoing attempts at decoding its verbal surface."

210. Wheeler, Burton M. "The Text and Plan of **Oliver Twist**." DSA, 12 (1983), 41-61.

Wheeler takes as his starting point **Oliver Twist**'s lack of unity and advances an original hypothesis to account for the work's structural flaws and lack of form. The melodramatic plot, with its "lockets, wills, villains, and bucolic conclusion," he suggests, strains the reader's credulity because Dickens radically altered his plans when he decided to convert a short serial about a parish boy into an extended piece of prose fiction, whose design he never originally formulated. Only after the appearance of the opening numbers in the **Miscellany** and no sooner than October 1837 did Dickens

decide to alter course when he found a new central focus in Nancy. This
shift, Wheeler believes, also coincided with Dickens's determination to make
Bentley accept Oliver Twist as one of the two novels he owed him under the
agreement of August 1836 (I. 6), a concession Bentley finally made on 28
September 1837 only after repeated attempts by Dickens to force him to
comply. With this victory in hand, Wheeler continues, Dickens then worked
hard to re-shape Oliver Twist, using the plot as "a conjurer's trick" to convert
a serial of uncertain length into "a novel with the superficial appearance of a
unified plan."

To support his contention, Wheeler cites the "significant revisions"
Dickens made when he prepared the text of Oliver Twist as it first appeared
in the Miscellany for republication as a three-volume novel in November
1838. The principal cancellations, he argues, show how Dickens, in the course
of composition, rescued Oliver from a representative "Parish Boy's Progress"
and expanded the short serial into a novel by shifting the focus to Nancy. Yet
despite the attempts Dickens made to realign the novel's focus and remove its
loose ends, Wheeler finds Oliver Twist structurally flawed because Dickens
never conceived it as a full-length work. If he had, why did he omit any
reference to the mystery of Oliver's parents in the first ten chapters, delay
the introduction of the conspiracy between Monks and Fagin, and make such a
profound shift in the narrative mode following the opening chapters?

As a study of the passages Dickens dropped from the Miscellany text
Wheeler's has no rival. His careful analysis reveals many significant loose
ends and contradictions, all of which Wheeler uses to support his thesis about
Dickens's change in plans. At the same time, Wheeler's essay invites
qualification on some important points. He remains elusive about the details
of the proposed "short serial" of a representative parish boy, for which no
external evidence exists, unless we assume that Dickens's plan for the earlier
chapters resembled the story Cruikshank claims he originated (XIII. 10, and
11). Wheeler also overplays the significance of the agreement Dickens signed
with Bentley in September 1837, which he emphasizes as the sole external
cause permitting Dickens to give his undivided attention to Oliver Twist,
making no reference to The Pickwick Papers and to the fact that Dickens
finished writing its final double number shortly after he concluded his truce
with Bentley. Wheeler makes a plausible case but discounts entirely the
counter arguments of those who represent Oliver Twist as a planned and
unified work. Cf. Tillotson (XII. 201).

211. Whitlow, Roger. "Animal and Human Personalities in Dickens' Novels."
     CLAJ, 19 (September 1975), 65-74.

Expands Gibson's argument (XII. 90) that the dogs in Dickens's fiction
reflect the characteristics of their owners and suggests that Dickens
also uses the animals to supplement "the intellect of their human associates"
and give an added dimension to their owners. Whitlow cites Bull's-eye as an
example of an animal with a double function. While Sikes's surly companion
reflects his master's outlook, the dog also endows the housebreaker with "a
sense of duty, dependability, and even devotion" when he leaps towards his
dangling master in Chapter 50. Although Sikes remains alien to these qualities, Whitlow argues, he becomes "a more tolerable character" because of
his association with Bull's-eye's loyalty evident in his misdirected but dutiful
leap.

212. Williams, Guy. "Introduction." In 1983 Macmillan Edition (II. 56), pp.
     ix-xxiv.

Marshalls miscellaneous and occasionally erroneous facts about the novel under topics presumed useful for the intended audience of British students preparing for national examinations. Williams writes predictably and unhelpfully about Dickens's shameless use of "million-to-one coincidence." He also makes the novel claim that his interest in an East London gang of robbers--"the Old Nicol Street Gang"--prompted the decision to send Oliver to a thieves' kitchen after he left the undertaker's. Equally dubious is Williams's assertion that when Dickens started to plan **Oliver Twist** he intended Rose Maylie to die tragically but that after Mary Hogarth's death he found himself unable to kill her off.

213. Williamson, Colin. "Two Missing Links in **Oliver Twist.**" NCF, 22 (December 1967), 225-34.

This analysis of two seemingly loose narrative threads in the text rests on two assumptions: (1) that Dickens saw himself, in Williamson's words, as "the spokesman of the spontaneous, the impulsive, the emotionally committed" and the enemy of "the cautious, the calculating, the scientifically detached and the coldly reasoning"; (2) that unconsciously Dickens wished to qualify this position because he realized that impulsive actions can have unfortunate consequences. To illustrate his hypothesis, Williamson suggests that the episode describing Losberne's impulsive attempt to search the house where Oliver was taken before the attempted robbery at Chertsey (ch. 32) really exists to criticize the worthy doctor's behavior. His impetuous assault on the house, Williamson believes, allows the hump-backed man to see Oliver, identify him, and track him down. As an associate of Sikes--Williamson assumes this too--the ugly little man passes on the information to the gang, thus providing a naturalistic explanation for the miraculous appearance of Fagin and Monks at Oliver's window two chapters later. But if this was Dickens's intention, the writer asks, why did he not make explicit the link between Oliver's stopping at the hump-back's and the villains' sudden materialization in Chertsey?

Williamson finds another apparent mystery in the way the narrator condemns mob violence and also portrays Harry Maylie, in the words of Losberne, as sallying forth on horseback "to join the first party" of those pursuing Sikes. On the strength of this evidence, Williamson identifies Harry Maylie as the unnamed man on horseback in the following chapter who reveals "such fury" and promises twenty guineas to the man who brings a ladder so the crowd can gain access to the murderer's stronghold. But if Dickens wanted to show "the almost effeminately correct Harry Maylie" transformed by the hue and cry of Sikes's pursuit, asks Williamson, why does he portray his metamorphosis so reticently? Williamson concludes that both episodes exist as indirect warnings that rash actions can lead to undesirable results. Losberne's lack of caution leads the villains to Oliver once again, while Harry Maylie's enthusiasm makes him one with the roaring mob.

214. Wilson, Angus. "Introduction." In 1966 Penguin Edition (II. 47), pp. 11-27.

A wide-ranging, informative introduction touching on many issues relevant to an understanding and assessment of the book. After commenting briefly on Dickens as he is about to embark on his career as a full-time novelist, Wilson examines **Oliver Twist**'s literary ancestors. Among them, he distinguishes the influence of Bunyan, the picaresque plots of the eighteenth century novelists, and the Gothic and crime novels of the early nineteenth century. By doing so, Wilson deftly counters the old assertion that Dickens learned from life and not from books.

In an assessment of the opening chapters, Wilson differs from Kettle (XII. 125) and others in finding the irony too crude and the humor overdone, conceding that Dickens's instinctive attack on the injustices of the new Poor Law "seems to have been right." Later research by the Webbs (XV. 10-13), Wilson observes, corroborates Dickens's knowledge of the real state of affairs of poor law administration in the 1830's and undercuts the criticism of intellectuals like Harriet Martineau, who attacked Dickens for failing to distinguish between the provisions of the old and new Poor Law.

The remainder of Wilson's essay focuses on Dickens's treatment of crime in **Oliver Twist**. He notes that Dickens's view of the adult criminal was far from sentimental and writes informatively about the puzzling contradiction implicit in the implacable manner with which Dickens hunts down Sikes and Fagin and the imaginative sympathy he shows when exploring their feelings. "Nowhere more than in Sikes on the run and Fagin in the dock is Dickens so emotionally at one with Dostoyevsky, the creator of Raskolnikov and Dmitri Karamazov."

Of the novel's protagonist, Wilson writes of his difficulty reconciling creations like Paul Dombey and young David Copperfield with "so unreal a boy" as Oliver. Yet Oliver's passivity enhances the story, Wilson argues, and even if Oliver fails to engage our feelings on the surface level, "at a deeper level, as childhood is threatened by obscure evil," he is a satisfactory device.

215. ____. "Oliver Twist." In his **The World of Charles Dickens.** London, 1970; rpt. New York: Viking, 1972, pp. 124-32.

Wilson calls **Oliver Twist** "one of the great popular works of art of all time" but finds it artistically flawed because Dickens lacked the technical power to fuse its two plots. On the one hand, Dickens presents in brilliant journalistic scenes a story of Victorian cruelty grown routine and deadly extending from baby-farmers to the wider world of apprentices. On the other, he shows the "strange evil world of the thieves," fictional characters vividly brought to life and superbly realized. A "preposterous plot of coincidence and improvised mystery" fails to join these two elements, but the figure of Oliver, he asserts, provides the necessary connection. The gulf between the two groups owes its origin, Wilson thinks, to two views of crime not easily reconciled: crime as the result of ignorance and poverty, and crime caused by the evil nature of those Dickens termed "utterly and incurably bad." By arousing compassion for the exploited but not facing the full implications of the social causes of crime, Dickens tapped instincts which made **Oliver Twist** "a great 'pop' novel."

216. Wilson, John R. "Dickens and Christian Mystery." **South Atlantic Quarterly,** 73 (Autumn 1974), 528-40.

Examines an evolving pattern of salvation in **Oliver Twist, Bleak House, Great Expectations,** and **Our Mutual Friend.** In the first, Wilson argues that Oliver achieves salvation by journeying to heaven "on the backs of others" and by surviving primarily because of the efforts of Mr. Brownlow. Because he embodies good, Oliver need not act nor seek salvation "by means of self-knowledge or introspection"; he need only remain "quiescent" in order to be saved. For Esther, Pip, and Eugene Wrayburn, however, the expiation of sin and move towards grace prove far more complicated, requiring action rather than passivity and the acquisition of self-knowledge. On these grounds,

Wilson concludes that Dickens appears as "a hesitant Christian," one who half believes in the reality of supernatural salvation and also admits the efficacy of "self-realization" as a means of coming to terms with oneself in this world. In the end, Wilson concludes, Dickens's belief in "the Christian supernatural is subsumed by a stronger belief in the self."

217. Winters, Warrington. "The Death Hug in Charles Dickens." L&P, 16 (Spring 1966), 109-15.

Comments briefly on an Oedipal motif in Dickens's fiction which Winters characterizes as a chain of "little devils" who engage in "a terrible death embrace" with a big devil. Of the elder devils, Winters points to Fagin, Sikes, and Jasper, each of whom either literally or figuratively engages in a "death hug" with his respective victim. The characters in **Oliver Twist** figure prominently in Winters's analysis, which attempts to explain Nancy's wish to protect and save Oliver from Sikes and Fagin and Bates's struggle with the murderer in Chapter 50 as acts of atonement for the iniquities of their elders, a motif Winters also sees behind Dickens's personal enthusiasm for the reading version of **Oliver Twist** constructed around Nancy's violent death.

218. Worth, George J. "**Oliver Twist** and **Nicholas Nickleby**." In his Dickensian Melodrama: A Reading of the Novels. Univ. of Kansas Humanistic Studies, 50. Lawrence, Kansas: Univ. of Kansas, 1978, pp. 39-51.

Worth calls attention to the general imprecision with which critics discuss melodrama, variously employing it as a term of disparagement for Dickens's offenses against the art of fiction and good taste. In response, Worth proposes to study how Dickens uses melodrama with its "moral polarities" and "language peculiar to stage melodrama." Early works such as **Oliver Twist** and **Nicholas Nickleby**, he suggests, rely on the conflict between "clear good and clear evil." At the same time, they also illustrate artful and surprising modifications, features which anticipate the increasing complexity of the later works. With respect to **Oliver Twist**, Worth notes mixed results, faulting Dickens when he strains too hard for pathetic effects. Among the many examples the novel provides, Worth points to the sardonic asides and strident exclamations that characterize the narrator's voice in the early chapters and the high-flown speeches of Rose, Harry Maylie, Mr. Brownlow, and Monks (chs. 30, 34, 49 and 51). On the other hand, some melodramatic scenes succeed "when they are energized by the participation of vividly depicted characters [such as Nancy] in states of high feeling" (chs. 16, 40, and 46). Also among Dickens's successes, Worth includes his use of "the melodrama of mystery" (Monks's midnight meeting with the Bumbles) and "melodramatic narrative" (Sikes's flight). By substituting clipped language for "formulaic verbal padding," Dickens gains power and arouses a corresponding response in the reader, Worth argues.

219. Wright, Thomas. "**Oliver Twist** Considered." In his The Life of Charles Dickens. New York: Charles Scribner's, 1936, pp. 116-21.

Wright offers his work as a corrective to Forster's biography (XII. 7), especially in his treatment of "a number of very important events" relative to Dickens's life to which Forster did not even allude. Wright refers primarily to Ellen Ternan, whose relationship with Dickens he is the first to chronicle. As a critic, Wright has little to say about **Oliver Twist**, offering a few dubious assertions--the main idea of the novel "was, no doubt, borrowed from

Smollett's **Humphry Clinker**"--and rehearsing Cruikshank's claim to have created **Oliver Twist.** See XIII. 9-11. In support of this, he quotes from a letter he received from R.H. Gooch, a friend of the artist. "I have often sat in Cruikshank's parlour which numbered among its visitors the burglar Sikes," writes Gooch. "His first name, it seems, was Bill, though his surname has not come down to us." "Jaw away, Bill," Dickens would say, and Dickens took shorthand notes while Cruikshank did the sketching. Both Nancy and Oliver were also veritable characters and used to make their way to this room." Wright grants the verity of "all this" but adds that the text remains "none the less Dickens's."

XIII. SPECIAL STUDIES

DICKENS, CRUIKSHANK, AND THE ILLUSTRATIONS

1. Blackall, Jean Frantz. "Cruikshank's **Oliver** and 'The Turn of the Screw.'" AL, 51 (May 1979), 161-78.

    Makes a convincing case for James's indebtedness to his early reading of **Oliver Twist** and "his highly charged reaction in childhood to Cruikshank's illustrations" in "The Turn of the Screw." Blackall argues for the "primitive origins" of James's story and stresses how its essentially pictorial character and essence characterize the work as a Gothic tableau full of terror rather than as "a psychical probing of the governess."

2. Borowitz, David. "George Cruikshank: Mirror of an Age." In **Charles Dickens and George Cruikshank.** Los Angeles: William Andrews Clark Memorial Library, 1971, pp. 73-95.

    A useful introduction to the highlights of Cruikshank's life and his work.

3. Burton, Anthony. "Cruikshank as an Illustrator of Fiction." In PULC (XIII. 44), pp. 93-128.

    Surveys the great range of subjects Cruikshank illustrated from the fiction of his day and comments on his ability to accommodate a comparable diversity of styles and subjects in the plates he produced. Burton argues that Cruikshank responded with special intensity to certain situations, themes, and states of mind, producing his best designs when he focused on adversity, imprisonment, escape, encounters, and opposing passions. "All these qualities," he adds, "are most vividly seen in his illustrations to **Oliver Twist.**" Discussing Dickens's novel, Burton takes care to emphasize that the measure of Cruikshank's achievement lies in the sum of the illustrations and not in just one or two brilliantly executed plates. There is much more to his work in **Oliver Twist,** he writes, than the frantic gloom of "Fagin in the condemned Cell." The plates, considered as a whole, reveal how Cruikshank composes figures in recurring patterns of grouping and gesture, which serve to express the novel's themes of loneliness, isolation, captivity, exclusion, and Oliver's relation with the adult world. The repetition of details also works so that various themes gather symbolic force, thus making the plates a sustained sequence rather than isolated moments superbly visualized.

4. **Charles Dickens: An Exhibition to Commemorate the Centenary of his Death.** June-September 1970. London: Victoria and Albert Museum, 1970, pp. 23-25.

    Assembles an interesting sample of the range of work Cruikshank executed in the course of illustrating **Oliver Twist.** Succinct and informative notes comment on Cruikshank's professional relationship with Dickens and recount the story of how inspiration came to him for "Fagin in the condemned Cell." See also Hodder (XIII. 23) and Jerrold (XIII. 27).

5.   Chesson, W.H. **George Cruikshank.** London: Duckworth & Co., 1908, passim.

A chronological survey of Cruikshank's career which includes brief comments on his illustrations to **Oliver Twist.** Chesson expresses little sympathy for Cruikshank's claims concerning the novel. He agrees that Cruikshank may have supplied some suggestions and "local colour" but accuses the artist of collecting fame in his attempt to deprive Dickens of his authorship. "The subject really belongs to the pathology of egoism," he concludes.

6.   Cohen, Jane R. "'All-of-Twist': The Relationship of George Cruikshank and Charles Dickens." HLB, 17 (April, July 1969), 169-94, 320-42.

A detailed account of Cruikshank's personal and professional relationship with Dickens clearly superseded by Cohen's revised study of Cruikshank in her book on Dickens's illustrators. See next entry (XIII. 7).

7.   ____. "George Cruikshank." In her **Charles Dickens and His Original Illustrators.** Columbus: Ohio State Univ. Press, 1980, pp. 15-38.

Provides a comprehensive and scholarly account of Cruikshank's professional and personal relationship with Dickens from the period of their first collaboration over **Sketches by Boz** to Cruikshank's later attempts to reshape the outlines of his partnership with Dickens. Cohen notes that the two began harmoniously and worked well together, carrying the amicable relationship established in 1836 into the early period of their joint work for Richard Bentley. Matters between them changed, however, as Dickens tried tactfully but clearly to assert control over the illustrations for **Oliver Twist** by dictating his preferences for subjects instead of consulting with the artist. Cohen suggests that Dickens lost his initial deference because he had gained his own reputation, but notes a degree of defensiveness in Dickens the neophyte jealously determined not to bow to Cruikshank's superior knowledge of the haunts of London's criminals. Useful comments on Cruikshank's work follow, especially on the final six plates he designed for **Oliver Twist** and executed in Dickens's absence in October 1838. See XIII. 14.
Perhaps the distinguishing feature of Cohen's account of the Cruikshank-Dickens relationship lies in her convincing analysis of Cruikshank's outlook from 1838 onwards. After his collaboration with Dickens ended with an "intolerable" challenge to his authority and the artist's sense of a loss of independence, Cruikshank, Cohen argues, came gradually to make Dickens "a prime scapegoat for his tormented ego." Cruikshank did so, she continues, by earnestly overstating his claims to have originated **Oliver Twist** and by introducing other "distortions" into their relationship in whose petty triumphs Cruikshank sought psychic satisfaction for having submitted himself in the past "to Dickens's schedules, tastes, and texts." This analysis of the artist's apparent state of mind makes plausible the inflated claims he advanced about his role in **Oliver Twist** and explains the combativeness that marks the statements he issued in his later years about Dickens. See also Harvey (XIII. 20) and Vogler (XIII. 58-61), who reject psychological interpretations of Cruikshank's behavior and offer different accounts of his claims.

8.   Cohn, Albert M. **George Cruikshank: A Catalogue Raisonne.** London: Office of the Bookman's Journal, 1924, pp. 78-80.

The definitive catalogue raisonne of Cruikshank's works. Part I lists by authors (arranged alphabetically) all the books Cruikshank illustrated. Cohn provides the main bibliographical facts about Bentley's 1838 edition of **Oliver Twist** and the other editions of the novel to which Cruikshank contributed illustrations.

9.   Cruikshank, George. **The Artist and the Illustrator: A Statement of Facts.** London: Bell and Daldy, 1872. 16 pp.

A short pamphlet which reprints Cruikshank's correspondence in the **Times** with William Harrison Ainsworth stating the artist's belief that he originated several of the latter's novels and Ainsworth's two emphatic denials. In his additional comments, Cruikshank makes only passing references to **Oliver Twist.** He repeats his claim that the novel's "original ideas and characters" emanated from him, and he concentrates instead on making credible his charge that Ainsworth, like Dickens, owed him a far greater debt than he would acknowledge.

10.   _____. "A Bit of Literary History." **New York Daily Tribune,** 8 February 1871, p. 6.

Includes Cruikshank's letter to the Editor, dated 12 November 1870, which Cruikshank wrote in response to one W.J. McClellan. Earlier that year, McClellan had placed a bet with friends that Cruikshank had illustrated no less than six of Dickens's novels. Correcting him, Cruikshank noted that his role as illustrator for Dickens was far smaller than people supposed, although he added that he understood why members of the public could easily be misled because Dickens's other illustrators imitated his style. For the record, Cruikshank affirmed that he was the first artist to illustrate Dickens (**Sketches by Boz**), that "the greater part" of the second series of **Sketches by Boz** was written from his "hints and suggestions," and that the first plate Cruikshank did for the **Miscellany** was a work of his design, "which Mr. Dickens wrote up to" (the "Public Life of Mr. Tulrumble, Once Mayor of Mudfog"). After this followed **Oliver Twist,** which, wrote Cruikshank, "was entirely my own idea and suggestion, and all the characters are mine." Cruikshank ended his letter by commenting that he was preparing a statement about why he did not illustrate the whole of Dickens's writing, adding ominously that "this explanation will not at all redound to [Dickens's] credit."

11.   _____. "The Origin of **Oliver Twist.**" **Times** [London], 30 December 1871, p. 8.

When the reviewer in the London **Times** concurred with Forster's dismissal of MacKenzie's anecdote about Cruikshank's role in the novel (XIII. 17) in his notice of the first volume of Forster's **Life,** Cruikshank felt compelled to respond. His motive, he explained, was to defend MacKenzie and to clear him of Forster's charge of lying. The account by MacKenzie, he countered, confounded "some circumstances" but did not err in its assertion that "I was the originator of the story of 'Oliver Twist.'"

Cruikshank's proof rests on his contention that he supplied Dickens not just with the germ of the story but with a plot and cast of characters, material which both the novelist and artist could adapt to the proposed serial for the new **Miscellany.** The life of a London boy, Cruikshank argued, would serve admirably, sketching the idea of a protagonist who rose from poverty to respectability through his ability, industry, and good conduct.

After falling in with thieves but escaping their evil influence the boy would rise steadily. Cruikshank liked the idea of an encounter with the underworld because, he argued, he could use it to introduce adult thieves and their women, young thieves, and a receiver of stolen goods.

Cruikshank claims that Dickens responded warmly to this outline but differed in his conception of the hero, preferring "rather a queer kind of chap" to Cruikshank's "nice pretty little boy." Such a figure as the latter, Cruikshank maintained, held greater appeal to readers, an argument Dickens belatedly recognized. As proof of his original conception and of Dickens's conversion Cruikshank cites the alteration of Oliver's appearance after the first two illustrations, when Oliver began as Dickens's "queer chap" and evolved into Cruikshank's "pretty boy."

Cruikshank also takes the credit for introducing the workhouse scenes, noting that he drew Dickens's attention to a recent scandal in St. James's parish, Westminster, where workhouse children had died after being "farmed out" (XIII. 38). Making the fence a Jew represents yet another of the artist's contributions. For Dickens's convenience Cruikshank impersonated a Jewish receiver he had observed in Field Lane, Holborn, who, Cruikshank insisted, must end up in the condemned cell at Newgate. On this point Cruikshank admits to "the greatest difficulty" in getting Dickens to agree to let the public see "what sort of places these cells were." "I said I must have either what is called a Christian or what is called a Jew in a condemned cell, and therefore it must be 'Bill Sikes' or 'Fagin'; at length he allowed me to exhibit the latter."

Cruikshank conceded the characters' names to Dickens, but he added that Dickens had overheard an omnibus conductor refer to one Oliver Twist and preferred it to Frank Foundling or Frank Steadfast, Cruikshank's choices. Cruikshank admitted his disappointment that Dickens did not "fully carry out my first suggestion," but he concluded that without further particulars readers would allow him his claim to have originated the novel and invented "all the principal characters."

12.   Dalziel, George, and Edward Dalziel. **The Brothers Dalziel: A Record of Fifty Years' Work 1840-1890.** London: Methuen, 1901, p. 48.

Records, without comment, Cruikshank's remarks to the Dalziels about his role in **Oliver Twist.** Cruikshank maintained, they write, that he not only suggested the subject to Dickens, "but that he had also given him the entire plot, sketched the characters, arranged all the incidents, and, in fact, constructed the entire story," so that all Dickens had to do with it "was TO WRITE IT OUT, and any man who could hold a pen might have done it better." Those were Cruikshank's identical words, they conclude, "as spoken to us."

13.   D[exter], W[alter]. "Author and Artist: The Claims of George Cruik-shank Definitely Refuted After One Hundred Years and the Discovery of a New Work by Dickens." **The Dickensian**, 34 (Spring 1938), 97-100.

Uses a series of forty-three letters Dickens wrote Cruikshank mainly relating to the illustrations of **Oliver Twist,** to show the hollowness of Cruikshank's claim to have invented the story and supplied Dickens with many of the characters.

14.   Dickens, Charles. Letters to George Cruikshank. In **Pilgrim Letters** (I. 1), I, passim.

The decision to choose George Cruikshank as the illustrator for the Miscellany appears to have been solely that of Richard Bentley, who followed his contract with Dickens on 4 November 1836 to edit the new monthly publication with a separate formal agreement with the artist. On 29 November 1836, Bentley contracted to pay Cruikshank fifty pounds for the use of his name and twelve guineas for supplying one plate for each monthly publication. See Tillotson (II. 48), p. 392n.

By combining two well-known names, Bentley made almost certain the appeal of his new journal, offering readers a partnership they had already recognized. When Sketches by Boz appeared in 1836 Cruikshank stood at the height of his powers and helped launch the career of the unknown "Boz." Now with the extraordinary success of The Pickwick Papers to his credit, Dickens matched Cruikshank in reputation, thus providing Bentley with a formidable pair of stars, the envy of his fellow publishers.

This partnership, however, did not survive beyond the serial publication of Oliver Twist, despite Dickens's good intentions to cooperate fully with Cruikshank by sending him each installment of the novel by the fifth of every month. Nothing in Dickens's correspondence suggests that he deliberately tried to thwart Cruikshank. The two, in fact, lived on amicable terms and frequently visited each other on both professional and personal occasions. But as the editorial work of running a monthly and the pressure of completing the serial numbers of Oliver Twist combined to push the completion date of each installment later and later into the month, Dickens's good resolutions and promises to "behave better next time" came to nothing.

Reading the extant correspondence makes one realize how quickly Dickens appears to have wrested control over the illustrations away from Cruikshank. Although their initial procedure called for Dickens and Cruikshank to confer over appropriate scenes and work together, Dickens soon substituted direct instructions instead. "We had better not give Oliver's real master and mistress this number," Dickens wrote in February 1837, referring to the third installment, "because we shall want them in the next plate; and for this reason I have substituted a preliminary negociation with Mr. Gamfield the Sweep" (p. 234). In the same vein, Dickens noted several months later that "I think you will find a very good subject at page 10, which we will call 'Oliver's reception by Fagin and the boys" (p. 319). Even down to the minutest detail, Dickens appears to have retained control. "I have described a small kettle for one on the fire--and a small black teapot on the table with a little tray & so forth and a two ounce tin tea cannister," Dickens emphasized as he gave Cruikshank orders for the illustration to Chapter 23 (p. 353). Later in the serial, Dickens offered Cruikshank the freedom to select scenes for the plates without consulting him, but he did so admitting that he was "of necessity in that part of the story which is not so productive of subjects for illustration" (p. 426).

Apparently Cruikshank responded gracefully and showed little resentment. When Dickens quarrelled with Bentley in the fall of 1837, Cruikshank offered his help as a mediator, serving in this capacity until Forster assumed the role of Dickens's arbitrator and advocate. When matters respecting Oliver Twist were finally settled, Dickens acknowledged Cruikshank's role by inviting him to a dinner with Bentley to celebrate, the occasion also being marked by the fourth Miscellany Agreement of 22 September 1838, which, among other stipulations, named 25 October as the delivery date for the completed manuscript of Oliver Twist.

By applying himself to the task with "such hearty energy," Dickens met this deadline, finding time also to plan an excursion to Wales and the Midlands and to attend to the last details of the novel, scheduled now to appear in three volumes in November 1838 before the serial finished in the **Miscellany** the following April. Before Dickens left London he consulted with Cruikshank about the remaining six plates. Three subjects, Dickens thought, might be taken from the interview between Rose and Nancy, their subsequent meeting in the streets, and Oliver's happy discovery that Rose was his aunt. The remaining three Dickens selected from among the criminals. He suggested Monk's nocturnal meeting with Mr. and Mrs. Bumble, "The Last Chance," and a final scene devoted to Fagin.

Dickens evidently proposed these topics before finishing the novel because after writing the scene of Sikes's escape he told Cruikshank that it would not do for an illustration. "It is so very complicated," Dickens wrote early in October 1838, "with such a multitude of figures, such violent action, and torch-light to boot, that a small plate could not take in the slightest idea of it" (p. 440). Cruikshank, however, ignored the advice and etched Sikes trying to escape from his pursuers, a plate many critics consider one of the most fascinating of the series. He also substituted "Sikes attempting to destroy his dog" for the interview between Rose and Nancy.

By shifting the emphasis to the criminals and away from the virtuous characters, Cruikshank acted in his professional interests, preferring to work with his own evident strengths rather than complying with the novelist's apparent wish to achieve a balance between the two groups. In Dickens's absence, Cruikshank's independence went unchallenged until Dickens unexpectedly returned to oversee the final details of the book's production. From Forster's letter to Bentley (p. 451n), we can infer Dickens's annoyance at Cruikshank's disobedience and at the plates themselves. Forster claims that he prevailed on Dickens to restrict his objections just to the dog--a "tail-less baboon," in Forster's words--and to the last illustration depicting Rose Maylie and Oliver. Subsequently Dickens modified this position, for, when he wrote to Cruikshank the day after he returned, he omitted any reference to Bull's-eye and tactfully asked him to design "afresh" the scene of Oliver standing next to Rose, now Mrs. Maylie, seated by the fireside in her new home. "I feel confident you know me too well," Dickens added, "to feel hurt by this enquiry, and with equal confidence in you I have lost no time in preferring it" (p. 451).

Cruikshank complied with reluctance. At first he tried to improve the original by adding stippled shadows before drawing an entirely new plate representing Oliver and Rose Maylie standing before a memorial to Oliver's mother on the wall of a church. Since Bentley had already prepared a number of copies of the novel to meet the demands of those who already had subscribed to the book, Dickens had no recourse other than to agree to their distribution before Cruikshank finished the new plate. Accordingly, 528 copies with the cancelled "Fireside" plate went forth (p. 453n), some of which survive and are preserved in libraries and in private collections.

Cruikshank's involvement with **Oliver Twist** ceased after he submitted the "Church" plate. In 1845 he agreed to design a new cover showing eleven scenes from the novel for the 1846 edition of **Oliver Twist** published by Bradbury and Evans in monthly parts (II. 12). In 1850 he contributed a new frontispiece showing Oliver standing before the Beadle and Mrs. Mann in the latter's parlor for the Cheap edition of the novel (II. 13), while in 1866 he made water-color copies of all his original illustrations for his friend F.W. Cosens. Cruikshank excluded the "Fireside" plate but designed a new title-page using thirteen illustrations. The originals of these are now in the Pierpont Morgan Library, New York; in 1849 Chapman and Hall published a limited edition of **Oliver Twist** which reproduced the colored drawings in collotype facsimile, states Tillotson (XIII. 57). For a complete list of

Cruikshank's illustrations to the novel and for information about the holdings
of extant studies of sketches Cruikshank executed while working on Oliver
Twist, see Appendix E of Tillotson's Clarendon edition (XIII. 57).

15.   Ellis, S.M.   William Harrison Ainsworth and His Friends (X. 23), II,
      105-06.

Records the comments of the painter W.P. Frith on the claims
Cruikshank made about works by Dickens (XIII. 10-11) and Ainsworth (XIII. 9).
Frith, who knew Cruikshank intimately, expressed the view that he suffered
from an "absurd delusion," but added that Cruikshank would not intentionally
deviate from the truth. Frith noted that Cruikshank, referring to Oliver
Twist, would say, "Dickens just gave it a little literary touching up, but
persisted in calling the hero Oliver Twist. I wanted him to be called Frank
Steadfast."

16.   Evans, Hilary, and Mary Evans.   "Cruikshank and Dickens" and "Claims
      and Counter-claims." In their The Life and Art of George Cruikshank
      1792-1878: The Man Who Drew the Drunkard's Daughter. New York:
      S.G. Phillips, Inc., 1978, pp. 81-85 and 92-96.

Brief comments about Cruikshank's partnership with Dickens and praise
for the plates in Oliver Twist as some of Cruikshank's most memorable
illustrations. The authors call Cruikshank's claims concerning the novel "one
of the rare regrettable incidents" in his career and express the view that little
can be gained from examining them in detail. The Evanses recognize the
probability that Cruikshank supplied some useful suggestions but argue that it
is "a long step" from partial collaboration to "instigation on the scale that
George claimed."

17.   Forster, John.   The Life of Charles Dickens (XII. 7), passim.

Forster makes three brief derisive references to Cruikshank's alleged
role in Oliver Twist. In Volume One, published in 1871, he "disposes" of that
"wonderful story" of Cruikshank's claims as they were first made public by
MacKenzie in his Round Table article (XIII. 35) and later spread by Hotten
(XIII. 24) by referring to the chronology of the composition of the last third of
Oliver Twist. With uncustomary obtuseness, Forster seems to imply that
because Dickens wrote the last volume of Oliver Twist in advance of the
monthly installments for the Miscellany and because Cruikshank completed
the plates for this part of the novel without Dickens's ever having seen them,
Cruikshank's drawings could not have prompted Dickens to change his plot and
show Fagin in the condemned cell, as Cruikshank claimed. To prove his
contention, Forster refers to the letter he received from Dickens on 9
November 1838 in which the novelist expressed his objections to Cruikshank's
plates and declared that he had never seen them in the book until Oliver Twist
was on "the eve of its publication" in three volumes.
     In Volume Two (1873), Forster returns to the topic when he takes up the
question of the extent to which Dickens kept his illustrators in a subordinate
position. Of all the notions to entertain, "the most preposterous," he argues,
would be that which directly reversed the relationship by showing the
illustrator as inspiring the author instead of vice versa. To counter the
further misconceptions caused by Cruikshank reopening the subject of his
contribution to Oliver Twist in the columns of the Times (XIII. 11), Forster
reproduces in facsimile Dickens's letter of 9 November, juxtaposing with it

the "strange language" Cruikshank used to advance his claims. Finally, in a prefatory note to the same volume, Forster adds that the existence of Dickens's letter spares him the necessity of characterizing the whole anecdote "by the only word [a lie] which would have been applicable to it." MacKenzie receives no direct apology from Forster, although the latter concedes that MacKenzie is not responsible for the "worst part" of the "incredible and monstrous absurdity" that one of Dickens's masterpieces "had been merely an illustration of etchings by Mr. Cruikshank!"

18.   Fowles, John.   "Introduction: Remembering Cruikshank."   In PULC (XIII. 44), pp. xiii-xvi.

Writes briefly but evocatively of the phases of Cruikshank's career and expresses a preference for the artist who bristled with social concern, the foe of hypocrisy and complacency, and the bitter satirist who never lost his faith in people's essential humanity. In contrast to H.K. Browne, whom Fowles calls "a soft center," Cruikshank revealed a more direct knowledge of reality and resisted "the schmaltz in Dickens more successfully." Comparing two plates on similar themes by each artist--Cruikshank's "Oliver asking for more" and Browne's "The internal economy of Dotheboys Hall" in Nicholas Nickleby--is "like comparing a Goya to a David," Fowles states.

19.   Fraser, W.A.   "The Illustrators of Dickens I: Cruikshank."   The Dickensian, 2 (May 1906), 117-22.

Disputes Forster's estimate of Cruikshank as a "distinguished artist" and a "great caricaturist" (XII. 7). Cruikshank, writes Fraser, was "absolutely incapable" of drawing a pretty girl or handsome woman, as the Rose Maylie plates show, and equally unable to draw a horse or a dog.

20.   Harvey, J.R.   "Appendix II: Cruikshank and Oliver Twist."   In his Victorian Novelists and their Illustrators (XIII. 21), 199-210.

Takes a less polemical view of Cruikshank's claims than Vogler (XIII. 58-61), writing more as an arbitrator than an advocate. Harvey focuses on Cruikshank's letter to the Times (XIII. 11), the "central document," he suggests, because it constitutes a public statement with five specific assertions, which, Harvey believes, contain a bizarre mixture of justifiable "minor claims," "honest mistakes," and "falsifications of evidence." Harvey draws the following conclusions: (1) Cruikshank's claim to have suggested the novel's subject "rings true" because the plot he outlines about an honest London boy bears a close resemblance to Hogarth's series "The Industrious and Idle Apprentice," a work Cruikshank obviously knew. But Oliver, Harvey notes, is not a London boy, and Oliver Twist ends where Cruikshank's story begins. (2) Suggestions from Cruikshank about introducing criminals appear "very likely" because the artist was knowledgeable about the seamy side of London life. Dickens may well have used some details for local color, but there is no evidence, Harvey points out, that Cruikshank was the first to suggest that Oliver fall among thieves. (3) A glance at the first three plates of Oliver Twist reveals a change in Oliver's appearance, but the degree of change is not as great as Cruikshank suggests, nor is the reason for it quite as straightforward as the artist claimed. Pettigrew's pamphlet (XIII. 38), Harvey comments, appeared in 1836, not 1837 as Cruikshank maintained, so possibly Dickens knew about the workhouse scandal in St. James's parish independently of Cruikshank. The possibility also exists that the change in

Oliver's appearance was made at Dickens's insistence, not Cruikshank's. Harvey grants, however, that the artist's hostility to Dickens's rather queer kind of chap and his preference for a pretty boy "may have contributed to the change." (4) Harvey thinks that Cruikshank told the truth about the Jewish fence in Field Lane, Holborn, upon whom he "had long had [his] eye." Cruikshank introduced Ainsworth as a witness, and Ainsworth never denied the validity of the story. (5) Finally, the credit Cruikshank takes for introducing the climactic scene in the condemned cell raises for Harvey "the delicate question of Cruikshank's honesty." Harvey examines the complicated evidence of two sketches ("Bill Sikes in the condemned Cell" and "First idea and sketch for Fagin in the condemned Cell"), discusses the validity of the labelling of each, and concludes that while no absolute deception was involved, probably some mis-titling occurred. In fairness to Cruikshank, he adds, the artist may well have suggested the condemned cell climax, and Dickens may well have decided on Fagin's form of death at a late stage in writing the novel. But if Dickens did change his plans this way, there is "not the slightest evidence ... he was at all influenced by Cruikshank."

21. _____. Victorian Novelists and their Illustrators. London, 1970; New York: New York Univ. Press, 1971, passim.

Harvey's account of the origin of the illustrated serial novel provides fascinating reading for both the literary critic and the reader interested in graphic art and Victorian book illustration. This study also deftly summarizes Dickens's relations with his main illustrators and connects literary works with the pictorial tradition that runs from Hogarth through the nineteenth century.

Harvey points out that the "artist's realm of creation" had a dramatic side which overlapped with that of the novelist, a fact Dickens recognized and responded to by wanting to rule alone. Only by doing so, writes Harvey, could Dickens's genius "properly ... fulfill itself in the kind of publication he had chosen." Thus, H.K. Browne, young and malleable, proved a more enduring partner than Cruikshank, a mature artist when Dickens first met him, one with his own style and vision. While Cruikshank's reputation proved initially useful to the unknown Boz, Dickens, Harvey believes, quickly moved to throw off the older man's influence as he fought for control of Oliver Twist. Unwittingly, contemporary reviewers, Harvey suggests, intensified Dickens's desire for independence by frequently praising him as the Cruikshank of writers. In Chapter 3, Harvey makes some provocative connections between Hogarth and Dickens when he discusses the legacy of graphic satire as it appears in aspects of Dickens's style and in his use of contrast as an organizational technique. For further comments on Cruikshank's contribution to Oliver Twist, see Harvey's Appendix II (XIII. 20).

22. Hill, Nancy K. "Heightened Reality: Oliver Twist." In her A Reformer's Art: Dickens' Picturesque and Grotesque Imagery. Athens: Ohio Univ. Press, 1981, pp. 55-62, and passim.

Argues for the prevalence of picturesque satire and the grotesque as a "double-edged visual rhetoric" in Dickens's work. The purpose of the first, suggests Hill, exists to cast doubt on art reflecting an attitude of ease and comfort such as that often favored by the Royal Academy; the second, she thinks, Dickens uses to widen readers' awareness of the outside world.

In the section on Oliver Twist Hill presents Hogarth as Dickens's master in the grotesque, who "paved the way for Dickens' treatment of street life." From Hogarth Dickens absorbed various techniques (such as animism,

making people appear as beasts), and learned to temper the grotesque by
juxtaposing with it the beautiful. Hill sees further evidence of Dickens's debt
to Hogarth in Mrs. Thingummy, the doctor who attends Oliver's birth,
Bumble, and Sowerberry, all of whom, she suggests, have antecedents in minor
characters in "The Harlot's Progress." Juxtaposing Oliver's rescue by Mr.
Brownlow with his possible fall reminds Hill of "Industry and Idleness," in
which series Hogarth relates the alternating fortunes of Francis Goodchild
and Thomas Idle. Furthermore, Nancy's nobility, Hill adds, indicates how well
Dickens internalized Hogarth's lesson that beauty within scenes of squalor can
profoundly affect the beholder. However, Dickens's stress that unhappy
consequences are partially reversible departs from Hogarth, who placed less
emphasis on the possibility of moral improvement once characters committed
immoral or unfeeling acts.

23.   Hodder, George. **Memories of My Time.** London: Tinsley Brothers,
      1870, pp. 107-08.

Reports the story Cruikshank told the author and journalist Horace
Mayhew about the fortuitous events that led to his depiction of Fagin sitting
dejectedly in the condemned cell. After pondering the subject for several
days, and beginning almost to despair, Cruikshank recalled how, on sitting up
in bed one morning, his hand covering his chin and the tips of his fingers
between his lips, he espied his own face in the cheval glass opposite him.
"'That's it,' he involuntarily exclaimed, 'that's just the expression I want!' and
by this accidental process the picture was formed in his mind." For
Cruikshank's later denial of this story, see Jerrold (XIII. 27).

24.   Hotten, John Camden. **Charles Dickens: The Story of His Life.** Lon-
      don: J.C. Hotten, 1870, p. 27.

Reprints MacKenzie's story (XIII. 33) of his interview with Cruikshank in
1847 and discovery of the sketches Cruikshank used to substantiate his role in
the origin of **Oliver Twist.** Hotten bases his reference to Cruikshank's claims
on the 1865 **Round Table** report (XIII. 35).

25.   Hunt, John Dixon. "Dickens and the Graphic Imagination." **Times**
      [London], June 1970, p. 19.

A much abridged version of Hunt's essay in **Encounters.** See next entry
(XIII. 26).

26.   ____. "Dickens and the Traditions of Graphic Satire." In **Encounters:
      Essays on Literature and the Visual Arts.** Ed. John Dixon Hunt. New
      York: W.W. Norton, 1971, pp. 124-55.

Like Harvey (XIII. 21), Hunt discusses connections between Dickens's art
and Hogarth's in this exploration of affinities between Dickens's vision and
various traditions in the graphic arts. Hunt refers briefly to **Oliver Twist** as
an early work "fully and unambiguously Hogarthian" in its structure and use of
emblematic detail. The careers of Oliver and Noah Claypole, he argues,
recall Hogarth's two rival apprentices, Nancy's squandered life replicates
Moll Hackabout's, and Dickens's use of details from ordinary life as a form of
moral commentary is reminiscent of Hogarth's work. Hunt also detects a
typically Hogarthian idea in Dickens's presentation of the intricate
interconnections of society. The most notable moment occurs, he writes,

after Oliver's recapture, when Charley Bates produced "the identical old suit of clothes which Oliver had so much congratulated himself upon leaving off at Mr. Brownlow's; and the accidental display of which, to Fagin, by the Jew who purchased them, had been the very first clue received, of his whereabout" (Oliver Twist, ch. 16).

27.   Jerrold, Blanchard. **The Life of George Cruikshank in Two Epochs.** London, 1882; rpt. London: Chatto & Windus, 1892, pp. 137-58.

Attempts an impartial account of Cruikshank's contention concerning his role in Oliver Twist, quoting in full Cruikshank's letter to the Times (XIII. 11), Forster's "summary dismissal" (XIII. 17), and accounts from others about the artist's involvement in the novel. Chief among them are Hodder's anecdote as told to him by Horace Mayhew (XIII. 23) about how Cruikshank accidentally hit on Fagin's pose in the condemned cell and Austin Dobson's report of the artist's subsequent denial of the popular story. "False!" responded Cruikshank to Dobson, who asked the artist about it on 14 December 1877. In a letter about the meeting he sent to Jerrold, Dobson described how Cruikshank tenaciously held to his denial, arguing that he knew what pose he wanted but puzzled only about the position of Fagin's hands. Cruikshank settled this, he explained, by studying the position of his own knuckles in the mirror, thus reinforcing his contention that the plate was not "a happy accident" but the result of his "own persistent and minute habit of realization." Jerrold refers to Cruikshank's extraordinarily strong sense of identification with Fagin, agrees that there is "truth in all these stories" about his role in Oliver Twist, and surmises that Cruikshank "probably fixed his model of Fagin" during his frequent studies in Petticoat Lane.

28.   Johnson, E.D.H. "The George Cruikshank Collection at Princeton." In PULC (XIII. 44), pp. 1-33.

Surveys the highlights of an important and rich collection of book illustrations, prints, trial proofs, and sketch-books. Johnson refers to the library's holdings of several sheets of pencil sketches Cruikshank made while at work on Oliver Twist. One, on a folded sheet, shows on its facing halves a version of the supressed "Fireside Plate" and four rough sketches for the cut which replaced it. These sketches, Johnson infers, "would seem to offer evidence that the artist had these alternate designs in mind at the outset." Cohen (XIII. 7) questions in a footnote (p. 241) whether this sheet contains a "version" of the suppressed plate, offering instead the view that the sketch looks like a transitional drawing from the "Fireside" to the "Church" plate. Vogler notes in his dissertation (XIII. 59) that the "Fireside" plate possibly represents Cruikshank's return to an earlier idea rejected by Dickens, which might explain the author's anger (p. 244). Alternatively, Johnson's idea could explain the artist's reluctance to execute a finished drawing of a subject he had already considered and rejected for whatever reason. For an interesting and different interpretation of Dickens's rejection of the "Fireside" plate, see Steig (XIII. 54).

29.   Kitton, Frederic G. "George Cruikshank." In his **Dickens and His Illustrators.** 2nd ed. London, 1899; rpt. New York: AMS Press, Inc., 1975, pp. 1-28.

Combines a brief but useful survey of Cruikshank's career as a book illustrator with a reliable introduction to Cruikshank's partnership with

Dickens. Kitton takes an interest in Cruikshank's working habits and provides a wide selection of his trial designs and first ideas, making possible the study of the evolution of many of the plates that appear in **Oliver Twist.** Kitton indicates Cruikshank's strengths and weaknesses, noting his success with drawing criminal types, and his lack of convincing pretty women and good people. Quiet humor, fabled accuracy in the rendering of details, and an ability to portray drama, however, compensate for the latter, Kitton thinks, and account for **Oliver Twist's** power. "In considering the story as a whole," Kitton writes, "it is difficult to say how much of the powerful impression we are conscious of may be due to the illustrator."

No such uncertainty characterizes Kitton's judgment about Dickens's literary indebtedness to his illustrator. That Cruikshank could have offered hints Kitton finds "not improbable." He also argues that one can never satisfactorily determine the extent to which artist and author interchanged ideas. But he voices skepticism about Cruikshank's claim, quoting in full the text of his **Times** letter (XIII. 11), and ascribes Cruikshank's story to the illustrator's "habit of exaggeration" and eagerness to over-estimate the effect of his own work.

30.   Layard, George Soames. "Suppressed Plates III. Dickens Cancelled
      Plates: Oliver Twist, Martin Chuzzlewit, "The Strange Gentleman,"
      Pictures from Italy, and **Sketches by Boz.**" **Pall Mall Magazine,** 17
      (March 1899), 341-48.

Corrects George William Reid's note in his **A Descriptive Catalogue of the Works of George Cruikshank** (London, 1871) about the order of the appearance of the "Fireside" plate and "Rose Maylie and Oliver at the Tomb" and tells the story of Dickens's response to the plates Cruikshank executed in his absence. Layard also argues convincingly against Francis Phillimore's contention in his **Dickens Memento** (London, 1884) that Cruikshank responded immediately to Dickens's request to execute another plate in lieu of the "Fireside" scene. The existence of "a unique impression" of the Fireside plate Layard saw in 1892 led him to conclude from "a large amount of added work ... principally of a stipply nature" that Cruikshank tried hard to improve the original plate before acting on Dickens's demand to design the plate afresh. Layard speculated that this proof was submitted to Dickens and again rejected "for no impressions of the plate with stippled additions are known to have been published." A reproduction of the stippled plate accompanies the article, as do two reproductions of the substituted plate. The first shows Rose wearing a light dress, except for a dark shawl, and the second, touched up and shaded, portrays her dress as black. Layard points out that this is the old plate altered and used again and "not a new plate copied from the old, for every line and every dot in the illustration to the earlier editions reappear in this."

31.   Leavis, Q.D. "The Dickens Illustrations: Their Function." In **Dickens
      the Novelist** (XII. 133), pp. 332-71.

Explores the reasons for the acknowledged success Dickens had with his illustrators and examines why his publishers insisted on having his novels illustrated. Leavis argues that Dickens's work grew out of the satiric art of the eighteenth century and remained close to Hogarth, in whom visual and literary traditions met and flourished. Dickens's illustrators, too, belonged to the same tradition of "visual-literary moralistic-satiric art" which publish- ers adapted successfully to the cheap part-publication system as a popular alternative to the expensive three-volume novel. Leavis admires Cruikshank's work but judges him a less suitable partner for Dickens than Browne because the former's independence and egotism made him less inclined to take direction from the novelist than "Phiz." Cruikshank failed to help the reader sufficiently at key points in Oliver Twist (Oliver's recapture and the scene of Monks and Fagin spying on Oliver asleep at his desk), but he produced admirable work in "Oliver asking for More" and "Fagin in the condemned Cell."

32. Ley, J.W.T. "George Cruikshank." In his The Dickens Circle: A Narrative of the Novelist's Friendships. New York: E.P. Dutton, 1919, pp. 20-26.

Recounts briefly Cruikshank's partnership with Dickens and presents the artist's claims in the charged language frequently used by Cruikshank's detractors.

33. MacKenzie, R. Shelton. "George Cruikshank." The London Journal; And Weekly Record of Literature, Science, and Art, 6 (20 November 1847), 177-82.

A survey of Cruikshank's principal works up to the publication of "The Bottle" in 1847. MacKenzie notes Cruikshank's successes, declares his high opinion of his genius, and suggests that his tremendous popularity played a significant role in establishing the books he illustrated. MacKenzie cites Sketches by Boz as an example and recognizes Dickens's debt to Cruikshank in Oliver Twist. The "thrilling earnestness" of Cruikshank's plates, he argues, leaves a lasting impression on the minds of readers, before whom Cruikshank places Fagin, Sikes, and Nancy "bodily," as if the characters were "as much creations of his mind as the author's." MacKenzie adds that he does not wish to undervalue Dickens, but he says seriously that the illustrations "have very materially contributed to make him popular." They place before the reader, writes MacKenzie, "in a sort of bodily presence, the parties whom he described, and thus enable us to realize, without any difficulty, the creations which the author was bringing up."

34. ____. "George Cruikshank vs. Charles Dickens." The Press, 19 December 1871, p. 2.

MacKenzie's only public statement refuting the charges of lying Forster made against him (XIII. 17) when he first published his story of Cruikshank's claims concerning Oliver Twist in the Round Table article (XIII. 35). "Mr. Forster, who lives in London, where Mr. Cruikshank also resides, appears not to have taken the trouble of asking that distinguished artist whether what I wrote was caluminous or fabulous," MacKenzie comments. "But Mr. Cruikshank, fortunately for me, has confirmed my statement." MacKenzie also reprints the text of Cruikshank's letter to W.J. McClellan (XIII. 10) as further confirmation in the artist's own words of the claims he described in 1865.

35. ____. "Philadelphia." The Round Table, 11 November 1865, pp. 155-56.

MacKenzie's first account, signed R.S.M., of a "curious bit of literary history" involving Cruikshank's claims to have influenced Oliver Twist and suggested the novel's main criminal characters. See Cruikshank (XIII. 10-11).

While at Cruikshank's house in connection with the article he published about the artist in **The London Journal** in 1847 (XIII. 33), MacKenzie describes how he examined one of his portfolios. In it he discovered "a series of some twenty-five to thirty drawings, very carefully finished" of the now-familiar portraits of Fagin, Sikes, Nancy, the Artful Dodger, and Charley Bates.

In explanation, MacKenzie recounts how Cruikshank told him the story of Dickens's examining the same drawings one day, works Cruikshank had intended to use as a projected series illustrating the life of a London thief. See Vogler (XIII. 61). When Dickens came to the one representing Fagin in the condemned cell, Cruikshank recalled, "he silently studied it for half an hour, and told me that he was tempted to change the whole plot of his story; not to carry Oliver Twist through adventures in the country, but to take him up into the thieves' den in London, show what their life was, and bring Oliver safely through it without sin or shame." MacKenzie accepts Cruikshank's story without comment and closes with the artist's final assertion that he thought up Fagin, Sikes, and Nancy. "My drawings suggested them," he observed, rather than Dickens's "individuality suggesting my drawings." Tillotson, in Appendix E in the Clarendon edition (XIII. 57), incorrectly states that MacKenzie's claim was not first brought forward in the American **Round Table** (p. 394, n. 3).

36. ———. "Relations with Artists." In his **Life of Charles Dickens.** Philadelphia: T.B. Peterson, 1870, pp. 161-75.

Republishes the version of Cruikshank's claims concerning **Oliver Twist** that he first issued in his 1865 **Round Table** article (XII. 35).

37. McLean, Ruari. "IV. Cruikshank and Dickens." In his **George Cruikshank: His Life and Work as a Book Illustrator.** New York: Pellegrine and Cudahy, 1948, pp. 21-28.

Discusses the partnership of Dickens and Cruikshank in a brief essay surveying Cruikshank's career as a book illustrator. McLean provides no detailed examination of Cruikshank's later claims about originating **Oliver Twist.** He grants that the artist might easily have thought up the plot, but adds his view that Cruikshank "could never have written all the chapters of **Oliver Twist** if he had lived to the age of Methuselah."

38. "Meeting at St. James's Parish Respecting the Poor Law Amendment Act." Times [London], 4 March 1836, p. 5.

Cruikshank cites the troubles in the parish of St. James's, Westminster, and the subsequent inquiry into the charges of abuse and maltreatment suffered by a number of children when the authorities farmed them out to an establishment in Norwood, London, as the specific circumstances behind the workhouse chapters of **Oliver Twist.** "I called the attention of Mr. Dickens to this inquiry," Cruikshank wrote in his letter to the **Times** of 30 December 1871 (XIII. 11), alleging that he, not Dickens, should take the credit for the idea of exposing the harsh conditions to which workhouse children were frequently subject.

The report in the **Times** refers briefly to the high mortality rate of those children sent to Norwood and to the diseased state of many of them, as recorded by parish medical authorities. Vogler, who reproduces this article in full (XIII. 59), notes that an examination of the actual parish records (now in a branch of the Westminster City Libraries) confirms the information in the

Times, as does Thomas Joseph Pettigrew, surgeon, a friend of Cruikshank who resided in the neighborhood. Pettigrew attacked the practice of farming out children in his pamphlet, The Pauper Farming System. A Letter to ... J. Russell ... on the Condition of the Pauper Children of St. James's Westminster, London, 1836.

While these reports document conditions that apparently prevailed in London during the early years of the Poor Law Amendment Act of 1834, they do not prove any close connection between the practices in St. James's and those Dickens attacks in the opening of the novel. Stories about abuses were not uncommon at the time and Dickens could have as easily learned about them from sources other than Cruikshank.

39. Miller, George Eric. "Postcard Dickensiana, 1900-1920." The Dickensian, 71 (May 1975), 91-99.

Describes the vogue for Dickensian postcards which flourished, Miller notes, particularly in the years before World War I. Sets specifically designed for the collector featured the water-color drawings of Joseph Clayton Clarke ("Kyd" or "Stylus"), photographs of places associated with Dickens, and cards of actors and actresses well-known for their roles in the dramatic adaptations of Dickens's novels. Among the last, Miller singles out one especially popular set of nine cards devoted to Comyn Carr's 1905 adaptation of Oliver Twist (VI. 18).

40. Miller, J. Hillis. "The Fiction of Realism: Sketches by Boz, Oliver Twist, and Cruikshank's Illustrations." In Dickens Centennial Essays (XII. 101), pp. 85-153.

A retitled version of the same paper Miller gave at the Clark seminar on Cruikshank. See XIII. 41.

41. _____. "Sketches by Boz, Oliver Twist, and Cruikshank's Illustrations." In Charles Dickens and George Cruikshank (XIII. 2), pp. 1-69.

Despite the presence of Oliver Twist in the title, Miller makes little reference to the novel in his lengthy demonstration of the fictional qualities of Sketches by Boz. Miller's concern focuses on his attempt to reveal the fallacy of valuing Dickens's Sketches for their realism, preferring to read them as essays full of graphic, literary, and theatrical conventions rather than documents presenting the authenticity of middle class life in London in the 1830's.

Particularly convincing are Miller's "readings" of Cruikshank's illustrations, images which, in his words, refer not directly to the scenes and objects they depict but to the world as seen by Cruikshank's unique sensibility. Miller defines that particular angle of vision as one which expresses itself in the centered, centripetal, circular compositions, their evocative sense of enclosure and confinement, and their distinctive use of a double structure. This structure, Miller argues, typically combines figures at the center caught in the immediacy of an action or moment and those outside the action, often present as portraits on the walls, whose detachment suggests a tension "between mimesis and fiction."

42. "Mr. Forster's 'Life of Dickens,' Vol. II." Nation, 16 (9 January 1873), 29.

Cited by Vogler (XIII. 58) as one of at least two contemporary American writers who charged Forster with failing to meet the point at issue over Cruikshank's claims in reference to **Oliver Twist.** This reviewer chides Forster for his unmannerly treatment of MacKenzie, to whom he never apologized for calling him a liar, and for evading the charge against Cruikshank's role "in a fashion which is curious rather than laudable or sagacious." See also XIII. 17 and XIII. 46.

43.   Olmsted, John Charles, and Jeffrey Egan Welch. **Victorian Novel Illustration: A Selected Checklist, 1900-1976.** New York: Garland, 1979. xv + 124 pp.

Annotates books and articles treating various aspects of Victorian novel illustration. Individual entries are generally brief; where they are longer, the editors use the authors' own words. Olmsted contributes a short but useful Introduction in which he surveys how attitudes towards illustrations changed from indifference and even contempt to a growing appreciation of the integral role played by artists like Cruikshank and Browne, whom critics now recognize as interpreters of the texts they illustrated.

44.   Patten, Robert L., guest ed. "George Cruikshank: A Revaluation." In PULC, 35 (Autumn, Winter 1973-74), pp. vii-xii.

Writes briefly in his "Foreword" of Cruikshank's unjustified neglect and the tendency to reduce Cruikshank's whole career "to a series of hoary anecdotes about eccentric behavior" and expresses his hope that this special double issue of PULC signals the beginning of "a major and continued revaluation of Cruikshank's vast contributions to the nineteenth century." Patten's collection of first-class essays appeared in conjunction with an exhibition of items from the Meir collection of Cruikshank's work at Princeton University. For annotations of essays relevant to Dickens, Cruikshank, and **Oliver Twist,** see individual entries under Burton (XIII. 3), Fowles (XIII. 18), Johnson (XIII. 28), Paulson (XIII. 45), and Vogler (XIII. 58).

45.   Paulson, Ronald. "The Tradition of Comic Illustration from Hogarth to Cruikshank." In PULC (XIII. 44), pp. 35-60.

Complements Harvey's analysis (XIII. 21) of Hogarth's impact on Victorian book illustration by referring more specifically to a tradition of comic illustration and by concentrating on the relationship between the plates and the text. Paulson argues that the advent of **The Pickwick Papers** and **Oliver Twist** signalled a new departure for the artist, who in these works collaborated with the novelist for a "visual-verbal effect" and did not simply represent something in a known text in the tradition of his earlier forebears. In the sort of collaboration Dickens and Cruikshank and Dickens and Browne personify, the illustrators had access of their own to the emblem tradition, just as Dickens could introduce emblems of his own that did not appear in the plates. Paulson's closing remarks suggest the extent to which the role Dickens assumes as a narrator and even the means by which his characters "come to terms with a place and situation" have assimilated "the Hogarth way." As an example, Paulson compares the perceptual process of Fagin entering the Three Cripples in Chapter 26 with the way the "reader" responds to the sixth plate of "A Rake's Progress." In each, the interpreter discerns "an increasing intensity of moral significance" as he explores the multiplicity of experience and comes to terms with it.

46.   "Recent Literature." **Atlantic Monthly,** 31 (February 1873), 238-39.

Comments on Forster's **Life** (XIII. 17) in a survey of recent publications and expresses dissatisfaction with Forster's handling of Cruikshank's claims to have played a role in **Oliver Twist.** This reviewer, the second of at least two American writers to come to MacKenzie's defense, admits that Cruikshank overstated his contribution by saying that he furnished the principal characters and scenes, but he finds "not at all improbable" some aspects of the story MacKenzie reported. See also XIII. 42.

47.   Robb, Brian. "George Cruikshank's etchings for **Oliver Twist.**" **The Listener,** 74 (22 July 1965), 131.

A general appreciation of Cruikshank's work and account of his career. Robb comments on Cruikshank's collaboration with Dickens and discusses briefly his illustrations for the burglary, Sikes on the roof, and Fagin in the condemned cell. Cruikshank manages to involve the spectator so closely in his interior world, Robb observes, "that you have almost the illusion that if you keep your eye on the page the characters will go on to enact the scene which must follow this momentary episode."

48.   Sala, George Augustus. "George Cruikshank: A Life Memory." **The Gentleman's Magazine,** 242 (January to June 1878), 544-68.

A warm, personal account of Sala's fondness for Cruikshank and an appreciation of the work of an artist he characterizes as "a walking Directory in low-life London." Sala remarks briefly on Cruikshank's contributions to **Oliver Twist,** noting the illustrator's tendency to develop great enthusiasm for the criminal figures he depicted, inventing, in a graphic, not in a literary sense, "Sikes and Fagin, Charley Bates, and the Artful Dodger." "The types of all these criminal characters," Sala adds, "to their very counterparts, with Nancy and Mr. Bumble to boot, may be traced in many of George's etchings and wood drawings published between 1825 and 1830. The truth is, that he had acquired by that time a visual acquaintance of more than a quarter of a century's standing with the criminal classes."

49.   Sauerberg, Annette Juel. "On the Literariness of Illustrations: A Study of Rowlandson and Cruikshank." **Semiotica,** 14 (1975), 364-86.

A comparative study of Rowlandson and Cruikshank as book illustrators based on a corpus of illustrations drawn from contributions each made to novels by Fielding, Goldsmith, and Dickens (**Oliver Twist**). Sauerberg's quantitative analysis reveals that Rowlandson prefers, above all else, to render atmosphere in his plates by concentrating not so much on the figures and aspects of the plot but on a feeling he attempts to express by use of moving lines and caricature. Cruikshank, by contrast, shows a preference for situations which bear directly on the novel's plot, preferring to create characters and help the reader by "mediating the author's created universe as pregnantly as possible." Sauerberg proceeds on rigorously scientific lines but cloaks her observations in obfuscating jargon.

50.   Solberg, Sarah A. "Bull's-eye's 'Eyes' in **Oliver Twist.**" N&Q, NS 27 (June 1980), 211-12.

Notes Cruikshank's inaccurate representation of Bull's-eye staring at

Sikes from the apex of the roof in "The Last Chance." Apparently Cruikshank overlooked Dickens's reference to the dog, three paragraphs after the description of Sikes falling to his death, as lying "concealed" until his master fell. As a result, suggests Solberg, readers may easily take Sikes's cry, "'The eyes again'" as referring to the dog's instead of to Nancy's eyes. Two chapters before, Sikes had been haunted by the vision of Nancy's widely staring eyes; seeing them again, as he looked behind him on the roof, caused Sikes to stagger and fall. Solberg speculates that Dickens's dissatisfaction with the plates Cruikshank designed for the third volume of **Oliver Twist** so absorbed him that he missed this error.

51.   "Some Unpublished Sketches by George Cruikshank." **Strand Magazine,**
        14 (July-August 1897), 183-91.

Reproduces a small collection of Cruikshank's sketches and impromptu drawings, two of which relate to **Oliver Twist.** The first shows several rough attempts at the figure and pose of Oliver in preparation for the first plate, "Oliver asking for more," while the second portrays Bill Sikes in the condemned cell. The author of this piece takes this latter drawing as proof against Cruikshank's claims concerning the novel because, he explains, MacKenzie spoke of the completed drawing of Fagin in the condemned cell and not Sikes as the one Dickens saw before he wrote the novel (XIII. 35). For a different interpretation of this drawing, see Harvey (XIII. 20).

52.   Steig, Michael. "A Chapter of Noses: George Cruikshank's Psycho-
        nography of the Nose." **Criticism,** 17 (Fall 1975), 308-25.

Steig coins "psychonography" to designate the range of largely unconscious meanings he sees in Cruikshank's apparent fascination with noses and his tendency to show them in various stages of tumescence and detumescence. Steig points to several protean noses in Cruikshank's earlier works, whose phallic associations he unmasks. Later in the essay, he puts aside the equation of nose with penis and explores other implications. Steig denies that Cruikshank invented a "comprehensive system of nasal allegory," but he finds two patterns in **Oliver Twist.** Noses in the plates clearly indicate class and race; they also, in the case of the protagonist, frequently change in size. Of the first, Steig suggests that long, straight noses signal respectability, pug noses with prominent nostrils indicate the animal proclivities of the lower classes, and villainously hooked noses serve as the obvious stereotype for Jews. Why Oliver's olfactory organ should alternate between a proboscis and a distinguished straight nose proves more elusive. The explanation Steig advances lies in the ambiguity Cruikshank expressed towards the hero. Cruikshank was drawn to Oliver's inherent respectability and goodness; he also identified, in part, with the underworld and suggested Oliver's affinity with the criminals by relating him through his nose to Fagin. Behind this oscillation, Steig speculates, lies a personal interest indicative of a series of swings between respectability and rebelliousness that a broad view of Cruikshank's work reveals.

53.   ——. "Cruikshank's Nancy." **The Dickensian,** 72 (May 1976),
        87-92.

In the 1841 Preface Dickens stated explicitly that Nancy "is a prostitute" (II. 10), although nothing as specific about her profession appears in the novel. Beyond a general reference he made to her face as heavily rouged (she and

Bet are introduced in Chapter 9 as "not exactly pretty," but with "a great deal
of colour in their faces"), Dickens apparently thought he had to soften or
conceal details of her criminal life. This deliberate vagueness, Steig argues,
left Cruikshank with little opportunity to make visually explicit in the four
graphic appearances Nancy makes what Dickens dodged verbally. Yet in the
third, "Mr. Fagin and his pupils recovering Nancy" (ch. 39), Cruikshank
represents her as a prostitute in a convincing yet esoteric manner.

Steig's proof rests on his analysis of the portrayal of Nancy in this plate,
for which he claims "a definite prototype": Cruikshank's 1816 "The Night
Ma[yor]re," an intriguing parody of Henry Fuseli's The Nightmare, 1783.
Cruikshank's satiric print represents Matthew Wood (twice Lord Mayor of
London), a nineteenth-century Mr. Clean, whose reformist inclinations
manifested themselves in an attempt to rid the City of prostitutes.
Cruikshank ridiculed Wood's motives by showing him alighting on the "downy
Breast" of a gin-soaked "Love-bewildered Maid," his Mayor's staff erect
between his legs, and an accomplice looking on with vicarious pleasure. The
similarities between Nancy and the sleeping prostitute of 1816, whose posture
parodies the sleeping form in Fuseli's painting, provide, for Steig,
Cruikshank's "most explicit acknowledgement of what she [Nancy] is." Both
have fleshy faces and large, heavy breasts, details obviously at odds with
Dickens's description of Nancy as "pale and reduced with watching and
privation." In this manner Cruikshank makes his point; and by implying "a
predominant sympathy for the prostitute," he conveys an attitude independent
of the text.

54. _____. "Cruikshank's Peacock Feathers in Oliver Twist." Ariel,
     4 (April 1973), 49-53.

Calls attention to the symbols of misfortune traditionally associated with
peacock feathers in Victorian graphic art. In "Oliver recovering from the
fever," Cruikshank places peacock feathers over the picture of the Good
Samaritan, an appropriate graphic means of suggesting the fate that awaits
Oliver shortly afterwards when he is recaptured and returned to Fagin. But
why, therefore, include them so prominently in the rejected "Fireside" plate?
Steig grants that the feathers have no iconographic function in this scene of
domestic happiness but speculates that they serve instead as a private
comment. The feathers suggest Cruikshank's curse upon the novel, the
illustrator's symbolic revenge for having to submit to the will of the novelist
during the period of their partnership. Although Cruikshank had to redesign
the plate, the feathers represent, Steig surmises, his having "something of a
last laugh."

55. Sutherland, Guilland. "Cruikshank and London." In Victorian Artists
     in the City: A Collection of Critical Essays. Ed. Ira Bruce Nadel and
     F.S. Schwarzbach. New York: Pergamon Press, 1980, pp. 105-25.

Argues for a general pattern in Cruikshank's career evident in his
changing attitudes towards London. As a Regency buck, Cruikshank's work
emphasized the amusing and satirical aspects of the metropolis (see his
illustrations to Pierce Egan's Life in London, 1821). Following this phase, he
developed greater sympathy for the commonplace before assuming the role of
a social investigator with an educational purpose. Sutherland suggests that
this third aspect coincides with Cruikshank's work for Dickens and notes that
Oliver Twist, if read simply as a delineation of lower-class life for
middle-class readers, consolidates rather than departs from the traditions he

discerns among graphic artists and other novelists. Sutherland avoids a detailed discussion of Cruikshank's claim to have "authored" **Oliver Twist** but grants "an element of plausibility" in his contention. Cruikshank, he explains, can be seen as Dickens's forerunner because Cruikshank explored London in a way similar to the writer long before Dickens began **Oliver Twist.**

56.   [Thackeray, W. M.]. "George Cruikshank." **Westminster Review,** 34 (June 1840), 1-60.

Treats in detail the range of Cruikshank's work, including his contributions to **Oliver Twist** as an illustrator. Thackeray admires Cruikshank's "energetic fecundity" and his remarkable ability "for telling the truth after his own manner," to which he attributes much of his success. Dickens himself, Thackeray thinks, "would admit as readily as any man" the assistance he has had from his illustrator, whose figures, once seen, "remain impressed on the memory, which otherwise would have no hold upon them, and the heroes and heroines of Boz become personal acquaintances with each of us." Among Cruikshank's "famous designs" for the novel, Thackeray singles out the sausage scene at Fagin's, Nancy seizing the boy, Bumble's courtship, Sikes's farewell to the dog, and Fagin in the condemned cell. "For Jews, ... little boys, beadles, policemen ... [and] charity children Mr. Cruikshank has a special predeliction," writes Thackeray, calling Fagin's portrait "immortal" and concluding that the illustrator has studied the "tribe of Israelites ... with amazing gusto."

57.   Tillotson, Kathleen. "The Illustrations." Appendix E. In the Clarendon edition of **Oliver Twist** (II. 48), pp. 392-97.

Gives the factual details of Cruikshank's contract to illustrate the serial publication of **Oliver Twist** in the **Miscellany** (fifty pounds for the use of his name and twelve guineas for each plate), together with his involvement with the subsequent editions of the novel. Cruikshank designed a new cover for the 1846 edition in ten monthly parts (II. 12) from a list of scenes drafted by Dickens; he also executed a new frontispiece for the 1850 Cheap edition (II. 13) and made water-color copies of all his original illustrations in 1866.
Tillotson also comments on the history of Cruikshank's relationship with the novelist, referring briefly to Dickens's dissatisfaction with the "Fireside" plate and to Cruikshank's "preposterous claim" to have originated the story of **Oliver Twist.** Tillotson notes that copies of the rejected plate appeared in Lea and Blanchard's one-volume edition of 1839 but omits any reference in her footnote to the distribution of some copies of the plate in England. Appendix E also includes a list of Cruikshank's original illustrations with the date of their first appearance and provides information about the locations of the surviving preliminary sketches, tracings, and sketches. Vogler (XIII. 58) corrects information Tillotson gives about MacKenzie (XIII. 35) and refers to several letters unnoted in the Appendix that bear on Cruikshank's controversial claims. The letters are significant, Vogler argues, because they document the neglected Cruikshank side of the dispute and refer to information that adds plausibility to aspects of the role he claimed in originating **Oliver Twist.**

58.   Vogler, Richard A. "Cruikshank and Dickens: A Reassessment of the Role of the Artist and the Author." In PULC (XIII. 44), pp. 61-91.

Vogler writes as an articulate proponent of Cruikshank's claim for the role he played in **Oliver Twist**. He grants at the outset that the artist distorted his case by exaggeration and by furnishing contradictory statements, but he finds Cruikshank's arguments "frequently valid." If we start with the assumption on which Anglo-American justice rests--that no one is guilty until proved so--Cruikshank, writes Vogler, is certainly innocent of the charge of "willful mendacity."

The defense Vogler provides covers several topics. He rebuts the biased accusations of Dickens partisans like Forster (XIII. 17); and he challenges those who characterize the relationship between Dickens and Cruikshank as that of dominant author and subordinate artist, suggesting that this simplification of roles distorts a more complex reality. That reality Vogler defines as one based on the model of cooperation-collaboration rather than order-execution implicit in the accounts of their partnership provided by Tillotson (XIII. 57), Cohen (XIII. 7), and others. Vogler also refers briefly to the matter of pictorial prototypes, which, he believes, offer "strong collateral evidence that discussions about characters or events must have taken place during consultations if not through prearranged outright collaboration."

Additional new material comes from an unpublished rough draft of a letter Cruikshank addressed to the agent who acted for Richard Bentley. This draft, undated but written before Cruikshank left the **Miscellany** in 1841 after quarrelling with Bentley, appears to document Cruikshank's working arrangements with his two editors, first Dickens and then Ainsworth, whose serials he illustrated in the journal. Cruikshank's practice, Vogler suggests, and the one Cruikshank states he never departed from since the first number of the **Miscellany**, was to produce his plates after consulting with the author and not after reading the text. The significance of this document, as Vogler shows, lies in Cruikshank's emphatic rejection of being asked to select a subject for illustration after reading the text instead of etching something "before the author had written a line." By granting this procedure, argues Vogler, we admit the necessary preconditions for an exchange of opinion between artist and author and for a degree of reciprocity in the ensuing discussion that allows Cruikshank to speak plausibly about "influence."

Further points include an examination of the extant correspondence between Dickens and Cruikshank and the introduction of more new evidence. From the first, Vogler draws inferences quite different from those of Tillotson (XIII. 57) and Cohen (XIII. 7), who cite Dickens's letters to document Cruikshank's essentially subordinate role, and from the second--a hitherto neglected slip of paper Vogler found in the Print Room of the Victoria and Albert Museum--dramatic proof of the list Cruikshank showed MacKenzie in 1847 of the proposed illustrations for "The Life of a London Thief." This paper, tentatively dated 1819 by Vogler, depicts an outline of a "progress" or narrative series of compartmentalized drawings with captions revolving around criminal life, all of which constitute "strong corroboration" of Cruikshank's claims as they were first published by MacKenzie in 1865 (XIII. 35). This document, Vogler surmises, formed the basis of the "suggestions" Cruikshank offered the young author, "whose imaginative literary genius translated them into the novel we know as **Oliver Twist**."

Vogler concludes his essay by noting that literary critics accept without question the fact that Shakespeare, Defoe, Smollett, and Carlyle "influenced" the novelist. Why not, therefore, accept similar claims from a graphic artist without vilifying him as a "preposterous," "deluded," "senile" liar or reducing him to a caricature of a comic drunk or a Temperance fanatic? "No one," Vogler observes, "can survive such designations with dignity," not even "the colossus of graphic art of the last century." For a less polemical appraisal of Cruikshank's claims, consult Harvey's Appendix II (XIII. 20).

59. ——. Cruikshank and Dickens: A Review of the Role of the Artist
     and Author. Diss. UCLA 1970.

Vogler's first attempt to redress the bias of Forster and other Dickens
partisans in their derisive response to Cruikshank's claims about his
contribution to **Oliver Twist** (XIII. 10-11). The significant parts of Vogler's
reassessment of Cruikshank's role as an illustrator have already appeared in
print--see XIII. 58 and XIII. 61--but the dissertation usefully reproduces many
of the published and unpublished documents that bear on the Dickens
Cruikshank controversy. In Appendix I, Vogler lists in brief form the original
tracings and drawings for and related to the illustrations Cruikshank did for
Dickens. See pp. 283-92 for those relating to **Oliver Twist.**

60. ——. "148-159. Illustrations from **Oliver Twist, or the Parish Boy's
     Progress.**" In his **Graphic Works of George Cruikshank.** New York:
     Dover, 1979, pp. 148-51.

Useful notes on twelve of the twenty-four etchings Cruikshank executed
for **Oliver Twist.** Vogler's commentary on the plates calls attention to the
visual devices Cruikshank used to capture the novel's main themes; he also
points out how small details not in the text elaborate themes in the passages
being visualized. In "Mr. Bumble and Mrs. Corney taking tea," for example,
Cruikshank, not Dickens, is responsible for the porcelain figure of Paul Pry on
the mantel, a well-known dramatic character who repeatedly turns up at
inopportune moments, just as Mr. Bumble does in the next plate, when he
pries into Noah Claypole's feast with Charlotte. Vogler argues aggressively
for the active role Cruikshank played but occasionally strains too hard, as
when he praises the catchy titles for the plates invented by the artist and
denigrates Dickens's preference for "rather bland, generic titles." An
introductory essay presenting Cruikshank as caricaturist, illustrator, and
reformer (pp. vii-xviii), makes a persuasive case for Cruikshank as an
independent graphic artist and not simply as the man who illustrated a number
of famous books.

61. ——. Oliver Twist: Cruikshank's Pictorial Prototypes." DSA,
     2 (1972), 98-118.

Vogler uses the evidence of Cruikshank's pictorial prototypes, all of
which he published before Dickens wrote **Oliver Twist,** to illustrate the error
of arguing that Cruikshank slavishly followed Dickens's directions or the
text. Vogler also explores the nature of Cruikshank's contributions to the
novel. While he avoids endorsing Cruikshank's claim to have originated both
the plot and the characters of **Oliver Twist,** he raises points that compel us to
think seriously about Cruikshank's role as a contributor instead of dismissing
it with Podsnappian indignation.
  The case Vogler presents rests on the similarities in appearance of
various Cruikshankian characters frequently found in his work prior to his
collaboration with Dickens and those later described in **Oliver Twist** and
also illustrated by the artist. Perhaps the most convincing example remains that of the burly thug and housebreaker, a familiar figure in
Cruikshank's work, whose physical appearance, clothing, and female
companions bear a strong relationship to Bill Sikes well before Dickens
introduced him in the July 1837 number of **Bentley's Miscellany.** The
striking resemblance between the two, writes Vogler, "raises the important
question of how the two men arrived at such similar concepts of characters

unless they settled upon them (as Cruikshank contended) by discussion and mutual agreement prior to the writing of the novel."

Vogler builds a similar case for Fagin, whose stereotypical Jewish features and occupations show up in Cruikshank's pictures long before the appearance of Dickens's fence. Even Bull's-eye, Sikes's dog, and several of the novel's minor characters can be associated in the same way with stock figures in Cruikshank's work. Vogler closes by emphasizing the impossibility of absolute conclusions about the extent of Cruikshank's role and Dickens's debt. But even the most skeptical, as he notes, ought to recognize that the artist's conception of many of the characters existed independently of the text.

62. ____. An Oliver Twist Exhibition: A Momento for the Dickens Centennial 1970. Los Angeles: UCLA Univ. Research Library, 1970. 15 pp.

Vogler's essay provides a useful commentary on an exhibition of materials principally drawn from the holdings of the UCLA Library and the William Andrews Clark Memorial Library. The exhibits center on Oliver Twist and document the diverse visual appeal of Dickensian caricature evident in the widespread reproduction of characters from the novel, who reentered the public imagination after its publication in media ranging from Punch cartoons, porcelain, brass, and plaster reproductions, to wallpaper and games of "Snap" or slap jack for children. As Vogler observes, "Whatever the artistic merits of these tributes ... Dickens remains--aside from Shakespeare--almost the only writer in our language accorded such attention."

The essay also presents a brief but informative history of the illustrations Oliver Twist inspired, ranging from the work of Cruikshank, his associate F.W. Pailthorpe, and the drawings of J.C. Clarke or "Kyd," to the more recent drawings of Barnet Freedman for the Heritage Club Edition of the novel in 1939, and Ronald Searle (II. 44). Vogler notes how the later artists, even when they were not deliberate imitators, seldom escaped Cruikshank's pervasive influence, which continued despite the change in concept of illustration from attempts to illuminate the text to the inclusion of decorative scenes or character portraits unrelated to specific incidents in the novel. Referring to Cruikshank's claim to have originated Oliver Twist, Vogler acknowledges the artist's reputation for exaggeration but comments that not all his arguments can be dismissed "as without substance." Vogler also notes how Cruikshank had established a repertoire of pictorial types--criminals, beadles, Jews--before he began to work with Dickens, a point whose implications he discusses more fully elsewhere (XIII. 61).

63. Waugh, Arthur. "Charles Dickens and His Illustrators." In The Nonesuch Dickens: Retrospectus and Prospectus. London: The Nonesuch Press, 1937, pp. 9-52.

Narrates how the Nonesuch Press acquired the original plates--steels and wood blocks--for use in this edition, noting that by doing so it "will never be possible for a more complete and perfect Dickens to be put on the market." Waugh provides a brief history of Dickens's partnership with Cruikshank and praises the latter as an ideal illustrator for Oliver Twist because he had "an almost unequalled knowledge of the under side of London life." But Waugh calls Cruikshank's claim to have invented the book "impossible," excusing it as "one of the foibles of an old age which had already outlived the trust- worthy support of human memory."

64. Wechter, Sidney. "Cruikshank's Fagin--The Illustrator as Creator."
     Courier, (Syracuse Univ. Lib.), 14 (1977), 28-31.

A brief, uninformed comment about Cruikshank's preliminary sketches of
Fagin in the condemned cell and the final plate he drew for the novel.

65. Wilkins, William Glyde. "Cruikshank Versus Dickens." **The Dickensian,**
     16 (April 1920), 80-81.

Gives the text of Cruikshank's letter of 12 November 1870 to W.J.
McClellan in which Cruikshank advances his claim to have originated **Oliver
Twist.** Wilkins notes that MacKenzie published Cruikshank's letter in his
column in the **Philadelphia Press** on 19 December 1871 (XIII. 34), but he does
not refer to the letter's earlier appearance in the **New York Daily Tribune**
(XIII. 10) or in the second American Edition of Forster's **Life of Charles
Dickens** (Philadelphia: J.B. Lippincott, 1872).

66. _____. "Variations in the Cruikshank Plates to **Oliver Twist.**" The
     Dickensian, 15 (April 1919), 71-74.

Reconstructs Cruikshank's response to Dickens's rejection of the
"Fireside" plate, noting that Cruikshank added "a large amount of work of a
stipply nature" before abandoning the plate altogether. Wilkins also includes
a reproduction of the drawing Cruikshank submitted to Dickens as a substitute
for the "Fireside" plate. This sketch, now part of The Henry W. and Albert A.
Berg Collection, The New York Public Library, includes Dickens's signature of
approval, together with other comments by Dickens which Cruikshank later
rubbed out, leaving only the note in Cruikshank's hand: "'Rose and Oliver'
Twist too old."
     The remainder of Wilkins's essay details the difference he notes between
the illustrations as they accompanied the text in the **Miscellany** and their
appearance in the 1846 edition. For that occasion, Cruikshank touched up
some of the plates and added different backgrounds. Generally, the later
plates appear darker; Rose's dress in the last illustration was almost all white
in 1838; by 1846 it had become entirely black, writes Wilkins.

FAGIN AND ANTI-SEMITISM

67. Aronstein, Philipp. "Charles Dickens' Weltanschauung: Part IV. Dickens
     und die Juden." **Anglia,** 18 (1896), 246-47.

Provides a factual account of Mrs. Davis's complaints about Fagin (XIII.
78) and notes that after she charged Dickens with anti-Semitism he
recommended in the columns of **All the Year Round** the importance of
treating Jews without bias.

68. Belloc, Hilaire. The **Jews.** Boston: Houghton Mifflin, 1922, pp. 135-36.

In a chapter describing British disingenuousness and unintelligence in
dealing with the Jews, Belloc cites Dickens as an example of these qualities
extended to literature, where, trying to make amends to the Jews for their
former persecution, he creates an imaginary Jew as hero. His "offense,"
writes Belloc, "was grave," referring to Dickens's treatment of Jews in **Oliver
Twist.** "He disliked Jews instinctively; when he wrote of a Jew according

to his inclination [Fagin] he made him out a criminal. Hearing that he must
make amends for this action [see XIII. 78], he introduced [in Our Mutual
Friend] a Jew who is like nothing on earth--a sort of compound of an Arab
Sheik and a Family Bible picture from the Old Testament, and the whole
embroidered on an utterly non-Jewish--a purely English character."

69.   Blum, Samuel. "As Great Christian Writers Saw the Jews." The Jewish
      Tribune, 94 (19 April 1929), p. 16.

Notes briefly how when Dickens needed a despicable character in Oliver
Twist he "chose a Jew for the role" and expresses the opinion that "In all
probability" Dickens knew no Jews since in his day their population in England
did not exceed 50,000.

70.   Calisch, Edward N. "Oliver Twist and Our Mutual Friend." In his
      The Jew in English Literature as Author and as Subject. Richmond,
      Va., 1909; rpt. Port Washington, N.Y.: Kennikat Press, Inc., 1969, pp.
      127-29.

Faults Dickens not for the accuracy of the picture of Fagin but for the
presentation of him as "a Jewish type." "A Jew may be all that Fagin was, ...
but his being a Jew does not make him so." This truth, Calisch argues,
Dickens undermines by creating the contrary impression, "even as
Shakespeare had done before him." Shylock and Fagin, he states, have gone
abroad "as types, not only among English-speaking peoples, but throughout the
world," synonymous "of relentless usury and thievery." It is "more than
probable," Calisch concludes, that Oliver Twist "intensified the struggle and
delayed the victory of Jewish emancipation for at least a decade." Cf. Landa
(XIII. 94).

71.   Charles Dickens: An Appreciation. A Sunday lecture by the Rabbi
      of the Rodeph Shalom Congregation. Series 11, No. 14. Pittsburgh,
      Pennsylvania, 4 February 1912. 19 pp.

Summarizes briefly the main events of Dickens's life and adds a short
passage called "Dickens and the Jew." The author notes how a dear friend of
his father, the father of Sir Philip Magnus, once asked Dickens how it
happened that he could paint two such different Jews as Fagin and Riah.
Dickens reportedly replied, as Sir Philip told the author of this essay, "If I
have drawn a Fagin it is because I have known a Fagin; if I have drawn a Riah
it is because I have known a Riah."

72.   Charles Dickens and His Jewish Characters. Introd. Cumberland
      Clark. London: Chiswick Press, 1918, pp. 1-39.

Describes the incident of Mrs. Davis's protest against the portrayal of
Fagin (XIII. 78) and provides the complete text of the ensuing correspondence
between her and Dickens. See also XIII. 79.

73.   Chesterton, G.K. "Introduction." In his Appreciations and Criticisms
      of the Works of Charles Dickens (XII. 54), passim.

A general essay on Dickens in which Chesterton records his puzzlement
about the novelist's intentions toward Jews in Our Mutual Friend. If Dickens
introduced Riah to redress the affront given by "the great gargoyle

of Fagin," Chesterton reasons, why did Dickens pack Our Mutual Friend "literally full of Jews"? Chesterton sees Veneering, Lammles, and Fledgeby as the "particular types that people hate in Jewry," bad Jews, "whom nobody could fail to recognise." One explanation, Chesterton thinks, may lie in Dickens's sensitivity to British society, whose oriental and cosmopolitan financiers he portrayed without ever knowing that they were oriental or cosmopolitan.

74.   Coppock, Barbara M. "Dickens' Attitude to Jews." Common Ground, 24 (Autumn, 1970), 23-26.

Praises the portrayal of Riah in Our Mutual Friend and offers the suggestion that recent history has given a prominence to Fagin's Jewishness that Dickens never intended. For example, showing a film version of the novel shortly after the second world war in which a Jew is caricatured and given greater emphasis than he received in the book constitutes for Coppock "the height of folly." Lean's film (VII. 18) she finds "devoid of imagination" and "damaging to the memory of a great writer."

75.   Dachslager, E.L. "Teaching Literary Antisemitism." College English, 39 (November 1977), 315-25.

With only passing references to Fagin, Dachslager argues that teaching works which depict Jews in negative and offensive terms promotes anti-Semitic practices, unless the instructor puts the character into its proper context and deals objectively with the portrayal. Ideally, he states, literary anti-Semitism should not be taught "if it is taught as something other than what it really is," i.e., anti-Semitism in literature.

76.   ____. "To teach or not teach antisemitism." Sh'ma: A Journal of Jewish Responsibility, 8 (24 December 1976), 25-26.

Rejects censorship and argues that those teaching literature with anti-Semitic elements should first recognize how Chaucer, Marlowe, Shakespeare, Dickens, and others stereotyped Jews and then come to terms with the issue of anti-Semitism rather than avoid it. Excusing an author's antagonism to Jews by saying that he was simply expressing the conventional views of his day, Dachslager thinks, evades history and reinforces a reader's negative image of the Jews. Dachslager also argues against justifying anti-Semitism in literature "as simply a literary device" subservient to artistic necessity and rejects the defense of Fagin which stresses that the plot needed a villain and that Dickens's character is only incidentally Jewish.

77.   Davis, Helen I. "When Charles Dickens Atoned: The Story of his Sinister Character, Fagin, Which he Offset with the Benign Figure of Riah." American Hebrew, 122 (May 1928), 980, 1008, 1024-25.

Draws on the correspondence between Mrs. Eliza Davis and Dickens (XIII. 78) to argue that Dickens genuinely repented his error in unintentionally giving through Fagin the impression that he hated Jews.

78.   Dickens, Charles. The Letters of Charles Dickens. Ed. Walter Dexter. Vol. III. 1858-1870 (V. 5), passim.

Almost three years after Dickens sold Tavistock House in August 1860,

Mrs. Eliza Davis, the wife of the Jewish banker who bought the novelist's London residence, wrote to Dickens asking him to subscribe to a Convalescent Home for the Jewish poor. The home, she explained, would also serve as a memorial to Lady Montefiore, whose efforts on behalf of Jews throughout the world British Jews wished to acknowledge when she died in 1862. Eliza Davis also took this occasion to express the feeling common among Jews that "large hearted" Dickens, so noble and so eloquent in his pleas for "the oppressed of his country" has "encouraged a vile prejudice against the despised Hebrew." In her view, she added, the portrait of Fagin admitted only a negative interpretation, which she thought would continue unless Dickens either justified himself or atoned "for a great wrong on a whole though scattered nation." See also XIII. 79.

First, Dickens responded with a justification. Fagin, he argued, "is a Jew, because it unfortunately was true of the time to which the story refers, that that class of criminal almost invariably was a Jew." Dickens also added that the remaining villains in the novel were Christians and that he called Fagin "The Jew" not because of his religion, but because of his race. Dickens attached importance to the epithet because he thought it conveyed the idea that Fagin was "one of the Jewish people," just as he would give his readers an idea of "a Chinaman, by calling him a Chinese" (N, III, 357).

In a quick response, Mrs. Davis conceded that Jews received stolen property at the time of Oliver Twist and then turned to the flaw in Dickens's case. "If, as you remark, 'all must observe that the other Criminals were Christians,' they at least contrasted with characters of good Christians; this poor, wretched Fagin stands alone--'The Jew.'" She then closed her comments about Fagin with the observation that her fellow countrymen remain ignorant of the Jews around them and suggested that "an author of reputation" would do well to examine the manner and character of British Jews and represent them "as they really are to 'Nothing extenuate nor aught set down in Malice.'" See also XIII. 79.

This appeal, skillfully backed by the quotation from Othello, evidently prompted Dickens to examine some of his unconscious assumptions about Jews. Already the exemplary conduct of Mr. Davis, the purchaser of Tavistock House, had caused him to admit that in all things Davis "has behaved thoroughly well" (N, III, 176). As Dickens concedes in the same letter of 19 August 1860, Davis's behavior contradicted his expectations. "I cannot call to mind," Dickens wrote to W.H. Wills, "any occasion when I have had money-dealings with any one that have been so satisfactory, considerate, and trusting," a sentiment markedly different in tone from his initial doubt, also expressed to Wills, about "a Jew Money-lender" whose word to buy the house Dickens would never believe "until he has paid the money" (N, III, 172).

Further evidence of Dickens's changed attitude to Jews appears in Our Mutual Friend, in the character of the good Jew, Riah, whom he worked into the novel as an apology to the race he unintentionally insulted. Although Mrs. Davis found Riah unrealistic, she took the portrait in the spirit Dickens intended and thanked him for "a great compliment paid to myself and to my people." As a further expression of gratitude, she later sent Dickens a copy of the Scriptures in Hebrew as "a New Year offering." For her inscription, see XIII. 79. The arrival of this present, Stone argues (XIII. 120), jogged Dickens's memory of his intention to remove the epithet "The Jew" from the new 1867 Charles Dickens Edition of Oliver Twist. For the revisions to the text, see II. 15.

Dickens's letters contain a few other prejudicial comments about Jews. In 1837 Dickens referred to Richard Bentley, the owner of the Miscellany and publisher of the first edition of Oliver Twist, as the "infernal, rich,

232

plundering, thundering old Jew" in a note to Forster (P, I, 292). Bentley, a Gentile, earned Dickens's hostility for trying to profit as fully as he could from Dickens's labors. Similarly, another publisher, Henry Colburn, earned Dickens's scorn for a business agreement between himself and Thomas Hood, in which Colburn, wrote Dickens on 12 September 1843, "took a money-lending, billbroking, Jew clothes-bagging, Saturday Night pawnbroking advantage" of Hood's situation (P, III, 559).

79.   "Fagin and Riah." The Dickensian, 17 (July 1921), 144-52.

   Provides a complete record of the exchange of letters between Mrs. Eliza Davis and Dickens about Fagin and her praise for Riah in Our Mutual Friend (XIII. 78), together with her comments about the errors Dickens made in Riah's character. The article also gives the text of Mrs. Davis's letter of 8 February 1867, in which she thanked Dickens for his nobility and sent him a copy of the only complete Jewish translation of the Bible into English collated with the Hebrew. Inside she wrote:

6 February, 1867.

Presented to
Charles Dickens, Esq.

in grateful and admiring recognition of his having exercised the noblest quality man can possess; that of atoning for an injury as soon as conscious of having inflicted it,

by a Jewess.

80.   Fiedler, Leslie A. "What Can We Do About Fagin? The Jew-Villain in Western Tradition." Commentary, 7 (January 1949-June, 1949), 411-18.

   Refers to Fagin directly only in the title but poses important questions relevant to both Oliver Twist and any work tainted by anti-Semitism. How does the Western literary tradition appear to Jews, asks Fiedler, and what constitutes an appropriate response to a culture in which "so terrible and perilous a myth" of Jews predominates?
   Although Fiedler remains unwilling to resign from Western culture, he and other Jews wince when they re-examine their literary heritage "as Jewish writers and readers of English." Looking again at "Lawrence or Pound, Shakespeare, Chaucer, Marlowe, Pope, Wordsworth, Scott or Dickens, T.S. Eliot, Charles Williams or Graham Greene," Fiedler sees "a myth of the Jew" before which Jews are "embarrassed, dumb." The momentary labels of Usurer, "the Jew with the knife, [and] the Jew as Beast," he thinks, do not matter. Rather the compulsive figure of a creature of "fear and guilt" disturbs him because this image "haunts the English imagination" and inhabits the collective unconscious of the English-speaking peoples.
   The essay then traces two motifs: the de-humanization of the Jew apparent in the bestial or animal imagery so frequently used to characterize stage or literary Jews, and "the myth of the Jew with the knife." Fiedler traces the latter pattern from Chaucer's Prioress' Tale to Marlowe, Shakespeare, and, via Dickens, to Graham Greene and speculates that the sense of threat the myth embodies represents a threat to sexuality, in which "even the standard atrocity attributed to the Jew, the ritual murder of a

child, is a rationalization of that original nightmare of the circumcisor, ritual blade in hand." Fiedler thinks that for Marlowe and Shakespeare the vilification of this figure reflects "the lynch spirit" out of which their anti-Jew sentiments arose, whereas in "most respectable modern literature," the writers convey "an irrepressible vestigial shudder rather than lust for a pogrom."

How, therefore, should Jews respond to a culture nurturing such prejudice? Fiedler examines various possibilities--withdrawal, acceptance, "kidnapping" the myth and turning it to Jews' advantage, and censorship. The last, he sensibly concludes, would probably release "a perilous hysteria" difficult to keep within reasonable bounds. Besides, he values, for example, The Merchant of Venice or Pound's poems for "their beauty and a degree of true vision" despite their evil doctrine. The soundest course, he thinks, lies in the recognition that "moral darkness" cannot be confined to one race. Instead, the Gentile must learn "for himself that Shylock is the creature of his fantasy and fear; his stratagem to transfer the evil that haunts us all to an alien, an Other." See also XIII. 91.

81. Fisch, Harold. The Dual Image: The Figure of the Jew in English and American Literature. New York: KTVA Publishing House, 1971, pp. 63-65.

Cites Fagin as an example of "the continuing vitality of the Judas-Devil myth," which Dickens exploits, working not so much from a contemporary type as from a stock figure "associated in the public imagination with the word 'Jew.'" Fisch finds Dickens's presentation of the medieval details of the bad Jew "curiously incorrect" in Fagin's red hair, blasphemies, penchant for drugs and poisoning, blood-guiltiness, and grotesque humor. But, he notes, Fagin is secularized and portrayed as "the villain writ large" rather than as the enemy of Christianity. After his rebuke by Mrs. Davis (XIII. 78), Fisch adds, Dickens reversed his picture of the Jew, contributing one who protects rather than exploits the weak. "But in a way," he comments, both Fagin and Riah are "neutral portraits--they have neither of them much specific Jewish quality." Fagin, with a few alterations, could be interchanged with another particularly detestable villain, just as Riah could be metamorphosed into another one of Dickens's kindly old gentlemen.

82. Fleissner, Robert F. "Dickens' Oliver Twist." The Explicator, 41 (Spring 1983), 30-32.

Suggests two associations implicit in Fagin's name. As the derivative of the German Veigelchen or Veigelein, the name had numerous variations, of which Fagin, a Jewish name, was one, thus providing linguistic justification for Dickens's description of Fagin as a Jew. Secondly, the fact that Veigelchen meant violet in Old German, a flower with inherent erotic connotations, leads Fleissner to speculate that Dickens subtly associated his archvillain with effeminacy and homosexuality. Could it not be, Fleissner asks, that the violet in Fagin's name "points to his having a flowery or ... swishy air?"

83. Forster, John. "Hard Experiences in Boyhood 1822-4." In his The Life of Charles Dickens (XII. 7), I, 19-33.

Refers briefly to Bob Fagin, Dickens's protector at the blacking factory, whose name, writes Forster, the novelist "took the liberty of using ... long afterwards, in **Oliver Twist**." When Charles arrived at Warren's, in early 1824, Bob Fagin showed him "the trick of using the string and tying the knot" around the pots of paste-blacking, as the boys covered them first with oil-paper and then with a piece of blue paper before pasting on a printed label. Bob, whom Dickens describes as "much bigger and older than I," stood up for Charles when he was teased by another of the boys for receiving superior treatment from the foreman; he also kindly applied bottles of hot water to his side when Charles suffered one day from a "bad attack" of his old kidney disorder at work. Dickens refers to Bob as "an orphan ... [who] lived with his brother-in-law, a waterman." The two boys worked side by side when the blacking business moved to new premises in Chandos Street. Before an open window, where they stood to take advantage of the light, Dickens and Fagin demonstrated their "great dexterity in tying up the pots" to the passers by, who used to stop and look in on them. Cf. Carey (XII. 48).

84.   Frank, Maude. "The Jew in English Fiction." **The Critic**, 39 (July-
        December 1901), 79-81.

Claims that Dickens's Jewish characters "have little significance" and that Fagin "has absolutely nothing of the Jew--not even his name is characteristic." Without altering a line of the portrait, she adds, Dickens could have made his thief-trainer "a pure-blooded Londoner." Calling him a Jew merely adds "to the Hogarthian grotesqueness of the thieves' den."

85.   Gelber, Mark. "Teaching 'Literary Anti-Semitism': Dickens' **Oliver
        Twist** and Freytag's **Soll und Haben**." **Comparative Literature Studies**,
        16 (March 1979), 1-11.

Offers little useful advice other than a common sense plea to confront anti-Semitic attitudes as they occur in a text. Gelber suggests that an analysis of Fagin's realistic and symbolic roles, his debt to stereotyping, and Dickens's textual emendations (II. 15) and correspondence with Mrs. Davis (XIII. 78 and 79) will give readers more insight into both "the nature of literature and anti-Semitism" than excluding **Oliver Twist** from syllabi in the belief that such a book should be eliminated from "the canon."

86.   Hirsch, S.A. "Some Literary Trifles." **The Jewish Quarterly Review**,
        13 (1901), 595-619.

Glosses two expressions used by the narrator in Chapter 52 of **Oliver Twist** when he describes Fagin's response to the "Venerable men of his own persuasion" who come to pray beside the criminal in the condemned cell. Fagin, we are told "[drove] them away with curses" and "beat them off" after they renewed their charitable efforts. Both recall, Hirsch argues, a passage in Maimonides's (or Moses ben Maimon, 1135-1204) **Mishneh** Torah or **The Strong Hand**, a reference book based on Talmudic precepts. In **The Strong Hand** Maimonides advises his readers that they are duty bound to reprove gently a fellow sinner and should continue to do so, making successive efforts if ignored until the well-meaning mentor is finally beaten off and "driven away by curses." These verbal echoes, Hirsch concludes, represent not coincidence but evidence that Dickens--"a careful and painstaking author"--consulted "some Jew, learned in the Law, and asked him what the Jews would do were a case like that of Fagin brought before them."

87.   Hobsbaum, Philip.   "The Two Faces of Charles Dickens." **Jewish Chronicle**, Literary Supplement, 4 December 1970, pp. i-ii. Also published as "Charles Dickens and the Jews: A Centenary Essay." **Jewish Affairs**, 26 (February 1971), 17-20.

Summarizes briefly the content of Stone's essay (XIII. 120) and presents three main points: (1) Dickens's treatment of Jews in his early fiction suggests "unthinking prejudice" rather than deep-seated intolerance; (2) Dickens drew on current stereotypes when he created Fagin; (3) his attitude began to change after he sold Tavistock House to Mr. Davis and after Mrs. Davis rebuked Dickens for the wrong Fagin did to Jews, for which Dickens apologized in both Our Mutual Friend and in the revisions to Oliver Twist.

88.   Hurwitz, Solomon T.H.   "The Jews and Jewesses of Scott and Dickens: Part II of A Critical Survey of the Important Types of Jewish Character in English Literature."   **The Jewish Forum: A Monthly Magazine**, 5 (1922), 243-46.

Comments briefly on Fagin as representative of Dickens's ignorance of Jewry. Hurwitz finds Fagin's name "non-Jewish," sees no evidence of Jewish characteristics in him, and concludes that the only single Jewish feature of Oliver Twist is Barney, who, "just fresh from a foreign soil, speaks with a remarkably good Jewish accent."

89.   Isaacs, Myer S.   "An Ancient Grudge." In his The Old Guard and Other Addresses. New York: The Knickerbocker Press, 1906, pp. 76-124.

Treats briefly "the effect of works of fiction upon the popular mind" and cites the portrait of Fagin as second to that of Shylock in English literature for its offensiveness to Jews. Myers calls the delineation of Fagin "a shocking libel upon the Jewish character" and a blot on Dickens's fame which he tardily tried to efface by creating "the comparatively good but essentially feeble Riah."

90.   "The Jew on the English Stage." **Jewish Comment** [Baltimore], 21 (22 September 1905), 3.

An anonymous review of Tree's production of Oliver Twist (VI. 18) in which Tree takes the part of "the hideous Jew 'Fagin.'" The writer attacks the stage version of the novel for its crude melodrama and "almost primitive" pathos and humor. He also describes Fagin played with "the usual lisp" and the "usual thick voice." In conclusion he states: "It is difficult to see what glory Mr. Tree hoped to gain from presenting his impossible Jew to the theatre-going public. Nor can one imagine that the profits of the production are likely to be large."

91.   "The Jewish Writer and the English Literary Tradition." A Symposium. Part I and II. **Commentary**, 8 (July 1949-December 1949), 209-19, 361-70.

Twenty Jewish writers take up some of the questions raised by Fiedler (XIII. 80) and comment on his sense of the dilemma Jews face as writers and readers of a literary tradition "shot through with the notion of the Jew as a creature of darkness." Louis Kronenberger sees Barabas and Fagin as crude and extravagant but not really menacing until anti-Semitism in society grows virulent. They are, he thinks, "fuel for a fire that literature itself ... never starts. Indeed, observed **inside** literary tradition, Barabas and Fagin involve not how anti-Semitic but only how anti-realistic a Marlowe and a Dickens are."

Diana Trilling notes that "The Jewish issue" brings out a particular sensitivity in people's reactions but can see no reason to give more weight to, say, Dickens's anti-Semitism than to his anti-parliamentarianism. "[T]he latter," she writes, "is just as much a threat to my security as the former," yet no one ever suggests that Dickens should perhaps be boycotted "because of his animus against the democratic process."

Harry Levin thinks Fiedler goes out of his way to "darken the picture" by arbitrarily omitting "the brighter touches" of Riah and Jews in the work of George Eliot and Browning. Irving Howe finds himself uneasy with the tradition of gross caricatures of Jews in English literature but adds: "There is, however, nothing we should 'do' or wish to 'do' about Fagin [and others] ... They are to be forever with us, a stab of pain, a reminder of evil."

92.   Johnson, Edgar. "Dickens, Fagin, and Mr. Riah: The Intention of the Novelist." Commentary, 9 (January 1950-June 1950), 47-50.

Provides no analysis of the extent to which the novel's text is or is not anti-Semitic. Instead, Johnson sidesteps the issue by describing Dickens as "an advanced liberal" in social thought and as a man with a strong humanitarian tendency whose sympathies for "the unhappy and injured" are everywhere apparent. While Johnson admits that someone with these beliefs could also be anti-Semitic, such an attitude, he thinks, "would at least be incongruous." Johnson grants that Dickens made careless remarks about Jews in his letters (XIII. 78) but stresses that such "thoughtlessness" dwindles to "insignificance in the enormous bulk of his correspondence." Johnson summarizes Dickens's response to Mrs. Davis's criticism and the evolution of Riah (XIII. 79), from which he concludes: "Surely the man whose developing awareness of the injustices of his time grew even more acute and painful throughout the years ... was no intolerant anti-Semite and Jew-baiter."

93.   Kohut, George Alexander. **Charles Dickens and The Jews.** Philadelphia: n.p., 1912. 18 pp. Rpt. from **The Review** [Philadelphia], March 1912 as "A Contribution to the Dicken's [sic] Centenary (February 7, 1912)."

Reprints the correspondence between Dickens and Mrs. Davis (XIII. 79) "just as it was printed in the **Jewish Chronicle** of London in June 1870" with a brief comment about Dickens's treatment of Jews in his fiction. Kohut argues that Fagin resembles Shylock as "a synonym of villainy and unscrupulousness" but lacks the latter's tragic stature. Because Fagin has no redeemable qualities, Kohut argues, he has aroused "far more racial prejudice and has cast a deeper shadow on the people whom he is alleged to typify, than Shylock." Kohut also includes a short passage from **Barnaby Rudge** Chapter 37, in which Lord Gordon speaks of his dream of being a Jew, and reprints Sergeant Dornton's anecdote in "A Detective Police Party" (XIV. 7) about his capture of Aaron Mesheck, a Jewish thief. Kohut points out that Dickens is among the first writers to use "Gonoph," the Hebrew equivalent for the word thief, and "gonophing" in "On Duty with Inspector Field" and "A Detective Police Party." (The OED cites Dickens's use of "gonoph" in **Bleak House** Chapter 19, as the earliest recorded use of the term.)

94.   Landa, M.J. "The Original of Fagin." In his **The Jew in Drama.** London: P.S. King, 1926, pp. 159-69, and passim.

Argues that Fagin sprang from "the boards" and not from any living model, cf. Pugh (XIII. 110), although Landa sees the trial of Ikey Solomons at London's Old Bailey as an influence on Victorian melodrama and so, in turn, on Dickens, whose portrait of Fagin owes, in his view, much to an obscure play by W.T. Moncrieff (XIII. 142). The latter's **Van Diemen's Land** contained a minor figure, one Barney Fence, whose name would probably have gone unnoticed had it not been for Solomons. Soon after the play opened in London on 10 February 1830, Moncrieff renamed Barney "Ikey Solomons" as he cashed in on public interest in the real fence and thus saved his play from obscurity.

Landa plausibly assumes that Dickens saw one of the play's frequent revivals in the following years and speculates that Moncrieff's villain provided him with a conventional stage Jew readily adaptable to **Oliver Twist**. As proof of this assertion, Landa cites the ease with which dramatists adapted **Oliver Twist** for the stage and argues that Dickens's own anxiety to see the novel performed "justifies the contention that the character of Fagin was invented with an eye to the theatre."

Dickens, Landa believes, never intended Fagin to be harmful to Jews, but through his "sheer ignorance and thoughtlessness, he saddled the stage with a wretched character who has become second in command to Shylock." Landa contends that Fagin's evil influence both in fiction and on stage set back Jewish emancipation and delayed the admission of Jews to Parliament until 1858. In the 1830's Jews made striking gains in civil liberties, he points out, until the advent of Fagin, whose negative impact "appears to have been instantaneous." Cf. Calisch (XIII. 70). Landa also holds Dickens responsible for spreading the belief that fences were always Jews and states that he must bear the blame for "the libel of the lisp," a caricature and supposed racial peculiarity for which Landa finds no validity.

95. Lane, Lauriat, Jr. "The Devil in **Oliver Twist**." **The Dickensian**, 52 (June 1956), 132-36.

Argues that Law (XIII. 98) overstates her case about the influence on **Oliver Twist** of Defoe's **History of the Devil**. Dickens had already established the satanic quality of Fagin's character, Lane points out, **before** he wrote enthusiastically to Forster on 3 November 1837 about Defoe's book (P, I, 328). Prior to Chapter 19, Dickens's focus at the time of the letter, Dickens referred repeatedly to Fagin as "the old gentleman," spoke of his red beard, and showed Nancy and Sikes talking of Fagin's diabolical nature. Lane also suggests that lore about the devil was so deeply rooted in the language and traditions of Dickens's culture that the novelist probably "found little in Defoe's **History of the Devil** that he was not already aware of."

Lane also comments on Dickens's use of Fagin's diabolism. By combining this aspect of Fagin with "the implicit villainy of the traditional Jew," Dickens establishes "an archetypal antithesis" between the corrupt world of the city and the restorative world of the country. As one who tries to entice and trap Oliver, Fagin falls into the traditional role of Satan; as an extension of the novel's "mythical-theological meaning," Oliver manages to escape by earning first partial and then "total redemption." His salvation comes to him, Lane suggests, "only after receiving a serious wound" and thereby being "purged of his corruption."

96. ____. "Dickens' Archetypal Jew." **PMLA**, 73 (March 1958), 94-100.

Lane analyzes the elements of which Fagin is composed and argues that Dickens drew on "an ancient literary and cultural tradition" to make his first great villain a union of two archetypal figures, the Jew and the devil. Dickens also impresses Fagin's Jewishness on the reader by constantly repeating the epithet "the Jew" and by representing him through the eyes of a child, Lane suggests. When Oliver sees him, Fagin becomes "an even more exaggerated and archetypal image of evil."

Lane thinks that Dickens's intentions with Fagin remain primarily aesthetic and argues that if Dickens sinned he did so as a beginner "writing rapidly under the pressure of serial publication." However, by examining a "much fuller pattern of Jewish materials and allusions" in Dickens's fiction, together with slurring references to Jews in his letters (XIII. 78), Lane detects "unthinking prejudice" and the author's tendency to reflect "the general attitudes [to Jews] and prejudice of his age." In fact, even in the case of Riah in **Our Mutual Friend**, "Dickens' one attempt to work counter to the anti-Jewish tradition in English literature," Lane finds "Unwitting but deeply held bias and prejudice." As evidence he cites the passage where the narrator describes financial manipulators as "asthmatic and thick lipped" (Bk. II, ch. 9), an odd stereotype for a writer trying to reverse his attitudes towards Jews in response to Mrs. Davis's criticism.

Two problems characterize Lane's study. First, his insistence on finding an archetypal Jew in Dickens's fiction seems to blind him to the possibility that Dickens's attitude to Jews did change later in life. Second, the evidence Lane presents of Dickens's pejorative references to Jews runs counter to his statement that Dickens's anti-Semitism lies not in the author but in his readers, whom Lane divides into two classes. Some, he contends, are over-zealous guardians of the public weal busily introducing into our response to Fagin "problems that are not only insoluble but perhaps irrelevant." Others, he regrets, seem to share Dickens's view that "certain kinds of social evil" justifiably tend to be associated with Jews. For further comments on Lane's essay, see Stone (XIII. 120).

97. _____. "Oliver Twist: A Revision." TLS, 20 July 1951, p. 460.

Draws attention to the implications of the changes Dickens made in Chapter 52 when he revised **Oliver Twist** in 1867 for the Charles Dickens Edition of his novels. See II. 15. By removing the epithet "the Jew," Dickens subdues "the racial characteristics of the villain" and makes Fagin "a real person" identified by his name instead of a type based on racial hatred. Lane incorrectly states that Dickens confines his changes to that part of the text portraying "our final picture of Fagin." The revisions begin in Chapter 32 but are not made in Chapters 34 and 35. See also XIII. 104 and 115.

98. Law, Marie Hamilton. "The Indebtedness of **Oliver Twist** to Defoe's **History of the Devil.**" PMLA, 40 (1925), 892-97.

Argues that Dickens invests Fagin, Sikes, and the Dodger with a sinister appeal that owes more to their "satanic quality" than to their realism, a trait Law sees increasingly present in Dickens's later villains. Nevertheless, the evil figures in **Oliver Twist** prove effective, she thinks, because of "the psychological truth" of their reaction to their wicked deeds, in which growing consciousness of their crimes undermines their characters.

Law suggests that Dickens's "exposition of sin in its effect upon the individual" parallels the philosophy of sin in Defoe's **History of the Devil,** a book Dickens read while at work on the novel. See Lane (XIII. 95). As proof of her contention, she argues for the resemblance between Defoe's belief that the Devil "manifests himself through human agency" and Dickens's "satanic conception" of Fagin, whose crimes link him with the Devil. She also points, unconvincingly, to Defoe's interest in ghosts and apparitions, which she sees reflected in Sikes's hallucinations after he killed Nancy.

99. Levi, Rabbi Harry. "Lesson VI: Oliver Twist, by Charles Dickens." In his Jewish Characters in Fiction: English Literature. Philadelphia: The Jewish Chautauqua Society, 1930, pp. 51-57.

A booklet of little help to modern readers offering a syllabus and study guide to works treating Jews. Levi comments that Dickens presented Fagin as a Jew he knew and suggests that he wrote without personal prejudice.

100. Mabon, Doris. "The Jew in Fiction." The Jewish Chronicle, suppl. 21 (June 1929), pp. ii-iii.

Suggests that moral considerations rather than realism affected Dickens's treatment of Jews in his fiction. In Oliver Twist he "pilloried Evil" (Fagin); later, he "exalted Good" in his characterization of Riah in Our Mutual Friend.

101. Marcus, Steven. "Who is Fagin?" Commentary, 34 (July 1962), 48-59. Also published as an Appendix in his Dickens: From Pickwick To Dombey (XII. 146), pp. 358-78.

This essay offers an account of Fagin, whose genesis Marcus traces to details of Dickens's personal experiences, the effect of which is to minimize the significance of Fagin's Jewishness. The most accessible source appears in the novelist's Autobiographical Fragment (XIII. 83), where Dickens mentions that Bob Fagin, one of his "every-day associates," taught Charles how to wrap and tie "the pots of paste-blacking." Bob Fagin also befriended Charles, protecting him against taunts from their companions and caring for him when kidney pains prevented young Dickens from working. From these and other passages Marcus points to both "myriad analogies" and significant differences between the Fragment and Oliver Twist. He cites, for example, the similarity between the lesson in tying pots and the class in picking pockets; he emphasizes the contrast between Dickens's ambiguous response to Bob Fagin, the well-intentioned older boy, and Oliver's terror at Fagin the old man, "Jew, devil, demon and master criminal."

Marcus then argues for the existence of a much deeper level of experience, whose multiple "meanings and motives" converge upon two passages in the text rich in "some private resonance." The scenes to which Marcus refers are Oliver, half waking, observing Fagin gloating over his box of jewels (ch. 9), and Oliver, waking from sleep, transfixed by the sight of Monks and Fagin peering at him through the Maylies' window (ch. 34). These incidents, Marcus suggests, represent "a screen memory," a term psychiatrists apply to the mind's curious manner of both revealing and concealing something buried deep in the psyche. In this case, Marcus asserts, Dickens's depiction of an "intense experience of watching and being watched, which gives way to emotions of threat and terror," represents "the decomposed elements" of the "primal scene," Freud's term for the child who observes sexual intercourse between his parents, is frightened by what he sees, and then imagines what would occur if he were noticed. One obvious consequence is fear, a fantasy Marcus connects with Fagin "the terrible, frightening old Jew," whose traditional representation as the devil, Anti-Christ, and "castrator and murderer of good little Christian boys" corresponds with the image of "the terrible father of infancy." This argument, Marcus concedes, does not account for the power of Fagin "as an imaginative creation," but it does show, if one accepts his hypothesis about the use to which Dickens puts his unconscious memories, that the part of Fagin which is Jewish "turns out to be not merely minor but almost fortuitous."

102. McLean, Robert S. "Fagin: An Early View of Evil." The Lock Haven Review, 9 (1967), 29-36.

Presents Fagin as a composite villain whose evil characteristics Dickens drew from three readily available sources: the theater, the Newgate novel, and traditional literary or folk materials. This resulting "early and superficial view of wickedness," McLean concludes, reveals little serious social criticism and originates in Dickens's inexperience, which led the young novelist to rely on a stereotypical view of evil. In his later fiction, McLean contends, Dickens abandoned the use of devil figures, unfavorable Jewish stereotypes, and other simplified versions of evil, portraying instead convincing villains drawn from "the respectable rulers of an exploitive society." McLean sees no personal malice towards Jews in the portrait of Fagin, arguing that he is "simply a vivid embodiment of individual evil." In no way does Dickens state or imply that Fagin is typical of Jews, writes McLean, "or that Jews as a group are villainous or culpable."

103. Modder, Montagu Frank. "Charles Dickens and the Realistic School." In his The Jew in the Literature of England to the End of the 19th Century. Philadelphia: The Jewish Publication Society of America, 1939, pp. 217-36.

Against a richly documented background of references to Jews by early Victorian authors, Modder comments on Oliver Twist and states his view that "It is absurd to say ... that Dickens disliked Jews" and that in creating Fagin "he shows a prejudice unworthy of a humanitarian novelist." Modder accepts the accuracy of Dickens's statement that fences were frequently "persons commonly designated as Jews"--cf. Van der Veen (XIII. 126)--and argues, as Dickens did to Mrs. Davis (XIII. 78), that the novelist was "merely describing a reprobate in the dens of London ... who, it so happens, is of Jewish origin." Modder also believes that "Thoughtful readers" will see that although Fagin is a Jew, he "retains no distinctive peculiarities of his religion" and that as a Jew Fagin "lacks actuality." Modder suggests that Dickens's letters to Mrs. Davis express his true sentiments about Jews and concludes that in calling Fagin a Jew, the novelist expressed "neither forethought nor malice" towards the Jewish community. Modder grants that Dickens and his fellow novelists recognized the value of the Jew as a literary type, but as realists truthfully representing contemporary life "Dickens and his followers ... succeed to a great extent in breaking away from the old patterns, and in giving a less unjust and more tolerant delineation of Jewish character." Such changes, Modder argues, reflect the attitude of contemporary society as increasingly liberal treatment of Jews followed social and economic developments.

104. Morse, J. Mitchell. "A Doubtful Case: Dickens." In his Prejudice and Literature. Philadelphia: Temple Univ. Press, 1976, pp. 160-66. Also published in College English, 37 (April 1976), 789-93.

Following his preliminary remarks about how prejudice tends to disable a writer "as writer" because it "involves a defect of perception," Morse

categorizes three ways writers cheapen their work by resorting to cliches that
signify distrust of "a whole race or sex or religion or nation." Some, like
Valery Larbaud, James Joyce, and Charles Lamb, he calls "inadvertent
offenders," who fail to see women or Jews as individuals and who represent
them unintentionally and unconsciously as types. Others, like T.S. Eliot,
Pound, and Shakespeare, deliberately offend Jews with remarks of calculated
enmity. And in the middle he places Dickens, "a doubtful case," whose
anti-Semitism, Morse thinks, may be accurately compared to the
anti-Semitism of a child, "believing as a matter of course what he was taught
at home and in Sunday school."

Morse notes the Dickens-Mrs. Davis exchange of letters (XIII. 79) and
comments on Dickens's switch from "the Jew" to "Fagin" in **Oliver Twist.** He
includes a footnote in which a commentator on the novel guesses correctly
that there was "almost no chance at all" that the change was "a random
thing," without knowing that Dickens deliberately revised the text in 1867 (II.
15). At the same time, Morse speculates incorrectly that "the effects of
serial publication" may account for the alterations. Morse, whose arresting
study examines some of the cultural metaphors and abstractions that haunt
us, concludes this section of his book by suggesting that we take Dickens's
disavowal to Mrs. Davis "at his word," even though his portrait of Fagin
continues "to feed the most vulgar prejudices" in present-day readers. Let us
agree with the Dickensians who argue that his purpose as a novelist was to
make the world better by encouraging people to be more decent in their
attitudes, he resolves; "Then we are left with the conclusion that in creating
Fagin he inadvertently counteracted his purpose. That was a literary
inadvertency."

105. Naman, Anne Aresty. "Charles Dickens: Prejudiced Imagination."
In her **The Jew in the Victorian Novel: Some Relationships Between
Prejudice and Art.** New York: AMS Press, Inc., 1980, pp. 57-95.

Can an author who creates a major character deeply rooted in the
anti-Semitism of English history successfully defend himself against charges
of defamation and prejudice? Naman addresses this problem by distinguishing
between prejudice in society and prejudice in art. While several correlations
between the two worlds exist, she argues that they are "never considered to
be absolutely the same in intention, function, or achievement." Prejudice in
life may serve what psychologists term "the scapegoating process," whose
aetiology may be either personal or social. By contrast, in serious literature
prejudice can serve artistic ends compatible with wholesome moral views.
Oliver Twist, like most Victorian novels, reflects a belief in a rational world,
where events follow as a result of causes and are attended by a moral order.
Naman concedes that while Dickens oversimplifies the dichotomy of good and
evil in **Oliver Twist,** his portrait of Fagin nevertheless serves the book's
structure in which evil, after disrupting the status quo, is eventually
defeated. Negative propaganda against the Jews as a group plays no part in
this scheme because such a purpose does not enter the novel's artistic needs.

A second argument stresses that because the portrait of Fagin differs
from that of other literary representations of Jews, even within the context
of Jewish stereotypes, Fagin cannot be described as representative. Those
negative characteristics Dickens seized upon serve to identify Fagin's evil
nature and reappear among other Dickensian villains. Fagin, she concludes,
"is as much a product of a Dickensian conception of evil as he is of social
stereotypes." Dickens's technique of rendering palpable external traits
accords completely with the distinctive nature of his characterization and

leads Naman to confront the paradox that the achievement of his art is
enhanced by his ability to manipulate prejudicial traits. Despite Fagin's red
hair, avarice, and identification with the devil, a sense of the inner man
emerges, whose lively, changing, and pleasing surface makes him a human
being. Some may reject Naman's premise that negative prejudice can serve
an acceptable purpose in literature, but few will deny her preference for
Fagin, whose richness remains far more compelling than the portrait of Riah,
the good Jew in Our Mutual Friend.

106. Niman,   Archie.   "A   Case   for   Shakespeare   and   Dickens."
     Midstream, 27 (October 1981), 52-55.

Comments on the general reputation of Shylock and Fagin as "the
archetypes of villainy" most people would cite if asked to offer names.
Niman, however, absolves both authors of anti-Semitism, arguing that
Shakespeare created a character with "humanity and depth" and that Dickens
invented Riah to make amends for Fagin.

107. Panitz, Esther L. "Fagin and Philistinism." In her The Alien in
     Their Midst: Images of Jews in English Literature. London and
     Toronto: Associated Univ. Presses, 1981, pp. 103-26.

Identifies two principal elements in Fagin's composition. Complete with
red hair and beard, he functions as the devil, a miser, and tempter of little
boys, the stock figure "of the old Morality play." At the same time, Panitz
argues, Fagin also represents Dickens's first sustained attack on the
privileged, the "fiscal ogres" who oppress the poor and justify their actions by
referring to "a fact-filled, emotionless, utilitarian philosophy." From the
seeds of Fagin's obsession with money and jewels, she argues, "there grew
whole hothouses of noxious weeds," middle-class villains whom Dickens
continued to attack throughout his career. With such negative views of
wealth, she concludes, the question of Dickens's overt anti-Semitism becomes
"irrelevant."

108. Paroissien, David. "'What's in a Name?' Some Speculations about
     Fagin." The Dickensian, 80 (Spring 1984), 41-45.

Argues that the German matronym Feige, of which Fagin is one of
several variants common among German Jews in the eighteenth century,
corroborates the Jewishness of Dickens's villain and supplements the
novelist's claim that criminals of Fagin's class were almost invariably
Jewish. Since Fagin and its variants appear to have been common names
among Ashkenazi Jews leaving the Continent in large numbers to escape
persecution and settle in England, Robert Fagin--the warehouse associate
after whom Dickens named his character--may well have had ancestors who
had arrived in London along with other Ashkenazi immigrants. Circumstances
forced many of these Jews into trading, peddling, and, frequently, crime, a
cause for alarm among magistrates such as Patrick Colquhoun and Henry
Fielding (XVI. 6 and 9), whose writings document the extent to which
immigrant Jews soon became implicated in the workings of London's
underworld. Perhaps familiar with their writings and drawing both on direct
personal observation and on the figure of the criminal Jew deeply embedded
in the popular imagination, Dickens reached into several sources when he
created Fagin, not least of which is the historical record showing receivers of
stolen goods who were also Jews.

109. Philipson, David. "Dickens's **Oliver Twist** and Our **Mutual Friend.**" In his **The Jew in English Fiction.** Cincinnati: Robert Clarke, 1899, pp. 88-102.

Notes the power of fiction to shape and mold opinion and laments how novels constitute "hidden thrusts" against Jews, who have "No worse enemy" than writers spreading anti-Semitic doctrine and misrepresenting Jews on the basis of only a slight acquaintance with them. Philipson expresses his puzzlement over why great English writers, when they had occasion to speak of Jews, did so "in derogatory terms" and classed them "with the lowest elements of society."

Fagin, Philipson thinks, reflects an idea of Jews drawn from "hostile writings" rather than personal ill will. The irony of such a portrait, which suggests to him that Dickens joined "the vulgar cry, and marked his worst character a Jew," confronts Philipson when he considers how Dickens's reputation rests on his fierce antagonism to social abuse and determination to oppose false opinion. But in Dickens's defense, Philipson points out that "if the novel is read carefully, it will be seen that he draws a Jew, not the Jew; that is, one man, not the type." He also credits Dickens for his later awareness of his unjust portrayal of Fagin and his wish to atone for it by representing Riah as the good Jew in **Our Mutual Friend.**

110. Pugh, Edwin. "Criminal Prototypes." In his **The Charles Dickens Originals.** London, 1912; 2nd imp. New York: Charles Scribner's, 1913, pp. 237-52.

Makes the first assertion that Fagin was founded "on the personality of a famous rogue named Ikey Solomons." Pugh admits that the case for the likeness between Solomons's career and Fagin's is "not too apparent" but argues for the connection on the basis of circumstantial evidence. Cf. Tobias (XIII. 123). At the turn of the century, Pugh claims, "a very plague of Jews" appears to have been engaged in receiving stolen property. Astute villains who trained young boys to steal and pick pockets were also known to have existed in numbers, a point Pugh makes by quoting from the testimony of Arthur George Frederick Griffiths, a former governor of Newgate. See XVI. 11.

Pugh also comments briefly on Dickens's depiction of Fagin as "the arch devil," a lurid and malignant figure "like Satan in mediaeval pageantry."

111. Rolfe, Franklin P. "More Letters to the Watsons." **The Dickensian,** 38 (Spring 1942), 113-123.

Among this collection of thirty-one previously unpublished letters appears Dickens's letter of 1 October 1850 to Mrs. Richard Watson in which he describes one Nathan, a "costume-maker" whom he employed for his amateur plays, as "a Jew, but for a Jew a very respectable man indeed."

112. Rosenberg, Edgar. "The Jew as Bogey." In his **From Shylock to Svengali: Jewish Stereotypes in English Fiction.** Stanford: Stanford Univ. Press, 1960, pp. 116-37, and passim.

This book's ostensibly modest focus--a study of the Jewish criminal and the Jewish paragon as they appear in the British novel between 1795 and 1895 unintentionally misrepresents the range of scholarship Rosenberg brings to the two stereotypes he selects, whose "massive durability" he brilliantly documents over a much greater period. Stereotypes, Rosenberg argues, are literary conventions a writer draws on and consciously manipulates for particular aesthetic purposes. How writers use these fundamentally anti-realistic components forms his central preoccupation, not why. Rosenberg ignores the question of authors' personal biases for or against Jews, and says of Dickens, for example, that he had no idea whether Dickens was an anti-Semite. Referring to the discrepancy between the portrayal of Fagin and Dickens's public denial of intolerance, he comments: "I suspect that the gulf ... defines the difference between metaphor and statement, creation and criticism, and that one of the defects endemic to earlier studies of the Jew in literature lies in the general failure to distinguish between the two."

The chapter on Fagin presents him as an atavistic figure who combines "two levels of reality." Part of Fagin belongs to the stage, immediately to the melodrama of Moncrieff (XIII. 142), and more remotely to dramatic villains with hooked noses and red hair, a Satanic character in a medieval play, a murderer, fiend, and diabolical miser divested of his theology "and patched up for purposes of Victorian sensation-drama." Fagin also operates as a distorted dream figure, whose terrifying unreality assumes compelling power when seen through the eyes of a child. Rosenberg finds a further prototype in Bob Fagin (XIII. 83), a friend at Warren's whose name Dickens used when he wrote **Oliver Twist,** his first partially autobiographical account of his boyhood rescue from despair, to which he later returned in **David Copperfield** and **Great Expectations.**

In spite of Rosenberg's persuasive survey of Fagin's prototypes--dramatic, historic, and psychic--he does not forget his earlier expression of critical humility. "But how **can** one account for Fagin?" he asked in his Introduction. This "hideous bogeyman with the red hair, and the hooked nose, and the devilish leer," he suggests, defies an ultimate explanation. When characters arise, like Riah, from clearly stated motives, dogma rather than art results. Products of the imagination, like Fagin, admit bafflement and compel respect for genius.

113. ____. "The Jew in Western Drama: An Essay and a Checklist." BNYPL, 72 (September 1968), 442-91. Reprinted in Coleman (IV. 6) in 1970.

Comments briefly on Fagin, noting how he, Squeers, and Quilp have "a good deal in common" with Marlowe's Barabas. All move, he suggests, "in rather the same atmosphere of sensational and cheerful criminality." Their appetite for "sinister wheeler-dealing" buoys them up as they brag loudly about their wickedness and congratulate themselves "on being as bad as you can get."

114. Roth, Cecil, ed. **Anglo-Jewish Letters (1158-1917).** London: The Soncino Press, 1938, pp. 304-09.

Includes the text, with no notes, of Mrs. Davis's two letters to Dickens about Fagin and Riah and his replies. See XIII. 78 and 79.

115. ____. "**Oliver Twist:** A Revision." TLS, 3 August 1951, 485.

Contends that "the full story" of Dickens's revisions to the novel is more complicated than Lane (XIII. 97) suggests. In the opening paragraph of Chapter 10, for example, an examination of the manuscript reveals that Dickens carefully scratched out "old gentleman" and substituted the word "Jew."

Roth also questions Dickens's assertion of verisimilitude when he told Mrs. Davis that Jews invariably were receivers of stolen property (XIII. 78). "I have come across instances of Jewish 'fences' in the early nineteenth century," writes Roth, "but still have to trace the Jewish prototype of Fagin's educational institution."

116. **Rubin, Abba.** "The Anti-Semitism of Charles Dickens: A Re-Examination." University of Portland Review, 31 (Spring 1979), 22-37.

Contributes usefully to the discussion of Fagin by making a sensible distinction between the novel's anti-Semitism and the author's attitude to Jews. Rubin finds **Oliver Twist** a powerfully anti-Semitic novel in its effects because Dickens makes Fagin's villainy inseparable from his Jewishness, uses the word "Jew" as an opprobrious epithet, and bases Fagin on literary stereotypes portraying Jews as "ugly, snivelling, greedy, cunning and suspicious, treacherous and revoltingly humble coward[s]." Fagin, he concludes, is a typically Jewish villain, whose anti-Semitic effect many Dickens admirers have denied because, loving his works, they have blinded themselves to the author's personal failing.

Can we justly ascribe the book's attitudes to Dickens? One passage in **Oliver Twist** makes Rubin qualify the supposition that the novel's hostility to Jews originates with the author. Referring to Chapter 52, in which the narrator describes the "Venerable men of his own persuasion" scorned by Fagin as he awaits his execution, Rubin writes: it is unlikely that an anti-Semite could write those lines." Rubin takes seriously Dickens's "unequivocal denial of anti-Semitism" in his response to Mrs. Davis (XIII. 78) and argues that, clearly, Dickens did not wish to be considered as an enemy of Jews. Rubin finds Dickens's intended "philo-semitic portrait" of Riah in Our Mutual Friend ineffective and unconvincing but recognizes that the flawed character originated in an impulse to make amends. "It is very likely," he concludes, "that Dickens was not a selfconscious anti-Semite."

117. Schneider, Rebecca. **Bibliography of Jewish Life in the Fiction of America and England.** Albany: New York State Library School, 1916, p. 16.

Lists **Oliver Twist** and describes Fagin as "one of the most prejudiced pictures of the Jew in fiction and one of the most repulsive."

118. Shillman, Bernard. "Legends of the Jew in English Literature." The Jewish Chronicle, suppl., 25 (January 1933), vi-viii. Reprinted in The Reflex, 9 (1939), 17-24.

Comments briefly on Dickens's portrayal of Jews in **Oliver Twist** and **Our Mutual Friend** as he surveys the depiction of Jews in English literature from the fourteenth to the nineteenth century.

119. Sokolsky, George E. **We Jews.** New York: Doubleday, Doran, 1935, pp. 25-28.

Comments on Dickens's hatred for Jews evident in both the portrait of Fagin and in the references to Jews in The Life of Our Lord (XIV. 7). In **Life of Our Lord**, writes Sokolsky, Dickens lets his hostility "go full force," citing the "stirring" picture of the crucifixion as evidence. "As long as such a book ... is read by children," he states, "so long will anti-Semitism be prevalent throughout the world."

120. Stone, Harry. "Dickens and the Jews." VS, 2 (March 1959), 223-52.

Stone vigorously rebuts Lane's analysis of Fagin and offers instead of Lane's contention that Dickens saw his villain wholly in archetypal terms (XIII. 96) an extensive and persuasive examination of the evolution of the novelist's attitudes to Jews. Stone sees Oliver Twist as the product of an anti-Semitic era and finds in Dickens's characterization "careless prejudice" and anti-Jewish sentiment typical of the age. Stone also comments that the pejorative allusions to Jews in Dickens's fiction from Sketches by Boz to Dombey and Son, the vicious articles about Jews that appeared in Bentley's Miscellany under Dickens's editorship (1837-39), and the references to Jews in his letters as sly, grasping, and picturesque all indicate Dickens's apparent insensitivity. Oliver Twist, concludes Stone, "was the work of an author who accepted and reflected the anti-Semitism of his milieu."
     During the next thirty years, attitudes toward Jews in Victorian England changed as Jews gradually won increasing civil and religious liberty and a greater degree of social acceptance. This development, Stone argues, appears in Dickens's work. Antagonism to the Jew in his fiction begins to decrease; under Dickens's editorship, Household Words published articles about Jews which were factual and neutral (XIV. 7), unlike the pieces appearing in Bentley's Miscellany. Stone sees the same moderation continue in All the Year Round See XIV. 7 for titles.
     Perhaps the most dramatic change of attitude occurred in Dickens's private life when in 1860 he sold Tavistock House, his London residence, to James P. Davis and his wife, Eliza. At first, Dickens's letters about Davis, a Jewish banker, contained snide references to the buyer as "a Jew Money-Lender," whom Dickens would never trust "until he has paid his money." But three years after the sale, Eliza Davis forced Dickens to rethink what he had previously written about Jews. As a result of her criticism (XIII. 78), Dickens, writes Stone, decided "to strike a blow for the Jews" in Our Mutual Friend (1864-65). Stone sees Riah, the good Jew of the novel, "as a measure of Dickens' conversion"; he also argues that Dickens's revisions to Oliver Twist reflect a similar gesture (II. 15). The silent excisions of "the Jew," argues Stone, "were one more way station in his journey; his voluntary emendations demonstrate again that intellectually at least he had come to understand and regret a prejudice more typical of an earlier day.... [B]y 1854 and Our Mutual Friend. ... he was urging forward the Victorian advance toward toleration." For a slightly expanded version of this essay, see Stone's "From Fagin to Riah: Jews and the Victorian Novel," Midstream, 6 (1960), 21-37.

121. [Thackeray, W.M.]. "Horae Catnachianae." Fraser's Magazine (X. 3), pp. 407-24.

Thackeray, a relentless but principled opponent of gallows fiction, attacked Fagin, despite his admiration for this character, because he thought Dickens ignored the rough facts of the life of one such as he and made his fence too attractive. "Dickens's Jew," wrote Thackeray, "is one of the cleverest actors that ever appeared on the stage; but, like a favourite actor, the Jew is always making points to tickle the ears of the audience. We laugh at his jokes, because we are a party to them, as it were, and receive at every fresh epigram a knowing wink from the old man's eye, which lets us into the whole secret." Such a presentation, Thackeray argued, undercut Dickens's seriousness. "Fagin is only a clever portrait, with some of the artist's mannerism--a mask, from behind which somebody is uttering bitterest epigrams, not an immortal man, like the celebrated Jonathan Wild" of Henry Fielding.

122. Thundyil, Zacharias. "Dickens, Fagin, and Critics." Thought:
     A Weekly Review of Politics & the Arts, 27 (16 February 1974), 15-17.

Summarizes briefly and sometimes confusingly the positions of Lane (XIII. 96), Stone (XIII. 120), Johnson (XIII. 92), and Marcus (XIII. 101). Thundyil states his own view about Dickens's anti-Semitism as follows: "I think the problem ... may be dropped with Dickens's own testimony on record," which, for him, appears definitively stated in the answer Johnson quotes Dickens as giving in 1854 to the Westminster Jewish Free School when the novelist was invited to the school's anniversary dinner. "I know of no reason that the Jews can have for regarding me as 'inimical' to them. On the contrary, I believe, I do my part towards the assertion of their civil and religious liberty, and in my Child's History of England [(XIV. 7)] I have expressed a strong abhorence of their persecution in old times."

123. Tobias, J.J. "Ikey Solomons--a real life Fagin." The Dickensian, 65
     (September 1969), 171-75.

Tobias provides a brief outline of the life of Isaac Solomons (?1785-1850), a notorious London criminal, pickpocket, and large-scale fence on whom Dickens ostensibly modelled Fagin. Tobias rebuts this suggestion first made by Pugh (XIII. 110) and repeated by Lane (XIII. 96) and Collins (XII. 60). No physical or biographical resemblance exist between Solomons and Fagin; Forster, in his discussion of Dickens's use of original people for characters, makes no reference to Solomons in his Life of Charles Dickens (Life, VI, vii); similarly, Dickens himself, when he rejected Mrs. Eliza Davis's charge of anti-Semitism (XIII. 78), ignored Solomons despite his claim of verisimilitude for Fagin. Tobias concludes that "no positive evidence" exists to support the connection: "We shall never know with certainty, but I suggest that there is no foundation for the claim that Dickens based Fagin on Ikey Solomons."

124. ____. "The Life and Exploits of Ikey Solomons." The
     Listener, 81 (3 April 1969), pp. 462-63.

A brief version of XIII. 123 and 125.

125. ____. Prince of Fences: The Life and Crimes of Ikey Solomons.
     London: Vallentine, Mitchell, 1974, passim.

A biography of a professional receiver of stolen goods in the early nineteenth century, whose notoriety earned him the nickname Tobias incorporates in his title. Tobias states that many fences regarded the training of young boys as their principal occupation and offers his view that Dickens's picture of Fagin "was in essence true." Tobias ends by reprinting his earlier essay (XIII. 124) in which he rebuts the claims of those who argue that Dickens uses Solomons as a model for Fagin.

126. Veen, H.R.S. van der. "The Early Eighteenth Century Prose-
     Writers." In his **Jewish Characters in Eighteenth Century English
     Fiction and Drama.** Groningen-Batavia, 1935; rpt. [New York]: KTAV
     Publishing House, Inc., 1973, pp. 99-116.

Assesses Fielding's possible contribution to **Oliver Twist** and suggests
that his **Enquiry** (XVI. 9) may provide "a clue to the origin of Fagin." Fielding
spoke of the Jews as receivers of stolen goods, referred to the trade in stolen
handkerchiefs, and lamented the impunity with which fences trained young
thieves in eighteenth-century London. For these reasons, van der Veen
concludes, Fielding's treatise on the increase of robbers more than probably
influenced "the conception of Fagin and his surroundings." At the same time,
van der Veen believes that Dickens exaggerated the extent to which fences
were "almost invariably" Jews, cf. Modder (XIII. 103), as the novelist
explained to Mrs. Davis (XIII. 78), and thinks that Fielding's statement
represents a more nearly accurate assessment. "Among the Jews," wrote
Fielding in 1751, "who live in a certain part of the city, there have been, and
perhaps still are, some notable dealers in this way."
     van der Veen notes that his theory about Fagin does not exclude Landa's
contention (XIII. 94) that Dickens drew on Ikey Solomons and the character
Barney Fence, a Jew in W.T. Moncrieff's **Van Dieman's Land** (XIII. 142). In
fact, van der Veen faults Landa for not pointing to Barney at The Three
Cripples as further evidence of Moncrieff's influence. He also points out that
Landa fails to notice how the names Ikey and Solomon occur in "A Passage in
the Life of Mr. Watkins Tottle," **Sketches by Boz** (1836), where Dickens
portrays Ikey as the factotum of Solomon Jacobs, a bailiff who runs a
sponging house. van der Veen notes Maria Edgeworth's "The Good Aunt,"
Moral Tales (1801), as another source from which Dickens may have borrowed
(XIII. 135). Elsewhere, van der Veen concludes that "The picture which the
average eighteenth-century author drew of the Israelites" made "an almost
indelible impression" on Edgeworth, Scott, Dickens, and Reade, who could not
disengage themselves from the anti-Semitic example of earlier plays and
novels about Jews, whose influence on those authors "has never perhaps been
fully realized."

127. Zatlin, Linda Gertner. The **Nineteenth-Century Anglo-Jewish
     Novel.** Boston: G.K. Hall, 1981, passim.

Includes comments on **Oliver Twist** in her survey of the work of fifteen
Anglo-Jewish novelists active between 1840 and 1900. Zatlin sees Fagin as
typical of the negative stereotyping Jewish writers tried to counter. In his
presentation of Fagin as an evil man, she argues, Dickens establishes Fagin's
affinity with the mercantile and criminal Jew popularized by English
dramatists, invests him with full Satanic powers, and also presents him as a
classic scapegoat. As such, Dickens transfers to Fagin blame for society's ills
and then removes him at the end of the novel in an act of "ritual cleansing."

LITERARY PARALLELS, SOURCES, AND INFLUENCES

128. Allen, Walter. The **English Novel: A Short Critical History.** New
     York: E.P. Dutton, 1954, pp. 164-67.

Contains a few brief though suggestive hints of an affinity in attitude and
humor between Dickens and Marryat. Allen finds some resemblance

between Peter Simple and David Copperfield, two young boys who share a similar innocent wonderment at and acceptance of a hostile adult world, and sees in Peter Smallbones of Snarleyyow (XIII. 141) a hero who has "obvious affinities with Dickens's oppressed and friendless waifs." But one goes too far, Allen thinks, to represent Smallbones as a prototype of Oliver because Snarleyyow appeared the year Dickens began Oliver Twist (although chs. 1-40 of Snarleyyow were published serially in The Metropolitan Magazine from January 1836 to June 1837). Allen also refers to Marryat's reformed prostitute, Nancy, calling her appearance "one of the earliest ... in fiction of a stock character in the nineteenth-century novel from Dickens to Gissing." See also Collins (XII. 60) and Lindsay (XII. 138), who also connect Marryat's Nancy with Dickens's figure.

129. Atherton, J.S. "Shem as 'Artful Dodger'?" A Wake Newslitter, NS 9 (October 1972), 99.

Notes a possible reference to Fagin's lament over the loss of the Dodger (ch. 43) in Joyce's Finnegans Wake (173, 27).

130. Bennett, Agnes Maria. The Beggar Girl and her Benefactors. 7 vols. London: William Lane, 1797.

A foundling story in vogue during Dickens's childhood which Colby (XII. 59) cites as seminal "in its mixture of philanthropy with picaresque adventure," doing much, Colby thinks, to fix in the minds of early nineteenth-century readers "the stereotypes of the outcast waif and benevolent gentleman." Dickens's writings contain no direct reference to this novel, but Colby notes that Dickens knew the genre well enough to laugh at the popularity of such tales in his digression on fathers in "Astley's," Sketches by Boz.

131. Blatchford, Robert. "On Realism." In his My Favourite Books. London: The Clarion Press, n.d., pp. 222-53.

Draws attention to parallels and differences between Josh Perrott and Fagin in an essay designed to qualify the extravagant claims made by some critics for Arthur Morrison's A Child of the Jago (XIII. 143) on its publication in 1896. Blatchford points out that Victorian novels abound in examples of realistic writing, many of which he finds superior to Morrison's. Think of the attempts of Josh Perrott to escape from the police, he suggests, read the attempted burglary, the murder, and Sikes's efforts to escape over the roof in Oliver Twist, "and tell me what you think of the French critic's claim that a new school of fiction has been founded by Mr. Morrison." As further proof of Dickens's superiority, Blatchford compares the reflections of Fagin in court with Morrison's presentation of Perrott also on trial for murder. He finds the latter's passage "very good" but pronounces it inferior to the one in Oliver Twist because Josh Perrott "scarcely thinks of death at all," while Dickens portrays Fagin obsessed with the thought of the gallows, a response Blatchford finds more convincing based on his own reaction to being "in great peril."

132. Brownlow, John. Hans Sloane: A Tale Illustrating the History of the Foundling Hospital. London: F. Warr, 1831. 147 pp.

Colby (XII. 59) argues that Brownlow's novel, "with its lurid intrigue joined to sentimental humanitarianism," was a more significant influence on Oliver Twist than the author's name and his real-life career as an employee of London's Foundling Hospital in Guildford Street, near Dickens's first home in Doughty Street. Colby finds in the novel "the germ of the much deplored Monks' plot of Oliver Twist" in the amulet tied around the baby's neck by its mother containing her miniature portrait. Brownlow's plot also includes a wicked uncle who wants Hans Sloane removed in order to circumvent Hans's claim on some property the uncle covets, a denouement similar to Dickens's, and a moral atmosphere characterized by the author's faith in human benevolence and divine providence. Colby notes that the British Museum copy of the novel is the only one he has ever seen.

133. Carlyle, Thomas. **Sartor Resartus: The Life and Opinions of Herr Teufelsdroch.** [1833-34]; rpt. in Vol. I of **Collected Works.** London: Chapman and Hall, n.d.

Scholars unanimously affirm Carlyle's impact on Dickens's later novels but they prove less united about the possible contribution of **Sartor Resartus** to **Oliver Twist.** The serial publication of Carlyle's first major work in **Fraser's Magazine** (1833-34) and Dickens's familiarity with periodical literature provide a case for influence on first sight, allowing Marcus (XII. 146) and Colby (XII. 59) to argue for direct connections between the two authors concerning their agreement about the power of dress to determine status, their scorn for Utilitarians and political economists, and their allegorical imaginations. At the same time, other aspects of Carlyle's social philosophy are broad enough for Dickens to have formulated similar notions independently, knowing perhaps nothing of Carlyle's work until after he wrote **Oliver Twist.** In this respect, Oddie's (XII. 157) assessment proves the more cautious, especially his admonition that "influence" is easier to assert than to ascertain. But see F. S. Schwarzbach, "Dickens and Carlyle: A Note on an Early Influence." **The Dickensian,** 73 (September 1977), 149-53.

134. Crabbe, George. "Letter XXII. The Poor of the Borough. Peter Grimes." In his **The Borough.** 1810; rpt. in Vol. IV of **Life and Poems of the Rev. George Crabbe.** London: John Murray, 1834, pp. 39-53.

Noted by Baker (XII. 25) and Lindsay (XII. 138) as a possible influence on **Oliver Twist,** who see in Peter Grimes some resemblance to Bill Sikes. Grimes, a solitary and morose fisherman, obtains in succession three parish boys from a London workhouse. Each, in turn, is severely ill-treated and dies in Grimes's employ, after which Grimes becomes an alienated outcast shunned by the townspeople. Eventually Grimes dies, untouched by pity and without shame for his misdeeds, although Crabbe conveys some sense of guilt in the man's tormented visions of the spirit of his father and the ghosts of the dead boys. Cf. also Williams (XII. 18).

135. Edgeworth, Maria. "The Good Aunt." In her **Moral Tales.** London, 1810; rpt. in Vol. I of **Tales and Novels.** The Longford Edition; rpt. New York: AMS Press, 1967, pp. 144-220.

A deliberately didactic story written to affirm the importance of a judicious early education. Edgeworth makes her point by juxtaposing Charles Howard, an upright orphan reared by his kind and sympathetic aunt, and Augustus Holloway, the son of a wealthy alderman. The two boys clash at

school, where Howard befriends a lonely Creole underling, Oliver, whom
Holloway bullies and makes his fag but relinquishes after several fights with
Howard. The presence of Aaron Carat, a Jewish jeweller and receiver of
stolen goods, superficial parallels between the two Olivers, and the recovery
of some missing jewels lead Rosenberg (XIII. 112) and van der Veen (XIII. 126)
to surmise that Dickens knew the story and assimilated elements of it into
Oliver Twist.

136. Gay, John. **The Beggar's Opera.** London, 1728; rpt. Ed. Peter Elfed
      Lewis. Edinburgh: Oliver & Boyd, 1973. 143 pp.

An important Newgate work which precedes Fielding's efforts in this
direction (X. 1) and one which makes similar connections between the
criminal activities of the underworld and the fashionable vices of the rich. In
his 1841 Preface (II. 10), Dickens argues that Gay glamorizes the life of
Macheath and his friends and so undermines his "witty satire on society" in a
self-serving attempt to save Oliver Twist from similar charges, made by those
who apparently refused to admit a serious purpose to works featuring whores
and criminals. Despite Dickens's disclaimer, The Beggar's Opera remains an
important forerunner of satirical works which, as Forster notes (XII. 7), set
forth the low "to pull down the false pretensions of the high."

137. Harbage, Alfred. "Shakespeare and the Early Dickens." In Shakes-
      peare: Aspects of Influence. Ed. G[wynne] B[lakemore] Evans.
      Harvard English Studies, 7. Cambridge, Mass.: Harvard Univ. Press,
      1967, pp. 109-34.

Harbage writes gracefully and intelligently about Dickens's introduction
to Shakespeare during his early years, estimating that by the 1840's he was
familiar with more than twenty plays. The essay makes no attempt to
inventory all the allusions Dickens made to the dramatist in his early writings
but hazards perceptive guesses about the nature of Dickens's indebtedness and
the distinction between what Dickens took and what he learned. He also
comments on the significance of Dickens's admiration for Shakespeare: "No
one is better qualified to recognize literary genius than a literary genius. To
grant to a Dickens (or a Shakespeare) a great imagination but no ideas, or a
great capacity to write but little capacity to read, is to say (as an abacus
might say to a computer) that the mind of a genius is not so remarkable after
all."
    Writing of references to Shakespeare in Oliver Twist, Harbage notes how
the portrait of Sikes draws on Dickens's news report of an actual London
gangster arrested for a lethal attack upon his trull, "The Hospital Patient"
(XIV. 1), and on recollections from the tragedies, when Dickens's imagination
turns to the murder of Nancy. Besides the reference to Othello, V, ii, 7,
about putting out the light noted by Senelick (XII. 182), Harbage points out
how Fagin steps momentarily into Iago's buskins when the former says of his
plot, which leads to Nancy's death, "I have it all. The means are ready, and
shall be set to work" (ch. 47; cf. Othello, I, iii, 397). Harbage also detects in
Sikes's cry, "Wot do they keep such ugly things above the ground for?--Who's
that knocking?" (ch. 50), when he is haunted by Nancy's ghost, an echo of
Macbeth's injunction to Banquo's spirit, "Avaunt, and quit my sight! Let the
earth hide thee!" (III, iv, 93). As an example of perhaps a less conscious
process of absorption, Harbage thinks unlikely the appearance of the slightly
archaic phrase "houseless wretches" in Oliver Twist Chapter 5 without
Shakespeare's "naked wretches and houseless heads" in King Lear

(III, iv, 28). Finally, he notes Dickens's use of the line "There is some soul of goodness in things evil" (Henry V, IV, i, 4) as a running head in Chapter 16 of the 1867 edition of Oliver Twist.

138. Hofland, Barbara. **Elizabeth and Her Three Beggar Boys.** London: n.p., [1830?].

Colby (XII. 59) calls this a "fiction-sermon" that attaches the foundling tale to the social agitation that preceded the enactment of the New Poor Law. Elements of the book also prepare us for Oliver Twist in other ways: the author shows parish boys preserved from sickness and starvation in the workhouse and saved from criminal careers; links, through contrasts, individuals from the top and bottom of society; and introduces a mean and avaricious parish beadle and his shrewish wife.

139. Hugo, Victor-Marie. **Le Dernier Jour d'un condamne.** Paris: Gosselin, 1829.

Hugo's indictment of capital punishment from the perspective of the condemned man, who recounts his last five weeks in the notorious prison of Bicetre on the outskirts of Paris. Hugo ignores the prisoner's unspecified crime but concentrates instead on the victim's psychological state, as his terror increases as days inexorably fade away before the final preparations for his execution commence.

No English translation of Hugo's book appeared until 1840, although the French text received considerable attention in the British periodical press, where Dickens may have learned about the tale. Alternatively, he may have had sufficient knowledge of French to have read the original, or perhaps he learned about it from George Hogarth, who worked for the **Morning Chronicle** when Dickens first met him. Among Dickens's contemporaries to have connected Hugo's work with "A Visit to Newgate" and **Oliver Twist** are George Hogarth and Elizabeth Barrett Browning. See Hogarth's review of **Sketches by Boz** in the **Morning Chronicle** of 11 February 1836 and Elizabeth Barrett's comment to Mary Russell Mitford on 27 November 1842. "And have you observed what I have observed," she wrote, "... that Charles Dickens had meditated deeply and not without advantage upon Victor Hugo,--and that some of his finest things, (all for instance of the Jew's condemnation-hours in Oliver Twist) are taken from Victor Hugo, .. "Les derniers jours d'un condamne' [sic] and **passim?"** See **Elizabeth Barrett to Miss Mitford,** ed. Betty Miller (London: John Murray, 1954), p. 147. For a list of reviews of Hugo's tale, see Hollingsworth (V. 17), p. 240 n. 72. See also Sucksmith (XIII. 146), and Kenneth W. Hooker, **The Fortunes of Victor Hugo in England** (New York: Columbia Univ. Press, 1938), p. 25.

140. James, Henry. "Julia Bride." In **Novels and Tales of Henry James.** Vol. XVII. New York: Charles Scribner's, 1909, p. 529.

Describes the heroine of his story and a former suitor fully at ease together "quite as if they had been Nancy and the Artful Dodger, or some nefarious pair of that sort, talking things over in the manner of Oliver Twist."

141. Marryat, Frederick. **Snarleyyow; or, The Dog Fiend.** London, 1837; rpt. London: J.M. Dent, 1906.

A loosely constructed adventure story centered around the farcical attempts of Mr. Vanslyperken, a naval lieutenant, to murder his cabin boy and the latter's retaliatory attacks on his master's vicious dog, Snarleyyow. Marryat sets his narrative in 1699 against a background of Jacobite plots to oust William III. Peter Smallbones, the ill-treated and wretched youth serving Vanslyperken, bears some slight resemblance to Oliver, while Snarleyyow, his canine enemy, possibly suggested Sikes's Bull's-eye. Collins (XII. 60) and Lindsay (XII. 138) suggest that Mrs. Corbet, nee Nancy Dawson, a repentant prostitute now decently married to a smuggler, provided the germ of Dickens's Nancy. Marryat based his character on an historic Portsmouth woman in the reign of William III, not on her celebrated namesake, Nancy Dawson (1730-67), the dancer who made her professional reputation performing the hornpipe in Gay's **Beggar's Opera**. For Dickens and Marryat, see also XIII. 128, and Donald Hawes's essay, "Marryat and Dickens: A Personal and Literary Relationship," DSA, 2 (1972), 39-68.

142. Moncrieff, William Thomas. **Van Dieman's Land; or, Tasmania in 1818.** A Drama in Four Acts. Dicks Standard Drama n. 914. n.p., n.p., [1830].

A melodrama of approximately three hours duration portraying life among the early settlers of Tasmania. Moncrieff's Ikey Solomons appears briefly as one of a group of transported convicts now employed by a landowner on his hemp plantation. Landa (XIII. 94), Rosenberg (XIII. 112), and van der Veen (XIII. 126) point to Ikey Solomons as an example of the stereotypical stage Jew--a former fence from Rosemary Lane, London, complete with a foreign accent--who possibly contributed to Dickens's notions about Jews when he created Fagin.

143. Morrison, Arthur. **A Child of the Jago.** London, 1896; rpt. London: MacGibbon & Kee, 1969. 208 pp.

A powerful tale of London slum life which illustrates Morrison's sense of the impossibility of escape from a vicious and corrupt environment. Unlike Oliver, whom the novel's protagonist superficially resembles, Dicky Perrott fails to escape from the clutches of Aaron Weech, a scheming fence bearing some likeness to Fagin. Other aspects of the novel apparently indebted to **Oliver Twist** include a scene in which Dicky flees from the crowd shouting "Stop thief!" and the murder of Weech by Dicky's father, Josh, whose final moments before his execution faintly suggest Fagin's last night alive. See also Blatchford (XIII. 131).

144. Penner, Talbot. "Dickens: An Early Influence." The **Dickensian,** 64 (September 1968), 157-62.

Penner reprints two vividly written police reports which appeared in both **The Morning Chronicle** and the **Times** on 3 January 1834. One includes an account of an amusing confrontation between the Lord Mayor and two street-wise youths accused of stealing fish; the other refers to a Negro and his son who trained young children to steal and put them to work. Penner speculates that John Wight (a former sub-editor or manager of the **Morning Herald** and author of **Mornings at Bow Street,** 1824, and **More Mornings at Bow Street,** 1827) might be the author. He also suggests that Wight's fresh and lively manner of conveying the idiosyncracies of Cockney and the speech of the criminal classes, together with the fact that Cruikshank illustrated both books, signify the existence of a style and tradition familiar to Dickens and one that served as a model for scenes in **Oliver Twist.**

145. Steig, Michael. "The Whitewashing of Inspector Bucket: Origins and Parallels." **Papers of the Michigan Academy of Science, Arts, and Letters,** 50 (1965), 575-84.

Argues for a lack of consistency in the portrayal of Bucket, whom Dickens admires for his spirited competence but criticizes as a "grotesque representative of the law." Bucket's admirable qualities, Steig suggests, have much in common with Sam Weller, the Artful Dodger, and Quilp, figures Steig finds "inimical to the forces of respectability, law, and authority." As outsiders, these three present no problems when they defy the social order, but their mastery of situations and cockiness create difficulties in Bucket, whose main role, Steig thinks, is to illustrate yet another dimension of the law's parasitic nature in **Bleak House.**

146. Sucksmith, Harvey Peter. "The Secret of Immediacy: Dickens' Debt to the Tale of Terror in **Blackwood's.**" NCF, 26 (September 1971), 145-57.

Argues that immediacy of concrete detail partially explains Dickens's remarkable narrative power and suggests an alternative to W.C. Phillip's thesis (XII. 166) that Dickens developed as "a sensation novelist" by following the Gothic tale through Byron and Bulwer. A more likely influence, counters Sucksmith, is the series of early tales published in **Blackwood's Edinburgh Magazine** between 1821 and 1837. While no conclusive evidence exists to show that Dickens read **Blackwood's,** Sucksmith presents a plausible argument for the influence of these tales on early Dickens. Part of his case rests on an analysis of Henry Thomson's "Le Revenant" (XIII. 147), which Sucksmith thinks is a more likely influence on "A Visit to Newgate" (XIV. 1) than Hugo's **Dernier Jour d'un condamne** (XIII. 139). Sucksmith admits that similarities occur between Dickens and Hugo when "gifted imaginations contemplate the same subject," but he finds more persuasive the parallels between "Le Revenant" and "A Visit to Newgate" and Chapter 52 of **Oliver Twist.** Each considers the theme of escape from the gallows, uses chiming clocks to create suspense, and employs a similar narrative method to convey the terrified mind of an accused prisoner in Newgate alternating between close attention to his trial and his inability to concentrate on the legal proceedings. Each also shows the prisoner in his cell, where the condemned man gives way to a violent protest as his mind oscillates between a dreamlike state and a morbid rehearsal of the sensations of being hanged.

147. [Thomson, Henry]. "Le Revenant." **Blackwood's Edinburgh Magazine,** 21 (April 1827), 409-16.

Sucksmith (XIII. 146) suggests this fictional piece as a possible influence on "A Visit to Newgate" (XIV. 1) and Chapter 52 of **Oliver Twist,** in which Dickens describes Fagin in the condemned cell. "Le Revenant" describes in first person narrative the unusual experience of one who survives his own death by hanging. Scenes include the narrator's state of mind during his trial, an account of his wandering thoughts as he tries to imagine the details of his execution, and his awareness of the clock in St. Sepulchre's chiming away the hours. The story also presents in realistic detail the sequence of events attending a condemned man's last hours.

148. Vernon, Sally. "Oliver Twist and The Golden Farmer." DSN, 8
     (September 1977), 65-68.

Vernon points out a number of elements the novel shares with The Golden
Farmer. The latter, a play by Benjamin Webster first performed at the
Coburg Theatre in December 1832, includes a young London thief called
Jemmy Twitcher, whose dress, twitch, and saucy manner resemble those of
the Artful Dodger. At the same time, other aspects of Twitcher appear in
different characters. After an attempted robbery, Twitcher's companions
abandon him when he catches his breeches on the spikes of a fence; later,
Twitcher, like Noah Claypole, turns informer. The plot of The Golden Farmer
intersperses crime and comic scenes; the play ends in the condemned cell.
Furthermore, resemblances between Webster's play and Gay's The Beggar's
Opera, which continued to be performed in the early nineteenth century,
suggest to Vernon a theatrical tradition of underworld characters and mixed
tones undoubtedly known to Dickens. Vernon makes no case for specific
influences but plausibly offers The Golden Farmer as one of many sources
Dickens vastly altered to fit his own conception of the novel.

149. Zambrano, Ana Laura. "Dickens and the Rise of Dramatic Realism:
     The Problem of Social Reform." Silliman Journal, 21 (First Quarter,
     1974), 66-82.

Comments on Dickens's interest in social reform in Oliver Twist and
notes how, despite his use of realism to that end, the novel shares many of the
artificial and contrived features one associates with the domestic melodramas
popular in the years predating the novel's composition. Zambrano presents no
sustained case for the influence of specific plays but notes motifs common to
Oliver Twist and popular domestic melodramas by Thomas Holcroft, Charles
Maturin, Douglas Jerrold, John B. Buckstone, and others.

TOPOGRAPHICAL STUDIES

150. Chancellor, E. Beresford. "Oliver Twist." In his The London of
     Charles Dickens. London, 1924; rpt. New York: Folcroft Library
     Editions, 1978, pp. 109-24.

A useful topographical reference book illustrating Chancellor's observation that almost every Dickens novel "has a pronounced London motif." The
particular London of Oliver Twist, he argues, belongs to the London of the
last years of William IV, a point he documents thoroughly by showing how
many of the novel's topographical settings belong to a London lost even to
Victorian readers. The Clerkenwell improvements in the 1890's obliterated
Fagin's haunt in Field Lane, much of the Saffron Hill area (Oliver Twist, ch.
26) was cleared away in 1867 when the Holborn Viaduct was constructed, and
the Bow Street Runners ceased soon after Sir Robert Peel's Police Act of
1829. Chancellor also points out that the London Bridge in the novel was the
structure designed by John Rennie and opened by William IV on 1 August 1831.

151. Dexter, Walter. "Rose Maylie's House at Chertsey." The Dickensian,
     1 (July 1905), 176-77.

Suggests that the detached villa surrounded by a wall about a quarter of a
mile from Guilford Street, Chertsey, served as Dickens's model for the
Maylies' house. Cf. Parr (XIII. 156).

152. Fitzgerald, Percy. "Pyecroft House, of **Oliver Twist**." The Magazine of Art, 18 (1895), 432-34.

Fitzgerald indulges himself in one of "the fancies of the day," tracing out some of the scenes in Dickens's novels. One "beautiful summer's Sunday," Fitzgerald visited Chertsey in search of Pyecroft House, the fine old Georgian brick mansion Dickens selected for the fictional home of Mrs. Maylie. Pictures accompany the text, including an exterior and interior sketch of the type of window Sikes forced Oliver to enter.

153. Harper, Charles G. "In the Track of Bill Sikes." The London Magazine, February 1906, pp. 45-48.

Retraces the route taken by Sikes and Oliver from Bethnal Green, through Shoreditch, and across London as they strike west towards Brentford, Hampton, and Chertsey, their eventual destination. Harper identifies the pub at Hampton where Sikes and Oliver ate dinner by the kitchen fire as probably the former Red Lion.

154. Kitton, Frederic G. "Notes Chiefly Topographical." In 1900 Rochester Edition (II. 22), pp. 503-23.

Particularly informative, as the title suggests, concerning buildings, streets, and the routes travelled by characters in the novel. Kitton also includes useful annotations about social customs, occupations, slang, and institutions, making these notes helpful to modern readers but far from comprehensive. See also Hill (XII. 104).

155. Manners-Smith, C. "In the Footsteps of Bill Sikes." Cassell's Magazine, March 1900, pp. 431-37.

A descriptive essay which comments on the topographical details of Sikes's journey from Bethnal Green to Chertsey in Chapter 21 and points out the main landmarks he passes as he travels to the scene of the attempted robbery. Several illustrations accompany the text.

156. Parr, John Sayce. "With Bill Sikes to Chertsey." The Dickensian, 1 (October 1905), 260-63.

Retraces the route of Sikes and Oliver as they travel from Bethnal Green to Chertsey, noting how the landscape has changed but also remarking on Dickens's "astonishing" topographical accuracy. Local legend, writes Parr, identifies the Maylies' house as Pycroft House, a redbrick, eighteenth-century mansion standing at the end of Pycroft Street, Chertsey. Cf. Dexter (XIII. 151).

157. Rimmer, Alfred. "**Oliver Twist**." In his **About England with Dickens.** 1883; rev. ed. London: Chatto and Windus, 1898, pp. 133-59.

Ample summary of the various journeys undertaken by different characters in the novel with close attention to topographical and geographical detail, treating each fictional expedition as if it really did happen.

158. Roffey, William J. "Facts About 'Fagin's Land.'" The Dickensian, 21 (July 1925), 158-59.

Responds to Williams (XIII. 161) by pointing out that St. Alban's church may stand on the site of a former thieves' kitchen but not on the location of the notorious den where pickpockets, burglars, and other criminals were trained by master thieves. This kitchen, Roffey claims, used to be in the center of Fox Court, nearby, and was demolished in 1884 or later. Dickens refers to Fox Court, he thinks, in "On Duty with Inspector Field," when the police visit Bark's house in "the innermost recesses of the worst part of London."

159. Sack, O. [pseud. B.W. Matz]. "Jacob's Island and Bill Sikes's House." The Dickensian, 14 (July 1918), 184-86.

Identifies a house in Metcalf Court, Bermondsey, as the one Dickens selected for Sikes's retreat and death. The association of this particular house with the novel was so strong, Sack notes, that a London County Council plan of Jacob's Island (dated 5 April 1855) officially designated the building as "Bill Sikes's House." Later in the twentieth century an official in Bermondsey Town Hall discovered the plan, thus prompting a series of articles in The Southwark and Bermondsey Record about Dickens's connections with the district. H.W. Jackson, the author of the pieces, later mounted them in a scrapbook and presented them to Dickens House, where the scrapbook currently resides.

160. Southton, J.Y. "Bill Sikes's Hampton Tavern." The Dickensian, 7 (May 1911), 128-30.

Notes how Dickens's description in Bentley's Miscellany and in early texts of the novel clearly and distinctly locates the Hampton public house where Sikes takes Oliver to eat before they set out for Chertsey to rob the Maylies' house. (See Clarendon Oliver Twist, ch. 21, pp. 137-38.) In 1846 Dickens dropped the sentences describing the inn's setting, thus accounting, Southton thinks, for the difficulty some readers have had identifying the tavern and finding a real location for the place where Sikes and Oliver ordered dinner by the kitchen fire.

161. Williams, A. "Facts about 'Fagin's Land.'" The Dickensian, 21 (April 1925), 80-81.

Corrects an assumption, evidently current among some journalists at the time, that the church of St. Alban's, between Brook Street, Holborn, and Baldwin's Gardens, stands on the former site of Fagin's den. Field Lane, Williams points out, represents the location Dickens specified in Chapter 8 when he first describes the house to which the Dodger took Oliver. Cf. Roffey (XIII. 158).

STUDY GUIDES

162. Brown, Suzanne. Notes on Oliver Twist. York Notes, no. 101. Harlow: Longman, 1981. 88 pp.

A recent study guide fully representative of this species of academic spider, which caters to ignorant students in much the way that the father of Grandfather Smallweed spun webs to catch unwary flies and retired into holes "until they were trapped." Brown provides three main parts to her study: a biographical introduction, chapter-by-chapter summaries of the novel, and "Commentary." The first lacks distinction except for its misinformation (John Dickens drew a Custom House salary while in jail). The second provides enough detail to fool the lazy reader into believing that he has read the book, and the third serves up some prepackaged ideas about crime, coincidence, and characters. Like the facts put away into the mind of the son, Smallweed's grandfather, these academic cribs begin as grubs, remain as grubs, and rarely breed a single butterfly.

163. **Dickens: Oliver Twist: Notes.** Toronto: Coles Publishing Company, 1980. 128 pp.

The strength of these Notes lies in the chapter summaries, which combine a detailed condensation of each chapter together with a commentary discussing stylistic devices, social issues, and other points of interest about the novel. Shorter chapters are frequently paired; longer ones receive individual attention. The publishers credit no individual with these chapter summaries, although when Cliffs Notes (XIII. 166) published the identical text in 1965, Harry Kaste appeared as the author of the commentaries.

The supporting Notes provided by the Coles Editorial Board include an informative explanation of the treatment of the poor in Victorian England and a brief history of the Poor Laws since Elizabeth I. The Notes also refer to the Poor Law Commission of 1832, describe its recommendations, and outline clearly the basis of Dickens's disagreement with the policies adopted by the British Government in 1834.

Against this contribution we must offset a weak biographical introduction to Dickens's life. The writers usefully focus on Dickens's early years but present their information amidst hazy statements about his class background and curious factual errors. We are misinformed about the size of Mrs. John Dickens's family; we are told that the district of Chatham and Rochester "forms the setting for part of every novel [Dickens] ever wrote." Treating literary matters, the Editorial Board fares equally badly, passing off casual judgments about the novel's construction drawn from inferences about the speed of Dickens's composition and the story's appearance as a serial. The editors also hide behind the passive voice to tell us that it seems that Dickens was so absorbed in Bill Sikes that he identified himself with the murderer; when they appear, they state boldly that "We know that Dickens originally intended" to let Rose Maylie die. She survives, they continue, because the novelist was so distressed by the death of Mary Hogarth that he decided to keep her fictional counterpart alive, inventing as a consequence "the elaborate genealogical tangle" between Rose and Oliver. The authors devote several pages to character summaries, which they preface with the injunction to the reader to study the characters as part of the novel's total design and not simply to label them flat or round. Review questions, discussion topics, and a short annotated bibliography conclude the book.

164. Handley, Graham. **Brodie's Notes on Charles Dickens's Oliver Twist.** Pan Study Aids. London: Pan Books, 1978. 88 pp.

Unique among study aids for succeeding in the professed aim of stimulating thought about the novel and not providing a substitute for lazy or reluctant readers. Handley achieves this goal by reading the novel closely himself and by showing others how to respond intelligently to Dickens's language and to the novel's construction. In a short section on style, Handley demonstrates how Dickens controls the narrator's voice, repeatedly shifts his tone, and how dialogue, imagery, and narrative work to convey ideas. Alone among the authors of such guides, Handley defies the hazy assumptions others frequently offer about serialization by sending readers to Tillotson's list of chapter divisions in her Clarendon edition of **Oliver Twist** (II. 48) and asking them to judge the effect of serial installments for themselves. He also offers sound advice of his own by calling attention to Dickens's use of alternating scenes and by making a convincing case for the novel's careful construction.

Students using these Notes will find only brief chapter summaries. "Brownlow brings Monks to his house and Monks is forced into a series of revelations," Handley writes of Chapter 49, unlike the other authors, who devote pages to the unravelling of the novel's main mystifications. In this manner Handley avoids giving readers what they can get for themselves by studying the text and concentrates on the words, phrases, and sentences he lists in bold type. Some of these simply gloss words unfamiliar to contemporary readers, but many entries direct our attention to aspects of Dickens's style and his narrative skill.

In a short section on character, Handley introduces useful critical concepts, helping the reader to understand how characters lead "well-defined lives of their own within the fictional medium" and how they should be judged by that and not by an imperfect sense of "the real." This part also contains sensible comments about how Dickens's unconscious ambivalence towards Fagin led him to reveal an abiding concern with Fagin's humanity "that overshadows [Dickens's] inherent conservatism and over-sentimentalized Christian affiliations." Handley keeps his biographical Introduction short by confining matters to the novelist's early career and by avoiding comments about his personal life. The study ends with thirty review questions.

165. Hanson, John L. **Notes on Dickens's Oliver Twist.** London: Normal Press, 1928.

Cited in Gold's **Centenary Bibliography** (IV. 13) but unavailable for annotation.

166. Kaste, Harry. **Oliver Twist Notes.** Lincoln, Nebraska: Cliffs Notes, 1965. 103 pp.

Presents in a series of brief paragraphs generally accurate information about Dickens's early life, the start of his literary career, and his subsequent pursuits. Kaste recirculates the familiar but erroneous story that the legacy from his mother enabled John Dickens to leave the Marshalsea, where he was imprisoned for debt; he also calls Charles Dickens a free-lance court reporter when the context suggests that he meant a legal reporter attached to Doctors' Commons. Kaste provides a wide interpretation of the novel's historical framework, setting **Oliver Twist** within the context of England's struggle towards parliamentary democracy and the forces of reform at work early in the nineteenth century. His explanation, however, lacks the full treatment Coles Notes gives to the clamor arising over the inadequate provisions for treating England's urban and industrial poor. This guide provides notes on the main characters standard among most of the current guides, a "Critical Introduction," and the lengthy chapter summaries and commentaries reprinted in the Coles Notes booklet (XIII. 163).

167. Mussoff, Lenore. **Charles Dickens: Oliver Twist.** Barnes & Noble Book Notes. New York: Barnes and Noble Inc., n.d. 95 pp.

Substitutes a brief chronological outline for the more familiar narrative of Dickens's life favored by other study aids, but manages within a very short Introduction to offer questionable assertions to the unwary reader. Mussoff endorses without qualification Edmund Wilson's contention that Dickens feverishly pursued "fame and fortune" to compensate for "some of the insecurity and privations of his childhood." She also gives the erroneous impression that John Dickens's imprisonment for debt preceded his son's stint at Warren's and states twice that Mary Hogarth died within a few days of her return from the theatre when in fact she died within a few hours.

In the selected chapter summaries, accurate and detailed information is juxtaposed with useful discussion sections, where Mussoff raises critical issues and comments on aspects of the novel's context. Mussoff, for example, remains the only author of such guides to allude briefly to the disadvantaged life young chimneysweeps led, despite Victorian legislation to improve the conditions of their apprenticeship and work. In the section labelled "Critical Analysis," Mussoff recirculates the cliches about the weaknesses of serial writing and Oliver Twist's lack of structure, writes indifferently about the novel's style, and provides brief character sketches. The guide ends with a desultory sample of "Critical Opinions" selected with no apparent rationale. Mussoff omits any systematic discussion of the novel's historical context, dealing instead with such matters when they occur in the novel.

168. Versfeld, Barbara. **Notes on Charles Dickens's Oliver Twist.** Methuen Notes Study-aid Series. London: Methuen, 1976. 67 pp.

Versfeld provides concise and accurate chapter summaries but little else of much value. The advertised "Textual Notes" prove to be nothing more than occasional glosses of unusual words or terms. And much of the matter surrounding the summaries qualifies as either inaccurate or substantially misleading. For example, Versfeld writes that Dickens was "barely eleven" when he began work at Warren's, claims that John Dickens was sent to the Marshalsea on "at least two occasions," gives 1867 as the date of Dickens's 1841 Introduction (II. 10) to Oliver Twist, and says that he missed only one contribution to **Bentley's Miscellany,** compounding this particular error by calling the journal a weekly, a statement she later repeats.

Making some "General Observations," Versfeld fares equally badly when she writes about the novel's historical background in a short section mired in generalizations of the sort that produce despair. By 1837, she writes, elementary education "had begun to reach the masses," the middle class "were coming into their own," and Dickens, profound neither in politics or philosophy, economics or law, nevertheless "caught the essence of current affairs" and thinking and "subjected it to his own strong set of values, coming out every time in support of the good in terms of the qualitative life."

For the main part, Versfeld avoids overt literary judgments, except for stating that some tragedy is necessary to a tale of such "epic scope" as Oliver Twist, both from an artistic point of view and to give weight to the moral. As one committed to an unspecified but firmly held belief in realism, she predictably attacks Dickens for dealing out some "rather clumsy coincidences." These Notes devote three pages to "Typical Examination Questions," published to help students study Oliver Twist for Examination purposes.

169. Wertheim, Lee Hilles. **Oliver Twist: Chapter Notes and Criticism.** A Study Master Publication. New York: American R.D. Corporation, 1965. 76 pp.

A prefatory Note by the publisher promises the reader "accurate information about the author, his times, and his work," an assurance more frequently disregarded than honored by Wertheim. The author misstates the number of children born to Mrs. John Dickens, presents falsely the order in which Dickens began work at Warren's and his father entered the Marshalsea prison, and gives the impression that Charles and Catherine lived in a cottage in the country after their marriage in 1836.

When Wertheim turns to literary matters in her critical Appraisal, the novel fares equally badly. We are told that the plot is one of the book's "fundamental weak points," that its construction is "so artificial, so riddled with coincidence" that we feel Dickens could not possibly have expected his readers to believe it, and that the jerky narrative originates in the requirements of serial publication. Perhaps most remarkable of all is Wertheim's contention that Graham Greene called Dickens a Manichean, that is "a member of a dualistic Persian religion." Such statements cannot be redeemed by the guide's accurate and concise chapter summaries, but one can find some relief in the fact that the part of most interest to students is the least offensive.

170. Winans, Edward. **Charles Dickens' Oliver Twist.** Monarch Notes. New York: Simon and Schuster, 1966. 102 pp.

Provides a serviceable summary of the plot, chapter-by-chapter, complete with detailed and accurate information. But the introductory and critical sections illustrate weaknesses common to almost all of these study aids. Winans writes that Dickens was forced to work in the blacking warehouse after his father went to prison, states that a small legacy secured John Dickens's release from the Marshalsea, calls Dickens an apprentice to an attorney rather than an office boy, and claims that Dickens worked as a reporter for the Court of Chancery.

On the positive side, Winans is the only author of such guides who indicates the serial divisions of **Oliver Twist**; still, despite listing correctly the dates of the monthly installments, he writes elsewhere that **Oliver Twist** began in January 1837 instead of February. Winans devotes several pages to the description and analysis of the novel's characters and a brief section to essay questions and model answers, of which the following may be cited as typical: "What plot weaknesses are probably the result of serial publication?" Imagine a paragraph about the horrors of cliff-hanging and the infelicities of manipulating readers by switching narratives and you will have the answer.

PART III
BACKGROUND AND RELATED STUDIES

XIV. RELATED WRITINGS OF DICKENS.

1. Dickens, Charles. **Sketches by Boz.** First and Second Series. 3 Vols. London: John Macrone, 1836.

As Tillotson suggests (XII. 201), "A number of the sketches have what is essentially the same background material" as **Oliver Twist** and show how Dickens explored areas of experience in 1834-36 similar to those he examined in the novel. To read the following essays, she argues, "is to enter the London of Fagin and Sikes" and experience a world that belongs to both the sketches and **Oliver Twist.** In "The Old Bailey" (**Morning Chronicle,** 23 October 1834), which Dickens later retitled "Criminal Courts," we find a prototype of the Artful Dodger in the sketch of a juvenile pickpocket spiritedly defending himself in court. "Gin Shops" (**Evening Chronicle,** 19 February 1835) and "Seven Dials" (**Bell's Life in London,** 27 September 1835) introduce middle-class readers to sights and scenes of violence that prove, the narrator thinks, astonishing to all but "a regular Londoner," who knows the obscure passages and wretched inhabitants of the slums near "the great thoroughfares ... of this mighty city." Two other sketches--"The Pawnbroker's Shop" (**Evening Chronicle,** 30 June 1835), and "The Hospital Patient" (**Carlton Chronicle,** 6 August 1836)--convey some documentary sense of the consequences of street life for young women, who, battered and abused, progress rapidly towards the last two stages of life: "the hospital and the grave." In the last sketch, in particular, which recounts the final moments of "a fine young woman" who dies after being savagely beaten by her lover, we see a germ of Nancy's loyalty to Sikes in the woman's defense of her companion, whom the police have brought to her hospital bed hoping that she could identify him as her assailant. "The Streets--Morning" (**Evening Chronicle,** 21 July 1835) suggests an early draft of the memorable description of London awakening in Chapter 21 of **Oliver Twist,** while "The Parish" (**Evening Chronicle,** 28 February 1835) contrasts the poor's fear of the workhouse with the power of the beadle, who, imposing in his uniform, acts insensitively to the very people whose needs his office is supposed to address. Finally, "A Visit to Newgate" (**Sketches by Boz,** First Series, 1836) describes Dickens's response to the prison, especially his imaginative portrayal of the feelings of the condemned man. Collins (XII. 60) calls this "a magnificent **tour de force,**" but inferior to "Fagin's Last Night Alive." This chapter, which Dickens wrote three years later, Collins thinks, surpasses the earlier one because it is less hurried, more insightful about the criminal's mind, and more willing to comment on the penal and judicial processes. Denying that the sketch and Chapter 52 of **Oliver Twist** reveal the morbid Dickens "indulging his own suppressed aggressive instincts," Collins argues tha the descriptions speak for "Everyman." How many people, "innocent of crime or criminal intent," would not speculate about the feelings of men spending their last night on earth "in this cell?"

2. ———. "The Paradise at Tooting," "The Tooting Farm," "A Recorder's Charge," and "The Verdict for Drouet." **The Examiner,** 20 and 27 January 1849, 3 March 1849, and 21 April 1849.

Four articles Dickens contributed anonymously to the front page of **The**

Examiner in 1849. B.W. Matz identified and reprinted all except "A
Recorder's Charge" in his Miscellaneous Papers, I (London, 1909). In Victorian
Studies, 12 (December 1968), 27-44, A.W.C. Brice and K.J. Fielding reprint
this one piece Matz overlooked and append a useful summary of Dickens's role
in "the Tooting Disaster."

The four essays provide an important factual counterpart to the baby
"farming" system Dickens satirized in Oliver Twist Chapter 2, where the
narrator describes briefly Oliver's first eight years under "the parental
superintendence" of Mrs. Mann. Bartholomew Drouet, who operated a much
larger farm than did Mrs. Mann, supervised over 1,300 children in his Juvenile
Pauper Asylum at Tooting, about eight miles southwest of London. For 4s. 6d.
a week he promised to keep and to clothe poor children sent to him by various
parishes and Poor Law unions in London. Drouet, however, so inadequately
fulfilled his obligations that 150 children died of cholera within a few weeks
of the first death from the disease at the establishment on 29 December
1848. In January 1849 the Morning Chronicle and the Times reported on the
conditions of Drouet's asylum; shortly afterwards he was charged with
manslaughter after a coroner's inquest but was subsequently acquitted on 16
April 1849.

Dickens's heavy sarcasm in the first article about "this Elysium" in
Tooting recalls the indignation apparent in the opening chapters of Oliver
Twist. Later essays satirize the law's indifference to the brutal conditions in
which the children lived and warn his readers of the consequences of failing to
act when abuses such as Drouet permitted gave further evidence to Chartists
and others disturbing the public peace of the state's indifference to the poor
and "swell[ed] the mischief [in England] to an extent that is incalculable."

3.   ———.   Household Words. A Weekly Journal, Vols. 1-19 (1 March
      1850-28 May 1859).

This journal, which Dickens founded, edited, and frequently contributed
to, provided a useful forum for his subsequent thoughts about the importance
of meeting the educational needs of poor children as he continued to comment
on topics he first explored in Oliver Twist. Typically his essays affirm the
superiority of practical and secular measures over religious indoctrination and
state the importance of training children so that they could learn to live
usefully and productively. Among the relevant essays in Household Words are:
Dickens "A Walk in a Workhouse," 25 May 1850; Dickens "A December Vision,"
14 December 1850; W.H. Wills and Dickens, "Small Beginnings," 5 April 1851;
H. Morley and Dickens, "Boys to Mend," 11 September 1852. See also: A.
Mackay, "The Devil's Acre," 22 June 1850; W.H. Wills, "The Power of Small
Beginnings," 20 July 1850; and H. Morley, "Tilling the Devil's Acre," 13 June
1857, all three of which refer to aspects of Miss Coutts's charitable work in
the parish of Westminster. Further relevant essays include: Taylor and W.H.
Wills, "A Day in Pauper Palace," 13 July 1850; F.K. Hunt, "London Pauper
Children," 31 August 1850; F.K. Hunt, "What a London Curate Can Do If He
Tries," 16 November 1850; J. Hannay, "Lambs to be Fed," 30 August 1851; H.
Morley, "Little Red Working-Coat," 27 December 1851; H. Morley, "How
Charity Begins at Home, near Hamburg," 17 January 1852; W.B. Jerrold,
"Anybody's Child," 4 February 1854; H. Morley and G.E. Jewsbury,
"Instructive Comparisons," 29 September 1855; and Mrs. Hill, "Ragged Robin,"
17 May 1856.

Also of use is Dickens's private correspondence with Angela Burdett
Coutts, where the reader can trace Dickens's growing joint efforts to
help outcast children receive some practical training and an elementary

education. See **Pilgrim Letters,** III, 554, 561, 562-64, 565, and 572. For Dickens's account of a later visit to Field Lane Ragged School, the first he visited, see his "A Sleep to Startle Us," **Household Words,** 13 March 1852, where he notes the various improvements made since 1843.

Useful secondary sources by Philip Collins include: **Dickens's Periodicals: Articles on Education,** Vaughan College Papers, No. 3 (Leicester, 1957); "Dickens and Ragged Schools," **The Dickensian,** 55 (1959), 94-109; and Chapter 4 of Collins's **Dickens and Education** (XII. 61).

4.   _____. **Our Mutual Friend.** Published in 19 as 20 Parts. London: Chapman and Hall, May 1864-November 1865.

Dickens reconsidered the problem of administering humanely to the poor in **Our Mutual Friend,** where he uses Betty Higden's repugnance for "the House" and her fear of "the appointed evader[s] of the public trust" to suggest the extent of England's failure to evolve a dignified policy for relieving those in distress. Rather than end her life bricked up in a Union workhouse and forced to accept the vindictive charity propounded by the Poor Law Board, Betty Higden proudly resolves to master her own fate. For Betty this means setting forth late in life as an itinerant worker, getting her own bread by knitting and selling "many little things." In this manner she cheats the parish from claiming her and frustrates the designs of its officers, those "Cruel Jacks" who dodge and drive "the decent poor" to death. As the narrator observes, life in "a great blank barren Union House" more nearly resembles life in a county jail, so much more penal is the former in its remoteness, its dietary, its lodgings, and its tending of the sick.

Dickens drives home his indignation in a series of ironic apostrophes to "My Lords and Gentlemen and Honourable Boards." He also uses Mr. Podsnap for a similar purpose, attacking through this well-fed champion of England's greatness the complacency of those who deny the widespread misery about them. When forced to acknowledge the truth of the Registrar General's reports that each week people starved to death in London's streets, Mr. Podsnap replied: "Then it was their own fault."

In a postscript completed after the novel's serial publication, Dickens restated his position so that no one could confuse his view of the Poor Law with Mr. Podsnap's. "I believe that there has been in England, since the days of the STUARTS, no law so often infamously administered, no law so often so openly violated, no law habitually so ill-supervised," he wrote. "In the majority of the shameful cases of disease and death from destitution, that shock the Public and disgrace the country, the illegality is quite equal to the inhumanity--and known language can say no more of their lawlessness."

For additional references to the Poor Laws in Dickens's journals, see H. Morley, "Parish Poor in London," **Household Words,** 5 June 1858; "A Sum in Fair Division," **All the Year Round,** 7 May 1859; Dickens "The Uncommercial Traveller" [Wapping Workhouse], **All the Year Round,** 18 February 1860; "A New Chamber of Horrors," 2 March 1861; and "Little Pauper Boarders," **All the Year Round,** 28 August 1869.

5.   _____. "An Appeal to Fallen Women." [1847] 4 pp.

An anonymous pamphlet printed on pale gray paper and distributed to prostitutes in the streets of London and given to them by the police after arrest.

Commentators have frequently remarked on Dickens's charitable interest in prostitutes, whom he first portrayed sympathetically in **Sketches by**

Boz (XIV. 1) and **Oliver Twist,** several years before he cooperated with Miss Coutts to open an asylum for the rehabilitation of young women in November 1847. For Dickens's long letters to Miss Coutts about the principles and policies of Urania Cottage, see **Pilgrim,** IV, 552-56, 587-89, 603, 629-30, and V, 177-79, 181-88, and passim. Later, Dickens wrote an account of the asylum, "Home for Homeless Women," which he published in **Household Words,** 23 April 1853. In it, he outlined the practical but "cheerful and hopeful" assumptions upon which the home was founded and furnished statistics about its success, noting that in 1855 of the fifty-seven girls who had left, thirty had done well in Australia or elsewhere, seven of them having also married.

Some further sense of Dickens's personal response to the problem of seduced and abandoned women may be inferred from Forster's account of Dickens's kindness as a London juror in 1840 to a young woman accused of infanticide (Forster, II, viii). See also **Pilgrim,** II, 9-10, and n., and Dickens's own reference to the event in his essay "The Uncommercial Traveller," **All the Year Round,** 16 May 1853, which is reprinted as "Some Recollections of Mortality," in **The Uncommercial Traveller.** Arthur A. Adrian writes about a comparable episode in New York, when in 1868 Dickens gave a chambermaid sixty dollars so that she could escape to California with her illegitimate child and start life afresh there. See **Georgina Hogarth and The Dickens Circle** (London: Oxford Univ. Press, 1957), p. 114. Dickens's efforts to help Caroline Maynard Thompson also provide further insight into his practical philanthropic attempts to rescue young women. A full account of the case, which involves a young woman who turned to prostitution solely in order to support herself after she was abandoned by the man she lived with, appears in Edward F. Payne and Henry H. Harper's **The Charity of Charles Dickens: His Interest in the Home for Fallen Women and a History of the Strange Case of Caroline Maynard Thompson** (Boston: The Bibliophile Society, 1929).

6. _____. "Letters on Social Questions. Capital Punishment." **Daily News** [London], 23 and 28 February 1846, and 9, 13, and 16 March 1846.

As Chapter 52 of **Oliver Twist** makes clear, the narrator finds something hideous about the "apparatus of death," affecting, in his view, both the condemned and those who attended the brutal spectacle of a public execution. First drawn to a consideration of the ethics of executing criminals in **Sketches by Boz** (XIV. 1), Dickens returned to the subject in fiction (**Oliver Twist, Barnaby Rudge, Little Dorrit,** and **The Mystery of Edwin Drood**) and also contributed polemical essays about the death penalty first to the **Daily News** in 1846 and then later to the **Times** in 1849. For the text of Dickens's first two letters to the **Daily News** of 23 and 28 February 1846, see, respectively, TLS, 12 August 1965, p. 704, and **The Literature of the Law: An Anthology of Great Writing in and About the Law,** selected and introduced by Louis Blom-Cooper (New York: Macmillan, 1965), pp. 382-87. The three letters of March 1846 appear in Matz's **Miscellaneous Papers,** I, 30-51; Dickens's letters to the Editor of the **Times** published on 14 and 19 November 1849 can be found in **Pilgrim,** V, 644-45, and 651-54.

In the thirty or so years spanning Dickens's career as a novelist and journalist we can detect three principal phases of his writing about capital punishment. He began by advocating "the total abolition of the Punishment of Death," as he declared in his last contribution to the **Daily News.** Three years later, the double execution of the Mannings on 13 November 1849 and the rowdy behavior of the 30,000 spectators outside Horsemonger Lane Gaol, London, where the Mannings were hanged, prompted Dickens to reformulate his views. Private executions, he now concluded in his letters in the Times, represented a more realistic position than the one he had urged in 1846 because the state of "the general mind," he thought, did not admit the advocacy of the total abolition of the death penalty. By 1864 Dickens revised his views again, coming to the conclusion that one had to accept the necessity of ridding society of those who shed blood because there was nothing one could do with "the Savages of Civilization" (N, III, 378).

Dickens discusses various aspects of capital punishment, the psychology of criminals, and prison discipline in the following Household Words essays: "Perfect Felicity. In a Bird's Eye View," 6 April 1850; "Pet Prisoners," 27 April 1850; "The Finishing Schoolmaster," 17 May 1851; "The Demeanour of Murderers," 14 June 1856; "The Murdered Person," 11 October 1856; and "Murderous Extremes," 3 January 1856. See also in Household Words: W.H. Wills, "The Great Penal Experiments," 8 June 1850; G.A. Sala, "Open-Air Entertainments," 8 May 1852; and E.S. Dixon, "To Hang or Not to Hang," 4 August 1855.

Relevant essays in All the Year Round by Dickens include "Five New Points of Criminal Law," 24 September 1859; "The Ruffian," 10 October 1868; and "On an Amateur Beat," 27 February 1869. The last two can also be found in The Uncommercial Traveller. Other unsigned essays dealing with various aspects of crime in All the Year Round include "Of Right Mind," 22 September 1860; "Incorrigible Rogues," 8 February 1862; "M.D. and M.A.D.," 22 February 1862; "Small-Beer Chronicles" [Transportation], 11 October 1862; [Garotting], 6 December 1862; and [The Convict System], 10 January 1863; "Home-Office Inspiration," 24 January 1863; "Street Terrors," 14 February 1863; "Fat Convicts," 25 March 1865; "Rough Doings," 23 November 1867; "Now," 15 August 1868; and "Injured Innocents," 3 April 1869.

Alec W. Brice and K.J. Fielding make the case for adding three anonymous pieces in The Examiner ("False Reliance," 2 June 1849, p. 338; "Rush's Conviction," 7 April 1849, p. 210; and "Capital Punishment," 5 May 1849, p. 273), to Dickens's contribution to the journal in "On Murder and Detection--New Articles by Dickens," Dickens Studies, 5 (May 1969), 45-61.

7.   Readers interested in Dickens's references to Jews outside Oliver Twist may wish to consider other fictional sources, which include comments about Jews in Sketches by Boz, The Pickwick Papers (chs. 2, 35, and 46), The Old Curiosity Shop, (ch. 21), Martin Chuzzlewit (ch. 13), Dombey and Son (ch. 59), David Copperfield (ch. 54), Bleak House (ch. 47), Hard Times (I, 7), Little Dorrit (II, 26), Great Expectations (ch. 20), and Our Mutual Friend. Dickens also refers to Jews in his The Life of Our Lord (1846-49) and A Child's History of England (1851-53), Chapters 13-16. Furthermore, during his editorship of Bentley's Miscellany, Dickens published "Bonomye the Usurer" and "The Professor of Toledo," two unpleasant instances of racial stereotyping. Later, as the editor of Household Words and All the Year Round, Dickens published many articles by various contributors which refer either directly or indirectly to Jews and express opinions and attitudes he evidently shared. Among the articles published in Household Words are: G.W. Jewsbury, "The Young Jew of Tunis," 27 April 1850; Dickens, "A Detective Police Party" [ii], 10 August 1850; Soutar, Keys, and H. Morley, "The Jews in China," 2 August 1851; R.H. Horne, "A Penitent Confession," 2 August 1851; G.A. Sala, "Phases of 'Public' Life," 16 October 1852; E.S. Dixon, "The Phalansterian Menagerie," 17 September 1853; E. Lynn, "Passing Faces," 14 April 1855; Dickens, "A Slight Depreciation of the Currency," 3 November 1855; G.E. Jewsbury, "The Seven Victims of Mittelbron," 22 March 1856; and G. Lumley, "Jews in Rome," 20 November 1858. For similar contributions to All the Year Round, see: "A

Trial of Jewry," 19 December 1863; "On Public Service," 12 March 1864; "How I Discounted My Bill," 8 July 1865; and "Mr. Whelks in the East," 21 July 1866, which contains an apology reminiscent of Dickens's attempt in **Our Mutual Friend** to make up for his presentation of Fagin. "The character of the Jews has too long been wronged by Christian communities," wrote the author of "Mr. Whelks in the East." "We take old-clothes men and thieves--there being none such among Christians, of course--as the types of an ancient, refined, and charitable people." See also: "The Purchase System. A Tale," 17 October 1868, and "Credit Moblier in Discredit," 27 June 1868.

XV. THE POOR LAWS

1.   Checkland, S.G., and E.O.A. Checkland, eds. **The Poor Law Report of**
       1834. Pelican Classics. Harmondsworth, Middlesex: Penguin Books,
       1974, passim.

An accessible modern edition of the 1834 Poor Law Report. The
Checklands reprint the text of 1905, which was revised by H.M. Stationary
Office, and modernize only the punctuation and remove all footnotes to the
Appendices. The Appendices ran to thirteen folio volumes and contained all
the documentary evidence gathered by the nine Commissioners and their
twenty-six Assistants. This edition also includes a short introduction by the
Checklands in which they comment on the new assumptions of
self-responsibility and individualism underlying the Report, discuss the
pressures that led up to the Royal Commission of 1832-34, and note how
subsequent historians have differed in their interpretations of what they call
"one of the classic documents of Western social history." The Checklands
identify two main sets of opponents: historians in the liberal intellectual
tradition, who see the treatment of the poor as "part of the continuous
adjustment of society in response to changing conditions," and Marxists, who
take the poor as an index to illustrate the internal contradictions of
capitalism, victims of a defective society who fail to realize their potential
because of their class. Much remains to be done, the editors suggest, in the
field of computer studies when historians of the Poor Law submit their work
to "the new discipline of mechanized quantification."

2.   Edsall, Nicholas C. **The Anti-Poor Law Movement 1834-44.** Man-
       chester: Manchester Univ. Press, 1971, passim.

Documents in detail the sustained but uncoordinated opposition to the
work of the Poor Law Commissioners and their efforts to enforce the
principles laid down by the 1834 Act. Edsall examines how discontent erupted
first as local disturbances in southern England and then spread to the North,
where the work of various leaders, different local conditions, and, later, the
depression of 1837 intensified the hostility to the efforts of the
Commissioners. This book usefully conveys the extent of the resistance to
the New Poor Law and provides a necessary corrective to those literary
historians who tend to assume that **Oliver Twist** singlehandedly stirred up
public opinion about conditions in the workhouse. Neither Dickens nor any
other novelist receives a single mention in this study.

3.   Engel, Monroe. "The Social and Political Issues." In his **Maturity of**
       Dickens (XII. 75), pp. 49-59.

Comments succinctly on the changes in the Poor Law of 1834 and
discusses Dickens's response to it in a chapter examining the development of
Dickens's political ideas. Engel calls attention to the fact that the Act of
1834 created an administration but failed to lay down as policy the Malthusian
and Benthamite principles implicit in the Commissioners' Report of 1834 (XV.
1). That document, Engel suggests, if strictly adhered to, would have

given the able-bodied pauper one choice: work or starve. Because public sentiments opposed the implementation of such a policy, those responsible for drawing up the Act of 1834 saw that able-bodied paupers did not starve, but they also made sure that individuals were not treated too well. In Dickens's view, this response combined inefficiency with a basic lack of charity, a criticism he makes in Oliver Twist and repeats in all the subsequent attacks on the Poor Law in Household Words, All the Year Round, and Our Mutual Friend.

4.   Longmate, Norman. The Workhouse. London: Maurice Temple Smith, 1974, passim.

Conveys a vivid sense of the actual conditions of life in the Victorian workhouse by drawing on a wide range of contemporary records and reports. Through striking anecdotes and details, Longmate shows how the system inflicted its deliberately harsh policies on children, unmarried mothers, the able, the infirm, the sick and the aged alike, as the various authorities worked to enforce the inhuman policy of "less eligibility." The book's focus on the workhouse as a nineteenth-century institution supplies much to interest the student of Dickens, although Longmate pays little attention to the novelist, even in Chapter 9, in which he surveys the range of opposition the 1834 Act provoked. In that same chapter, Longmate repeats the familiar error that Dickens dealt only with conditions prior to 1834, when, in fact, the cruelty and the unsympathetic response to the causes of poverty Dickens criticized typify the outlook of those who ran the system for much of the century. In a short Appendix, Richard Wildman contributes a useful note about workhouse buildings, whose prison-like architecture embodied the principles of threat and deterrence the New Poor Law sought to inculcate.

5.   Lubenow, William C. "Central and Local Government I: The Victorian Poor Law, 1834-1847." In his The Politics of Government Growth: Early Victorian Attitudes Toward State Intervention, 1833-1848. Newton Abbot: David & Charles, 1971, pp. 30-68.

Lubenow focuses on early Victorian Poor Law legislation to illustrate the positions taken by both advocates and opponents of the 1834 Act. His discussion of the opponents makes no reference to the humanitarian objections Dickens and other novelists raised to the 1834 legislation, but his analysis of the various political groups arguing against the innovations introduced by the Act provides a useful perspective on Dickens's views. Many strident voices joined the public opposition to Poor Law legislation outside Parliament; and some of the loudest, as Lubenow demonstrates, issued from the Tory Radicals, reactionaries who idealized England's agricultural past and closed their eyes to its industrial future. With these voices of unreason Dickens had nothing in common except determined opposition to the principles of the Commissioners.

6.   Nicholls, Sir George. A History of the English Poor Law. 3 vols. London 1898; rpt. New York: G.P. Putnam's, 1898, passim.

A massive history of the English Poor Law by one of the Poor Law Commissioners of 1834. Nicholl's first two volumes (London, 1854) summarize legislation from the time of the Tudors, comment in detail on the Report of the Royal Commission of 1832-34, and extend his history as far as 1853. Volume three (London, 1898), the work of Thomas Mackay,

supplements rather than continues Nicholls's work. Because Nicholls wrote
with reserve in the last portion of his narrative, Mackay gives a fuller account
of the passage of the 1834 Act and the opposition it provoked.

7.   Rose, Michael E. **The English Poor Law 1780-1930.** Newton Abbot:
      David & Charles, 1971, passim.

A collection of documents--drawn mainly from official sources--assem-
bled by Rose to illustrate what happened when the Old Poor Law confronted
the massive social and economic changes set in motion by the Industrial
Revolution. Rose concentrates on the last two decades of the eighteenth
century and follows the major developments in Victorian England, showing
how critics responded to the 1834 Poor Law, how the new Law operated, and
how the system was continually under modification throughout the century,
until massive unemployment in the 1930's eventually brought about the
collapse of the old practice of local control. This occurred in 1929 when
Parliament passed the Local Government Act, wnich dismantled the local
administrative structure of the nineteenth-century Poor Law and handed the
responsibilities of the old board of guardians to county and borough councils.

8.   Stone, Marcus. "Some Recollections of Dickens." **The Dickensian,** 6
      (1910), 61-64.

Stone, Dickens's illustrator for **Our Mutual Friend,** speaks of long walks
he took with the novelist around Rochester. On one occasion walking through
Cooling with Dickens, he recounts, the novelist referred to an incident that
had provided him with material for his account of the pauper's funeral in
Oliver Twist, Chapter 5. "You see that church?" Dickens remarked. "That is
where I saw the pauper's funeral in **Oliver Twist** exactly as it is written in the
book. Here is something more interesting still. A few months after I
received a letter from the clergyman who behaved in an unseemly way on that
occasion, asking me whether I conceived it possible that such a thing could
ever occur. I wrote back to him and said, 'Thou art the man.'" Cf. Cohen
(XIII. 6), who cites the incident of the pauper's funeral as an example of the
frequent connections between William Hogarth's engravings and Dickens's
writings. Cohen calls "The Harlot's Funeral" in Hogarth's progress "a visual
precursor" of Dickens's scene in **Oliver Twist.**

9.   Trevelyan, G.M. **English Social History: A Survey of Six Centuries
      Chaucer to Queen Victoria.** 1944; rpt. London: The Reprint Society,
      1948, passim.

Provides a brief overview of the new Poor Law of 1834 within a broad
historical framework. Trevelyan argues that the three Commissioners
appointed by the Act applied the knife "without anaesthetics" when they tried
to save society from the consequences of the Speenhamland policy established
in 1795 by a group of Berkshire magistrates. Instead of fixing and enforcing a
minimum wage, for which purpose the magistrates originally agreed to meet,
they were persuaded to rule that wages should be supplemented out of parish
rates, so that as the price of bread rose above one shilling a loaf, the dole
rose with it. Trevelyan notes that this "evil system" spread over perhaps half
rural England, pauperizing the employed workman and artificially keeping
wages down. The policy also placed an intolerable burden on the small
independent parishioner, whose taxes supported the poor.
When faced with redressing this problem, members of the 1832 Royal

Commission offered to help the parish taxpayer by giving the able-bodied workman the choice of either entering the workhouse or supporting himself by employment. To discourage people from seeking relief, members of the Commission deliberately proposed making life in the workhouse less attractive than employment in field or factory, rather than increasing people's incentive to work by enforcing a minimum wage. The hardships caused by the adoption of this principle, legalized by the Poor Law Amendment Act of 1834, provoked widespread suffering. At the same time, Trevelyan notes, the three Commissioners charged with implementing the plan, created "a central machine" which, by displacing the old system of local autonomy with a national and centralized bureaucracy, prepared the ground for a more humane philanthropic policy. This solution, writes Trevelyan, was "pure Benthamism," combining local, elective bodies (the board of guardians responsible for each workhouse) with bureaucrats representing the central government, who drew up the rules the local parties administered. "Imperfect and harsh as was the poor law in 1834," Trevelyan concludes, the Act "had been intellectually honest within its limits, and contained the seeds of its own reform."

10.   Webb, Sidney, and Beatrice Webb. **English Local Government: English Poor Law History: Part I The Old Poor Law.** Vol. 7. London: Longmans, Green, 1927, passim.

A survey of three centuries of "Laws relating to the Poor," tracing the evolution of English policy through three centuries. The Webbs begin with the country's earliest repressive statutes, designed to keep the propertyless mass in place; later, they focus on the revolutionary proposal of 1834, which introduces the idea of a central executive authority responsible for administering a national Poor Law. In their narrative, the Webbs note how the early attempts to repress vagrancy gradually broadened to include moderate national efforts to provide for orphans, the sick, and the aged; they also argue that the assimilation of the proletariat into the work force, made possible by the industrial revolution, led to a relaxation of the disciplinary and repressive character of the policies established by the Tudor and Stuart governments. The Allowance system and outdoor relief, typical of the latter part of the eighteenth century, proved too expensive and too local, however, to meet the demands placed on them by the crisis England faced after Waterloo. By 1815 the cost of public relief had risen to unprecedented heights, prompting a chorus of protests that led to the appointment of a Royal Commission in 1832 charged with investigating the workings of the Poor Laws.

11.   ———. **English Local Government: English Poor Law History: Part Two: The Last Hundred Years.** Vol. 8. London: Privately Printed, 1929, passim.

An authoritative and detailed study of the "Principles of 1834," which begins with an examination of the reasons contributing to the changed response to the poor implicit in the Report of the Royal Commission of 1832-34 and in the Poor Law Amendment Act. The Webbs analyze the impact of the new social theories of Jeremy Bentham, whose ideas provided much of the Report's intellectual framework, the positions taken by those who argued against continuing the old system of the dole and outdoor relief, and the main principles recommended to Parliament for adoption. They also comment briefly on the members of the Royal Commission and on the three men appointed as Commissioners in 1834, noting their Benthamite and Malthusian assumptions.

The authors of the Report, the Webbs point out, almost totally ignored the causes of poverty in their determination to prevent able-bodied workers from seeking relief. Had they gathered statistics about who the paupers were, the Webbs think, instead of seeking proof of the abuses of the old allowance system, they might have seen what Edwin Chadwick later revealed, that the bulk of paupers were not able-bodied men and their dependents but people incapacitated by old age or laid low by sickness. The Webbs also summarize the reaction of various newspapers to the Report and describe the debate that followed when Parliament passed the Poor Law Amendment Act on 14 August 1834.

12. ____. **English Local Government from the Revolution to the Municipal Corporations Act: The Parish and the County.** Vol. 1. London: Longmans, Green, 1906, passim.

A useful source for those interested in the administrative structure of an English parish up to the time of the 1830's. The Webbs define the parish as "an organ of local obligation" through which the national government and the Established Church sought to arrange such collective regulations and common services as were deemed necessary to the welfare of the state. Responsibility for carrying out these services fell upon various parish officers, of whom the Beadle was one, an archaic servant of the parish traditionally provided with a cocked hat, gold lace, and an official staff. In the eighteenth century, beadles generally worked for their superiors and took over various "menial outdoor duties"; by the time of Dickens's birth, they were more commonly assigned with overseeing the poor and administering relief to those in need of assistance. Such duties, the Webbs note, seem to have been characteristic of beadles in parishes in the Metropolis and the Southern Counties; in the Northern Counties, beadles appear to have served less frequently as parish officers.

13. ____. **English Poor Law Policy.** London: Longmans, Green, 1910, passim.

Analyzes in detail English Poor Law policy in the nineteenth century, tracing the evolution of its principles and practice from 1834 to the Royal Commission of 1905-09. As the Webbs comment, policy in the sense of a coherent and well-defined set of objectives is something of a misnomer when one considers the bewildering accumulation of Statutes, General Orders, Special Orders, Minutes, general reports, and official letters issued by the three Commissioners, the Poor Law Board, and the Local Government Board between 1834 and 1907. During this period, the different central authorities, the Webbs point out, generated a "simply overwhelming" number of directives, a fact worth remembering when one recalls the charges of those who dismiss Dickens's attack on the Poor Law Amendment Act in **Oliver Twist** because he blurred the distinction between conditions before and after the new legislation. The existence of contrary directives, the failure to define key terms exactly, and the Commissioners' inability to introduce, even as late as 1847, their new principles in over one hundred places--all suggest the chaos that evidently prevailed in many parishes throughout England some years after the Act was passed. Hence we should treat with caution the assurances of those who argue that Dickens blunted his criticism of the Poor Law in the opening chapters of the novel by attacking the new principle of a central authority while simultaneously introducing practices consistent with earlier policies before the Poor Laws were amended in 1834.

XVI. HISTORICAL BACKGROUND

1. Antrobus, Edmund Edward. **The Prison and the School.** London: Staunton & Sons, 1853, pp. 27-35.

Comments on the conditions prevailing in London's public lodging houses, "dens of infamy" which provided nightly accommodation for the destitute. Antrobus's special concern lies with the criminal children of the metropolis, for whom these places often served as a surrogate home. Frequently an adult woman presided, cooking for the children, accepting stolen goods in return for food, and harboring the younger ones until they were taught how to steal and trained in crime. In the comments Antrobus (a JP for Middlesex county) quotes from the boys he interviewed, several describe a typical Sunday as one on which they "play cards, dominoes, and pitch half-penny, read Jack Sheppard, Oliver Twist, Martha Willis, and publications of that kind, [and] plan robberies." Conditions in these houses did not begin to improve until the Public Lodging-House Act of 1851, and subsequent additions to it, which gave the metropolitan police power to inspect and visit the dwellings. Antrobus states that by 1854 some 3,300 persons keeping common lodging houses had come under police control. This number, estimated at "rather more than half" of the houses in existence, accommodated nearly 50,000 nightly lodgers.

2. Binny, John. "Thieves and Swindlers." In Henry Mayhew. **London Labour and The London Poor.** London, 1861-62; rpt. London: Frank Cass, 1967, IV, 273 ff.

Provides documentary evidence of the "game" Fagin used to instruct his pupils in the art of picking pockets. Urchins were taught to steal by trainers who suspended a coat on the wall with a bell attached to the garment, from which pupils tried to remove a handkerchief without ringing the bell. Alternatively, the trainer would walk up and down in a room with a handkerchief in the tail of his coat, while the boys learned how to extract it adroitly. Binny also mentions how young boys were employed to enter houses through fanlights and windows. Cf. NECNE (XVI. 18).

3. Bouchier, Jonathan. "Dickens on English Criminal Law." N&Q, 5th Ser., 12 (5 July 1879), 6.

Defends Dickens against the charge by the **Saturday Review** of 21 June 1879 that he hanged Fagin "for no definite offence except that he was one of the villains of the novel" (XVI. 4). In Chapter 50 of **Oliver Twist,** Bouchier notes, Kags observes that if Bolter turns King's evidence, the prosecution will be able to prove Fagin "an accessory before the fact" [of Nancy's murder], thus ensuring that "he'll swing in six days from this." As Bouchier comments, any accessory before the fact in the case of willful murder is "a very definite offender" and one subject to capital punishment, if convicted.

4. "Browning's Dramatic Idylls." **The Saturday Review,** 47 (21 June 1879), 774-75.

A review of Browning's 1897 volume of poems in which the writer complains about the picture of the judicial system in "Ned Bratts," the narrative of a criminal publican and his equally wicked wife. While Dickens hanged Fagin for no definite offence, writes the reviewer, at least he was tried "in due form." Browning, he remonstrates, goes one better and hangs the Bratts "at the discretion of the judge." Cf. Bouchier (XVI. 3), who responds to the reference to Fagin. Writing much later, Harvey (XIII. 20) makes a similar point, arguing that Dickens's vagueness about the legal grounds for Fagin's execution arises from his bad planning rather than from ignorance of the law. Had Dickens intended Fagin to end up in the condemned cell, contends Harvey, "we would expect him to have provided Fagin with some more substantial crime." See also Thackeray (IX. 35), Lucas (XII. 142), and Saintsbury (XII. 178).

5.   Chesney, Kellow. **The Anti-Society: An Account of the Victorian Underworld.** Boston: Gambit, 1970. 398 pp.

Provides an eminently readable account of London's dangerous classes-- "thieves, cheats, bullies, beggars, touts and tarts"--around the middle of the century. Offering "portraiture rather than analysis," Chesney covers topics of interest to readers of **Oliver Twist,** who can learn much about how thieves operated and initiated the young into crime, as well as numerous details about Victorian prostitution, gaming, the sporting underworld, and so on. This survey relies heavily on Parliamentary Reports and on noted Victorian observers like Mayhew (XVI. 16), Binney (XVI. 2), Griffiths (XVI. 11), and Dickens, whose accounts he cites with appropriate acknowledgment. Unfortunately, however, Chesney generally avoids documentation, thus leaving the reader curious about the sources for some of the more arcane details he supplies. The book includes a comprehensive glossary of colloquial and cant words used by the criminal classes.

6.   Colquhoun, Patrick. **A Treatise on the Police of the Metropolis.** 7th ed. London, 1806; rpt. Montclair, New Jersey: Patterson Smith, 1969, passim.

A documentary analysis of London's underworld which corroborates some of the criminal activities detailed in **Oliver Twist.** Colquhoun provides a particularly useful portrait of the receivers of stolen goods, many of whom, he asserts, were Jews, poor German immigrants who turned to peddling, selling second-hand clothes, and dealing in stolen property as one of the few means of livelihood open to those without education or capital. Colquhoun puts the number of German Jews in the metropolis at around 12,000-15,000, estimates the number of active fences at around 3,000, and states that by the middle of the eighteenth century burglars and highwaymen found a ready vent for their plunder "through the extensive connections of the Jew dealer" both in Britain and on the Continent. Although no references to Colquhoun's writings exist in Dickens's letters, he may have known the **Treatise,** a likely piece of reading for one aspiring, as Dickens did, to turn his social knowledge "to good practical account" and serve, like Colquhoun, as a police magistrate (P, III, 570, and IV, 567).

7.   Dickens, Charles. "Metropolitan Sanitary Association," 6 February 1850. In **The Speeches of Charles Dickens.** Ed. K.J. Fielding. Oxford: Clarendon Press, 1960, pp. 104-10.

Seconds a resolution passed at the Association's first public meeting deploring recent deaths in London from "preventable disease." In the course of his remarks, Dickens referred to Jacob's Island, the unsanitary Thames riverside district he describes in Chapter 50 of **Oliver Twist** and the site of London's first fatal cholera cases in 1832 and 1849. Shortly after the meeting, an opponent of sanitary improvement cited Dickens and his fellow speaker, Dr. Blomfield, the Bishop of London, as examples of "misguided and misinformed reformers." Jacob's Island, contended Sir Peter Laurie, "only existed in a work of fiction, written by Mr. Charles Dickens ten years ago." Dickens quickly responded in his Preface to the Cheap Edition of **Oliver Twist**, written in March 1850--see II. 13--where he ridiculed the ignorance of the former Lord Mayor of London and quoted his adversary's foolish comments before the members of Marylebone's parish vestry.

8.   "Fang and Laing Again." The Dickensian, 34 (Spring 1938), 84.

Reproduces a cartoon from **Figaro in London** (13 January 1838), depicting Laing symbolically kicked from office and forced into resignation by the boot of "Public Indignation." Following the picture are extracts from a long article which originally accompanied the sketch, crediting the journal with the magistrate's dismissal. **Figaro in London**, its editors note, frequently promised its readers "unwearied ... exertions" to procure Laing's removal, and they praise themselves for exposing his ferocities "in their true colours" and for forcing the government to act. Laing's expulsion, they conclude, represents "a grand triumph of our honesty and faultless integrity." See also Pugh (XVI. 21).

9.   Fielding, Henry. "Of the Punishment of Receivers of Stolen Goods."
        Sec. 5 of An Enquiry into the Causes of the Late Increase of Robbers
        [1751]. In Legal Writings. Vol. XIII of The Complete Works of Henry
        Fielding. New York: Barnes and Noble, 1967, pp. 76-82.

An authoritative account of London crime in the eighteenth century undoubtedly read by Dickens and possibly an influence on **Oliver Twist**. Fielding takes seriously the receiver's major role in contributing to crime and asserts that if the market for stolen goods could be closed, shoplifting, burglary, and highway robbery would come to "an absolute end." Fielding refers to the reputation Jews had gained by 1751 as notable fences, mentions how pickpockets disposed of stolen handkerchiefs through receivers, and called for an end of the pernicious work of the latter, especially since "many of the younger thieves" plainly appear to have been "taught, encouraged, and employed by the receivers."

10.   Goddard, Henry. "Robbery at the Travellers' Club." In his Memoirs of a
        Bow Street Runner. Introd. by Patrick Pringle. London: Museum
        Press, 1965, pp. 37-43.

Goddard's account of a robbery he investigated on 31 January 1828 provides useful documentary evidence of those "melancholy shades of life" Dickens drew upon in **Oliver Twist** and furnishes several details similar to those in the novel. The principals in Goddard's case include: a notorious Jewish receiver of stolen property, Samuel Solomons, who kept a "fence" in White Lion Street, Seven Dials; an infamous "cracksman," Thomas Samuel White; and his two younger accomplices, who stole seven massive silver candlesticks from the Travellers' Club, Pall Mall. White and the boys entered the Club at 5 am by posing as sweeps sent by a local company to clean the chimneys.

Goddard and some of his associates from Marlborough Street Police Office traced the thieves by acting on two tips. One led to Solomons, who was caught with two of the candlesticks in his possession, the other to Bethnal Green, where White lived with Nance Castle after abandoning his former mistress, from whom the police received the information that led to White's arrest. White fought off five Runners for twenty minutes after they spotted him among a large gang of striking weavers parading the streets of Bethnal Green and carrying banners saying: "Starvation," "The Workhouse," "We are in want of bread," etc. Goddard describes White as "a rough bull neck strong built man, drest in a short jacket." During the fight to subdue him, a sympathetic crowd urged White on with cries of "Rescue, rescue," while Nance threw up her arms and screamed: "They are taking my Sam, don't let them!" The prisoners stood trial at Marlborough Street; a report of their final hearing appears in the Times of 3 April 1827 (3a 4a). White and Solomons were both committed for trial at the Old Bailey. Pringle makes no mention of Solomons' fate; White was sentenced to death but later had his sentence commuted to transportation for life.

11.   Griffiths, Arthur. "Juvenile Depravity." In his The Chronicles of
        Newgate. London: Chapman and Hall, 1884, II, 45-47.

Comments on the magnitude of juvenile crime in the early part of the nineteenth century and attributes "This deplorable depravity" to various causes. Among them Griffiths cites "the artfulness of astute villains--prototypes of old Fagin--who trained" children "in their own devious ways." Griffiths, a former prison inspector and penologist, also describes how children frequented "flash houses," formed gangs, and lived in dens at St. Giles's, Drury Lane, Chick Lane, Saffron Hill, the Borough, and Ratcliff Highway.

12.   Hill, T.W. "Books that Dickens Read--VI." The Dickensian, 45
        (Autumn 1949), 201.

Judges Dickens fairly well read in English history and writes that he was "well read up in police history" early in his career. Hill states his view that Dickens "must have known a lot [about police matters] even before he met Inspector Field" since many documents about crime and social issues formed part of his library before he wrote Bleak House.

13.   Hollingsworth, Keith. Chapters 1-3. In his The Newgate Novel 1830-
        1847 (V. 17), pp. 3-63.

An informative introduction to various historical and social factors contributing to the reading public's growing interest in crime. Hollingsworth attributes some of the attention criminals received to the intense debate arising from the nation's reform of its Bloody Code in the 1820's. Other factors include the popularization of criminal protagonists by the publishers of ballads, the growing space devoted to crime reporting in publications as diverse as the Annual Register and cheap newspapers, and the growth of "Newgate Calendars," collections of criminal biographies that began in 1773 and enjoyed a great vogue through the 1830's. Hollingsworth notes that novelists quickly caught on to the public's taste for crime, and he traces the evolution of the genre from the initially serious Newgate work of Gay, Fielding, Godwin, and Bulwer to that of lesser figures eager to capitalize on a successful vein. Later chapters examine in detail works by Bulwer, Ainsworth, and Dickens (XII. 107). Hollingsworth also includes Thackeray in his survey, the genre's most sustained and determined opponent whose animadversions (X. 2-4, 11, 13, and 16) mark the beginning of a reaction against Newgate fiction which led to its extinction by the next decade. By 1850, Hollingsworth suggests that Britain's legal changes were so great that Bulwer and Dickens addressed themselves "not primarily to the conditions of the law, but to the vicious effect of public executions, to social injustice, and to the psychology of crime."

14.   Kitton, Frederic G. "Oliver Twist." In his The Novels of Charles Dickens: A Bibliography and Sketch (I. 4), pp. 38-39.

Credits Oliver Twist "(indirectly, perhaps)," for contributing to salutary reforms in workhouses and to the formation of institutions for the benefit of waifs and abandoned children like Oliver. Kitton also cites the opinion of Dr. Thomas John Barnardo, a prominent social reformer, whose experience with London orphans testifies to the authenticity of Dickens's depiction of their plight in the novel. "I know him [Oliver] intimately," writes Bernardo later in the century, "by many different names, and I also know Noah Claypole; and Fagin I meet in Houndsditch, Short's Gardens, and Fulwood's Rents. The Artful Dodger was an early capture in Fulwood's Rents. As for Mr. Bumble, he is not dead yet, though I am thankful to say that in many instances the autocratic official has been dismissed from his 'porochial' duties. Whereas poor Oliver Twist was the rule when I caught my first street arab, he is now the exception in the slums. Oliver has come into his rights."

15.   L., A. "Obselescence of the Jury in Criminal Cases." The Law Times, 157 (12 April 1924), 307-08.

A brief survey of the movement in British legal practice to substitute in criminal cases trial by judge for trial by jury. The writer dates this trend from the middle of the eighteenth century, when the growth of numerous "summary offences" transferred jurisdiction to judges and magistrates, mainly in the interests of efficiency. Judges also made use of the related practice of trying offenders for lesser crimes, where appropriate, when such crimes could be tried summarily and processed quickly and with greater certainty of punishment than prevailed with jury trials. In the view of A. L., Dickens documents the preference for proceeding summarily when he portrays Mr. Fang in Chapter 11 making use of the Vagrancy Act (loitering with intent) rather than recommending that Oliver go to trial for a felony. Cf. Squires (XII. 187).

16.   Mayhew, Henry. "Jacob's Island." In Voices of the Poor: Selections from the Morning Chronicle 'Labour and the Poor (1849-1950).' Ed. Anne Humphreys. London: Frank Cass, 1971, pp. 3-5.

Mayhew's brilliant description, originally published on 24 September 1849 in the Morning Chronicle, of the slum to which Dickens refers in Chapter 50 of Oliver Twist. This "Venice of drains," as Mayhew calls the neighborhood where cholera broke out in 1849, consisted of houses built on piles and streets flanked by sewers not canals. The poor endured these conditions, Mayhew explains, because the "small capitalists" who owned the property refused

282 Background and Related Studies

to improve the dwellings, knowing that they were "handy for a man's [water-side] work."

17. "Monthly Commentary: The Dregs of London." New Monthly Magazine, 38 (June 1833), 213-15.

Comments on a shift in emphasis in the reporting and focus of the Morning Chronicle, one that apparently occurred about a year before Dickens joined its staff as a reporter in August 1834. The paper, suggests the author of the Commentary, should "take away its old motto about holding up a mirror of fashion, and exhibiting 'the body of the time, its form and pressure,' from the top of the Court Circular, and place it over the Police Reports." This tendency, the writer argues, shows the country in no very flattering light, but the tales of "domestic broils, quarrels, and drunkenness" in Bow Street court, he thinks, are "a more accurate mirror of the age than the patent [theatre, i.e., Drury Lane] hard by." Similar scenes of domestic violence and debauchery also characterize life in a typical, lower-class London street, of which there are "many hundreds," while nearby is the flash-house--"the snug public [bar] where crimes are concocted and concealed. In such holes as these," the author continues, "also, are the academies of theft, where burglary is taught on scientific principles--where effigies, hung with wires and bells, are put to exemplify the practice of pocket-picking."

18. NECNE. "Fagin-ism in the Sixteenth Century." N&Q, 4th Ser., 11 (29 March 1873), 253.

Cites a passage from Sir Henry Ellis's Original Letters Illustrative of English History (1824-46), in which William Fleetwood, Recorder of London, informs Lord Burghley how young boys in London were trained "to cutt purses"and pick pockets. In a school set up for the purpose, boys were taught how to remove silver from purses without causing specially attached warning bells to jingle when the coins were removed. The writer concludes that Dickens noted this passage when he found it and "turned it to good account" in Oliver Twist. Cf. Binny (XVI. 2).

19. P., W.P.W. "Oliver Twist." N&Q, 5th Ser., 7 (9 June 1877), 446.

Notes an entry in the parish register of Shelford, Nottinghamshire, on 5 January 1563 of "Dorothie Twiste, daughter of Oliver Twiste."

20. Phillips, George Lewis. "Dickens and the Chimney-Sweepers." The Dickensian, 69 (January 1963), 28-44.

A detailed and useful documentary account of the growth of public opposition to the brutality commonly inflicted upon young boys forced to earn a living cleaning chimneys. The practice of using children began during the reign of James I and continued unchecked until 1875, when an Act requiring the licensing of all master sweeps finally put an end to child labor in the flues. Phillips also summarizes Dickens's interest in the young apprentices, noting how in Oliver Twist he created Mr. Gamfield as a figure typical of the brutal and sadistic master sweeps of the times but as one inconsistent, in some respects, with the novel's historical setting. Although Dickens attacks the new Poor Law of August 1834, he portrays Gamfield as more nearly representative of the abuses rampant under the Chimney Sweepers' Act of

1788, a piece of legislation repealed in July 1834 and replaced by a new Act. Under this one, parliamentary legislation fixed ten as the minimum age of employment and stipulated that boys could not be apprenticed unless they consented after having served a two-month probationary period. In the novel, Bumble brings Oliver before the Board not long after he was eight (later amended by Dickens to nine), and no probationary requirement is observed because Board members instruct Bumble to bring Oliver and the indenture papers that same afternoon to the magistrates for the necessary signatures. Phillips suggests that Dickens was familiar with the provisions of the new legislation but ignores these details in his powerful attack. Cf. Strange (XVI. 25).

21.   Pugh, Edwin. "About Squeers and Mr. Fang." In his **The Charles Dickens Originals** (XIII. 110), pp. 109-13.

Calls Mr. Fang, the police magistrate in Chapter 11, the one "wholly authentic portrait [in Dickens's works], as to the identity of which there can be no possible confusion." As proof, Pugh cites the letter Dickens wrote expressing his wish to be smuggled into Hatton Garden court to watch Allan Stewart Laing in action (I. 1) and Forster's comment about the incident in his **Life**. Not long after Dickens caricatured Laing as Fang, Forster wrote, the Home Secretary removed the magistrate from the bench (F, VI, vii, 100).

Forster's reference to Fang and Laing's dismissal could imply a connection, although as the Pilgrim editors sensibly note, the portrait alone was not directly responsible (P, I, 267n). The reference to Laing in **Oliver Twist**, the editors add, represents the second occasion Dickens drew attention to him, having referred mockingly to the magistrate in a review of a burletta which appeared in the **Morning Chronicle** of 24 November 1835 (P, I, 97n). See also "Fang and Laing Again" (XVI. 8) and IX. 24.

22.   Reith, Charles. **British Police and the Democratic Ideal.** London: Oxford Univ. Press, 1943, pp. 48-50.

Comments briefly on the underworld of London prior to the Metropolitan Police Act of 1829 and describes crime as "rampant and beyond control." Police and press records reveal, states Reith, many instances of the existence of child-corrupting organizations and "kitchens" of young thieves. "Compared with some of the factual characters who are described in the records as amassing wealth by child-exploitation," writes Reith, "Fagin was inoffensive and respectable."

23.   "Reports of the Society for the Suppression of Mendacity, London, 1838-39." Quarterly Review, 64 (1839), 341-69.

Documents the currency of the assertion Dickens made to Mrs. Davis that Jewish fences were common at the time he wrote **Oliver Twist** (XIII. 78). "A Jew seldom thieves," wrote the author of the report, "but is worse than a thief; he encourages others to thieve. In every town there is a Jew, either resident or tramping; sure to be a Jew within forty-eight hours in the town, somehow or other. If a robbery is effected, the property is hid till a Jew is found, and a bargain is then made."

24.   Rushton, Joseph. "Bill Sikes and Mr. Dick." **The Dickensian**, 7 (August 1911), 223-24.

In a separate note which refers only to Sikes, Rushton cites an entry in the **Annual Register** for 1760 concerning one William Sikes, a housebreaker in Newgate whose death sentence had been temporarily suspended. Rushton wonders if Dickens was aware of this entry. Cf. Ellis (X. 23).

25.   Strange, K.H.   **Climbing Boys: A Study of Sweeps' Apprentices 1773-1875.** London: Allison & Busby, 1982, passim.

Provides useful background about the conditions under which young boys were employed by notorious master sweeps, who, like Mr. Gamfield, looked to the workhouse for their apprentices and treated their charges with equal cruelty. Strange tells a moving story of extraordinary suffering--of how boys from five or six were forced to soak their elbows and knees in brine to harden them so they could wiggle, like caterpillars, up torturous flues no more than nine inches by nine, and how they worked, a brush held above their heads, with choking soot falling down on them, for as many as fifteen hours a day. Many perished on the job, while others died from cancer of the scrotum, an occupational hazard caused by constant exposure to soot and the enforced habit of "sleeping black," a consequence of the failure of the boys' masters to provide washing facilities, clean clothing, and fresh bedding. Thus in showing Oliver on his knees, "pale and terrified" at the prospect of being indentured to "that dreadful man" Gamfield, Dickens added to a growing body of literature and referred to an abuse already well documented by reformers and humanitarians protesting the cruelty to which chimney sweeps were customarily subjected. In his last chapter, Strange presents a collection of poems, prints, and prose extracts (including Mr. Gamfield's appearance before the workhouse board) calling for reform. Cf. Phillips (XVI. 20).

26.   Trollope, Thomas Adolphus.   "Early Days in London."   In his **What I Remember.** New York: Harper, 1888, I, 7-8.

Recollects the stories he heard as an eight year old about the "sundry mysteriously wicked regions" of the city and describes one of his own expeditions in 1818 to Saffron Hill, "a sort of unholy market" where stolen pocket-handkerchiefs "fluttered in all the colors of the rainbow" on lines stretched across the narrow street from every window. "The whole lane," Trollope writes, "was a long vista of pennon-like pocket-handkerchiefs."

27.   Trudgill, Eric.   "The Fortunes of the Magdalen."   In his **Madonnas and Magdalens: The Origins and Development of Victorian Sexual Attitudes.** New York: Holmes and Meider, 1976, pp. 277-306.

Traces the growth of public sympathy for prostitutes from the 1750's and surveys briefly various groups working to rehabilitate fallen women. Trudgill argues that the novelists contributed significantly by publically ventilating the problem of prostitution and comments on Dickens's "The Pawnbroker's Shop" (XIV. 1) and the portrait of Nancy as two influential literary treatments of the issue. Trudgill judges Dickens's reticence and "cautious ambiguity" a necessary literary strategy and one more likely to succeed at the time than vivid realism. Had Nancy remained the "coarse, tawdry, gin-swilling slut" of the earlier scenes and not become "a figure of Sunday school piety," he reasons, Dickens would have antagonized the fastidious and lost the chance to move the public to action. Trudgill ranges widely over other novelists in this chapter and presents in an earlier one (ch. 5) a useful analysis of the prostitute's complicated social role in Victorian England.

28. Vizetelly, Henry. **Glances Back Through Seventy Years: Autobio-
     graphical and Other Reminiscences.** 2 vols. London: Kegan, Paul,
     Trench, Trubner, & Co., 1893, I, 122.

Refers to London Bridge as a favored hunting ground for "fogle-fakers,"
youthful pickpockets who stole expensive silk handkerchiefs and sold them to
fences after removing their distinctive marks. Dickens writes about a similar
incident in Chapter 9 of **Oliver Twist,** where he describes Fagin directing the
boys to pick out the marks with a needle after a morning's "work."

APPENDIX

Appendix: Dickens's Involvement with Oliver Twist

	Personal	Publications	Political and Social Context
1822–1827	CD moves from Chatham to London. Schooling interrupted; works at Warren's for several months. Resumes education until March 1827.		
1829			Metropolitan Police Act
1831			1 Aug. New London Bridge opened 20 Oct. Privy Council issues instructions and regulations concerning cholera.
1831–1832	Joins staff of the **Mirror of Parliament** and later works as a Parliamentary reporter for the **True Sun.**		
1832			Feb. 40 cases of cholera reported in several Thames neighborhoods.
1832–1834			Royal Commission on the Poor Laws. Commisioners' **Report.**
1833		1 Dec. First story; eight more follow in the next two months.	
[1833	? Dec.] Tells H. W. Kolle of his plan to commence "a series of papers . . . called **The Parish.**"		

Political and Social Context

1834	July Chimney Sweep Act; repeals 1788 Act and establishes a new minimum age of ten. Apprentices must be "willing and "desirous" and first serve a two-month probationary period before indenture. 14 Aug. Poor Law Amendment Act. Provokes sporadic violence in Southern England.
1834–1837	Opposition to Poor Law Amendment Act intensifies, especially in the North after bad weather in the autumn of 1836. Many officials deny out-of-door relief.
1835–1836	Figaro in London attacks A. S. Laing, police magistrate at Hatton Gaden London.

Publications

| 1836 | 8 Feb. Sketches by Boz (First Series). 31 Mar.–30 Oct. 1837 The Pickwick Papers in twenty monthly installments. |

Personal

| 1834 | Aug.–Nov. 1836 Reporter for the Morning Chronicle. Gathers material that serves as background for OliverTwist. |
| 1835 | 5 Nov. Visits Newgate prison. 17 Nov. Meets George Cruikshank. |

Personal	Publications	Political and Social Context
1836 22 Aug. Agrees to write two three-volume novels for Richard Bentley. 4 Nov. Contracts to edit **Bentley's Miscellany** from Jan. 1837.	1836 5 Dec. Completes "Tulrumble" essay Jan. number of **Bentley's** for **Miscellany.** 17 Dec. **Sketches by Boz** (Second Series)	
1837 9 Jan. Contacts Cruikshank about the first illustration for **Oliver Twist.** 7 May Death of Mary Hogarth July Proposes the publication of **Oliver Twist** in book form in addition to the serial. 28 Sept. Bentley agrees to publish **Oliver Twist** as a three-volume novel.	1837 Feb.-Apr. 1839 **Oliver Twist** published serially in the **Miscellany.** June No **Oliver Twist** installment. Oct. No **Oliver Twist** installment.	
	1838 Sept. No **Oliver Twist** installment. 20 Oct. Delivers completed **Oliver Twist** to Bentley. 9 Nov. **Oliver Twist** published in three volumes.	1838 1 Jan. Laing forced to resign as London magistrate.
1839 31 Jan. Resigns as editor of <u>**Bentley's Miscellany.**</u>		
1840 2 July Released from all contractual obligations to Bentley.		

Political and Social Context

Publications

1841 April Writes Preface for "Third
       Edition" of **Oliver Twist**
       published by Chapman and Hall.
       15 May Publication of Third
       Edition.

? 1844–Revises text of**Oliver Twist**
1845   in preparation for new edition
       in ten parts by Bradbury and
       Evans, beginning 1 Jan. 1846.

1846 4 Feb. "Crime and Education" pub-
       lished in the **Daily News.**

1846 23 Feb.–16 Mar. Five letters in the
       Daily News advocating total
       abolition of capital punishment.
       26 May One-volume edition of
       Oliver Twist published.

? Oct. "An Appeal to Fallen
       Women."

Personal

1842 14 Sept. Visits Field Lane Ragged
       School. Begins philanthropic part-
       nership with Miss Coutts.

1846 26 May Responds to Miss Coutts's
       interest in an asylum for women,
       pledging advice and help.

1847 13 Nov. Urania Cottage opens.

Personal	Publications	Political and Social Context
	1849 20 Jan.–21 Apr. Contributes four essays to **The Examiner** about the Tooting Juvenile Pauper Asylum. 14 and 18 Nov. Two letters in **The Times** advocating private executions.	1849 13 Nov. Mannings executed.
	1850 6 Feb. Addresses the Metropolitan Sanitary Association. 30 Mar. **Household Words** begins. Weekly to 28 May 1859, when title changes to **All Year Round.** March New topical Preface to the Cheap Edition of **Oliver Twist** arguing for sanitary reform.	
1860 Aug. Sells Tavistock House to Mr. and Mrs. Davis.		
1863 24 May Refers in a letter to trying in private "the **Oliver Twist** murder." ? June Mrs. Davis accuses CD of treating Jews unjustly in **Oliver Twist.**		

Political and Social Context

Publications

1864 24 Jan. First two numbers of
Our Mutual Friend
completed. Published serially May
1864– Nov. 1865. Attack on Poor
Laws continues.

1867 1 Aug. Charles Dickens Edition of
Oliver Twist published.

1868 Sept. Sikes and Nancy (First version)
privately printed.

Personal

1867 1 Mar. Acknowledges gift of
Jewish translation of the Bible
from Mrs. Davis; CD revises
Oliver Twist again and removes
references to "The Jew," from
the Charles Dickens Edition,
beginning at Ch. 32.

1868 14 Nov. Trial reading of Sikes
and Nancy.
8 Dec. Revised ending of Sikes
and Nancy completed.

1869 5 Jan. First public performance of
Sikes and Nancy.

INDEXES

AUTHOR INDEX

This index of authors provides the numbered references to all main entries but excludes every instance when names appear within annotations. Authors whose names I furnish for further reference but do not annotate are also included here as "cited." In the case of anonymous works, I list these entries by titles with the exception of titles of the contemporary reviews of **Oliver Twist** annotated in Sections IX and X. Readers seeking access to those entries via the Index should consult the subject Index heading, "**Oliver Twist**, reviews," and its various sub-entries. Also see the Subject Index for the titles of Dickens's works and his relationship with other literary or artistic figures.

a Beckett, Gilbert A. VI. 1
Adrian, Arthur A. XIV. 5 (cited)
Adventures of Oliver Twist
(English version for Dutch schools), VIII. 34
Ainsworth, William Harrison XI. 1, 5
Alico, Stella Houghton VIII. 24
Allen, Walter XIII. 128
Almar, George VI. 3
Altick, Richard D. III. 1, XII. 19
Antrobus, Edmund Edward XVI. 1
Aronstein, Philipp XIII. 67
Aswell, Mary Louise VIII. 41
Atherton, J. S. XIII. 129
Auden, W. H. XII. 20
Austen, Zelda XII. 21, 22
Axton, William XII. 23, 24
Aytoun, W. E. X. 21

Bagehot, Walter XII. 1
Baker, Ernest A. XII. 25
Balmain, Rollo VI. 19
Barham, R. D. XI. 2
Barnett, Charles Zachary VI. 2
Barrett, Elizabeth XIII. 139
Basch, Francoise XII. 26
Bayley, John XII. 27
Bayne, Peter XII. 2, 3
Becker, May Lamberton II. 32
Beckett, Dan VI. 23
Belloc, Hilaire XIII. 68
Bennett, Agnes Maria XIII. 130
Benson, A. C. XII. 28
Bicanic, Sonia XII. 29
Billington, Michael VII. 2
Bill Sikes and the School Board VII. 35
Binny, John XV. 2

Bishop, Jonathan XII. 30
Blackall, Jean Frantz XIII. 1
Bland, Joellen VI. 38
Blatchford, Robert XIII. 131
Blount, Trevor XII. 31
Blum, Samuel XIII. 69
Bodeen, DeWitt VII. 3
Bodenheimer, Rosemarie XII. 32
Boll, Ernest XII. 33
Boll, Theophilus E. XII. 34
Borough, The XIII. 134
Borowitz, David XIII. 2
Borrow, George XI. 12
"Bos" [Thomas Peckett Prest] VIII. 1
Bouchier, Jonathan XVI. 3
Bowen, W. H. V. 1
Bowers, Fredson III .2
Brand, Oswald VI. 17
Brantlinger, Patrick XII. 35
Braybrooke, Peter VIII. 15
Brier, Peter A. XII. 36
Briggs, Katharine M. XII. 37
Brody, Benjamin XII. 38
Brogan, Colm XII. 39
Brown, Ivor XII. 40
Brown, Suzanne XIII. 162
"Browning's Dramatic Idylls" XVI. 4
Brownlow, John XIII. 132
Brueck, Katherine T. XII. 41, 42
Buller, Charles IX. 6
"Bumble on Old-Age Pensions, Mr." VIII. 39
Burdett, Sir Francis XI. 3
Burnett, Henry I. 3
Burton, Anthony XIII. 3
Burton, S. H. XII. 43
Busch, Frederick XII. 44
Butler, David VII. 4
Butler, Ivan VII. 4
Butt, John III. 3, 4, 5, 6

Thundyil, Zacharias XIII. 122
Thurley, Geoffrey XII. 196
Tick, Stanley XII. 197
Tillotson, Kathleen II. 48, III. 6, 17,
  18, IV. 10, V. 23, IX. 40, XII. 198,
  199, 200, 201, XIII. 57
Tobias, J. J. XIII. 123, 124, 125
Tomkins, A. R. XII. 202
Toole, J. L. VI. 13
Townsend, W. T. VII. 35
Toynbee, William XI. 16
Trevelyan, G. M. XV. 9
Trilling, Diana XIII. 91 (cited)
Trollope, Thomas Adolphus
  XVI. 26
Trudgill, Eric XVI. 27

Ursini, James VII. 25

Vail, R. W. G. IV. 11
Vance, Daisy Melville VI. 33
Vann, J. Don XII. 203
Veen, H. R. S. van der XIII. 126
Vermilye, Jerry VII. 29
Vernon, Sally XIII. 148
Versfeld, Barbara XIII. 168
Victoria, Queen XI. 6
Vizetelly, Henry XVI. 28
Vogler, Richard A. XIII. 58, 59,
  60, 61, 62
Vredenburg, Eric VIII. 19

Wagenknecht, Edward XII. 204
Walder, Dennis XII. 205
Walker, B. (publisher), VIII. 5
Walker, William (publisher), VIII. 3
Wall, Stephen IX. 41
Wallace, John Jr. VI. 41
Wallins, Roger P. XII. 206
Waugh, Arthur VI. 62, XII. 207,
  XIII. 63
Way, Brian VI. 36
Webb, Sidney and Beatrice Webb
  XV. 10, 11, 12, 13
Wechter, Sidney XIII. 64
Weedon, L. I. VIII. 32, 33
Wertheim, Lee Hilles XIII. 169
Westburg, Barry XII. 208, 209
Wheeler, Burton M. XII. 210
Whipple, Edwin P. XII. 17
Whitlow, Roger XII. 211

Whyte, Harold VI. 19
Wilkins, William Glyde IV. 23,
  XIII. 65, 66
Williams, A. XIII. 161
Williams, Bransby VIII. 50
Williams, Guy VI. 37, XII. 212
Williams, Nigel VII. 45
Williams, S. F. XII. 18
Williamson, Colin XII. 213
Wilson, Angus XII. 214, 215
Wilson, Edmund V. 24, XII. 214, 215
Wilson, John R. XII. 216
Winans, Edward XIII. 170
Winters, Warrington XII. 217
"Work of [Robert] Ball Hughes,
  The" VIII. 51
Worth, George J. XII. 218
Wright, Thomas XII. 219

Yates, Edmund V. 25
"Year's Work in Dickens Studies"
  IV. 24
Young, Vernon VII. 30

Zambrano, Ana Laura VII. 9
  (cited), 31, 32, 33, XIII. 149
Zatlin, Linda Gertner XIII. 127

SUBJECT INDEX

Acton, William XII. 203
adaptations see dramatizations,
   film versions, "Oliver!" radio
   adaptations, Sikes and Nancy,
   songs
Ainsworth, William Harrison
   Jack Sheppard succeeds Oliver
   Twist in Miscellany II. 1, 2;
   Sheppard attacked as Newgate
   fiction X. 3, 5, 6, 7, XI. 9; CD
   ranked above IX. 24; praises
   Oliver Twist XI. 1, 5; relations
   with Cruikshank XIII. 9, 20
allegory Oliver's role seen
   as XII. 61, 74, 112, 137, 214;
   Oliver's journey and struggle
   against evil XII. 146, 185; Oliver
   as Rousseauistic child of nature
   XII. 142, 156, 172
annotations Hill's notes XII. 104;
   Hebrew references XIII. 86, 93;
   pauper's funeral (ch. 5) XV. 8;
   "summary offences" (ch. 11) XII.
   187, XVI. 15; see also
   language--naming of characters,
   "By hand"
anti-Semitism CD accused of
   by Mrs. E. Davis XIII. 67, 72, 77,
   78, 79, 93, 114; CD's response
   XIII. 78; changes to 1867 edition
   of Oliver Twist II. 15, III. 2,
   XIII. 78, 97, 104, 115, 120;
   others repeat accusations II. 20,
   XIII. 67, 68, 69, 70, 89, 116, 117,
   119; bibliographical sources for
   IV. 6, 9, VI. 42, XIII. 113;
   charges questioned XII. 39, 112,
   136, XIII. 74, 91, 104, 105, 106,
   112, 116, 122; CD defended and
   exonerated XIII. 84, 92, 96, 99,
   101, 120; Fagin and "fiscal
   ogres" of middle class
   materialism XIII. 107; historical

justification for Jewish fences
   XIII. 71, 78, 103, 126, XVI. 6, 9,
   10, 23; literary tradition of
   anti-Semitism XIII. 70, 80, 87,
   88, 91, 98, 102, 109, 118, 120,
   127; stage tradition of IV. 6, 9,
   VI. 42, XIII. 90, 94, 102, 107,
   112, 113, 126, 142; mythic and
   theo- logical tradition XIII. 81,
   95, 96, 102, 112; pedagogical
   responses to XIII. 75, 76, 80, 85;
   sensitivity of modern readers
   XII. 136, XIII. 74, 96; see also
   dramatizations, Fagin, film
   versions
"Appeal to Fallen Women,
   An" XIV. 5
appreciative criticism XII.
   1, 2, 3, 8, 11, 16, 25, 28, 191
archetype Jungian archetype
   of the child XII. 88; Jung and
   the idyll XII. 93; Genesis
   mythology and Edens XII. 109;
   myth to intensify urban vision
   XII. 77; see also fairy tale,
   comedy and humor--comic
   purpose and Classical romances
Arnold, Matthew XII. 72
Artful Dodger see Dawkins,
   John

Barnaby Rudge XII. 172, XIII. 93
Bates, Charley Talfourd pleads for
   XII. 7; character change XII.
   183; pun on name XII. 203
Bennett, Agnes Maria (The Beggar
   Girl) XIII. 130
Bentham, Jeremy CD supports
   Benthamite objectives XII. 35,
   70; support qualified XII. 35;
   opposes Bentham and Malthus
   XII. 110, 162, 205; Bentham and

305